Coaching Youth Football

What Soccer Coaches Can Learn From The Professional Game

Ray Power

BENNION KEARNY

Published in 2020 by Bennion Kearny Limited.

Copyright © Bennion Kearny Ltd 2020

Ray Power has asserted his right under the Copyright, Designs and Patents Act, 1988 to be identified as the author of this book.

ISBN: 978–1–910515–84–6

Published by Bennion Kearny Limited
6 Woodside
Churnet View Road
Oakamoor
ST10 3AE

www.BennionKearny.com

Acknowledgements

To Lisa – this football game is a tough place to live at times – thank you for being there to keep my head straight.

To Georgia – thank you for the use of the laptop!

To Gracie – for being the one who always wants the latest football shirt!

To Finley – for making writing this book five times longer than it needed to be! Please sleep soon.

About the Author

Ray Power is one of the bestselling football authors in the world. With over a decade of experience working in football and education, coaching players from non-league to Premier League levels, and internationally, he is the author of *Making the Ball Roll*, and the *Deliberate Soccer Practice* series.

As a coach developer and educator, Ray has worked for, and consulted with, numerous national FAs, as well as governing bodies from other sports, including the NBA. He also works as a consultant - mentor - educator on a freelance basis, working with grassroots coaches all the way to professional teams.

Foreword
@CoachingBadges

"

There's always a better way.

"

Gavin Teehan • @CoachingBadges

I'll be totally honest with you, and admit that I've never written a foreword before… but when Ray approached me to see if I would do so for *Youth Football Coaching*, I had no hesitation in getting involved. I am a keen *Twitter* user and love the idea of sharing knowledge, whilst at the same time helping fellow coaches.

As a player, I was fortunate enough to play internationally at various levels, in the UK as a schoolboy/apprentice, and then later play in the League of Ireland for over eight years.

I was lucky enough to play the game we all love from the age of six up until injury curtailed my playing journey at the age of just 28. Having initially taken a few years break from the game, I returned to catch the coaching bug and I have been coaching for the last 17 years, probably enjoying it now more than I ever did. My one regret is not having access to Ray's books all those years ago, when I began my coaching journey.

As a coach, I have experience of dealing with boys, girls, men and women from Under–5 social players, right up to senior professionals. I have coached at various club and representative levels, recently embarking on a new challenge as the head coach of an Under–19 group in the National League of Ireland.

The reason I am always keen to help those who are brave enough to ask, and open enough to consider alternatives, is that I live by the mantra, "There is always a better way." No matter who you are, or how well you think you know something, there is generally a better way if you dare to discover it. Someone once told me, as a young coach, that your mind is like a parachute, it only works at its best when it is fully open!

I have often used Ray's previous books – *Making the Ball Roll* and the *Deliberate Soccer Practice* series – as a source of new learning and as a way of reflecting on my own philosophy, and challenging my thinking of the time. His books have become a permanent fixture in my coaching library and Ray himself has become a valued friend.

I was introduced to Ray, initially, via a trusted friend and fellow coach who suggested that we might get some external coaches in to do some workshops, talks, and sessions at a club we were both involved with at the time. I didn't know Ray personally before this, but quickly realised that we would work well together once we met.

Very early on in our dealings, he had me thinking about how we currently coached, what areas we would like to improve, and he challenged what we were prepared to do to make such changes. It was refreshing to say the least. To have someone so upfront and honest about how he worked and, indeed, how he could help us improve as coaches. We didn't always necessarily agree, but we certainly always walked away from such discussions with much food for thought. I often think that this friendly discord is often missing from modern coaching. We believe what we want, and shy away from things that challenge us. I guarantee you, regardless of your coaching level, experience or ability, this book will challenge your thoughts at some point along the way.

Now, it takes a particular person to accept this challenge, embrace change, and seek continued improvement through reflective learning. It also takes a particular person to be open–minded to all of this type of sharing and mutually challenging discussion.

We have come a long way from when I began to learn to be a coach. When I first started coaching, there was a distinct culture of secrecy within football circles. Very few people were willing to share anything and you had to go out and search for everything yourself. Rarely did coaches even show you their session plans and the websites full of football resources were in their infancy. Thankfully, things have improved radically in recent times, and there is now an abundance of material floating around bookshelves and the internet. The trick now is to learn how to spot the good stuff, and filter out the bad.

I sometimes glance through my phone, Dropbox, and computer files and wonder where on earth I got all the documents, pictures, articles and videos from – and wonder further about how I will ever get through them all! The truth is I probably never will, but this is where coaches like Ray come into their own. Ray has produced a series of books that are invaluable to coaches of all levels, pulling all the topics that relate to football together into one place. This newest addition to this suite of resources is as good, if not better, than any I have read before.

I hope you find, as I did, that this book will become a valued resource in your coaching armoury. It is brimming with great game–related topics, well laid out and presented, with thought provoking ideas throughout. You can use and adapt all these to suit the age and ability of your players, regardless of the stage of their playing careers. I have always found Ray's books to be easy to read and follow. He presents his topics in detail, enabling you to relate everything on the page to your players, quickly and easily, as appropriate. The following pages are no different.

Whether you want a coaching bible aligned with current best practice within the world of coaching, or simply a quick reference for good guidelines, this book will improve your knowledge of the game and your ability to deliver fun, quality, engaging sessions and experiences to your players.

I have no doubt that coaches will value this book and make it a part of their own continued development, whether working as a part–time community coach or a full–time professional. Take what your players need from it and make it work. After all, no one knows them as well as you do.

Coaches like Ray and books like this, help to make our game a better place. We, as coaches, gain invaluable knowledge or simply have our current knowledge challenged. Players get taught in a better, more enjoyable and engaging way. All stakeholders see the results as we start to develop not only better players but better people. The smallest of improvements on how we all interact with each other, can make the biggest and most rewarding improvements.

Ray has followed up *Making the Ball Roll* brilliantly, and this latest edition is sure to be even more successful than its predecessor. I hope it makes you think. I hope it makes you a better coach. I hope it makes your players better. I know it did all of these things for me.

It only remains for me to wish you continued growth on your coaching journey, whatever stage you may be at currently, and I encourage you to embrace the knowledge within this superb book.

Remember, there is always a better way!

Gavin

@coachingbadges

Table of Contents

Chapter 3 – The Feet Are Just the Tools | 39

Chapter 4 – A Growth Mindset Environment | 53

Chapter 5 – The Power of Failing | 73

Chapter 6 – Building a Player | 97

Chapter 7 – Psychology in Action | 119

Chapter 8 – Football Fitness | 141

Chapter 10 – Football Intelligence | 183

Chapter 11 – The 'I' in Team | 201

Chapter 12 – The 'We' in Team | 223

Chapter 13 – Modern Playing Positions | 239

Chapter 14 – Modern Team Tactics | 261

Conclusion – For the Love of the Game | 331

Introduction

Before you can coach others,
first you must learn to coach yourself.

Johan Cruyff

In my early 20s, I made football coaching my professional aim in life. Even back then, I was absorbed in the game. I felt I knew everything – not in an arrogant way, but having played and watched and studied it all my life, I couldn't possibly imagine what was out there that I had left to know. How wrong I was.

Football coaching is, of course, more than just being familiar with the game. It is about much, much more than that. A colleague once asked me, after the publication of *Making the Ball Roll*, whether this was everything I had to share. Is the content of the book the end? It was not. There is always new content out there – new angles, new takes, new research. This book, although with a different title, is very much a follow-up to *Making the Ball Roll* (and I'll reference the first book a lot over the following chapters! Please bear with me!). There is masses of new material here (90%+), but there is also some material which is either reproduced or re-adapted from my first effort. Without doing this, important continuity would have fallen flat.

From thinking I knew all there was, to accepting that I will never, *ever* know everything, was an important watershed in my journey. Being open-minded to all avenues of knowledge and improvement should form the foundation of the work and development of any coach, at any level.

Anyone who stops learning is old,
whether at twenty or eighty.

Henry Ford

Our Coaching Lens

I recently presented at a coaching event in Asia. I was asked to feedback to a national association about the performance of their Under-18 team, the morning after the game.

I have always had a problem with parachuting into another environment, telling coaches what I believe is 'wrong' then parachuting out again. It is too easy. When you go somewhere to find fault in something, you will find it pretty easily and pretty quickly. The feedback can lack context, a full understanding of what is happening behind the scenes, and, critically, people are biased. I was never afraid to receive feedback as a coach, but rarely did I appreciate somebody watching my teams train or play, and basing all their judgements on that alone.

So, as you can imagine, feeding back to the personnel above, in the presence of about 30 other football people, made me feel quite uneasy. It was while preparing this presentation that I first spoke about our *coaching lens*.

Whether we like it, or not, or whether we know it, or not, we see the game through our own thoughts, experiences, and preferences. So, had Pep Guardiola been presenting in my place, he may have watched the game and focused heavily on ball possession, for example. Jürgen Klopp may have focused on counter-pressing. Jose Mourinho on compactness, etc.

Introduction

We will all have our respective lenses. We see the game the way we want to see it, and therefore coach it the way we are familiar with. This is 100% ok provided we are not just dismissing alternatives along the way.

This is probably a big reason why spectators or maybe parents around your team, complain when you require your team to play out from the back and express themselves in possession. Their experience of the game may be a different one from yours. It may even be quite old-fashioned. When they played, maybe it was all about physical dominance, direct play, or one particular formation. So when they see you encouraging short kick-outs, dribblers, or playing a certain system, they don't like it as it doesn't represent the game as they know and understand it. Maybe they believe that coaches should shout and narrate every kick of the ball, so do not understand a more subtle, composed approach. Opening our minds and allowing a widening of our lens is essential to progress.

Confirmation Bias

As you read through this book, I would ask you to be as aware of your own lens and your own biases as you can. I am certain that at least one thing in this book will challenge the way you coach or think about the game. Even if on first reading you disagree with something entirely, work hard not to reject it immediately. Allow the conflicting theories to have a 'punch-up' in your mind and see then if it changes or adds further layers to your view. If it doesn't, then this is also acceptable. You have learned by considering and then rejecting information. Even if it does not change how you operate, the reinforcement makes your work stronger.

Those of you who are keen users of social media will note the many debates that surround coaching – opposed practice versus unopposed practice, blocked practice versus game-related, etc. There are often two camps – those who would argue to the death for one view or the other. Ironically, however, to have a balanced opinion and to learn, we need both these people. We need that polarised conflict to help us come to our own conclusions.

Often we search for the evidence that only backs up our opinion – this is our confirmation bias. We highlight, agree with, and allow information that supports our opinion to grow and anchor in our minds, but immediately dismiss anything that does not fit into our lens. This does not allow us to grow as we might.

"

Discover your gift, develop your gift, and then give
it away every day.

Don Meyer

The Professional Game

"

Children are not mini-adults.

Youth coaching mantra

Coaching youth football is very different from coaching the adult version of the game, and coaching amateur players is very different from coaching professionals. Training methods, the pressure put on players, and a 'win-at-all-costs' mentality is different. Indeed, quite often, what we see in professional environments will be completely inappropriate for young players. I subscribe wholeheartedly to the quote above – children are not mini-adults and should not be treated as such.

Throughout this book, we will nonetheless look at a lot of examples from the professional game, but apply them *carefully* to our youth environments. This includes well-known professional teams and coaches, the work of international football associations, and the academy game (for clarity, I use the term 'academy' to represent the youth section of professional clubs).

Your team will not be as tactically astute as Pep Guardiola's, but maybe we can learn from his game model nonetheless. Your young attacker may not have a lot in common with Harry Kane or Antoine Griezmann at the moment, but maybe anecdotes from when they were teenage boys making their way through the game will have relevance to you and your players. There may be a sense of survivorship bias (focusing on those who 'made it' through one system and ignoring those who did not) throughout, but I do not believe we should ignore the journeys and work of those who have reached the top of their profession. If Richard Branson was to give a lecture on developing a successful business model, I would expect every entrepreneur to listen. Today, we have more access to the best coaches and the best players, so why wouldn't we try to glean best practice from them?

It's Your Game

Story-telling is a powerful learning tool. In any coach education course I took, there was always a saying that "You learn as much in the bar in the evening, as you do in the classroom." Whilst arguable, the angle was that sharing experiences with others, and listening to theirs, gives you first-hand accounts of what has been successful or unsuccessful for actual coaches working in a similar environment to you, again promoting learning and broadening horizons.

Throughout the book, we will hear from coaches of all levels – ex-professional players, players who never played at elite level, and other experts in their field. We will also hear from part-time coaches who work with amateur, grassroots players, who simply have something they want to share – and they are certainly worth listening to. We will also hear from authors, academics, coach educators, and a referee!

Those familiar with *Making the Ball Roll* will remember the *Real Coach Experience* segments at the end of each chapter. Here, real coaches tell us about a snippet of their work, helping to bring the theory of the chapter to life. Due to the popularity of the segments, they have been expanded here. The majority of chapters have at least two 'real coach experience' segments, now called *It's Your Game*, due to our link with the wonderful football website and resource, www.football4football.com. I have included their Twitter handles, and also the handles of others mentioned throughout the book.

On a personal note from me, I would like to thank all of those who contributed to the content of the following chapters. Your time, whether face-to-face, over the phone, email, or through various message services, is truly appreciated!

Enjoy the book, and you can always find me on Twitter (@power_ray).

Chapter 1
Coaching in the Magic

"
The creative process is also the most terrifying part because you don't know exactly what's going to happen or where it is going to lead. You don't know what new dangers and challenges you'll find. It takes an enormous amount of internal security to begin with the spirit of adventure, the spirit of discovery, the spirit of creativity. Without doubt, you have to leave the comfort zone of base camp and confront an entirely new and unknown wilderness. You become a trailblazer, a pathfinder. You open new possibilities…
"

Stephen R. Covey, *The Seven Habits of Highly Effective People*

We are all familiar with the work and dedication required from players to be the best that they can be. It is probably something that all coaches will have asked of them at some point along the journey. We cannot turn all players into professionals, and for the overwhelming percentage of football coaches, this will not be on their radar at all.

Maybe your aim for them, instead, is to send them to the next level on the pyramid – to an 'elite'[1] academy, on a scholarship at university, or to play at an age group that is older. Instead, maybe you coach to keep kids out of trouble, to turn lives around, or to help them make better life decisions – or many other reasons you might coach the game.

While we are familiar with asking for the best from our players, and imploring them to improve, do we ask the best of ourselves?

The final chapter of *Making the Ball Roll* encouraged the coach to self-reflect – to analyse his/her performance first, before attributing blame to others. The purpose of *this* chapter, and its position at the beginning of the book instead, is to encourage you to self-reflect as you read, noting – physically or mentally – the information that captures your imagination as you go along. When presenting coach development seminars, I begin by asking the participants to tune into any 'lightbulb' moments they may have – the ones that resonate and spark further investigation. All coaches will have different lightbulb moments, and all coaches reading this book will have different elements that will stick with them.

---

[1] In this book you will note the word 'elite' referenced. When applied to young players, it means those who have been chosen for select groups – normally academies attached to professional clubs. There is currently a large-scale argument about naming and treating youth as elite, when the reality is they are far from that. The elite are those right at the very top of the pyramid, but, for the sake of semantics, I will use the term throughout.

Chapter 1 – Coaching in the Magic

This chapter is a preamble for that and will thus provide you with more questions than answers – in a guided discovery type of way. Get your highlighter and notepad ready.

Comfort and Learning

Most of us are probably familiar with the *2% Mindset* graphic below. It is generally used as a motivational 'hit' encouraging people to get the most out of life. The concept is that, unlike 98% of the population, you should live outside your comfort zone, "living without limits" and "going for your dreams".

The 2% Mindset

Infographic adapted from WhoisCH!CK.com

As I surfed through several books and articles about becoming better, a familiar term kept staring back at me – *comfort zone*. Psychologically, the comfort zone is a state in which we feel in control, experience low levels of anxiety, and can exist without challenge. We are safe in there – blocking out any threats, whether they exist or not. Risk-taking is unnecessary. The threat of the unknown is not in the equation.

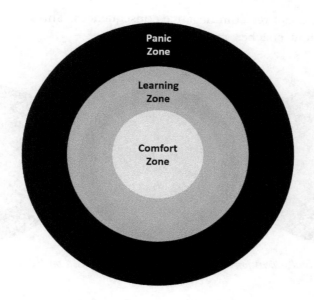

Senninger's Learning Zone Model

The 'unknown', however, is a great place to learn, but it resides outside of your comfort zone. In 2000, German learning expert, Tom Senninger, designed a simple model around *The Learning Zone* (above). When we nudge ourselves from the comfort zone into the learning zone, we put ourselves in a place where we can grow and develop – it gives us challenges and experiences that we can bank, and which help us improve. Psychologist Lev Vygotsky called this *The Zone of Proximal Development* – it is where the magic happens.

However, beyond the learning zone is The Panic Zone. This is where we have pushed our level of challenge too far, causing a heightened level of anxiety and fear. Learning in this zone is impossible – our brain becomes more concerned with our survival than with developing and extending our capabilities.

In the brain, the greater the challenges, the
greater the changes – up to a point.

Anders Ericsson and Robert Pool, *Peak*

Shape Shifters

Although Senninger's model, above, is neat and well-shaped, the reality, however, is that we all contain several different comfort zones, depending on the situation we are in. The one you may have professionally may be different to your romantic relationship one, for example. While you may be able to talk-the-talk amongst high-level boardroom CEOs, you may have trouble approaching a love interest in a bar.

In addition, all people will have differently-sized zones, depending on the situation they are faced with. Try to convince someone who is afraid of flying to board a plane (although *you* feel there's nothing to it), and no sooner is your idea rejected than you get asked to join him or her in a thrill-seeking mountain climb (inciting panic with you!). If you force yourself or others beyond their boundaries prematurely, it can result in negative consequences. This is worth remembering when working with players, fellow coaches, mentors and mentees.

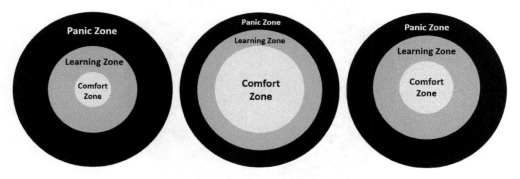

Every individual's limit for each zone will be different based on the situation at hand

Our Coaching Comfort Zone

It is important, firstly, to point out that the comfort zone we are going to focus on from here is one that relates exclusively to our coaching, not our everyday life. I am not arrogant enough or qualified enough to lecture an agoraphobic, for example, on why they should leave the fortitude of their house, or why a grief-stricken person should just jump out of bed.

Everyday life will, however, affect your coaching comfort zone. Although the comfort zone is much slandered, it *is important* as it gives us – all of us – somewhere safe, reliable, and predictable to return to. We all need it.

We read a lot about how family life, social life, and the school life of players affects their football playing, but it will affect the coach's approach to coaching too. If you feel there are 'bigger' issues that need addressing before challenging your coaching needs, please do so. In the meantime, let's look at comfort, learning, and panic in a coaching context.

Coaching in The Learning Zone

The avoidance of new things, new ideas, outside influences, or challenges are normal strategies that come with those who are 'trapped' in their comfort zone. As a coach, your comfort zone is a very noticeable place. It is probably a place where sessions you know (and are good at) are repeated. They are conducted, as much as possible, beyond the watching eyes of parents and fellow coaches. Anything or anyone that challenges you gets pushed away or sidelined.

All coaches expect that they should know everything. Being comfortable with what you do not know is a highly-tuned skill. Sports coaching can be a hard place to be. Many coaches are territorial and are quick to judge and criticise. An ex-colleague of mine told me that men hate being criticised for three things – driving, sex, and football. However unscientific and slightly sexist that may sound, the attitude may result in a culture where being left open to criticism is avoided. If you don't want criticism, you don't take risks; you stay in the shadows and confine yourself to your comfort zone.

In 1978, Pauline Clance and Suzanne Imes, two female psychologists, coined the phrase 'Imposter Syndrome'. It initially referred to women in high-powered positions who doubted their accomplishments and abilities, and who thought they were frauds in their roles. Since then, the theory has been extended into many other fields and genders. The infographic below highlights this nicely.

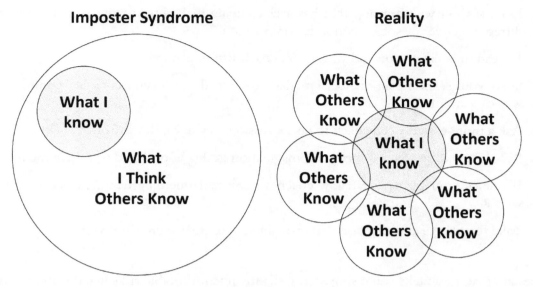

The term was coined in 1978 by clinical psychologists Pauline Clance and Suzanne Imes, mainly focusing on high performing women

Remember, some of the top coaches in world football are regularly openly criticised by those who know a mere fraction about their job or have only a tiny portion of their ability. I have seen Guardiola nicknamed 'Fraudiola', Mourinho lambasted for his tactics, and Bielsa castigated for having great ideas but no trophies to show for it. They handle it, secure in the knowledge that they are doing the right thing.

The challenge of leaving your comfort zone is a positive thing in the long-term, although short-term it may cause us some stress or discomfort. What is crucial to know, however, is that being vulnerable (in a safe way!) and entering the *Learning Zone* can help you improve your performance.

Simple ways to tiptoe from Comfort to Learning Zone

Because all coaches will have differently-sized zones and different boundaries, it is almost impossible to list suggestions that will completely meet the needs of *all* coaches. This is one of those times where I encourage you to find your lightbulb moment. I have suggested some below, but this list is arguably endless. A great start would be to take one of these ideas, explore it – and, crucially – action it!

- Get a mentor who gives you feedback, or seek feedback from a fellow coach or colleague[2]

- Video/audio record yourself – and watch/listen back

- Do a session with an age group much older or much younger than the team you would normally coach

- Do a session, or part of a session, with a team playing at a higher level than you are used to[3]

---

[2] If you put yourself out there for feedback, actioning and being open to it is paramount. Make the short-term discomfort you feel worth it over the long-term.

- Do a session with a group that has a challenging make up to what you are used to – a different gender or socio-economic composition

- Instead of isolating you and your team, coach within plain view

- Share your session plan on social media – treat feedback, even the critical comments, as a way of learning

- Ask a more experienced coach to take a session so you can learn from it

- Record any ideas that capture your imagination in this book – and test drive them

- If one of your players or fellow coaches suggests something new (and meaningful!), go with it

- Take the plunge and enrol on that coaching course that intimidates you

Chances are that if you take some short-term, slightly uncomfortable risks like the above, you will likely walk away from the experience feeling positive about yourself, more confident to adapt, and will be able to bank some learning. In short, you will be better. This is significant – it is all about the learning. With enough practice, you will expand your coaching comfort zone. What was once daunting is now something you can do contentedly. For example, your first unnerving plunge into taking a session with 'elite' players may pave the way for you to work in an academy environment in the future. Your first uncomfortable session with senior professionals may allow you to work consistently in that company as your career progresses.

If you take action and feel like you have failed, that is ok too. Maybe the experiences make you realise that the environment you have dabbled in simply does not suit you. It may or may not surprise you to know that many coaches who dream of coaching elite players quickly change plan; the wrong professional football environment can be a pretty negative place.

"   **"**

> I don't want to hear that someone can't "handle pressure". Everyone can handle pressure. Most people choose not to because it's easier to stay safe in the comfort zone. But if you want to be successful, to have that place in the sun, then you have to leave the shade. It's not easy to leave the shade; it's cool and comfortable, compared to the hot discomfort of the sun. But you can't be relentless if you can't take discomfort, and you can't be unstoppable if you only deal with pressure when you have no choice.

Tim S. Grover, *Relentless*

---

[3] As territorial as football can be, elite coaches are often very open to mentee coaches becoming involved in their sessions – network and use this. Ensure, however, that if you arrange something with them, you follow it through. As quickly as the door opens, it will close if you are unreliable.

Marginal Gains

Between 2003 and 2014, Sir David Brailsford was the Performance Director at British Cycling. In Athens 2004, Team GB won just four Olympic medals across road and track cycling. Since then, however, they have won a combined 38 medals at the three games from 2008 to 2016. In 2009, Team Sky – a road cycling team – was launched, again with Brailsford at the helm, with the aim of winning the Tour de France by 2014. At this point, no Brit had ever won the prestigious road race. Three years ahead of schedule, Bradley Wiggins became the first-ever Briton to win it, starting a streak where British cyclists won five of the six races between 2012 and 2017. Something had changed – but what?

It was during Brailsford's time at British Cycling,[4] and his subsequent role with Team Sky, that the term 'marginal gains' became popularised in sport. The culture of organisations changed from looking at the bigger, overall picture, to focusing on the minute details. The details that the other teams had missed (and which could help give your team an overall advantage over others) were actively looked for.

"

The whole principle came from the idea that if you broke down everything you could think of that goes into riding a bike, and then improved it by 1%, you will get a significant increase when you put them all together.

"

David Brailsford

Not only did Brailsford oversee the development of a wind tunnel to isolate and test various bike designs under different weather conditions, but Team Sky also ensured that all cyclists slept on the same mattress each night when travelling, that hotel rooms were hoovered immediately before their arrival, and that the clothes detergent used was skin-friendly. Together, athletes enjoyed marginal gains in sleep quality, the prevention of infection, and body comfort, respectively. All before any of the riders even looked at a bike, ate a meal, or donned their cycling attire.[5]

Brailsford was the first to admit that each gain was very, very small, but cumulatively, they led to a significant upturn in overall performance. It is breaking big goals down into smaller, more manageable ones. It is not only these 1% gains themselves that are a success, it leads to what Matthew Syed calls a "deeper understanding", not just of the bigger picture, but of its smaller components. So, while British Cycling went in search of each improvement, they gave themselves a more profound knowledge of their entire professional operation.

Other examples from sport, again highlighted by Syed, include the Mercedes Formula 1 motor racing team. In *Black Box Thinking*, Paddy Lowe, the Technical Leader at Mercedes, highlighted how they recorded 16,000 channels of data (in 2015), versus the eight that they did when he first arrived in 2013. Pitstops, for example, can be measured in ways that drill down to how far off-angle the mechanic has applied the wheel gun to remove a wheel nut – we are talking absolute

---

[4] British Cycling is not without its controversy. In 2017, former coach Shane Sutton admitted that anti-doping rules may have been bent in search of another marginal gain.
[5] Matthew Syed, *Black Box Thinking*

fractions of a second to compensate. But when aggregated and improved with the rest of the data, these minuscule improvements add up to significant overall advantages.

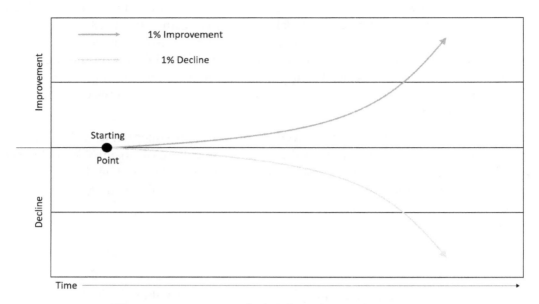

*1% improvements vary only slightly on day one, but over time,
these aggregate to a much bigger difference.*

Marginal Gains in Football

Without necessarily using the term 'marginal gains', many of us will use certain routines that we feel give us an edge. Some coaches will produce the same pre-match warm-up with the players so that players remain comfortable in a routine. Others I have met will change this routine if they feel the players need brightening up. In the professional game, these 1%s may include being an expert team at set-plays; using the 'Moneyball' theory when recruiting players; or Liverpool hiring a specialist throw-in coach. In 2013, Real Madrid consulted sleep expert, Nick Littlehales,[6] in an effort to find marginal gains around recovery, fatigue, and injury prevention.

As is usual within professional sport, once a concept becomes championed, it is quickly questioned by others. When you search 'marginal gains football', for example, you get a series of links from blogs, newspapers, and websites that pick the theory apart. One such article quotes Rasmus Ankersen's *The Gold Mine Effect*, slating professional football players for not training enough (or effectively enough) across multi-disciplines. There is a culture of leaving their own improvement in the hands of the coaches. Martin Samuel, the much-respected Chief Football Writer for the *Daily Mail* newspaper, argues that if every team is looking at the same gains, it will eventually come back to who is better at the game. He looks at Italian football in the 1980s, who were championing sleep habits, correct nutrition and recovery long before the rest; but once everything is done, one team still comes first and another 20th. Not everyone can be a champion at the same time. At the end of the article *Attention to Detail is Old Hat … It Won't Make You A Champion,* Samuel notes simply that Bradley Wiggins is "really, really good at pedaling fast."

---

[6] bbc.com – *How Gareth Bale and Real Madrid sleep their way to the top*

Searching for YOUR 1%s

Where the critics are right is that all improvement begins with the desire to improve. Buying this book, for example, is a good way to start and suggests that you are committed to becoming a better coach.

Thinking of some of the brightest, forward-thinking coaches I have met on the coaching circuit, two spring to mind immediately. One would frequently use his phone to record his verbal communication. At that moment, that was his 1%, his marginal gain in an effort to improve. The second would time his interventions with players to ensure they were hitting the "70% ball rolling time" as championed by England DNA (see below). To justify matters, he said: "We train three times a week for about 42 weeks of the year. If the players are experiencing the ball for five minutes more per session, that equates to over 10 hours extra playing time per season". He went on to explain how a 15-minute warm-up without the ball was replaced by a ball warm-up, which adds another 30-hours of ball-time the players wouldn't otherwise have had. These were small acts and small measures but designed to make a big impact. How, as a coach, can you find 1%s in your game to improve?

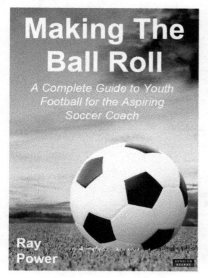

Chances are that, stored away with your coaching resources and paperwork from coaching programmes, you will have a coaching checklist, often as part of a coaching assessment. These can be useful resources, well beyond the completion of your course, and can be highly valuable in your search for your 1% improvements.

In the final chapter of *Making The Ball Roll*, I included coach evaluation forms from *Manchester United Soccer Schools*. I have included them again, below, as well as an interesting self-evaluation produced by former Manchester United and England Sport Psychologist, Bill Beswick. Also, below is the *England DNA Coaching Fundamentals* that all English coaches are now being encouraged to follow – with some very impressive recent results across youth international tournaments. If you search for your 1%, these resources can provide a good starting point.

Manchester United Soccer Schools

Since 1999, Manchester United Soccer Schools began their coaching programs in the UK and internationally. The programs are not elite-driven and are separate from the elite academy, but coach young players to 'Play the United Way'. Their staff are encouraged to reflect on their own performances with the evaluation form below, grouped under headings around planning, technical topics, management, and coaching styles. Across the 23 points, where can *you* add 1%s?

A. PLANNING & PREPARATION		Comments
Appearance	1 2 3 4 5	
Session Plan	1 2 3 4 5	
Organisation Space	1 2 3 4 5	
Organisation of players	1 2 3 4 5	
Use of MUSS Equipment	1 2 3 4 5	
Welfare & Safety of Players	1 2 3 4 5	
Registration of Players	1 2 3 4 5	
B. SUBJECT / TOPIC KNOWLEDGE		
Warm-up session	1 2 3 4 5	
Technical detail demonstrated and taught	1 2 3 4 5	
Skill practice progression	1 2 3 4 5	
Coaching in small-sided games	1 2 3 4 5	
Evidence of progressing to needs of players	1 2 3 4 5	
C. MANAGEMENT OF GROUP		
Coaching position	1 2 3 4 5	
Questions – right way, right time, right question	1 2 3 4 5	
Communication with group	1 2 3 4 5	
Control of group	1 2 3 4 5	
Rapport with group	1 2 3 4 5	
Encourages player-led learning	1 2 3 4 5	
D. COACHING STYLES USED		
Guided Discovery	1 2 3 4 5	
Command	1 2 3 4 5	
Question & Answer	1 2 3 4 5	
Positive environment created?	1 2 3 4 5	
Adaptability to session plan	1 2 3 4 5	

Manchester United Soccer School (MUSS) Coach Evaluation Form

Bill Beswick

If you ever have the opportunity to attend a seminar run by former England, Manchester United, and Middlesbrough sports psychologist, Bill Beswick, please take it. His lectures are some of the most inspiring, engaging, and thought-provoking I have ever attended. Some of his videos are available online.

Beswick has worked not only in football, but in other sports as well, and has a range of experience from young participation players to elite players playing on the world stage. In one of his *Sportsmind* workbooks, Beswick offers the following 15 points to evaluate yourself. Are there some marginal gains in here for you to improve?

	Where are you now? A Coach's Self Evaluation (Bill Beswick)					
	SA – Strongly Agree; **A** – Agree; **M** – Maybe; **D** – Disagree; **SD** – Strongly Disagree					
		SA	A	M	D	SD
1	Everyone knows how passionate and committed I am to coaching football					
2	My personality and behavior always reflect a positive model to the players					
3	I have clear goals and am tough enough to drive the program forward					
4	I am a good communicator and always get my message across					
5	Players enjoy playing for me players enjoy playing for me					
6	I have a clear understanding of how to develop players and teams					
7	My strength is being able to plan, organise and coach practices well					
8	I have a good track record of identifying and recruiting talent					
9	I am tactically sound and can teach a variety of formations					
10	I coach game day well and always give the team the best chance to *meet their goals*[7]					
11	I pride myself on developing positive and productive relationships with players					
12	Players who have played for me will say that I got the best out of them					
13	As far as possible I always try to share 'ownership' with the players					

---

[7] Changed 'win' to 'meet their goals'. The focus as a youth coach won't always be to win, as opposed to a senior coach.

14	I communicate constantly with the players, but especially, I listen					
15	The power of my player relationships is shown by their motivation to play					

Taken and slightly adapted from Bill Beswick's Soccer Masterclass Series[8]

England DNA

After a succession of underperformances at World Cups and European Championship finals, the English FA set about developing their own playing and coaching philosophy. The aim was to take influences from successful nations and fuse them with what they saw as the 'English' way of playing. Overall, there are five core elements:

1. Who We Are
2. How We Play
3. The Future England Player
4. How We Coach
5. How We Support

Part of this endeavor includes the 12 coaching 'fundamentals' below, the last one around 'ball rolling time' we touched on earlier in the chapter. Explore the fundamentals and see if it offers any marginal gain that resonates with you.

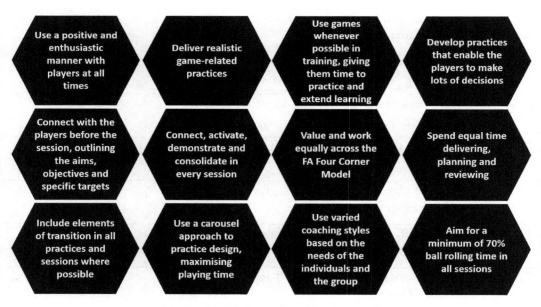

England DNA Coaching Fundamentals

---

[8] Full Title – *Soccer Master Series for Coaches and Players; Volume 1 The Modern Coach; Workbook 5 Creating the Perfect Coaching Environment*

More tellingly, and fittingly as I ask you to explore your improvement areas, is the final section of the leading DNA presentation. This section implores coaches to 'play their part', encouraging individual coaches to assess themselves across the five core elements. You can use this as you see fit, and in a way that works best for you, but identifying your strengths and areas of improvement is highly recommended.

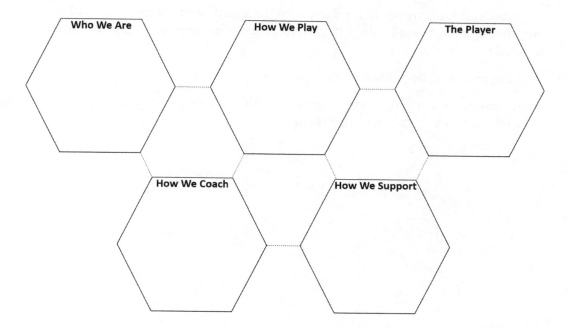

Conclusion – Challenge Yourself to Challenge Your Players

Ultimately, as a youth and a player-centred coach, everything must circle back to the players you engage with. Although much of this chapter has been about you, the coach, we must eventually take this back to the players. Hopefully, the players are the ones that develop further and faster as a result of *your* aggregated improvement. By exploring and looking for the small details, we get a deeper understanding of the whole coaching process.

So, whether the resources above from MUSS, Bill Beswick, The England DNA, the resources from your previous coach development courses, or the rest of this book inspires lightbulb moments, your players should be the winners throughout. As you go through this book, your coaching journey, and your life, I challenge you to find *your* marginal gains.

Summary

- We ask for the best from our players and implore *them* to improve – do we ask for the best from ourselves?

- Your comfort zone is a safe place, and it is necessary, but moving beyond it inspires learning and improvement.

- Beyond our comfort zone is the learning zone – beyond that, however, is the panic zone.

- We all have different comfort, learning, and panic zones, depending on the situation.

Chapter 1 – Coaching in the Magic

- There is a culture in football where coaches feel they must know everything, confining themselves to their comfort zone to avoid criticism. Imposter Syndrome shows us that this feeling of inadequacy is different in reality.

- There are many simple ways to take your coaching self from the comfort to the learning zone – identify them, but, crucially, action them!

- David Brailsford made the concept of marginal gains a priority within cycling – improving lots of small things by 1% to create large aggregate improvements. This has filtered into football also.

- Use the resources available to you to find *your* 1% gains.

- Your improvements must circle back to ultimately improve your players – challenge yourself so that you can challenge them.

It's Your Game #1

Audio Recording

Alex Trukan • @AlexTrukan

Academy Coach

A couple of years ago, at the beginning of my coaching journey, I had started coaching one of the academy teams. I was doing the UEFA B Licence and completing the FA Youth Awards. Although inexperienced, I was very keen on personal development and challenging myself as a coach.

At that time, I was introduced to the idea of videoing sessions and watching them back for my own benefit. I found this very useful but also shocking when I first saw myself coaching for the first time!

Although very useful, videoing sessions can be challenging and time-consuming to arrange, especially for grassroots coaches where equipment, parent's consent, as well as time for reflection, can be very hard to find. It probably took me another 18 months to video myself again.

I continued to look at ways to analyse my own coaching performance. One idea that came to my mind – quite spontaneously – was recording audio. I took my phone, switched on the voice recorder and put it in my pocket. An hour and a half later, I had all the voice interventions recorded and ready to review. It was very easy to organise, is available for most of the coaches nowadays, and is useful to listen to whether in the car, talking the dog for a walk, or on away journeys with your team.

I was able to analyse my verbal communication in depth – the words and phrases I used, along with my tone, volume, and clarity. It was also helpful purely for recalling some parts of the session and helping me to reflect on the session itself. It provided a reference from which further reflection can be started.

This is a good starting point for coaches with limited access to video equipment or opportunities for somebody else to video their coaching. There are obvious pitfalls of this method, though – no visual context, no body language, the absence of a player's non-verbal reactions. However, given the time, efficiency and accessibility of this method, I found it very useful and would highly recommend it for any beginners or advanced coaches.

> ### It's Your Game #2
> # Mentor
> ## Brian Nyabvure • @NyabvureBrian
> ## Head Coach, Trident FC, Zambia

Being based in Africa, opportunities for personal and professional development in football can be scarce. Formal coaching courses are infrequent and those privileged to work in professional or semi-professional football here often spend their time protecting their livelihood. Very little is shared, and you see the same methods repeated over and over again.

Somehow the game I was seeing at the professional level here was not being replicated by the big, big clubs that I would watch in the Champions League, or the leagues in England, Spain, or elsewhere. I felt that if I could import some of the methods from abroad, I could have the edge on many others in the profession here.

As head coach, it is sometimes difficult (but not unheard of) to have your daily ideas and methods challenged. You work in the way that you are used to, that you think is right, and do so without the feedback of a more senior member of staff. I can see why many young coaches bring in experienced ones to work alongside them to help harvest good practice from their knowledge and background.

I decided to challenge myself in a different way. I sought a European mentor, which is where I met Ray. We spoke weekly about tactics, training methods, coaching courses, my future prospects, and he connected me with other relevant coaches, websites, and coaching groups. He inspired me and helped me be different to every other coach at my level.

I was challenged and often overwhelmed once we finished speaking, but I learned so much in our time together. I was certainly outside my comfort zone at times, but it was worth it. I know Ray has mentors, too, that he calls upon to improve himself. I realised a trusted mentor is one of the most important figures for a football coach.

It's Your Game #3

24/7 Learner

Laurie McGinley • @LaurieMcGinley1

Head Coach, Glasgow Girls FC

I start each day the night before. Prior to going to bed, I make a to-do list for the following day, especially if I happen to have a free day. I see and engage with many magnificent coaches, both near and far, and I feel like I need to go the extra mile to give myself the edge – to become a better coach.

I wake up at 6am every morning, and go to the gym. On the drive there, and during the workout, I will listen to a podcast to help set up my day of learning. I like music and some radio, but I think that these podcasts get my brain firing. Depending on the topic – football-specific, psychology, coaching methodology, or stuff from other sports – I am always left with questions, and it makes me want to learn more.

Once back home, I will analyse a game and put together an analysis for my portfolio. This helps to hone my own analytical skills, but also helps to keep me abreast of how the game is developing.

A few years ago, I was not much of a reader. I always thought I never had the time. That was until I came across a performance coach named Jamie Alderton. His point about reading was that instead of aiming to read 40 books a year, you should break the goal down into reading one or two chapters a day. Therefore, before lunch, I look to read three or four chapters of whatever is on my reading list at that moment.

After a healthy lunch, I relax for 30 minutes or so then go for a walk – again listening to a podcast. Ensuring my body is healthy helps my mind stay healthy.

In the afternoon, I will send messages to coaches on social media to learn from them too. You would be surprised by the responses you can get when you reach out to those you admire. This networking challenges me to keep on top of my game.

If there is a professional or reserve game on locally, I will attend that and make notes on both teams. If there isn't a game, then I will try to study a new language. Once home, I watch videos or read internet interviews or articles. I particularly like *The Coaches' Voice* masterclass series and read one of their CV stories.

This is a physical and mental day of learning, but for those wondering, I do make sure that when my wife is home that I spend time with her. Having a support network is key.

I once read a 70-year-old Bobby Robson say he was always learning. If it was good enough for him, it's good enough for me.

It's Your Game #4

Being Me

Annie Zaidi • @CoachAnnieZ

@Womeninfootball National Ambassador

I have vast coaching experience across the game – from foundation phase to professional development and Head Coach at National League level. I have coached in grassroots and elite environments.

When I started coaching, I initially struggled with having a coaching identity. I did what every coach can relate to – I started to copy other coaches' styles. However, as they weren't mine, I didn't really believe in them and it showed in my sessions. A valuable lesson I learnt, when reflecting back, was that to be an authentic coach is to be me – to have my own style – so I am able to own it, embrace it, and more importantly, believe that it will make my players trust me more.

When I initially failed my UEFA B License (2015), despite the heartache and my confidence being knocked, it was a blessing in disguise. It gave me the opportunity to strip everything back and question myself: 'How does Annie learn best?' 'What learning environment suits Annie?'

Answers to both questions were simple – I excel best when everything is simple and less chaotic. There I found my coaching identity – keep it simple regardless of who, or where, I am coaching. This may be amended but not changed.

My session plans can be perceived as unconventional, but the method has never failed me. I believe in it, and own it, and because of this, I can sell messages to players.

I hand-draw all my sessions plans, as I have never been a fan of using my iPad in training – I feel that there is something very disconnected about it. I use coloured pens to draw my sessions onto a whiteboard that contains all the key information.

I use a lot of bright post-it notes, which reflects my personality. I write the schedule of what we are doing on green post-it notes – this way, when the players arrive for the session, they already have an idea of what we are doing and when we are doing it. They can psychologically prepare for the session immediately.

On other colourful post-it notes, I write each coaching point – one principle per post-it, stuck brightly next to the sessions plan on my board. On blue post-it notes, I include individual, unit, or team challenges depending on what segment of the session we are on.

Using my new-formed coaching identity has helped immensely with my confidence as I can always go back to the tactics board to refresh myself on the next scenario or coaching point. Most importantly, it has been an excellent learning tool for all my players, regardless of their age or ability, as I am able to amend it accordingly.

I'm not the best coach, and I have a long way to go, but the key thing I've learnt is to be myself, and bring my own coaching style onto the pitch. I can't be anyone else, no matter how hard I have tried. I am not other coaches; I am just being me.

Chapter 2
From Participation to Pro

"
We all talk about professional football. 98% of
the people who play football in their life have
no chance to be a professional football player,
but this game is only the game we love because
everybody can play. You give them the
opportunity to learn it as good as they can.
"

Jürgen Klopp

The children and adolescents who arrive in our care, and at our clubs, each week are the centrepiece of the whole youth coaching system. We, as coaches, are there for them – not the other way around.

There is, however, something of a disconnect between this – the coach working for the player – and the behaviour of a percentage of the coaching fraternity. Some coaches make themselves the focal point of everything, rather than the children.

Before we start any discussions around how to develop players technically, how to teach them tactics, or how to maximise their mental resilience (all done in later chapters), we must first look at the reasons why those young players turn up to your practice at all.

Player-Centred Coaching

The idea of *player-centred* coaching has become widely accepted within most coach development programmes since the turn of the millennium. The core principle is that the environment focuses on the player and ensures that the developmental environment stimulates each player and allows them to flourish. Importantly, the environment takes account of a player's perceived ability, or lack thereof. Lynn Kidman, author of *The Coaching Process – Developing Decision Makers,* angles that this is a more humanistic approach, where coaches are willing to share power with the players, and thus develop more independent, decision-makers. The table below highlights the differences.

Coach-Centred Approach	Player-Centred Approach
The game revolves exclusively around the coach ("pass here", "dribble there", "run here" etc.)	Players are encouraged to make their own decisions
Treats youth players like 'mini-adults'	Recognises the age considerations of young players
Plays his best team with the purpose of winning games	Gives all his players equal playing time with the purpose of development

Criticises players who struggle, and substitutes players after mistakes	Is patient with players and guides them through difficult periods
Uses command coaching style only	Uses a range of coaching styles, selecting which one is appropriate in any given circumstance
Focuses on team performances	Focuses on individual development, within a team context
Sets goals for the players	Allows players to set their own goals, offering guidance when required
Produces players that are robotic, lack decision-making skills, are defensive, easy to anger, and prone to frustration	Produces players that make their own decisions and are open-minded to new ideas
Produces players that may lack enthusiasm	Produces players that are enthusiastic and show a commitment to excellence
Rarely listens to opinions or advice from players	Listens to players' opinions, producing a 'buy-in' to the project

The players that arrive at your session will have a lot going on in their lives – school-life, home-life, and social-life – all interacting simultaneously. Recognising that each individual is not just a player, and certainly not just "my player" is an important step in the process. Recently, I read a very revealing, honest, and somewhat disturbing interview with former German international defender, Per Mertesacker, originally featured in the German *Der Spiegel* publication. The 6'6" colossus of a defender (hailed as *die Abwehrlatte – The Defence Pole* by the German tabloids, or the BFG – Big F***ing German by Arsenal fans), who has a World Cup winners medal to his name amongst other accolades including three FA Cups, talks about how coaches, fans and the media see players as "reduced to your performance" and, most tellingly, "You're always just the player and never the person behind the jersey." Behind the jersey, Mertesacker opened-up about the constant, debilitating diarrhoea, nausea and stress he experienced before games.

Many may argue that a professional player, and certainly one of Mertesacker's stature, fame, track record, bank balance, and macho nicknames, should be able to deal with this pressure, and that it comes with the privileged territory they inhabit. However, to dismiss this is to miss the point when considering young players. Are we reducing the players in front of us simply to their performances? Does the scoreline, the league table, or the 'hustle' the players bring to games and practice cloud our judgment of them as young people, with limited life experience?

The illustration below was taken from a presentation made by Birmingham City FC's Academy Manager, Kristjaan Speakman (@krespeakman),[1] to highlight the importance of recognising the 'boy' (or girl) first, before we consider them as a player, student or son/daughter. This is arguably even more pertinent in an elite academy environment where the overwhelming expectation is for the young player to become a professional player. This expectation brings its own pressure, which needs managing by both coaches and parents.

---

[1] I have edited the graphic to include the word 'girl' as well as boy. Speakman's presentation showed the work done in a male-only environment.

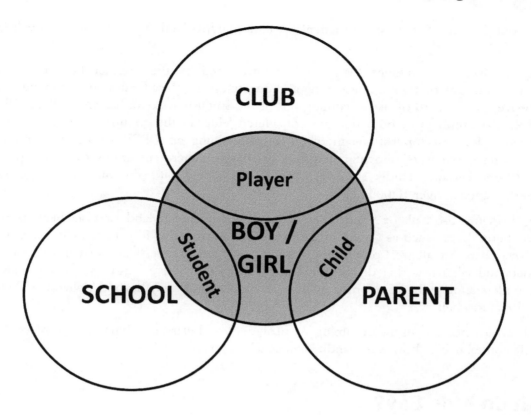

Becoming a Professional

As coaches, we can take it for granted that *all* the players in front of us want to consciously rise to the top end of the game and become professionals – regardless of what age they are. It is true that a lot of young players would like to emulate their heroes – the Messis and Ronaldos of this world – however, this does not equate to them seeking to be judged and measured purely against superstar professionals.

Becoming a professional player is *a lot* harder and *a lot* more unlikely than most of us can even imagine. Michael Calvin's book on the journey of young boys in professional English academies, *No Hunger in Paradise*, is particularly sobering. His research shows that only 180 of the 1.5 million players involved in organised youth football around the country will become professionals in the Premier League.[2] Claudia Romeo, writing for *Business Insider UK*, likens this minuscule 0.012% success rate as statistically similar to being hit by a meteorite! Furthermore, of all the boys that enter professional academies at age nine, only 0.5% will make a living from the game.

So, with the chances of the nine-year-old standing in front of you becoming a star in the Premier League put into place, what about the players who are older and further along their elite pathway journeys?

In England, the players who play at professional clubs beyond 16 are known as 'scholars' and will mainly play in the Under-18 professional league system. Although they are, largely, full-time young professionals, they marry training and playing with study, a measure put in place to ensure they have a fall-back option if they do not make the grade; a contingency that is altogether necessary, if not perfect.

The Professional Footballers Association (PFA), the trade union for professional players in England and Wales, states that not only will most of these boys not become full Premier League

---

[2] Note that this statistic refers to the Premier League only and does not consider the three other fully professional leagues in England – the Championship, League 1 and League 2, nor other professional leagues around the rest of Britain or abroad.

players, but five out of every six of them also will not be involved in professional football *at all* by the age of 21!

The Elite Player Performance Plan (EPPP), introduced by the Premier League and FA in England as a means of grading, measuring and quality-assuring academies (and ultimately seeking to improve the standard of player coming out of the English system), has and will actually work to reduce the numbers of boys that are considered 'elite' in the country. Due to the stringent criteria and the cost-implications involved in maintaining an EPPP Academy, a number of academies have extensively downgraded their provisions. There are simply too many players, at Under-18 and certainly Under-16 level, who are considered elite (this number across the UK, frequently stands at over 10,000). [3]

Slating academy football, or youth football as a whole in England or elsewhere, is not the purpose here. Books such as Calvin's, Matthew Whitehouse's *The Way Forward*, or Chris Green's *Every Boy's Dream* are all great publications should you want to investigate further. Our job here is to understand what it is that drives the young players that arrive before us on a weekly basis, whilst understanding that outcomes in coaches' minds must go beyond delivering them into professional football.

This does not prevent us from aiming to provide world-class coaching to our players, but it certainly contextualises how we, as individual coaches, go about it.

What do Kids Say?

You do not have to look far to discover studies and articles that address the simple question that is posed above. Although there are variations based on the actual survey and where the results hail from, the main reasons given by kids for participating in sport or football are:

- To have fun

- To play and socialise with their friends

- To learn new skills and practice existing ones

- To play the game they love

- To stay fit and healthy

Nick Levett, amongst several other roles, was the FA's National Development Manager for Youth and Mini Soccer between 2009 and 2015, and is currently the Head of Talent and Performance for UK Coaching. Much can be read online about Levett's findings on why children play football, and he is a prolific 'sharer' of some very thoughtful pieces through social media (@nlevett).

During his time working with, and researching the motivations of, eight to 12-year-olds playing football in the UK, Levett surveyed 55 groups of children who played football – including boys and girls, elite and grassroots players, from both urban and rural environments – from all over the country.

The children were given 16 options regarding their experiences of playing football, of which they needed to select the nine that applied the most to them. In a presentation of his findings, Levett flagged up how:

---

[3] Calvin, *No Hunger in Paradise*

- Six options were chosen far more than the others

- Three options were not chosen by a single participant

Below, I have included two tables with the 16 options offered to the young players. From the first table, can you identify the six most frequently chosen responses, and then the three that were never chosen? You can check your answers by using the second table. The six most frequently answered are in white, the three not chosen at all are in grey.

Table 1 – the 16 options given to players

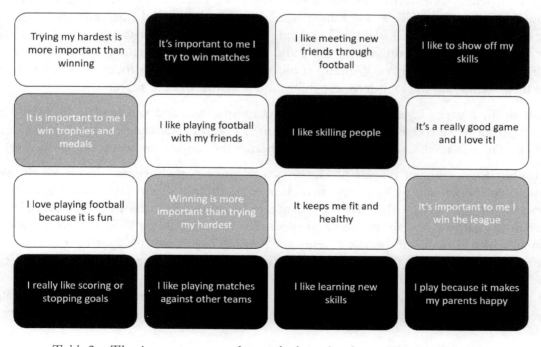

Table 2 – The six responses most frequently chosen by players (white) and the three options not chosen by any player (grey)

From these findings, from around 800 children, we see a clear pattern. Children are more interested in enjoying themselves, playing with their friends, and keeping active, than with trophies and winning leagues. Another study, led by Professor Amanda J. Visek of the Milken Institute School of Public Health, came to similar conclusions. Of the 81 reasons that kids, parents, and coaches gave as to why sports were "fun", winning came 48th, and playing in tournaments came 63rd.[4]

The Paradox of Winning and Competition

The first chapter of *Making the Ball Roll* delved straight into an issue that has been circling youth football across the world – whether the use of scorelines and league tables is beneficial to the development of young players.

The issue has caused a searing debate amongst everyone from school teachers to politicians, from football coaches to those in the media. Surely, we watch football to see who wins, just like any other sport? The match result of Liverpool, Barcelona, Inter Milan, or LA Galaxy has the potential to make a weekend, or completely break it. So why should we discount results in youth football? If there are no scores recorded, how do we know who wins? If there are no league tables, how do we know which team is the best?

Those who advocate the abolishment of scorelines and league tables look beyond the questions that have just been asked. They look towards the long-term development of players, rather than short-term results.

Winning at all Costs

The 'win at all costs' attitude of a significant number within the coaching community can actually hamper the long-term development of players and fly in the face of the player-centred environment. Winning (and trying to win) is not the enemy, but making poor long-term decisions in the quest for short-term glory can be.

We will talk about the effects of Relative Age Effect in a later chapter, but it raises its head here also. Often, when short-term winning is prioritised, the effect it has on a coach's decisions is profound. Firstly, especially at a younger age, it is the physically bigger and more developed players that are most readily identified as being the ones who affect games. Their size, and the impact of their physicality on games, will stand out and it takes a trained and disciplined eye to identify the potential of others. Winning at all costs leads coaches to focus on short-term ability rather than identifying the long-term capability and potential of each player.

The physically bigger players are selected to play more often, and will tend to be placed in key 'tactical' positions (through the centre of the pitch – central defender, central midfielder, and striker) leaving the smaller ones on the sides (although they will often be left out altogether).

This preference for bigger players produces two negative consequences – both for the smaller and the bigger boys and girls. Firstly, it reinforces to the physically-developed player (whether consciously or subconsciously) that this advantage alone will help him or her succeed and get further in the game. They are praised and applauded for their ability to kick the ball hard, high, and long, which connects to people's desire for praise – if you are applauded for it, you will feel encouraged to do it again. Improving in key long-term areas in terms of technical and tactical abilities takes a back seat, until later in youth football when a person's innate physical advantage starts to diminish. Suddenly, when the player is 16, 18 or 21, his powerhouse style of play no longer has the same impact, as the majority of his peers will have caught up with him physically,

---

[4] BBC article by Tom Farrey, *Have Adults Ruined Children's Sport?*

and, with little technique or tactical nous to fall back on, the player only has a fraction of the impact he once had. In turn, it's often too late to catch up technically or tactically. This can be a real blow to confidence and can lead to higher drop-out rates from this category of player.

Secondly, the smaller player who is struggling to compete physically, even before adolescence, gets less and less game time. He isn't 'rated' by the coach, even if he may be technically very proficient. He is simply too small *at that moment* to affect and help the team win games, the story goes. He may drop out of the game or have very little 'stage time' to become selected to play for regional or elite development teams. He, therefore, misses opportunities to get extra coaching, mix more frequently with 'talented' players, or perform at a higher level – stunting his development even further.

So, not only does the game lose the bigger player, the smaller ones can drift away too. As an amateur adult player, not many would sit on the sidelines on a regular basis – we would just go elsewhere and do something more rewarding and more productive. As will children.

" **"**

Let us say that you and I coach two teams with kids that are 10, 11, and 12 years-old and all are about equally good. You try to teach them to play good football, a passing game and with tactical basics, while I tell mine to only play long balls and to try to shoot. I can assure you that, at first, I will always win against you, by using your mistakes – break a bad pass and goal!

If we, however, continue with the same training methods during a three year period, you will most likely win every game against us. Your players will have learned how to play, while mine haven't. That's how easy it is.

Laureano Ruiz, former FC Barcelona Academy Director

Child-Centred Competition

In a paradox that some can find difficult to understand, the children who openly state that winning is not important, or that winning is some way down the list of priorities, are probably the most competitive group around. Chances are, in everyday life as a parent, older sibling, or teacher, you use the inherent competitiveness of children to your advantage. (My cousin, ten years my elder, would make me chase the ball down the street when it went too far, on the promise that he would time me, appealing to my desire to beat my previous time! As a 10-year-old, I duly ran to fetch the ball back, over and over again!)

In my *Deliberate Soccer Practice* series of session plans, each of the 200 sessions I put together includes a way of keeping score to add an extra layer of motivation and performance level to coaching sessions, and this kind of approach can be very useful in maintaining motivation and desire in youngsters. It just needs to be used wisely.

Despite this intense competitive streak, children let the disappointment of a scoreline defeat go quicker than most adults. I have lost count of the number of times that I've overheard a player asking what the score is during the game, often to the incredulity of the surrounding adults!

Coaches and clubs at a junior level, while promoting inclusion and development, can still be openly seen celebrating results, clean sheets, winning streaks, etc. Games that end in huge victories for one side, also end in huge defeats for another. I would go so far as to suggest that beyond a certain point (5-0, 6-0, 10-0?), the game no longer benefits either group of players. The team on the losing end clearly suffers, but the lack of relevant challenge has very little long-term benefit for the winning team either.

Certainly, scorelines that involve significant double-figure victories do little to develop anyone. Close games (that may be in terms of the scoreline, or just the natural competitiveness of the game), where things go right and wrong for everyone, produce mistakes that are learning opportunities; successes that are earned through hard work and challenge, and analysed beyond whether the ball went into the net or not, produce a much more conducive developmental environment. A succession of high-scoring, dominant wins for youth teams, mean that when an inevitable loss eventually comes, it can become completely debilitating. If winning by big margins becomes the norm, any kind of loss involves a big fall from grace. This links to Carol Dweck's study around *Growth Mindset* (more on that later!), where loss and struggle are important to the mental development of young players.

Learning to Lose

The paradox around winning and losing in youth football continues when we look at losing. Losing is not just a part of sport, it is also a part of life. Taking defeat and negativity in your stride is a skill, and one that needs honing. This can happen through explicit discussions, or through the natural ebb and flow of winning and losing. Most psychologists would highlight the ability to recover from setbacks as being one of the most important mental skills in sport. Finely-tuned elite athletes have been identified with their ability to 'doublethink' – having the supreme confidence to win and believe in their ability, but also being very able to deal with defeat and individual mistakes.

Being good at sport for one child is akin to another being good at maths or science. From an early age, children are judged and scored – whether that be in a spelling bee, or whether it is points to enter university. Shouldn't we be permitted to celebrate the athletic achievement of the academic underachiever in the same way that we celebrate the academic successes of the classroom's 'brainboxes' without undue scrutiny? If I put in all the effort to winning a race, jumping higher, or honing my football skills more than others, why should I get the same participation trophy as the ones who delivered some half-assed commitment to it?

This is the central *acceptable* argument that comes from those who believe that winning games and judging performances are positive for children. Please note that this is not the same argument that comes from those coaches who simply want to win medals and trophies for their own advancement, and at the expense of players' long-term development – we have seen how treacherous that can be. Winning medals and trophies is far more important to adults than it is to kids.

In a *Guardian* newspaper article, Alex Clapham (@alexclapham), having played and coached in England and Spain, asked quite a cutting question – *by not developing winners, are we subconsciously encouraging losers?* I have direct experience of this one.

The first, was when I was a relatively young, inexperienced coach, working with a professional Under-18 team. We travelled to a much bigger club, with an ex-Manchester United player as the coach in the opposite dugout – and lost 8-0. After 20 minutes of silence on the bus journey home, the atmosphere quickly changed. Almost like flicking a switch, the mood transformed to a semi-jubilant, I'm-on-a-bus-with-my-mates type ride, full of jokes, games, and group laughter. I couldn't understand how a group of players, whose next significant step was into an adult professional environment, could take such a beating so well. I never want a result to 'kill' a group of young men, but it should hurt, especially at that age. Looking back, maybe they were just masking their embarrassment, or maybe a lack of emphasis throughout their academy journey fostered a 'loser' mentality.

A second occasion was again within a professional academy, but this time with a group of Under-10s who I was not directly coaching. They were suffering a heavy defeat – it was still unfolding and becoming quite bruising – but the coach behaved like nothing untoward was happening, and the atmosphere was one of smiles, high-fives, and jokes. In an environment like this, fostering a desire to win (not to be confused with going all out to win, no matter what) is nothing to be ashamed of. Maybe as 18-year-olds, they would not accept defeat so readily?

It is important not to confuse the need to win at all costs – judging players' performances prematurely and based on the scoreline only – with the broader will to win. As coaches, we need to put winning – and losing – into perspective. The scoreline is only one way of measuring performance and, often, quite a false reflection on performance. I am convinced that a 7-a-side Under-11 team that would have contained Xavi, Iniesta, Messi, Jordi Alba, Fabregas, and Dani Alves would have lost a significant number of games. I would hate to be the coach that, concerned only with winning *now*, replaced those six players with physically bigger but technically limited boys, just to win an Under-11 league; risking the future involvement of the core of one of the greatest teams to ever play.

The Wider the Base, The Higher the Peak

Sometimes, as a coach, when working with your local team, it is very hard to feel as though you are part of a larger system or football development program. Depending on what country or region you are reading this from, your governing sports or football federation will have a vision and system about the progression of youth players from grassroots to the professional game.

As we have discovered above, the journey from a local underage team to the top professional leagues is a long, difficult, and unlikely one. Nor is it a journey that every player will want to make.

Below is a common sports development pyramid that is widespread amongst sports development organisations. The central concept is that entry-level and mass participation players are represented by the wider base of the pyramid. As the system progresses, the best players are filtered up the pyramid, slowly decreasing in numbers until the very best are playing at the top, usually meaning at professional or international level.

Common Sport Development Pyramid

Many organisations will use a variant of this model, be that for general sport development, or to pin down a talent development pathway. More and more football governing bodies are starting to recognise the positive impact that focusing on the larger foundation and participation segments has, and understanding that *the wider the base, the higher the peak*. The more cows you have, the more cream you produce, and it is the higher standard of the cream that ultimately rises to the top. The more children that are playing football, the more productive the system is. An adapted pyramid model below, from the Belgian FA, shows their emphasis on the base of the pyramid as part of their strategy, recognising that 95% of their football community will be from this segment.

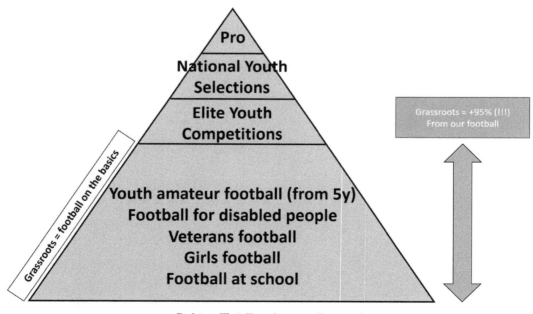

Belgian FA Development Pyramid

The numbers of children participating in organised sport, in Western countries around the world, is in decline. A study by the *Aspen Institute* in 2017, showed decreasing figures in major sports (apart from ice hockey). Football participation levels waned by 9% in a five-year period between 2011 and 2016. While 9% doesn't seem a significant figure – it equates to over 400,000 players. The result: a narrowing of the base.

Some time back, I read an excellent blog by Mark O'Sullivan (@markstkhlm), an Irish-born coach educator, based in Sweden. In that particular part of Scandinavia, the governing bodies are beginning to review the traditional methods of such a pyramid, and changing their thought processes with regards to the relationship between participation and elite development. O'Sullivan called their impetus on this "A Quiet Revolution". This revolution involves a focus on keeping as many players playing the game for as long as possible. Johan Johqvist, Chairman of The Hallands Fotbollförbund (Halland Football Association), is quoted in the blogs as saying that there is a huge focus on retaining players, rather than excluding them as he is "…convinced that under the present system we are losing young people that can become elite players."

Not only did this district FA aim to reduce the exclusion of participants, they also reduced the selection process by dismantling their district team, citing that it promotes early selection that reinforces the Relative Age Effect problem. Rather than seeing the district select team simply as promoting the best, they were seen as making selections too early, and ultimately increasing the numbers of players who didn't 'make it'. Since 2017, one of the top goals of the Stockholm-based club AIK, is "We want all children in AIK to feel good… to keep them playing football in AIK for as long as possible and to continue playing sport as much as possible through life."[5]

By focusing on the child first, and the talent later, the Swedish football bodies are not only tending to the wider social issue of obesity and associated ill-health, they are somewhat disturbing the traditional view of the pyramid as a linear pathway: "Development is nonlinear, learning is nonlinear. Therefore, talent is nonlinear".

Your Role within the Pyramid

Depending on the level of the pyramid that you currently coach at, you, as a single coach, will play a local role within whatever system you are a part of – whether that be a local or national structure. For this reason, it is certainly worth familiarising yourself with your local or national development model to ensure that you understand the wider implications of your coaching.

If you are coaching within the Foundation or Participation segments, one of your main jobs is to ensure that players are playing football for as long as possible. Ultimately, this will boil down to game time and game opportunities for *all* players – even if you may not feel that they are affecting games yet.

Much is made of the release policies and strategies of elite academies, as we discussed earlier, and there are indeed some stories of poor practice when handling such a sensitive issue. However, a player released from a professional club can still drop into a lower level of football that may suit them better at that moment. If we 'release' or exclude (intentionally or otherwise) players at grassroots level, however, they have nowhere to go. In previous generations, when street football was still strong, one could argue that players would drop back into playing in unorganised setups, before stepping back into organised clubs. Today, however, if we disengage players from participation-level football, the chances are that we may very well lose these players altogether.

If you are a coach working with 'elite' young players, you are still duty-bound to keep players involved in the game for as long as possible. Releasing players from such an environment is,

---

[5] Quotes and opinions taken from Mark O'Sullivan's blogs – *A Quiet Revolution – Swedish youth Football and the Idea of Avoiding Exclusion* and *The Quiet Revolution Starts to Bring the Noise!* Follow Mark on Twitter: @markstkhlm

obviously, par for the course, and one that nobody particularly relishes. If you are in this position, ask yourself whether you are serving the game, the system, and the players themselves, by ensuring they retain a love for the game, despite being rejected while still young.

In an article for the highly recommended football website, *These Football Times*, Arnar Bill Gunnarsson, Director of Education for the Icelandic Football Association (KSÍ), explains that much of the reason for their recent ascent in world football is down to new facilities and qualified coaches, but he also recognises these coaches' ability to inspire players:

"And, if kids get an experienced and qualified coach who is fun and entertaining, the kids love the game. What happens when you learn to love the game, you go out on the training pitch and do something extra. You play football outside of organised training sessions."

Inspiring and feeding a love of the game from coaches to the mass football-playing demographic, produces better players and a better experience for all. Circling back for a moment to the findings of Nick Levett, he added that when asked whether they would prefer to play and lose, or to be a substitute and win, 80% of the players would choose to play in any circumstance, rather than not play – highlighting the huge importance of *just playing*.

The Role of Play in Childhood Development

Play, whether that means organised sport, or unstructured play associated with younger children, is a vital part of a child's development. Children engage with play as it stimulates them and helps them to make sense of (and learn about) their surroundings. Most children have the innate ability to turn most situations they are presented with into a game, fostering creativity and imagination. Throw a group of kids a roll of toilet paper and a tin can, and they would probably come up with some sort of (competitive!) game.

Organised sport has an exhaustive list of benefits for youth, not just in a competitive sense, but in terms of social, physical, and emotional gains. Add to that the technical and tactical skills associated with particular sports and you have a well-rounded, heavily positive experience. The list below is taken from *Believe Perform*, a sports psychology platform that is popular online and on social media (@BelievePHQ).

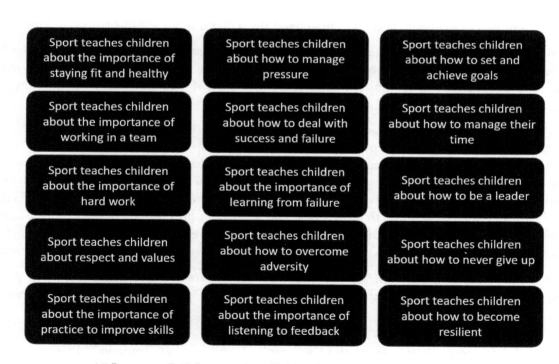

Sport teaches children about the importance of staying fit and healthy	Sport teaches children about how to manage pressure	Sport teaches children about how to set and achieve goals
Sport teaches children about the importance of working in a team	Sport teaches children about how to deal with success and failure	Sport teaches children about how to manage their time
Sport teaches children about the importance of hard work	Sport teaches children about the importance of learning from failure	Sport teaches children about how to be a leader
Sport teaches children about respect and values	Sport teaches children about how to overcome adversity	Sport teaches children about how to never give up
Sport teaches children about the importance of practice to improve skills	Sport teaches children about the importance of listening to feedback	Sport teaches children about how to become resilient

15 Important Life Lessons that Children Learn Through Playing Sport

Summary

- Before coaches worry about the technical, tactical, physical, or psychological development of their players, they should know why players are there.

- Make the players the centre of your environment, not yourself as coach.

- Coaches should consider that the players are children first and have other influences in their lives. Be careful when reducing your opinion of the boy/girl to their performance.

- Only a tiny percentage of players playing in organised football will play in the professional game – even if they are still involved with professional clubs in their late teens.

- Children place the value of winning medals, leagues, and trophies far lower on their list of priorities than you would expect. Their motivations focus more on enjoyment, socialising, and the health benefits of playing. 80% would rather play on a losing team than be a substitute for a winning one.

- A coach's win at all costs mentality negatively affects his/her decisions around team selection. Both physically-developed and under-developed players may suffer as a result.

- Children are inherently competitive, but we need to ensure that the competition we involve them in is child-centred and appropriate.

- Losing is an inherent part of playing football. It is important that winning and losing are managed correctly.

- The common Sports Developed Pyramid places foundation and participation players at the larger base, with elite players rising to the top.

- Some football decision-makers are challenging this model by focusing heavily on player retention in the sport – the wider the base, the higher the peak.

- Understanding *your* role in the pyramid and within the regional/national football development strategy is important.

- Play is important for children, and the benefits of sport for producing life lessons are significant.

> # It's Your Game #1
>
> # A One Man/Boy Team
>
> ## Anonymous

Every year, our school would play in an Under-11 schools league run by the local FA. For ten weeks, we would play every Thursday after school at a nearby sports facility. The games were 7v7 and involved six teams, all playing simultaneously.

All schools were pretty close geographically, so there was a respectable rivalry amongst the teachers/coaches and indeed the players themselves. Many of them, although from different schools, would play on the same teams at weekends and would probably train together later the same evening.

The most renowned player in the area was a 10-year-old fair-haired boy called Tom [not his real name]. Tom was a character – brash, outspoken, and a bit of a whirlwind, without being troublesome. Added to his lively character, he was a big kid – broad across the shoulders, and taller than most. You would certainly imagine him fitting in neatly with a team or class group two or three years his senior.

Tom played for one of the rival schools and was the heartbeat of his team. In fact, one could suggest that it was indeed *his* team! Although most players were rotated and offered reasonably equal playing time, Tom played every minute of every game. Positionally, he played everywhere the ball was – he was a central defender when the opposition attacked, and a mix of central midfielder and centre-forward when his team had the ball. What's more, the coach would happily admit that Tom had a "free role" to be an attacker and defender whenever required.

Tom would take all the team's corners, free-kicks, and could hurl a long, aggressive throw into the opponent's goal area. It was almost one man versus several kids, some of whom would still turn or avoid the ball if it was travelling too hard! After a drawn final game, the regular goalkeeper was replaced by Tom for the penalty shoot-out, and sure enough, he saved all three penalties as his team won the competition.

It was only after some time that I began to understand the pitfalls of the coach's behaviour with Tom. Not only was he being exceptionally unfair to the rest of the team, he was also setting Tom up for a big fall once his physical domination evened out over time. His total dominance of our league was due to powerful forward runs, hard shots, and robust defending; even when he lost control of the ball, his strength and pace allowed him to win it back quickly and effortlessly. What he lacked was the opportunity to develop close control, cleverness, deftness of touch – and he never had to find space where he may be unmarked.

The star of the show, I suspect, will be an also-ran within a few short years.

It's Your Game #2

The Holy S**t Effect

Peter Prickett • @PeterPrickett

Coach & Author

One of the books that had an early influence on my approach to coaching was *The Talent Code* by Daniel Coyle. One of the chapters described a phenomenon described as *The Holy S**t Effect* – when a player from seemingly nowhere jumps from somewhere near the back of the pack out to the front.

At the time, I thought it was a bit of nonsense. I felt it was a bit of fluff that gave hope to the triers, but mentally highlighted it anyway.

Then I experienced it first hand at an after-school session. A small 10-year-old boy suddenly started to excel in the ball mastery exercises. This transferred into the one v one sections, then the two v two. Within three weeks, he was one of the dominating players in matches. The boy had been coming for a year before that. What had changed?

The next time I witnessed the effect was at my own grassroots team. One player had been a bit of a joker at training. He was well-liked by his teammates, but even now, he describes his past self as: "the small, fat, right-footed left-back". He had some nice touches on the ball but little else. A summer passed, and he became a rampaging attacking left-back who scored a stunning goal from 40 yards. What had changed?

In the first case, I discovered that the boy had moved to a new house and now lived closer to his friends. He played football with them every day. His development had accelerated.

In the second case, the player had changed physically. Over that summer, the team moved from Under-12 to Under-13. Physical changes can be quite rapid at this age, and the summer break was from May to September – plenty of time for a teen to change. The 'puppy fat' had dropped off, and he had suddenly found acceleration no one knew existed. At the end of that season, his teammates voted for him as their player of the year.

Since these two early cases, I have witnessed the effect numerous times. It has convinced me that you just cannot tell what will happen with a player with any degree of certainty until they are close to physical maturation.

Are we prepared to wait?

It's Your Game #3

Not a Race

Debbie Sayers • @Salisburyrovers

Club Secretary & Welfare Officer, Salisbury Rovers FC

Our club, Salisbury Rovers, was established in 2016. We wanted to be different from the endless number of kid's football clubs that were "releasing" young players, letting the "poorer" ones warm the bench, and constantly trialling and poaching players.

We describe our philosophy as 'football environmentalism'. Our role as coach-facilitators is to create an environment which is fun, inclusive, and which facilitates empowerment and the child's ownership of their own game. We believe that, in line with self-determination theory and children's fundamental human rights (e.g., those in the UN Convention on the Rights of the Child), a fun and empowering environment is most likely to meet the innate human needs of competence, relatedness, and autonomy. This will facilitate the optimal function and growth of the individual (the person and player) by fostering risk-taking, creativity, and by supporting whole child development.

From a football perspective, we think this approach will increase retention in the game, allowing kids to reach their potential and encouraging them to be bold, self-motivated, and independent decision-makers in sport and in life. Any adult who coaches kids at our club is committed to our strap-line *the game belongs to the kids who play it*. For example:

- Coach-facilitators act inclusively and encourage *all* children to play. They use small sided-games and a constraints-led approach and avoid games with feeders or queues, or games where only a few kids are actively participating. They understand the dynamic of play and its importance for skill acquisition.

- Coach-facilitators value free play. Our #freeplaypledge affirms that "free play is a childhood right" which is "not objective based".

- Coach-facilitators prioritise relationships with children, allowing time for conversation. They encourage children to have and express their views. They respect and act upon these views within the course of sessions, and in session planning.

- Coach-facilitators design games for, and often *with*, children to allow them to explore the technical, physical, psychological, and social aspects of football independently. Coach-facilitators reflect and evaluate on these games with the children who have played them.

- Coach-facilitators do not direct play or, generally, provide explicit technical instruction: the coach is not a 'guru' with all the football answers. This limits children's potential to the capacity of their coach. Coach-facilitators observe rather than intervene and use their observations to inform the dialogue with children about play, adaptation, and progressions. They pose questions, and prompt exploration, encouraging children to find their own voice and answers.

At Salisbury Rovers FC, we believe fun starts with respecting the right of all children to play their game, their way.

Our approach is long-term. Youth football is not a race.

Chapter 3
The Feet Are Just the Tools

"   **"**

Football is played with the head.
Your feet are just the tools.

Andrea Pirlo

In 2012, Pep Guardiola left his role as Head Coach of FC Barcelona. During his four-year tenure with the first team, the club's trophy cabinet swelled.[1] Under his guidance, the Catalan club won 14 major honours, including three La Liga titles and two Champions League trophies.

Not only did 'Pep' bring a brand of technical football to the fore that was rarely seen alongside such success, but he also brought a brand of intelligent football into the living rooms of coaches across the globe. The sight of physically smaller players utterly dominating the football world, further compounded by the success of the Spanish national team, set the scene for a new way of looking at, and coaching, the game. The role of the mind and football intelligence was popularised.

Furthermore, in a fascinating article, *Why Understanding the Teenage Brain is Key to Coaching*, writer Simon Austin (@sport_simon) quoted a 2016 research paper pointing to a player's mindset as the underlying driver in those that made the step from Academy to professional football. In the same article, Dr. Perry Walters pointed out that football programmes will actively tailor for technical or physical defects within a player's game, but nearly always neglect brain-related, psychological issues. Understanding what is happening in the brain is a big plus for modern coaches looking to advance their players psychologically; awareness helps create the intelligent players popularised by the likes of Guardiola.

The Developing Brain

None of us need to be neuroscientists to note that the way children think is different to the way teenagers do. Which is, in turn, different to the way adults think.

By the time children are six years old, their brain is already 90 – 95% the *size* of an adult brain.[2] The size, however, should not be confused with how much it is developed or how it functions. Six-year-olds are not 90% of adults in the way they behave or think. From then until their mid-twenties, the brain is still growing and remodelling, which happens more intensely during adolescence. All the way through, this causes changes in behaviour; the way youngsters think, how they react in situations, what is important to them, etc. As much as we would like it, we cannot expect adult thinking from young people. When you hear the phrase 'kids are not mini-

---

[1] A year prior to his appointment as the club's Head Coach, Guardiola spent a season in charge of the club's second team, Barca B.
[2] www.raisingchildren.net.au

adults' – as is often referenced when it comes to inappropriate coaching in football – this is where it stems from.

The *prefrontal cortex* part of the brain is the area that is responsible for decision-making, behavioural regulation, and expression. Critically, this is the part of the brain that deals in rationality and is the part that *adults* predominantly think with. In the teenage brain, however, the prefrontal cortex is still under construction. Teenagers rely more on the *amygdala* part of the brain to make decisions and solve problems. This part of the brain is characterised by emotion and instinctive, impulsive behaviour. Risk-taking and experimentation are more prevalent, and the concept of 'cause and effect' is still evolving.

For those of us who work with teenagers, or even parent them, this will resonate. We will all have stories of teenagers making poor, irrational, overly-emotional, impulsive decisions on a daily basis. It is our job to guide, help, motivate, and influence young people on this journey.

During the early years of my coaching, I did some guest sessions in a 'secure unit', which housed eight teenagers of both genders convicted of various serious criminal offences. On day one, I was told that instead of two hours with all eight, I would have back-to-back one-hour sessions with four of them at a time. Having all eight taking part at once would be a recipe for potential disaster, I was told. Not only did these young teens have complicated pasts and display regular, challenging behaviour anyway, but their responses also tended to be straight from the amygdala – highly emotional, over-the-top, impulsive, and unpredictable. There were fights – verbal and physical – cases of non-compliance, and aggressive showmanship in view of their peers; a tough afternoon for all! The sessions, as a result, were fractious and littered with interruptions.

Day to day, you might find your pre-teen daughter challenges your authority more than ever before. In your coaching environment, that 11-year-old you coached two years ago, is now a more aggressive 13-year-old with ideas of his own and the impulse and emotion to challenge you.

Risk-taking and experimentation is a key feature of the teenage brain – making mistakes is a huge opportunity for learning and is actually something that can be welcomed (and even embraced). If we take the focus away from winning, and the focus away from trying to make kids football look like adult football, we can use any mistakes along the way as a major source of improvement.

Teenagers are highly sensitive to criticism, especially from their peers. Social rejection hurts, so the need to please peers is often high on the agenda of adolescents. Purdue University psychologist Kip Williams developed a very simple 'ball toss' experiment to test the effects of social exclusion on teens. The experiment involved three participants throwing the ball back and forth. Two of the participants, however, followed a script and began tossing the ball back and forth to each other, excluding Player 3. After a very short time, the experiment induced negative reactions from the excluded teen, from internal sadness to outward frustration and anger. So, when a player complains that he is never passed the ball by his teammates, however illogical you may feel it is, remember this. Such is the power of social rejection, and the need for acceptance; often, the advice of peers is valued more than that of an adult, regardless of life experience, knowledge, qualifications, and everything else!

Coaching 21st Century Children

Most of you reading this book will be coaching players born after 2000 – real 21st century children. I am not necessarily happy in making widespread generalisations about groups of people, and certainly not about whole generations. I am also conscious that this book will be read in countries that differ culturally, and a child's life will vary significantly depending on where they grew up. Nonetheless, there are many commonalities, especially in children who grow up in the 'west'.

When I was growing up, I could not quite comprehend the thought of the older members of my family huddled around a black and white TV, or listening to the 'wireless'. Today, the children we are working with will snigger at a TV that is not a flat screen, and 'wireless' means something completely different.

They can 'shazam' their favourite song and download it to a tiny hand-held music player that also functions as a phone, camera, and personal TV. They have never lived in a world without Wi-Fi, smartphones, or games consoles. We can sometimes go heavy on this generation for retreating indoors on media devices, rather than embracing the great outdoors but (however true) this criticism does not help the situation, and *has* an impact on our engagement with them.

21st century kids expect immediate answers – that is simply what they are used to – and frown at having to wait for anything. They are constantly in receipt of information – often in short bursts – and are incessantly stimulated by pictures, videos, and instant communications. They are infrequently bored. A teenager waiting for a bus will text friends, use social media, watch videos or utilise the thousands of other entertainment options that their smartphone offers. A toddler will sit on mum's lap and watch episodes of whatever TV show keeps them quiet and entertained at the doctor's surgery or on a flight. They are not used to waiting, being bored, or needing to be patient.

If we drag this concept back to our coaching environment, some elements may begin to resonate. We need to offer this generation stimuli that we ourselves probably didn't need. Long queues of players waiting their turn to pass, shoot or cross goes against their nature, and they will seek other ways to quench any boredom they may feel. Nor does it replicate the 'street football' environments where previous generations learned the game. Listening to a football monologue from a coach, without other stimuli, also goes against their day-to-day experience of life.

Talent and the Brain

"

When Ronaldinho and Ronaldo played futsal, they were firing and optimising their circuits more often and more precisely than when they played the outdoor game. They were growing more myelin.

"

Daniel Coyle, *The Talent Code*

I often cite the work of Daniel Coyle (@DanielCoyle) and the role of the brain as a game-changer when it comes to coaching. He champions myelin ("the stuff of talent") – a white, fatty substance involved in the learning process – and the plasticity of the brain (i.e., its ability to grow, change and mould).

During the skill development process, neural pathways and connections are built to reinforce learning. The more (and better) you practice, and the more you learn, these connections become layered in myelin. The thicker this coating of myelin, the faster and more accurately you can perform a skill. In a football sense, *the more we activate the brains of players, the better they will become.* This is done by putting players in situations that require decision-making and problem-solving, as well as deliberate repetition, and the making of mistakes.

Brain-Centred Training

According to Coyle, the key facilitators or "talent whisperers" in the development of talent are "master coaches". These coaches – you and me – through deliberate practice, can engage players on a higher cognitive level than others.

Chapter 3 – The Feet Are Just the Tools

As coaches, we can learn a lot from the high-profile figures in the game – I constantly refer to the likes of Guardiola, Ancelotti, and Bielsa – however, the majority of youth development experts work predominantly behind the scenes, away from TV cameras and the media spotlight.

Michel Bruyninckx is a Belgian football coach, who was the Academy Director at Standard Liège and who also had a spell at the Aspire Academy in Qatar. His methods have been utilised by giants Real Madrid and AC Milan, as well as football federations the world over. Bruyninckx himself claims that 25% of his graduates have become professional players, or national level female players. His early work and influence on Belgian internationals Steven Dufour and Dries Mertens, both of whom came through an intensive pilot study led by the Belgian, is particularly eye-opening. Between 2000 and 2011, both were part of a sample group of 200 children (140 boys and 60 girls) "whom were not naturally gifted at the outset" (www.senseball.com). They were then immersed in Bruyninckx's methods. Six of the 140 boys played for the Belgian national team, and half of the female national team have been made up of players from this sample. When you consider the low percentages we discussed in the *Participation to Pro* chapter, these numbers are truly impressive – as is a further statistic from the sample group, which found that the school grades of participants also increased by 10%.

Bruyninckx himself outlines his speciality as being: "Brain central learning based on cognitive neurology, neuropsychology and neurobiology in sports" – language that is more familiar to the world of science than the football pitch.

The central concept of Bruyninckx's technique is, in layman's language, 'Brain-Centred Training'. This includes innovative methods designed to 'stress' and multitask the brain within football sessions, focusing on the development of intelligent players who can think and execute technical demands quicker. In the first instance, he recognises football as a highly cognitive sport, and the Belgian is irked by the over-focus on physical factors. He speaks of many players whom he has worked with, who were released from the game because of easy-to-measure physical characteristics, and who went on to play at the highest professional levels. All football players, he says, have a "unique body and brain organisation" – both of which can be shaped and which must be considered.

Bruyninckx's method echoes much of the work from Coyle – the need to create and hardwire circuitry in the brain to improve the long-term performance of players. Indeed, myelination is a key phase in his language. In a practical training sense, Bruyninckx's method is to overload the brain in training, thus making complex game situations significantly easier. More extreme examples of his training methods include having the players converse in up to four different languages as they practice!

While this would be entirely impractical for most coaches, many use other ways to overload players' brains during training. Kevin McGreskin, quoted in the article *Standard Liege's Bruyninckx Leads Way in Developing Mental Capacity*, suggests the use of tennis balls and calling out colours as players pass and control the ball with their feet.

"

By constantly challenging the brain and making use of its plasticity, you discover a world that you thought was never available. Once the brain picks up the challenge, you create new connections and gives remarkable results.

"

Michel Bruyninckx

The session below is from the 2014 NSCAA Soccer Convention, run by Bruyninckx, and was shared by Neil Cooper (@NCHammer1980), slightly adapted for use here. For other sample sessions from this event, Neil's document is available online, and further sessions are available to view on YouTube. The session focuses on combination passing.

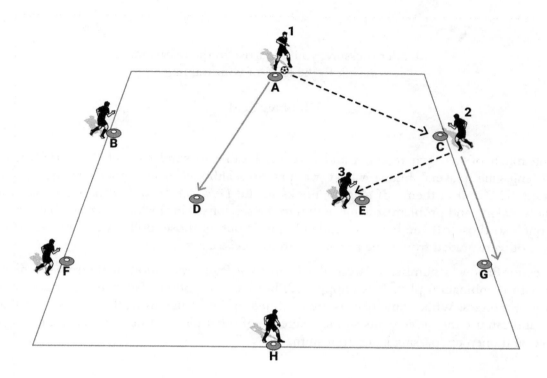

Set-Up – Grid area. All players are placed on a separate cone, with two free cones. In the session above, there are 6 players and 8 cones.

Practice – Player 1 can pass to any player within the group, but it cannot be a 'straight' pass (A-H, B-C, D-E, F-G). He then moves to a free cone. Player 2 receives and repeats, and the session continues.

Progressions – Coach shouts "out" and the player who just passed the ball must leave the grid. On the shout of "in" the player re-joins a free cone.

Other Possible Progressions – Add a second ball that plays simultaneously.

Other Options – In reality, we will have more than six players in our sessions, and most of the time we will not have multiples of six players. To manage this, you can use all your players, making the grid bigger, and adding more free cones. The more players you have, the more balls you can use and the greater the stress on the brain.

Deliberate Soccer Practice

Football is complex. The possibilities and variables, within the laws of the game, are almost endless. It is about solving problems in the face of constant obstacles, and interference. While players will find themselves in similar situations, they will rarely, if ever, face the *exact* same situation twice. When a player faces a problem on the pitch, he must have the ability to solve this problem – the more solutions he has to solve this problem, the better equipped he will be. In a 2011 interview with *US Soccer*, Daniel Coyle describes football as a "constant chain" of problems and solutions. A player's ability to improvise in situations that he may not have an exact experience of, before, is constantly tested.

" "

Under pressure, you don't rise to the occasion;
you sink to the level of your training.

US Navy Seal

During much of my own research and practice, I came to similar conclusions as Bruyninckx about engaging players' brains whilst we practice, although some concepts are noticeably different. The central theme of all four books in the *Deliberate Soccer Practice* series,[3] is to make decision-making and problem-solving central to the sessions. This includes players that are on the ball, but also those off the ball. I confidently threw out all those 'drills' where players stood in queues, or were guided from cone to cone, with no decisions to make.

The session below is number 13 from the *Passing and Possession* edition of the series, which also deals with combination play. It is unopposed, but has the option of becoming opposed as the session progresses. While some players are confined to the corner areas, they are not confined to cones and can use the movements and interference of other players to find space, create angles to receive, and open up 'passing lanes' to teammates.

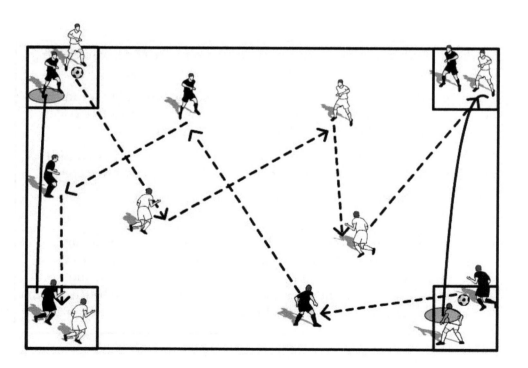

---

[3] *Deliberate Soccer Practice: 50 Passing and Possession Practices to Improve Decision-Making*

Set-Up – The group is split in half, with one player from each 'team' locked in the corners. Each team has a ball.

Practice – The ball is passed from one corner to the opposite one, with the internal players combining to get it there. The corner player switches the play and the practice resumes.

Progressions –

1. Once the pass gets to a corner player, he swaps position with a) the player who plays the pass, or b) with a different outfield player (non-passer).

2. Once a corner player receives the ball, he is 'unlocked'. Can all the players work to unlock all their teammates?

3. The game can progress to a possession game, where the first team to pass to, and 'unlock', all four of their corner players wins.

Decision-Making

In his book, *Sources of Power – How People Make Decisions*, author Gary Klein reveals something quite unsettling. During a pre-interview about his decision-making process, a firefighter revealed, "I don't make decisions." At first, this is quite disturbing. Surely, someone in that position needs clear analytical thinking? Given two options, for example, you would expect a firefighter to choose the best one based on A, B, C and D. If my house is burning down, I want to know that the guys charged with putting the fire out are competent decision-makers.

In reality, we would not want people in such a position – at the moment when it mattered most – to be bogged down with making *conscious* decisions. What we actually look for from people in such a position is intuitive, automated thinking, based on a variable problem that is in front of them.

This type of thinking is echoed by many senior professional football players. Their decision-making, like the firefighter's, is in the *unconscious competence* stage.

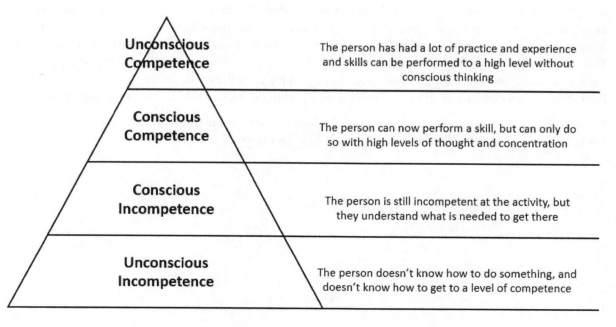

The Four Stages of Competence / Hierarchy of Competence

Professional players' experience of the game allows them to make automatic decisions (just like most of us have when we drive a car) – based on the many variables – quickly and efficiently. If we spend all our coaching time placing players in queues, telling them what to do, and shouting the solution to every problem they face, we are not allowing them to discover these things for themselves. We are stunting their ability to problem-solve and make decisions – and we also minimise their chances of making mistakes, learning from mistakes, and self-correcting.

As a youth coach, moving our players through the four stages of competency is a valuable process. Moving away from queues and cone-to-cone practices gives players better, and more, experience of the chaotic side of the game. By exposing players to variable and random situations more often, they will make sense of the game that others see as messy. The chaos is not chaotic for them at all, even if they cannot fully explain verbally why they made a particular decision. An answer of "I don't know, I just did it" will not make for much of a group chat around a tactics board, but it is an entirely acceptable one. Remember, whether players can answer your questions in a team meeting is not important, it is whether they can carry out the requirements of the game physically that is important.

The Paradox of Praise and 'Talent'

"

If the coach values passion, learning, and improvement, these are things that players can work together to produce.

"

Carol Dweck

I am a big advocate of using praise with youth players – and all players for that matter. Throughout my football journey, I have come across negative people who just suck the life out of you. Nothing is ever right, and every silver lining has a cloud. As Albert Einstein once said, negative people "have a problem for every solution." I made a decision quite early that these 'energy sappers' have no place near me, or near the players and teams I am involved with.

Critically, however, being positive does not mean that you sidestep negative things, or that you avoid discussions that require the addressing of indiscipline, poor behaviour, or a poor approach. You do not have to ignore undesirable elements or dress them up to be something they are not. You do not have to accept irrational, emotional conduct just because a teenager's amygdala is in play. Coaching means that, at times, you have a duty to tell people what they may not want to hear – that is an obligation. It just doesn't mean you have to mentally 'kill' people along the way.

Former Premier League striker, Uwe Rösler, when entering a professional first-team environment for the first time at 18, tells this story of his lasting memory of his first day.

"

The first day of preseason, the assistant coach did something I never forgot. Something that stayed with me for the rest of my career. "This is Uwe Rösler. Don't worry, he will never make it," he said, in front of the whole team. At the time, it crushed me. A few years later, I met him and asked him why he did it. He told me he only did it to players who he believed in a lot because either they came through it or they fell apart. I'm not saying it's the right way to do it, but it helped me in my career because I've always been out to prove a point. And, actually, to prove a point to him

"

Uwe Rösler

The story from Rösler above, I am certain, will generate a mixed response. Many people's views of professional footballers are that they should have a thick skin; that anything goes. They should have super-human mental strength to go with their super-human wage packets. However, this haphazard, inconsiderate way of testing resilience will see more casualties than survivors – more 18-year-olds that will stay "crushed" rather than pushing on through. This type of intervention, while not detrimental on this occasion, is *not* the acid test of whether an 18-year-old can make a career from the game. Motivating anyone using a balance of carrot and stick is one thing, but risking the career of someone you believe in, with such a public and humiliating crack of the stick, is quite another. For every teenage player that this unnamed German coach used this 'technique' with, I would be interested to see how many failed to fulfil their potential after such an inauspicious beginning.

Developing mental skills, such as the resilience shown by Rösler, is an important part of growing up. Whether in football or in the real world, we all face challenges, make mistakes, or feel like giving up. This calls for a *growth mindset*.

Fixed v. Growth Mindset

Sport is full of opinions. Players are judged frequently and judged early. At first glance, we see a boy/girl who 'looks like a player' or is a 'natural'. They are really 'talented'. The inspiration for *Moneyball*, the extraordinary achievements of baseball's Oakland Athletics, came from the quick, early judgement of their general manager, Billy Beane, as a player. Beane, as a young athlete, was a so-called natural – not only the best 'hitter' on the baseball team in high school, he was the quarterback of the American Football team, and the highest scorer on the basketball team. Beane was deemed a *natural* from an early age, and was a first-round draft by the New York Mets in 1980. Across his playing career, Beane never managed to achieve the heights that his feted status suggested he would reach.

If you are a natural, you do not have to work. Your ability is innate. It is just a matter of showing up, doing your thing, and getting the praise at the end. Failure is seldom seen and, if it does occur, it will be somebody else's fault. Or maybe the weather was not ideal. Or maybe there was a bug going around. Or maybe it just didn't matter too much in the first place. Go to the excuses box, find an excuse that even loosely fits, and go about preserving oneself and your natural talent.

Chapter 3 – The Feet Are Just the Tools

For a natural, with a fear of (or an aversion to) failure, every moment can turn into a risk of humiliation. Every failure a nail in the coffin for your untouchable reputation. Effort is for the others – the foot soldiers – not for you: the gifted and talented one. Ability is defined, so the notion of improvement is pointless.

The mindset adopted, subconsciously, by Beane and others, is known as a *Fixed Mindset*, as presented by Dr. Carol Dweck in her million-copy bestseller, *Mindset – Changing the Way You Think to Fulfil Your Potential*.

Because of this fixed mindset, players can be difficult to coach. They do not respond well to challenges. If you suggest ways they can improve, they take it as criticism. Trying such players in new positions or trying to take them out of their comfort zone, will cause negativity and pushback. They will give up when things get difficult – things should be easy for them. They would rather not try their best, in case their best isn't good enough. They would rather avoid challenges than test themselves. If they are unsuccessful, they will no longer be considered talented. They will only give you 50% of their effort, and you will know it. If they give you everything, and it is not good enough, they may cave. When others in the same field succeed, they are jealous.

Along with self-confessed fixed mindset sports stars, like Beane and former tennis legend John McEnroe, Dweck presents others to us. The others, those with a *growth mindset*, have a deep desire to improve and push themselves. They embrace challenge and define themselves by their effort, not their talent. They celebrate the success of others and use it as inspiration. They heed advice and suggestions from coaches and understand that improvement and learning require work – and are happy to do that work.

Mia Hamm was the youngest player to have represented the US Women's National Soccer Team at the age of 15. During a career that straddled three decades, Hamm achieved a staggering 276 caps, and is often cited as the greatest female player of all time. Among all her individual accolades, including 158 international goals, and her achievements as part of the national team (two Olympic gold medals and two World Cups), her growth mindset is evident to see. She had a dream, worked hard, and made it happen, even in the face of adversity.

"

All my life, I've been playing up, meaning I've challenged myself with players older, bigger, more skilful, more experienced – in short, better than me. Each day, I attempted to play up to their level … and I was improving faster than I ever dreamed possible.

"

Mia Hamm

Even at the peak of her powers, and all the accolades afforded to her at a very young age, Hamm remained focused on improvement. Likewise, Roy Keane, former captain and serial winner at Manchester United, faced challenges throughout his youth because of his size. His autobiography, *Keane*, is a sport psychologist's dream when it comes to resilience and overcoming adversity to succeed. It includes references to how Keane would visualise himself walking out at Wembley Stadium, when, in reality, he was entering the local pitches around Cork, Ireland. In turn, videos have appeared online of the likes of Steven Gerrard and Andrea Pirlo, both in their 30s, training alone to improve their games, at a stage in their careers when they had nothing to prove to anyone. In a *Big Interview* with journalist Graham Hunter, Damien Duff confessed to still practicing with his right foot, long after his playing career was over.

Growth Mindset		Fixed Mindset
Embrace challenges and use them to grow and improve	*Challenges*	Avoid challenges due to fear of failure
Believe that effort and hard work are the keys to improvement	*Effort*	Do not value the importance of effort to achieve success
Actively seek feedback and see it as a process to improve	*Feedback*	Gets frustrated easily and ignores feedback or criticism
Inspired by other athletes	*Inspiration*	Feels threatened by the success of others
View setbacks as opportunities to learn	*Setbacks*	Give up easily when things get difficult
Works hard and aims to succeed, even in the face of adversity	*Perseverance*	Underestimates the importance of perseverance
Shoulders responsibility and 'owns' their role in failure	*Blame*	Blames other people or other factors for their failures

Growth v Fixed Mindset Characteristics

A Lesson in Mindset – Cristiano Ronaldo

Many would be tempted to call Cristiano Ronaldo a natural. He was born with 'it'. Tests, conducted by Castrol, which were broadcast in the Sky Sports documentary *Tested to the Limit* in 2011 (available on YouTube!) seemed to back this up. These gruelling series of tests highlighted that the Portuguese had a unique skillset that set him apart from the rest. He had less body fat than a supermodel and could jump higher than the average NBA basketball player. Mentally, his brain was as sharp as a genius, predicting the movement of his opponent before his opponent even moved. Technically, he could successfully judge and control the flightpath of a ball – in the pitch dark!

Ronaldo, as a personality, divides opinion. He has an ego and can be openly petulant and stubborn. Where there can be no doubt, however, is around his ability and his place in the game as one of the greatest players of all time. This, however, is not due to natural, God-given talent and inherent ability (genetics, of course, play a part). This is down to his growth mindset.

At age 12, Ronaldo left his home on the Portuguese island of Madeira to join the academy at Sporting Lisbon. Leaving the island for mainland Portugal at such a tender age, without his family, was not easy and Ronaldo struggled at times. At one point, he even came close to leaving and going home. He was convinced by his godfather to stick it out as, having come from a poor family, "he was the future of that family." No pressure.

When you see interviews with former coaches from his youth days, many will admit to being surprised by Ronaldo's ascent from shy, humble kid to the greatest player in the world. This was all down to his mindset, and his work.

Chapter 3 – The Feet Are Just the Tools

In an interview for *goal.com*, former goalkeeper and teammate at Sporting Lisbon, Christopher de Almeida Pilar, told us that, "Ronaldo was different because of all the work he put in – not so much during the training sessions, but after the sessions. He would always stay and practice for an extra half an hour on the areas he had most difficulties."

In the summer of 2003, Ronaldo joined Manchester United after impressing both the players and then-manager Sir Alex Ferguson during a pre-season friendly. Ronaldo wanted shirt number 28, but was given number 7, vacated by departing superstar, David Beckham. No pressure. Those who witnessed his early performances could see lots of unique ability, but a lack of consistency and end-product. He would do tricks, promoting his own ability, rather than making decisions for the team. René Meulensteen, former youth and first-team coach at the club, takes up the story of working with the Portuguese during a time when he was suspended from playing:

"

I told him: 'The problem is also your attitude and therefore your decision-making. At the moment, you're playing to put yourself into the limelight, to say, "Look at me, how good I am." Therefore, Mr Ronaldo, you are doing a lot that doesn't mean anything for your teammates.

I've looked at your goals last season … you want to score the perfect goal all the time. "Look at me! Top corner!"

I needed him to get out of that. I told him: "It doesn't matter how you score, where you score, as long as the ball goes in the net."

"

**René Meulensteen, interview
for *The Telegraph***

Daniel Coyle speaks about master coaching as being the major conduit in getting the best from performers. After the intervention from Meulensteen above, Ronaldo surpassed his 23-goal tally from the previous season, with four months to spare. Meulensteen again intervened at this point and addressed his arrogant body language and challenged him to maintain his upward trajectory. Ronaldo accepted the challenge and went on to score 42 goals by the end of the 2007/2008 season. Since then, Ronaldo has scored well over 600 goals (and counting!) for his national team and his club sides.

During the 2011/12 season, when Ronaldo was at Real Madrid, Jesé Rodriguez broke through to the first-team squad at *Los Blancos*. On his first day of training with the senior players, Rodriguez described arriving two hours early to impress the coach, only to find Ronaldo, then the most expensive player in history, already in the gym.

Conclusion

The role of the mind, whether we (as practical football coaches) fully accept it or not, is front and centre when we are working with players. Understanding how players learn, how they operate in a cognitive sense, and the tools we can use to psychologically improve them, may be what sets you and them apart. In the following chapter, we will look at creating a culture and environment that encourages learning and a growth mindset.

Summary

- Understanding what is happening in the brain is a big plus for modern coaches looking to advance their players.

- As individuals move from child to adolescent to adult, the brain is always changing, growing, and remodelling.

- 21st century children receive a lot of stimuli through technology. This means that they are less patient than previous generations, have a greater need to be engaged, and bore more easily.

- As players learn, layers of myelin cover neural pathways in the brain, strengthening skill acquisition. Engaging the brain in sessions, as well as the feet, stimulates this process.

- Michel Bruyninckx's 'Brain Centred Training' method focuses on cognitive overload and stressing players mentally during sessions.

- The *Deliberate Soccer Practice* method also looks to engage the brain during training by invoking decision-making and problem-solving within football sessions.

- There are *Four Stages of Competence*. Many professional football players will note that their decision-making is not conscious but in the 'Unconscious Competence' zone.

- Players with a growth mindset are more coachable, will accept feedback more positively, and will strive to improve.

- Be careful with praise like 'talented' or a 'natural' or 'born with it' – this can induce a fixed mindset.

- Master coaching from "talent whisperers" can be the conduit between good and great, and help players become the best they can be.

It's Your Game #1

The Quiet Genius

David Sumpter • @Soccermatics

Coach and author of *Soccermatics*

Some time back, psychologist Torbjörn Vestberg, visited me and the futsal team I train on Monday evenings. Torbjörn's message was powerful. He told them that everyone has the mental ability to be a top player, such as Barcelona stars Xavi and Iniesta, with whom he had previously conducted a 'working memory test'. It isn't about training the brain to be better, but about understanding what you, as a player, experience as difficult and then finding the solutions.

When Torbjörn tested Xavi and Iniesta, he found that they both ranked highly in the completion of a task that involves connecting dots in as many different ways as possible. This tests a person's ability to find new solutions and suppress already-used solutions. More scientifically rigorous tests show that the youth players who score most goals are very good at this task and at another test of working memory.

Torbjörn could only test one of the players. Edvin, a left-footed player who now usually plays as a defensive midfielder in football, and as a single defender at the base of a diamond in futsal, was chosen, having won a dribbling contest to decide the winner.

Earlier, I had talked to Torbjörn about his research. He said that we shouldn't expect football players to verbalise what they do, to be able to explain their decision-making to us. He said that sometimes coaches prefer the kids who are good at talking about the game, who reliably repeat back the purpose of different exercises to their trainers. On the pitch, coaches want to see their players talk to each other. But Torbjörn's research indicates that this type of verbal intelligence is not important for predicting future performance; it is, instead, working memory that is the key.

Torbjörn was concerned that the players that were now being chosen for academy positions were talking their way in, using verbal intelligence, just as there has previously been a tendency for the stronger, more physical players to push their way in front of their peers.

He said that a player like Messi would be lost in an environment where an ability to communicate about the game was thought to reflect how well he can play. He saw little point in post-match interviews and is often annoyed by TV and newspaper commentary on football. The genius of a player isn't shown in how they explain what they have done; it is captured by their actions on the pitch and the many hours of training exercises that have shaped those actions.

Edvin is certainly never lost for words, before, after, or during our training sessions. But that wasn't the intelligence that he had now been tested on. Edvin was average in the number of questions he got correct but was two standard deviations better than the population average in how quickly he produced answers. He listened as Torbjörn Vestberg showed him the results:

"You are incredibly fast, a lot faster than most of the people I have tested."

Privately, to me, he elaborated: "He has a superfast brain, more than I told him, like … bloody fast."

I was proud of Edvin who I, together with a bunch of other dads, have trained since he was six. He won the dribbling competition narrowly, and I am sure several other lads would have done well in the test. It isn't just the training we do, but the hours we spend together. The players have a culture where they are competitive but supportive. Being a coach (and a parent) isn't so much about what you tell your kids, it is about providing an environment where they have the best chance to develop themselves.

Chapter 4
A Growth Mindset Environment

"   **"**

I will do everything I can to challenge young
players' mindsets. I want to challenge them so
that they are ready to take on new ideas.

Per Mertesacker

Many pictures don the walls of Manchester United's youth academy. The club are exceptionally proud of their record in youth development compared to many of their contemporaries. Indeed, at the time of writing, United have had players from their youth academy selected for the first team for almost 4,000 consecutive matches, dating back to October 1937. Pictures of current homegrown players Lingard, Pogba, and McTominay, not to mention past greats like Scholes, Giggs and the club's current Academy Manager, Nicky Butt, are there to show existing academy players that the journey from kid to pro – from where they are standing – is a real possibility.

This type of image is powerful. It shows you (as a player) that other individuals just like you have made the journey. The pathway is well established. The trail has been blazed. It could be *your* photograph hanging proudly on these walls one day.

Similar trailblazers in other sports have inspired whole districts. In *The Gold Mine Effect*, Rasmus Ankersen (@RasmusAnkersen), himself involved in professional football, researched why South Korea produces a disproportionate number of female golfers, why the world's greatest sprinters came from one athletics club in Kingston, Jamaica, and how a single Ethiopian village, Bekoji, has produced the world's best middle-distance runners. Other books, such as *The Sports Gene*, investigate similar phenomena. While lots of factors are at play in each environment, the inspiration of the initial trailblazer cannot be understated.

In Manchester, one particular photograph stands out among the rest, however. This is a rather out-of-place image of Lionel Messi, who clearly has no background or association with Manchester United. The picture of the Argentine was snapped in 2014 following a friendly match he had played for Argentina against Croatia at West Ham United's Upton Park. Messi, who had won the Ballon d'Or four times by this point and was also voted the best player at the World Cup that summer, is sitting there cleaning his boots.

The boot-cleaning image is a strong one in football. It is more about the message it conveys than the task itself. Traditionally, it was the job of apprentice youth players to clean the boots of the senior professionals. For the apprentice, it was a rite of passage. If you were cleaning their boots, you were nearly there. The next step was to walk in their shoes figuratively.

Having clean boots is football's version of making your bed in the morning – as made famous by Admiral William McRaven.[1] The concept does not seem important – it is not life-changing – but

---

[1] Admiral McRaven's *Change If You Want to Change the World, Start Off by Making Your Bed* speech is available on YouTube.

when attached to ideas of discipline and humility, it is a simple yet powerful task. A senior professional of status cleaning his own boots has become a metaphor for having a grounded personality – a humbleness and understanding that no matter what your perceived rank, looking after the small details and being self-effacing and grounded are values that are top priorities. Players like Messi sweep the sheds.

"   **"**

At Manchester United, we strive for perfection.
And if we fail, we might just have to
settle for excellence.

Sir Matt Busby

Leave a Legacy

During the writing of *Making the Ball Roll*, I made a conscious decision that most examples, quotes, and stories would be football-based. Not because I felt that you can't learn a lot from the likes of Michael Jordan, Tiger Woods, and Rodger Federer, or John Wooden, Sir Clive Woodward, and Vince Lombardi, but just to make the examples real to football. One of the main reasons I have relaxed this approach this time around is because of the All Blacks.

Rugby in New Zealand is almost religious in its influence and importance to the people. As a relatively small island, its rugby history has far outweighed its size and population of less than 5 million (23 US states have a larger population than New Zealand,[2] and its near-neighbour and rival Australia has around 25 million), certainly when compared to other powerhouse rugby-playing nations. They are the most successful team, pound for pound, in modern sport, however, with a win percentage peaking over 86% since 2004, and a 100-year win percentage of over 75%.

I would encourage any coach to read *Legacy*, by James Kerr. It is one of a handful of books I have read that makes you want to coach and engage with your players even as you are reading it. It is the story of the All Blacks' culture and the environment that is created there. Standards are high. The players, some of the best in the world and playing in the best team in the world, "sweep the sheds" (clean the changing rooms themselves) and carry their own baggage from the team bus.

"   **"**

No one looks after the All Blacks.
The All Blacks look after themselves.

New Zealand Rugby

To the man in the street, these menial tasks may not seem very impressive. Who cares if Kieran Read sweeps up, or carries his own bags, or whether Lionel Messi cleans his own boots? The point is, not many others do it. They have outgrown it. It is their time to have others do the lowly things, while they do the magical things.

Not the All Blacks.

---

[2] US Census Bureau

The culture and environment of learning in the New Zealand national squad is staggering. Players who are succeeding other world-class players in their position are challenged to "leave the jersey in a better place" for its next incumbent. Constant challenge, the drive for continuous improvement, respect, honesty, and class is inherent. The culture lives beyond individual players or coaches. This non-physical image is akin to the physical images hanging at Manchester United and in most other academy environments; this is what the top guys are doing, you can follow it.

Creating a Culture

Whether you are Nicky Butt at Manchester United, or the Technical Director at New Zealand Rugby, or simply a coach working with 15 kids twice a week, creating a culture is powerful.

From both the examples above, the culture superseded results. The long-term environment is more important than short-term winning. But when it all comes together, it would underpin the winning process inherent in both organisations at senior level. In 2018, Manchester United were demoted from Premier League 2 (the 'reserve league' aimed at Under-23 players, with some allowances for older players to play also) and to many outside observers this was shambolic – a sign of a club, at academy level, that was on the wane. Butt, however, was keen to point out that their promotion of players from the academy into the first team is their measure, not points in a league system that he sees as flawed. He also points to Tottenham Hotspur and Southampton, clubs renowned for graduating academy players also, as having struggled in terms of league position. Having home-grown players in their first team, when their rivals Manchester City and Chelsea had none, meant more to Butt and the club than relegation at that age.

Age-Appropriate Culture – No Dickheads!

The All Black culture contains a large number of elements that are conducive to an adult environment only, from the perspective of the words used to what is tolerated. Although a great example, not all of the All Blacks messaging is age-appropriate.

Frequently, the term 'No Dickheads' appears in their mantra. This is a broad rule where the group will not abide by inappropriate behaviour. There is no place for bad apples. You step out of line, and you are out, regardless of ability or stature. This works for the greatest rugby playing nation in the world. Adult players can be cut and replaced by another without making a splash. In 2016, New Zealand Rugby reported that there were record numbers of New Zealanders across ages, gender, cities, and the country, playing the sport. They will not run out of quality players to call upon. Their rugby trail was blazed a long time ago. Any shortfall in terms of ability can be absorbed – the culture and maintenance of their environment are more important.

Not every organisation has the luxury of being so hard-line and will need more flexibility when dealing with the multiple personalities that a dressing room contains. They cannot just cut talent on a whim – they need to get the best out of them. Many coaches have made a career by taking unfashionable players and working with them – warts and all. They smooth egos and motivate players to claim league points, or cup wins. Mario Balotelli, although likeable in many, many ways, is an obvious example. Despite being labelled "immature and unpredictable" by fans,[3] lots of coaches have given him a shot, including those at well-renowned clubs like Inter Milan, Manchester City, AC Milan, Liverpool and the French club, Nice. Many players could work ferociously for a lifetime and not come close to having a resumé like it. At the time of writing, Balotelli has over 30 caps and a highly respectable goal to game ratio of 1:3 for Italy. Some coaches have cast him aside, others have and will continue to take a gamble on his ability – they

---

[3] Massimiliano Nerozzi, *Mario Balotelli – Italy's Super Talented, Super Complicated Soccer Star.*

want to be there when the penny drops. Just because New Zealand Rugby does it one way, does not mean it will work for everyone – especially within youth environments.

If we are talking about youth development in football and the development of youngsters, then we must address all aspects of the game, not just the technical, tactical, and physical aspects. Coaches work tirelessly to improve the footballing ability of their players, but developing players' psychological and social aspects are also part of the process. You would not expect a youth player to have the same technical/tactical ability, or the same physique, as a grown man, so we cannot expect them to have the same behavioural skills.

Rather than being one that expects senior, professional behaviour *immediately*, your environment may be the one that has to teach young people how to behave, to be reliable, or promote simple life skills like being on time. Lots of young people will not turn up to your team or club and immediately fit into your way. They need work in that respect – and the kind of work coaches should be willing to do. The 'No Dickheads' mantra won't work. Values, like the 11 outlined below by Belgian Premier League side, Club Brugge,[4] are not rules – they are a roadmap, just like every other facet of football development. These values are what we expect during or at the end of the process, but we should also expect players to fall short of this standard from time to time. If a player shows disrespect, the youth coach will show him how to be respectful. If a player displays dishonesty, the youth coach will teach him how to be honest.

---

[4] The Club Brugge Academy vision is to produce "skilled and highly motivated players with a 'no sweat no glory' mentality" (*Club Brugge Academy Methodology* document).

---

11 Values of Club Brugge

RESPECT

Yourself and others

TRUST

Our belief and faith will lead to success

OPEN COMMUNICATION

Speak and listen

ENGAGEMENT

Sharing responsibility

POSITIVE

Think, act and be positive

HONESTY

In words, acts, feelings and thoughts

PRIDE

The engine and fuel

SELF-AWARENESS

Know your strengths and weaknesses

LEARNING ATTITUDE

Living is learning

PASSION

For achievement, detail, knowledge, life and play

TEAM

No single individual is bigger than the team as a whole

Today, as we watch the Premier League, Kevin De Bruyne is one of the stand-out players. He is a model professional, works extremely hard, and has an unquenchable desire to win. He has successfully married a very technical game with the desire to work hard. He has shown tactical flexibility by playing to a high level in a number of different positions, affecting the game on the right, left, or through the centre of the pitch. Psychologically, he has shown resilience when suffering fouls and has adapted well to coach Pep Guardiola's high energy style. He has excelled in a team that requires players to constantly concentrate and be aware of their roles in possession, out of possession, and in transition. In an interview on *Sky Sports Match Zone*, De Bruyne noted the strictness of Guardiola's regime where the players are not permitted to "do backheels or whatever – it's always good simple passes" during training exercises. In interviews, he speaks like a model professional, with discipline, intelligence, and respect.

Chapter 4 – A Growth Mindset Environment

From 2005 to 2008, however, De Bruyne was no adult and no angel. During this period, he was a teenager in the Academy of KRC Genk in Belgium and was infamous for arguing with teammates and coaches. He was often unhappy and temperamental. "Running and strength and conditioning tasks were never his favourite things to do – he didn't like to run," noted Academy Director, Roland Breugelmans. He had problems in his boarding school, and there were other difficult moments with families who hosted him while at the Academy. During both his first and second season at Genk, there were people at the club who were ready to let De Bruyne go; a truly extraordinary judgement with the benefit of hindsight.

Rules, Glorious Rules

"

The culture of any organisation is shaped by the
worst behaviour a leader is willing to tolerate.

"

Steve Gruenert & Todd Whitaker,
School Culture Rewired

Working *with* players' indiscipline, and understanding that they can still be shaped, does not mean that you have to tolerate everything. Rules are rules and if they are seriously breached, just like in a school environment, then the disciplinary process will kick into action. You may find that this is necessary to protect your values and culture and you will need to move players on. Lots of coaches have rules that are non-negotiable – they cannot be broken, and if they are, that is the end of the road.

Rules are a funny thing, however. The more you have, the more that can be broken, the more that need monitoring; they can prove a big distraction from the real reason you are all there – football.

Big academies and institutions can ask for almost anything and be as strict as they feel they need to be. I have worked in a professional academy in the UK that banned players from wearing gloves, woolly hats, or body warmers under their playing kit. The management at the time wanted to produce disciplined young men. Feeling the cold, however, is not a weakness or a sign of indiscipline. Those of you that have experienced a winter's evening in the UK will appreciate that the most appropriate way to teach the game would be to ensure the players' needs are met first. In *Making the Ball Roll*, I shared *Maslow's Hierarchy of Needs*, something I have shared again below. For significant learning, creativity, or problem-solving to take place in our environments, the young person's basic physiological needs and the need to feel safe and secure are required to be met first.

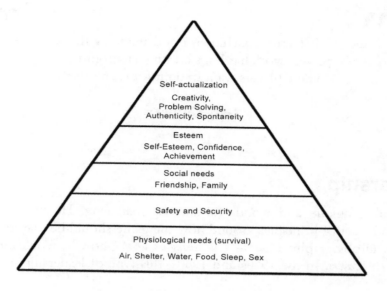

Maslow's Hierarchy of Needs

Around the same time (at the Academy referenced above) I witnessed an Under-12 player arrive at a venue five minutes late; he was unceremoniously sent home. The argument between parent and manager lasted less than 30 seconds. The threat of further upsetting the all-powerful club was too much for the parent to continue quarrelling. Certainly, at grassroots level, you may not have this power.

There is a certain protection that a big institution brings. Parents of young boys at Real Madrid, Chelsea, or Bayern Munich will fall into line with the club's rules without major fuss. However, trying to implement strict, gratuitous rules when in sole charge of a group of Under-10 players is difficult without the support and structure of a big organisation around you. KRC Genk, and many other academies, insist that all their players must wear black boots only. The theory being that this will keep them grounded and more focused on the game itself, rather than the cosmetic elements that surround football. Kids or parents in *your* environment, however, may not accept such a rule so easily. Why shouldn't Jonny wear the white boots, with Messi's name on the side, he got from grandma for Christmas? You could end up arguing about boot colour, or what percentage of the boot is black versus another colour (something I've witnessed with a parent), every time you meet your players.

Such rules may be very hard and time-consuming to manage if you are a coach at a local club. Other coaches will feel that allowing players to wear whatever boots they want will keep them happy. A happy player is one that performs.

Whatever rules you apply to your environment, ensure you can manage them effectively. If your rules are broken, and you cannot manage the situation when they are – or the same rules have not been applied to *all* of the players – your whole structure becomes jeopardised.

Brian Clough managed English teams Derby County and Nottingham Forest through the 1970s and 1980s, winning the 'First Division'[5] with both clubs, neither of whom were English powerhouses at the time. He also won successive European Cups with the Nottingham Club in 1979 and 1980 – an extraordinary feat. Much of this was down to his charisma, and he had a way of leading and managing environment rules that were ahead of his time.

---

[5] The 'First Division' was rebranded 'Premier League' in 1992.

"

"

Effective coaching is not demanding that
players work hard; it's creating environments
where players want to do it for each other.

Gary Curneen

Dual Leadership

Brian Clough had a unique and wonderful way of managing. He was sharp-witted, a real motivator, and had a set of principles around how the game should be played. Several years ago, he outlined in his autobiography, *Cloughie – Walking on Water*, how he would agree the team rules *in conjunction with the players*. In the 1970s and 1980s, this type of leadership, certainly in football, was rare.

In a team meeting early in the season, the players would outline their own code of conduct. For example, they decided what time they would train, and, because of that, they were bound to this time – being late was not breaking Clough's rule, they would be breaking their own. The players also agreed on the punishment or fine that was imposed. As this was driven by the players, they had no excuse and indiscipline could be dealt with smoothly and easily.

This type of leadership has positives beyond making and maintaining rules. As it is player-led, there is an automatic buy-in from them. They are responsible not only to the coach but to their teammates too. If there is anything young people hate, it is letting their peers down. You create the opportunity for the group to manage themselves. You change the leadership structure from 'them and us' to 'us'. This form of 'Dual Leadership', rather than the unilateral top-down model, is taking hold in modern sport.

Players should not *need* sanctions to adhere to rules – they should do it out of self-interest. This type of behaviour can take hold and seep positively into the culture of your environment. When new players arrive, they can be quickly brought up to speed on the way things work. This could be by being told explicitly what is (and what is not) acceptable, or they will feed off the behaviour of the players already there. Along with the playing part, new players in a new environment are picking up all sorts of social cues about what is expected, much like adults will do when going to a new restaurant, or to somebody else's home. How you behave in church is different from how you would behave in a local bar, which is different to how you would behave when you go to the movies.

Sir Alex Ferguson is remembered for his winning teams, 'Fergie time', and his use of the 'hairdryer' – a term used to reference his ferocious verbal blasts when dealing with poor discipline or under-par performance. Ferguson understood the role of rules and the synergy of the dressing room when it came to behaviour. He had rules, of course, and was strict with them, but he moved with the times if he thought there was a better way. Although famous for being harsh, he understood the value of inspiring his players. He understood the use of the carrot rather than the stick. Inspired by the environment, the famous class of '92 would go back to the training ground in the evening to train again. Eric Cantona, a free spirit and maverick player, went from turning up late and wearing incorrect travel wear for away trips, to always being on time and suitably dressed in a club suit or tracksuit. Steve McClaren, assistant manager for Manchester United from 1999 to 2001, frequently speaks of the environment there and the standards that were held. He describes club captain Roy Keane insisting that players report for training at 10.30, even after an away trip that would see them arrive home at 3am. No day off, no changes. While others are resting, we are working. These standards become ingrained from generation to generation.

"

Shared responsibility means shared ownership.
A sense of inclusion means individuals are
more willing to give themselves to a
common cause.

James Kerr

We changed totally from unilateral decision
making to dual management, and the players
had a big part of setting the standards, the life
standards, the behaviours that are acceptable.

Wayne Smith

Dual Leadership is a very important part of our
success. Perhaps the reason for that success.

Graham Henry

"

A Growth Mindset Environment

During the previous chapter about the concept of growth versus fixed mindset, you were probably mentally flicking through your squad, wondering if any of your players 'fit' either profile. Chances are, if you have identified one with a fixed mindset, you will be exploring ways of how you can positively aid him or her.

Interventions are best served with a long-term view in mind, but research has shown that even brief exposures can bear fruit.

Previously, Carol Dweck and colleagues, conducted a study with over 12,500 students aged 14 to 15, from 65 schools across the United States. They wanted to explore the effect of the exposure to a growth mindset on these students.

All the students watched two videos. Half of them were shown two growth mindset videos, and half watched a video about the brain, but which was not linked to a growth mindset. Accounting for certain variables, the study showed that the students who received the growth mindset intervention achieved, on average, a 0.03 higher grade point difference than the others. For "struggling students", this increased to 0.8.

Critically, those students who attended schools with a culture that endorsed high expectations and academic effort benefited most from the intervention. The take-home message is that a long-term vision, met with a series of short-term messages, can aid you in fostering growth players.

Talking the Talk

The normal term for our coaching environment across the literature is a 'positive learning environment'. Such is its frequency of use that I wonder if it has started to lose its meaning. The term is rather light. It brings positive and important things to mind for sure – players having fun, coaches being open and approachable, and the safety of the players being paramount – but (even though these elements are essential) I want more.

"

"

We create an open learning environment in every aspect of our operation. In doing so, our aim is to be the best at our level and surpass all expectations. We will make errors along the way but we learn from this and find solutions to problems rather than make excuses or creating a blame culture. We strive to help all players and staff to be their best by sharing best practice in every element of delivery and by providing feedback.

English Academy 'Performance Plan'

Earlier in the book, we touched on the EPPP – the Premier League's Elite Player Performance Plan – the framework upon which English academies receive their licences. Such is the value and focus on culture and environment, the EPPP guidelines stipulate the creation of an 'Academy Performance Plan'. This plan is aimed to "articulate the club's culture in terms of Youth Development". The environment is the starting point.

Below is the Mission Statement from Swansea City FC Academy. Most, if not all, academy performance documents talk about learning and a learning environment, but this one resonates more than others.

Swansea City FC Academy Mission Statement

The Academy, coupled with our scholarship programme, is an *educational establishment*. A player associated with the Academy is engaged to *learn and develop*.

The Academy's *programme for learning* is naturally centred on football activities, yet we consider that we can offer many other facets, which are important for a young person to *develop* as an individual within society.

In addition to helping young players enhance their football ability, we will also *educate them* on aspects of fitness, nutrition and health issues.

Significantly, also, we are committed to ensuring that all young players associated with the Academy acquire good values and standards, which will sustain them throughout their lives, irrespective of their ultimate achievements as football players.

We consider that a *central feature of our role as educators* is to ensure that all players acquire the value of tolerance, self-esteem, respect for others, loyalty, self-discipline and commitment to the cause.

A young player associated with Swansea City AFC Academy will be *embraced by a culture of learning*. We desire that all players are happy, content, enthusiastic and dedicated.

The Academy provides a welcoming environment, which is professionally structured to offer the opportunity for young players to thrive and gain success.

No one can reliably predict the future for any young player, but we hope that when a player leaves the Academy, at whatever age, he will be able to reflect on his association with the Academy as being positive, worthwhile and fruitful.

This statement is the first piece of material that players and parents will read upon entering the academy – and it is dripping with growth mindset material. A reader is left in no doubt as to what the environment entails. Along with other values and noble virtues, constant references are made to learning, improvement, and development. The players will be "embraced by a culture of learning". Right from the start – growth is key; a fixed mindset is shown the door.

Yet!

There are some words in the English language that are more powerful than others. In *Making the Ball Roll*, we noted that the words 'you' (well, more technically, the use of the players' names) and 'because' were powerful and persuasive, so let's add another to our coaching dictionary.

There is a huge difference between "You are not able to do this" and "You are not able to do this *yet*". The former can lay the foundations for a fixed mindset. It can induce thoughts that ability is rigid. The latter, by including the word 'yet', opens up possibilities of growth and improvement. It tells the player that, sometime in the future, he or she *will* be able to complete the task that they currently cannot. It encourages effort and creates a motivation to get there.

Not everyone has a growth mindset with everything, all the time. That simply cannot be expected. Just like when we discussed, in a previous chapter, about people having different comfort zones in different situations, the same applies here. A centre-back may have a growth mindset about passing out from the back but may have a fixed mindset about playing in another position. An attacker may have a growth mindset about ways of improving his goal-scoring but have a fixed mindset about what he should do when out of possession or when changing certain aspects of his game. The list is endless.

The language we, as coaches, use when engaging players can provide triggers that provoke either fixed or growth mindsets. Using 'yet' as a trigger to elicit improvement is one of those.

Yet helps players to deduce that improvement, understanding, and growth will come with effort and continuous determination. The poster below, from *Creative Access* (the original design is far more visually appealing than my adaptation below!), and ones similar to it, are popping up in classrooms all over the world and are referred to not only by teachers but also by students themselves who have been persuaded by the idea.

The Power of YET

I can't do this ... yet

This doesn't work ... yet

I don't know ... yet

It doesn't make sense ... yet

I don't get it ... yet

I'm not good at this ... yet

The Power of Yet, poster by Creative Access

Walking the Walk

Nothing can foster a growth mindset more than the environment you create. Words are all well and good, but walking the walk is the essential element. How do you, as a coach, handle players making mistakes? Is your mood determined by results and the number of faults that the players make? Or do you *genuinely* use mistakes as an opportunity for learning? If players make mistakes (which they will) and suffer from them, can you help them to reframe the errors and use them as opportunities to learn? It some cases, inwardly at least, you – as a coach – can celebrate errors as they present you and the player with the capacity for improvement. Within players' weaknesses, there is the opportunity to improve.

French football is particularly famous for its flagship development centre – Clairefontaine. Opened in 1988, the inner workings of the facility as a player development hub provided the green shoots for France to win its first World Cup in 1998.[6]

Along with Clairefontaine, eleven other regional hubs were developed by the French Football Federation. Known as INFs (Institut National du Football) these centres provide three-year residential training programmes for a select number of players in each region between the ages of

---

[6] It is often quoted by football administrators how it takes ten years for the fruits of a development programme to come to light!

13 and 15. Players live and are schooled there from Monday to Friday but are released at the weekend to go and play for their clubs.

Players usually spend the full three years within the programme, and the focus is entirely on learning. In year one, players are taught the game from scratch, with a high emphasis on technical training. During the second year, the training shifts towards playing in small groups and units. For the first two years, youngsters do not play any competitive matches with the INF. They believe that winning distracts from learning and if the coaches are preoccupied with a league table, then the training focus shifts. It is only in year three (aged 15), when they play competitive matches together, which coincides, not unintentionally, with the focus of their programme becoming about the tactical 11 v 11 game.

The INF's step-by-step learning programme takes winning out of the equation. The environment is one made up entirely of coaches teaching the game and players learning it. They walk the walk.

"

Those buildings are more than a fantastic tool.
They are a cornerstone, a vision, a philosophy,
a place of unity.

"

Gérard Houllier on Clairefontaine

Physical Environment

Clairefontaine, just like most high-level sports facilities, is a beautiful physical setting. Pitches are perfect and plentiful, as are classrooms, gym spaces, and social areas. These facilities are stacked with highly-qualified coaches as well as highly-qualified support staff.

Do not be fooled by appearances, however. There is a growing thought that pristine pitches and five-star hotel-like facilities actually diminish motivation and send the wrong message to young players. Players, exposed to a pampered environment at too early an age and on a constant basis, may lose a sense of humility and expect to be 'served', rather than doing the work. It may stimulate a fixed mindset. In 2017, Arsenal faced Sutton United in the FA Cup and suffered a backlash when they left the away dressing room at the Borough Sports Ground (aesthetically vastly different to the Emirates Stadium, the home of Arsenal) in an utter mess. They were accused of being prima donnas and that this behaviour reflected what some people saw as a major flaw in the attitude of the players, and their environment.

The Milanello Sports Centre is the training ground for Italian giants, AC Milan. Not only is it a well-stocked facility, it is traditionally known as a centre for innovation. Amongst some, the facility has been given a laboratory status, mainly due to their ability in the noughties to get the best out of their players, allowing them to perform at the highest level into their late 30s and even 40s. Within weeks of joining the Milan club in 2009, David Beckham's body fat had been reduced from 13.7% to 8.5%,[7] under the supervision of the club's doctor, Jean-Pierre Meersseman. He was also fitted with a small mouth support until certain dental work was completed, believing that a small gap in his tooth was affecting his balance. Separately, French left-back, Aly Cissokho,

---

[7] Independent.ie article *Beckham's career blooming with a little help from Milan fitness 'lab'* by Jeremy Wilson.

Chapter 4 – A Growth Mindset Environment

failed a medical prior to his transfer from FC Porto after a poor dentistry report. At Milan, nothing is left to chance.

Another innovation, this time in terms of the facility itself, was the construction of a sand pitch to replicate the modest environment where most Brazilian players learn their trade; it was inspired by Milan's former Brazilian wizard, Kaká. The current training ground contains a small side-pitch enclosed by a cage, where the ball never goes out of play, simulating the street football environment.

The reduction in street football,[8] especially in the western world, has long been the source of concern for developers. This is the environment where the greats first learned their trade – on the rough and tumble of a car park, communal green area, or down cul-de-sacs. Here, players played small-sided or large-sided games. They would hone their technique on surfaces that were far from perfect. This environment made them tougher and more agile – it was better to stay on your feet than to take a fall on the rough concrete. Games could last for hours on end, punctuated only by quick visits home to eat, and then play again. This environment is a far cry from Clairefontaine, St. George's Park, or Milanello, but it is where players were originally born.

Your Environment

Regardless of your physical environment, or the number of support staff you have around you, you can still create a vision – your own watered-down Clairefontaine. An environment where the vision and culture survive despite the lack of manicured pitches, unspoiled gyms, or plentiful staffing. Work with what you have, embrace it, see the positives and potential in it. Find a way.

From all the researchers that have explored talent-development environments, one word shines through (long before pretty surroundings) – and that word is passion. It is not about facilities – it is about the people that occupy them; master coaches, devoted to practice and to creating a place where motivation is high. It is a feeling that the environment produces – the need, will, and the possibility to excel. Physically, many development environments are made up of rough-and-ready buildings and meagre pitches. I have even seen the term "shantytown" used to describe some of them. The players are not given everything *now*; the reward for their effort brings all the nice stuff later on.

When we track the development of many of the high-level players of the modern era, they spent a childhood playing in less-than-perfect physical settings. A mural of Gabriel Jesus now stands at the spot where he once painted the kerb of a Sao Paulo favela; Steven Gerrard almost had to have his toe amputated when he kicked a garden fork when fetching a ball out of a bush at a local rough pitch at the age of nine; Dante practised in the car park of a supermarket where his mother worked as a cashier; Carlos Tevez attributes his dribbling skills to dribbling around syringes and broken glass. The list could go on.

I do not subscribe to the idea that you *have to* struggle in this way to become a success. These details, and many others, all go into a melting pot of reasons why players become successful. What it does show us, though, is that despite the money involved at the high end of football – physically dishevelled, ugly, disagreeable environments can be great places of learning and growth.

---

[8] To fill in the gap left by the disappearance of street football, several club academies started to try to replicate them. One particular academy had an evening where coaches would leave a ball with the players and let them at it – no drills, no bibs – just a space and a ball.

Conclusion

Later in this book, we will look at the concept of Individual Learning Plans, and how these work to create a growth mindset in players. Before then, however, I want to leave this chapter with a visual that I am sure most of you have come across somewhere before. I have seen this list presented in both glamourous academies and ramshackle, slum-like sports clubs. It helps us to look at talent in a different way and feeds directly into our mission to create growth mindset players.

10 Things That Require Zero Talent

BEING ON TIME
WORK ETHIC
EFFORT
BODY LANGUAGE
ENERGY
ATTITUDE
PASSION
BEING COACHABLE
DOING EXTRA
BEING PREPARED

Summary

- The culture you create around your team is important, like the one at Manchester United and with the All Blacks.

- Ensure your environment is age-appropriate – the All Blacks' 'No Dickheads' mantra will not be suitable for youth setups.

- As well as developing players technically, tactically, and physically, we need to also work with them psychologically and socially. Their behaviour may need guidance.

- Bigger clubs can use the institution around them to be as strict as they feel necessary. Only make rules that you can keep.

- 'Dual Leadership' methods can help you maintain rules, where players buy-in to the environment you are trying to develop. They will also help integrate new players into your group.

- Exposing players to growth mindset stimuli will help them to develop and reach their potential.

- Swansea City FC Academy understands the importance of creating a growth mindset environment, hitting their players with messages of development, learning, and improvement immediately.

- Adding the word 'yet' to player inadequacies gives them a strong message of improvement, rather than critique.

- Talking the talk is good, but not enough. Coaches need to walk the walk, like at Clairefontaine.

- Physical environments such as training grounds and national development centres give players everything they need. Having a fancy physical environment is not necessary to develop players – many talent hotbeds are ugly and underserved; use whatever facilities you have and inject them with passion.

It's Your Game #1

Fix Your Mindset When You're Eighty-Five

Ryan Baldi • @RyanBaldiFW

Football Writer and Author of *The Next Big Thing*

While researching for my book, *The Next Big Thing*, I spoke to a lot of players who were expected to grace the game with authority. One of them was John Curtis.

Curtis was considered one of the brightest prospects at Manchester United in the late 1990s, and was dubbed the 'future England captain' while still a teenager. However, the closest he ever got to the senior international stage was an infamous England 'B' outing versus Russia.

At club level, it was a similar tale of promising beginnings, where he was the recipient of the club's *Young Player of the Year* award in 1997 before impressing with his in early first-team outings. Instead of cutting it at the very top, however, Curtis's longest tenure at any one club was an 87-game spell with Nottingham Forest.

Former teammate Ben Thornley was quick to point out that he "still had a good career". Not having a successful career at Manchester United, Thornley adds, "was no slur on John whatsoever, with either his ability or attitude".

However, Curtis sees things differently. As a young player subjected to hype, 'destined for the very top', he believes he developed a fixed mindset. He was eager to protect this status, rather than opening himself to the trial-and-error process that breeds improvement. He feared mistakes rather than valuing them. And while he was flattered by individual accolades, he questions whether they were healthy for his psychological development. "Do these awards cement that fixed mindset?"

Now, the lessons Curtis learned the hard way as a player are not only being passed on to the players he works with, in his role with the United States Soccer Federation (USSF), but are also being applied to mould and improve coaches.

"A lot of the coaching I do focusses on the psychological aspect. It's nice that I can look back now, because I've lived those experiences, so I can pass those on."

"My son is on the verge of the England Under-18 squad for rugby. I do my best to try and protect him and not make the mistakes I did, not let him get fixed early.

"Fix your mindset when you're eighty-five, not when you are nineteen."

<u>It's Your Game #2</u>

Bleak Surroundings

Mick Browne • @tikitakafc1

UEFA B Licence Coach

When I first started coaching, after years of playing, I was invited down to a local youth football club, by a former teammate. He was running his son's Under-16s team and was struggling to keep them interested. They were not one of the elite teams, so it was more about keeping them playing and enjoying their football. They were losing more games than winning, and training attendance was poor.

At my first training session, there was full attendance which gave me some hope … until I saw our training area! This was a small plot of bumpy ground with hairy grass, tucked away in the corner of the park. It looked and felt pretty bleak – only streetlights were available for lighting. It measured no more than 20 metres x 12 metres. Horrified, I asked 'Is this it?' and mentally set about making my excuses to leave. The new all-weather pitches were being built so – in that moment – it was take it or leave it. Despite my reservations, I took it and now had 16 or so 16-year-olds to train in this area for the next 10 months.

As it turned out, it was the best season those lads ever had. The area forced me to rethink my sessions – to facilitate strength & conditioning, technical, some tactical, and goalkeeping work, in that small area. I even invented some short bounce games – with players on the outside – for such a tight area. The bumpy ground improved players' touch and control and the improvement in them was clearly evident. They were thinking quicker, and they grew to be comfortable receiving the ball under pressure. They loved playing the short sharp 'bounce games' and would relish the exercises on training nights. Attendance was up and so was their league position.

Not only did this experience benefit the players, it benefitted me hugely as a coach. I had to be positive and make the most of what I had. I learned that despite not having brilliant facilitates, we could find a way. I still use many of those small games in tight areas for improving players' speed of thought, movement, and execution. That small area for my first season's training nights turned out to be more beneficial for me, and the players, than I could have imagined.

It's Your Game #3

The Cliff, The Call, The Culture

Luke Chadwick

Former Player, Manchester Utd; Youth Coach, Cambridge Utd

From the second I walked into Manchester United's Cliff Training Ground, as a 15-year-old trialist, I could see it was special. It was like being immediately taken into a family; being made to feel welcome and accepted. The building at The Cliff was small and tight-knit, nothing like the incredible structures we see today. I was shown around and introduced to Ryan Giggs and David Beckham, players that I had only ever seen on TV. They were so accessible. It was surreal to meet these superstars and realise they are normal, good people. I thought – it could be me one day!

From my first few minutes at the club – from those important first impressions – I was desperate to sign for them. I played a trial game against Nottingham Forest and, after playing quite well, travelled home to Cambridge. By the time I got back, my mum said she had received a phone call from Sir Alex Ferguson who asked her permission for me to sign for the club. I couldn't believe it. I thought she was joking but, incredibly, it was true!

These are the little things that built the culture and environment at the club. The reason players would run a bit more, work a bit harder. You knew the manager cared about *you*. He had taken the time to personally call my mum – not the youth coach or recruitment officer, but Sir Alex himself! He would do this for all the young players. That personal touch, that extra bit of effort, tended to mean all the best young players in the country would sign for Manchester United at that time.

All the aspects that made the culture and environment so special were lived by the manager and his staff, day in day out – work ethic, high standards, discipline, how to treat people... whether that be a star player or the tea lady. When the leader of an organisation is doing this, everyone else follows suit. I am convinced that that's where the years of success came from.

After signing as a full-time scholar, one of the biggest memories I have was the high standards expected in *everything* that was done on and off the pitch. As a schoolboy, the coaches and staff worked hard developing your love for the game and the club. In the full-time programme, by comparison, it is about keeping that alive – but understanding it gets more serious now! It was a privilege to work at the club, and we were rightly reminded of this throughout the journey, whether that be physically pushing ourselves to the limit on the pitch, or cleaning the Cliff from top to bottom. Those long days were all to build character, preparing us for life and careers, whatever they ended up being.

Thinking back to my short time in the first-team squad, training was actually more demanding than the games. It was so intense, so competitive, with such a high level of technical ability. It was no wonder, when the games came along, that the opposition would be blown away, unable to compete with the levels United were at on a daily basis. Once a culture of hard work is developed on the training pitch at every session, it quickly develops technical ability as players have to be better on the ball to keep it against players working harder to win it back.

Looking back on what I have taken from my time at the club into my coaching, and life in general, is the *work ethic* and *character* required to be successful in anything you do. To have this, I believe you have to really love what you are doing. These are two things that can be worked on every day and require no football skill whatsoever, just an open mind. It is that which will keep the players there, and take them to the next level.

Chapter 5
The Power of Failing

"   **"**

I've missed more than 9,000 shots in my career.
I've lost almost 300 games. 26 times I've been
trusted with the game-winning shot –
and missed.

I've failed over and over and over again in my
life – and that is why I succeed.

Michael Jordan

In February 2018, *FourFourTwo* magazine published a list of the most successful Premier League managers, according to their win percentage. Although Antonio Conte and Pep Guardiola led the way with a win percentage of 70.3%, what is most interesting is that five of the top 20 most successful managers (Brendan Rodgers, Gianluca Vialli, Roy Evans, Kenny Dalglish, and Claudio Ranieri) actually came in with win percentages below 50%.

Rank	Coach	Club(s)	No. of Games	Win %
1=	Antonio Conte	Chelsea	64	70.3%
1=	Pep Guardiola	Manchester City	64	70.3%
3	Alex Ferguson	Manchester United	810	65.2%
4	José Mourinho	Chelsea, Manchester United	278	63.4%
5	Carlo Ancelotti	Chelsea	76	63.2%
6	Roberto Mancini	Manchester City	133	61.7%
7	Manuel Pellegrini	Manchester City	114	61.4%
8	Arsène Wenger	Arsenal	816	57.6%
9	Luiz Felipe Scolari	Chelsea	25	56%
10	Guus Hiddink	Chelsea	34	52.9%
11	Jürgen Klopp	Liverpool	96	52.1%
12	André Villas-Boas	Chelsea, Tottenham	81	51.9%
13	Rafael Benítez	Liverpool, Chelsea, Newcastle	290	51.7%

Rank	Coach	Club(s)	No. of Games	Win %
14	Louis van Gaal	Manchester United	76	51.3%
15	Mauricio Pochettino	Southampton, Tottenham	194	50%
16	Claudio Ranieri	Chelsea, Leicester	208	49.8%
17=	Kenny Dalglish	Blackburn, Newcastle, Liverpool	238	48.3%
17=	Roy Evans	Liverpool	172	48.3%
19	Gianluca Vialli	Chelsea	94	47.9%
20	Brendan Rodgers	Swansea, Liverpool	160	46.9%

FourFourTwo Magazine 'Ranked! The 20 Most Successful Premier League Managers'
by Alex Reid (published and correct as of February 6th 2018)

Who is on this list, who is not on the list, or whether they actually *are* the 20 best coaches in the Premier League is not the debate here. The central point is that *even the very best coaches, teams, and players lose. They fail. They make mistakes.* And they lose, fail and make mistakes all the time. Bouncing back from failure is an integral part of the process, and for young players, these un-successes are an integral part of the learning process.

Even the most successful teams in football, a sport where a draw or tie is more prevalent than a lot of other invasion-style sports, tend to have a win percentage of around 66%. Even the best should expect to lose, or not win, around one-third of their games. In fact, if you are a top-level player, playing in a middle-of-the-pack team, you *will lose* up to 50% of the games you play, and draw a further 25%.

During this chapter, we will look at failure, or more specifically, how football organisations handle big, systemic failures, right down to how players and coaches react to small mistakes. We will home in on how valuable it actually can be when things go wrong in the short-term, so we can learn and improve in the long-term.

Sometimes our biggest failures can result in our greatest achievements. Sometimes, hitting rock bottom allows us to rebuild bigger and better than ever.

Systemic Failure – Germany

During the 2000 European Championships, co-hosted by Belgium and the Netherlands, Germany were top seeds in Group A and would face-off against Romania, England, and Portugal – a tough, but surmountable group for a nation of their calibre.

An opening game draw against Romania – considered to be the weakest team in the group – was followed by two defeats, including a crushing 3-0 turn-around against an already qualified, second-string Portugal. Germany had hit rock bottom, both figuratively and in terms of championship points.

In his excellent book, *The Bundesliga Blueprint*, author Lee Price (@Lee_Price) describes Germany's Euro 2000 as "The Disaster Tournament". Inquests were held throughout the fan-base, the media, and the governing body, the *Deutschland Fussball Bund* (DFB). Their past successes had bred complacency, highlighted further by their 2004 European Championship defeats to the Czech Republic, a 0-0 draw with lowly Latvia, and a second Euros where the *Nationalmannschaft* (national team) failed to qualify to the knockout stages.

"

The pre-tournament preparation in Mallorca was bad. We broke up some training sessions because of disagreements in terms of tactics, how we played, the intensity of training. For me, as a young player, it was a *good experience* – not in terms of how it was, but how it should have been.

Michael Ballack

"

Complacency Sparks Action

Berti Vogts was head coach of the German national team for much of the 1990s, following spells as assistant coach and Under-21 coach when his playing career ended in 1979. Although famous for claiming that a United Germany would remain "unbeatable for years", his tune quickly changed as the 90s took shape. On several occasions, the experienced coach had warned that there was a lack of talent coming through at youth level.

Even mainstream football punditry in the country was deficient, failing to address the issues at hand with outdated, almost arrogant theories. This is outlined by German football expert Raphael Honigstein (@honigstein) in *Klopp: Bring the Noise*. According to a pre-2002 World Cup live TV game analysis with Paul Breitner, the former Bayern Munich and Real Madrid star insisted that top professional players were too good to be coached, and that coaches without a significant playing career could not improve, contribute or understand the national team (plus other "contradictory" reasons for the failures of *Die Mannschaft*). At first, Breitner – himself a World Cup winner – was even reluctant to share a stage with Klopp, then 'only' a Bundesliga 2 coach at Mainz 05. Klopp went on to transform the base level of football analysis the German public was exposed to.

From Short-Term Thinking to Long-Term Revolution

In *Das Reboot – How German Football Reinvented Itself and Conquered the World*, again by Honigstein, he describes a chaotic football scene in Germany during the nineties, with a playing style and sequence of results that were becoming an embarrassment around the turn of the century.

In between the two disastrous European Championship Finals, however, Germany had some success, reaching the World Cup Final in 2002. They ultimately lost to Brazil, but did chalk up an 8-0 group stage win over Saudi Arabia in the process, one of the biggest wins in the tournament's history.

For many countries, an appearance at a World Cup Final might deter any planned overhaul – short-termism that characterises football in the 21st century. Not in Germany. Complacency had been replaced with action, and no short-term positivity was going to change things. The DFB was undeterred, recognising that the 2002 journey was achieved with a group of underwhelming players, in a style that did not appeal (in their 1-0 win against the unfancied United States, they were outshot 11 to 6) and the results were too heavily reliant on spectacular performances by goalkeeper Oliver Kahn (who became the first goalkeeper to receive the competition's Golden Ball – the award for being the World Cup's best player).

The usual format for dealing with a disappointment like Germany's in 2000, at this level, would be to wait for the media storm to pass, sack the manager (Head Coach Erich Ribbeck actually resigned – a case of jumping before being pushed), and employ a coach with a big name or reputation. They would paper over the cracks and cross their fingers. The reaction to this failure, however, was not just some cosmetic, face-saving changes. It was a comprehensive overhaul of football in the country, and a focus on youth and coaching, despite the relative success of 2002. *The failures were recognised as systemic ones.* Long-termism replaced short-termism, something which is a key learning outcome for all coaches. If there are decisions to be made – any decisions around your team – make them for the long-term benefit, rather than for short-term, knee-jerk reasons.

As of 2001, professional Bundesliga clubs were required to have an operational youth academy in order to receive a licence permitting them to play in the country's top league. To take part, they had to get their youth division in line with what the DFB dictated. In 2002, Bundesliga 2 clubs were then subjected to the same rules. Such was the eventual buy-in from clubs (some took more time and convincing than others!) 18 of the 20 teams in the third tier of German football ran a fully operational academy by the 2015/16 season, even though they were not required to do so. A revolution had occurred.

In 2002, the DFB launched the *Extended Talent Promotion Programme.* Between 2002 and 2014, the year Germany won the World Cup in Brazil, the Germans built 52 centres of excellence and a further 366 regional coaching bases, in a systematic effort to increase the level of young players in the country. They were keen to ensure that a comprehensive talent programme would develop and 'catch' the very best players in the country. 1,300 coaches nationally, all with a minimum of a UEFA B Licence, watch 650,000 youngsters per year. Gone are the days when players of the calibre of Miroslav Klose, a player who would go on to break World Cup scoring records, was still playing fourth division amateur football with FC 08 Homburg at 21-years-old.

Critically, because of the clubs' development of young players, and because they were a cheaper option than importing average but expensive foreign players, German academy products were now getting their chance to play in the country's top division. Between the 2002/03 and 2015/16 seasons, the average age of Bundesliga players had dropped from over 27 to 24.5 years old, and the percentage of German players had risen 50% to 66%.

As part of the overall strategy, Jürgen Klinsmann was hired as the new national team Head Coach (assisted by his eventual successor Joachim Löw) in 2004. The fact that Löw was still in position for the 2018 World Cup shows the long-term thinking behind these appointments also. Klinsmann instilled a brand of football that steered Germany into the modern era. It was free-flowing, exciting, and preparation for tournaments intensified.[1] A young, almost unknown, and entirely Germany-based side travelled to South Africa for the 2010 World Cup with little media hype. They ended up wooing the football world with an attractive, attacking style, exposing us to the likes of Mesut Özil, Sami Khedira, Manuel Neuer, Thomas Müller, and Toni Kroos. By 2014, this group was the core of the team that took home Germany's fourth World Cup.

2018

During the 2018 World Cup, the German national team once again were looking towards rock bottom. The reigning World Champions and pre-tournament favorites were again knocked out in the group stages – losing to both Mexico and South Korea.

This time there was no hesitation – they had learned from previous mistakes. They did not sack the coach; they investigated, swiftly introducing further reforms into youth football, including the

---

[1] In preparation for the 2014 World Cup in Brazil, Germany did not hire a base to live and train, they *built* a purpose-built training facility and resort to use an in-country base for their preparations (taking marginal gains to a new level!).

initiation of the 3v3 format for the youngest players. They looked at their top professionals, asked what was missing, and went right back to the grassroots scene to solve it.

Implications for Coaches

Although Germany's widespread football reforms are not *directly* transferable to the readers here, its lessons are applicable to all of us.

Seeing through short-termism is our first port-of-call. If there is ever a decision to be made in your environment, ensure it is made for long-term reasons. While the German revolution, from an outside perspective, was focused on the elite level of the game, there was also considerable work done in terms of the grassroots game. The DFB recognised that to improve the overall standard, then grassroots development would be key. Coach education was improved, leading to a more open-minded recruitment process of young, modern-thinking, dynamic coaches. At the beginning of the 2017/18 season, five of the 18 Bundesliga clubs had a Head Coach in their 30s. Hoffenheim's Head Coach, Julian Nagelsmann was 29 – a sign that clubs had become more willing to recruit, or promote, academy coaches whose focus and success had been in developing and improving players. There was also a concerted, detailed effort made to improve players from the top of the pyramid to the bottom, like we spoke about in an earlier chapter.

For those interested, Germany's development documents are available online, in English, and detail much of what we include here. Two stand-out slides in their documentation are below, highlighting the effort and attention to detail paid to amateur youth coaches.

The first, identifying the children's coach as "key", identifies three significant areas needed to work with young players in grassroots settings – training, competitions, and care. The central theme is that football should be, in the first instance, fun; youngsters should learn the game by playing the game, and coaches' behaviour should be positive and enthusiastic.

DFB – The Key Aspects of a Children's Coach

Training	Competitions	Care
Key question: What do children want and what are they capable of	Promote the fun in football!	Be tutor and friend!
Develop ball-/skilled movement!	Be game organiser and companion!	Convey enthusiasm
Mediate the fun in football	Allow children to play long enough!	Support each child!
Teach football in small steps!	Simple tips – cheer and praise!	Be a role model in all situations!

(Circle diagram with segments labelled: Care, Training, Competitions)

The Children's Coach as Key, from the DFB youth development document,
Talent Development in the German Football Association

Along with the mainly social aspects required of a 21st century coach in Germany, above, the DFB also outlined six key principles within youth football development:

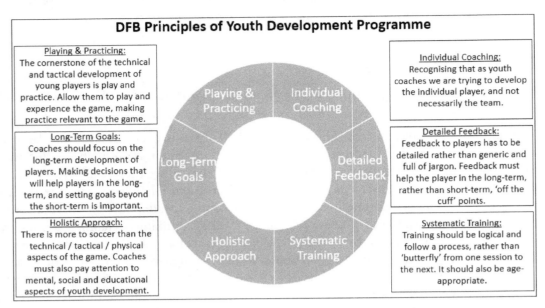

The Six Principles of Youth Development Programme outlined in the DFB document,
Youth Development Programme

Lessons from Hoffenheim

In 2010, Niklas Süle joined the Academy at TSG 1899 Hoffenheim. He spent a further seven years at the club and went on to represent them over 100 times before he was 21-years-old. He also represented his country at Under-16, 17, 18, 19, 21, and Under-23 level. In 2016, he became a full German international and his pedigree was enough to convince Bundesliga giants, Bayern Munich, to lure him to Bavaria.

Although Hoffenheim is a club with significant financial backing since the early 2000s,[2] the Academy remains a source of pride, and large-scale efforts have been made to export the Hoffenheim Academy philosophy around the world.

When most coaches are asked about their philosophy, the conversation drifts towards playing style, technical football, and a smattering of unconvincing references about holistic development. At Hoffenheim, and in line with the DFB concept that holistic development and education should be developed alongside football skills, the person, as well as the player, is advanced.

---

[2] Between 2000 and 2008, Hoffenheim ascended from the German fifth division to the Bundesiga, largely due to the backing of billionaire entrepreneur, Dietmar Hopp, who was once an Academy player at the club.

"

We cultivate and foster an honest relationship with our young players and assume a sincere responsibility for their development. In this way, we want to encourage an active lifelong learning approach and prepare them with a qualified holistic education for the demands of later life. The coordinated training aims to create a "Hoffenheim" mentality that pushes the players to excel as an athlete, whilst also teaching them important life skills such as self-discipline and social competence.

Hoffenheim Academy Philosophy document

The club outlines 11 values with which their players must abide and which get reinforced across academy programmes. More and more football programmes are now recognising that, if they can improve the person, they can improve the player – in fact, the player is the person. If they can encourage honest, coachable, self-aware young people, they can then mould them in a football sense[3].

Hoffenheim's 11 Values

1	Open and honest	7	Team-minded
2	Ready to learn	8	Respectful
3	Independent	9	Proactive
4	Critical	10	Passionate
5	Self-aware	11	Principled
6	Fair		

From a purely footballing point of view, Hoffenheim promote age-appropriate coaching, something we looked at extensively in *Making The Ball Roll*. They go so far as to divide their programme into three separate centres. Like in the DFB guidance, they commit to a process that is not driven by results. Education, holistically and from a football point of view, is of greater concern to coaches than the scoreline of games.

---

[3] One particular academy in England rewards players who are the best at displaying the club's values each month.

Fundamental Training	Kinderzentrum	Age 5 – 11
	(Kids Centre)	
Advanced Training	Förderzentrum	Age 12 – 15
	(Development Centre)	
Advanced Intensive Training	Nachwuchsleistungszentrum	Age 16 – 19
	(Centre of Excellence)	

Hoffenheim's Three Training Centres

Hoffenheim is one of two Bundesliga clubs that use the highly technical football machine, the *Footbonaut* (the other is Borussia Dortmund). At a seven-figure cost to install (I have seen estimated costs vary from $1.5-$3.5 million), it is unsurprising that very few have invested in this.

If you are not familiar with this machine, it is worth surfing YouTube for some videos, although the concept is quite straightforward. One player works within the 14x14 metre cage, receiving balls from any of eight different directions, heights, and angles. Once he receives the ball, he must place a pass into one of 72 square panels, one of which lights up. The frequency and speed of the balls that are played into the player can be altered by the machine's operator. A Bundesliga.com article boasted that the machine tests players in terms of their "reaction, vision, precision, and skill."

The merit of using such a machine in football development is often questioned (we will talk about action-perception coupling later). It's relevance to the game is often queried. Hoffenheim's aptly named Sports Coordinator for Innovation, Raphael Hoffner, uses statistics to back up an improvement in how the pace of play at both first team and youth team level has increased since installing the machine in 2014.

The speed of first-team players (from the ball being released to the moment it hits the target) has improved by 0.3 seconds. The youth team has improved by 0.5 seconds. He claims that you can deal with the ball more times in a three-minute footbonaut session (200 ball contacts) than in a full 90-minute game (100–120). To add further variables, up to four players are placed in the centre at once, and on occasions, defenders are also added. Hoffner claims that he has not witnessed one player who was fast in the footbonaut, and not on the pitch.

We noted in the last chapter that success is not necessarily aligned with money and snazzy facilities. Lots of 'talent hotbeds' are dilapidated and do not contain the best of everything. With that in mind, the session below, from a YouTube video from Planet Training, offers the regular grassroots coach – armed with balls, bibs, cones, and enthusiasm – an alternative to the footbonaut.

The coach's skill of seeing, then adapting sessions is very important. Many would argue that it is the essence of coaching. Making a session you see online, in a book, or in person, relevant to your group in terms of size, age, ability, and situation is the cornerstone of our planning. The rondo exercise that you see at Barcelona will not be the same with your Under-10s. The small-sided game you see at Bayern Munich will not produce the exact same outcomes for your Under-16s. Expecting the same time in the footbonaut from your Under-14s as the first-team at Hoffenheim is unrealistic. Borrowing ideas from other coaches and environments is great but making them relevant to your situation is the skill.

"
Ideas belong to everyone, and I have stolen
as many as I could.
"

Pep Guardiola

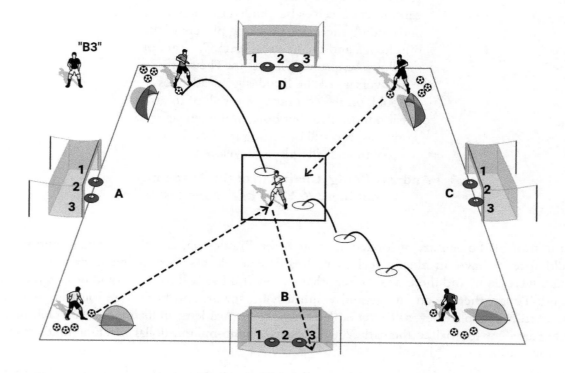

Setup:

One player (white) starts in the middle, and four different coloured players start with a stash of balls – one in each corner. The white receives passes from all four players, in order. The yellow and black players play passes along the ground. Blue bounces the ball into the white (can use hands if necessary), and the red plays an aerial pass.

Practice:

On the command of the coach (in this case, he shouts "B3"), the white player controls and passes the ball into this area. The coach may also call a colour (yellow / red / black / blue) where the white must pass into the relevant goal.

The player works for one minute, and the coach keeps score of the successful passes. The central player then rotates with another.

Warning:

A work ratio of one player to four is not ideal. This exercise should not be done with any more than five players. There is potential for the other players in your squad to take part in another practice at the same time. For example, if you have 15 players, five will be in the 'footbonaut', while the others play 5v5. Once the players are finished in the footbonaut, they swap over.

A practical version of the footbonaut machine, from Planet Training

Inspiring

"

The biggest mistakes in football are often the result of temporary hype. In that respect, we cannot let ourselves be blinded by the recent outstanding successes of young players in the Bundesliga and the national team. We cannot allow complacency to set in. The tenth anniversary of the Bundesliga academies should, on the contrary, be for all of us an occasion to think about how, in the ten years to come, we can still be setting the standard in youth and elite player development.

"

Andreas Rettig, Chairman of the Academies Committee, *10 Years of Academies*

At the turn of the century, it looked as though the Bundesliga, and the German national team, would forever have an elderly feel to it. Readymade players were given priority over youth. Tactics were dour, and there was a threat that a powerful football nation would be completely left behind. Today, there is an energy and youthful vibrancy around both – and lessons have been learned from complacency, as Rettig outlines above. An Academy in its infancy, at a club that was playing amateur football in the early 2000s, boasts a multi-million-dollar machine that's exclusive function is to improve players.

Out of failure can come great success, if that failure is acknowledged and actioned. The problem with many, however, is that failure is feared – from boardroom level right down to what happens with players on the grass.

Fear of Failure

None of us seek failure, and none of us are very happy about it once it comes around. When we let it get hold of us, however, it can lead to devastating consequences and is a prevalent characteristic of someone with a fixed mindset. A key strength, however, of successful football, and other sports players, is that they do not fear failing. This allows them to take risks and move towards success. Those who are afraid to fail – either in general or just situationally – tend to play safe, and thus struggle to hit their optimum performance levels.

"

If a superstar ever sees a slight opening, zip, he has the courage to go for the small hole. He won't hold back because he's afraid to fail.

"

NHL Coach

You, the coach, are standing on the side of the pitch having just seen your team draw a game after extra time – a penalty shootout beckons. You have already made a note of your five best technicians who you want to take the all-important kicks. Without being too suggestive or prescriptive, your list is probably made up of regular penalty takers, reliable passers, and strikers. You ask each one of them if they 'fancy' it. Some accept and even volunteer to go first or fifth, arguably the pressure kicks. Some, however, even one or two with 'big' characters and a strong skillset, outwardly reject the offer. Why?

I mentioned Susan Jeffers' book, *Feel the Fear and Do It Anyway* in *Making The Ball Roll*. The exercise we looked at was a very powerful one, where we displayed the effect of positive or negative feedback and self-talk on physical performance. A central point of Jeffers' book is that fear exists no matter what. What separates people is how they treat or 'hold' that fear.

The player who volunteers to take penalty number five is (despite his or her apparent enthusiasm), fearful – or nervous at the very least. It is a stressful situation. His positivity in dealing with it, however, is because he approaches the situation from a position of power (through choice, energy, and action). He fancies himself to score or wants the opportunity to be part of the drama. The player who refuses to even engage in a conversation about it is also clearly fearful and holds the fear from a position of pain (helplessness, depression, and paralysis), thus making him 'flee' from the situation. Many call this 'choking' under pressure.

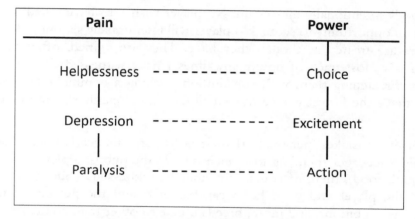

How We Hold Fear, from Feel the Fear and Do It Anyway

Our job then, as a coach, is to do all we can to ensure that players approach negative situations from a position of power. This goes beyond a penalty shoot-out situation (in reality, some players will still be 'cold' when it comes to volunteering for a shootout, no matter what!) and reaches into our environment as a whole. Our reaction and attitude towards players' mistakes, especially those of a technical/tactical nature, may help players see them in a new light.

Managing Players' Mistakes

In 1994, Nelson Mandela and Rick Stengel, author of Mandela's autobiography, *Long Walk to Freedom*, were travelling on a small propeller plane across South Africa to give a speech during an election campaign. En route, one of the engines failed. The concern onboard was obvious. The pilots prepared the airport for an emergency landing and emergency vehicles were on standby. Amid the panic, however, Mandela calmly read his newspaper, as if he didn't have a care in the world! The plane went on to land safely, and it was only when safe in his car that Mandela confided in Stengel that he was actually terrified.

This is what leaders do. They often repress their true reactions and emotions for the benefit of their followers. The travelling party, seeing Mandela, their leader, calm and collected, felt a sense of ease. It soothed people in the face of life and death.

As coaches, this type of behaviour is often needed, especially when things go wrong. Becoming openly angry, gesticulating, and being overly-dramatic around mistakes feeds those who look up to us with the same emotions, loading an already negative situation with more pessimism.

Environment

"You live, you learn," "nobody is perfect," and "to err is human" are terms that all of us are familiar with. The term "I never lose. I either win, or I learn," has positively filtered its way into many sport-specific environments, too.

Let's be honest, in the moment when a player has just made a mistake, even a small one, he will rarely consider it a "learning opportunity", not immediately at least. Embracing mistakes is a concept that needs to be learned, practiced, and backed up by the leader in their environment.

Rather than fearing failure, we can develop an environment where failure and mistakes help us to expand out of our comfort zone. Failure is evidence that we are challenging ourselves, growing, taking risks, and heading in the right direction. They can inspire us to find solutions. For some, the fear of failure can paralyse, but fear, managed effectively, can also heighten intensity.

First of all, nobody intentionally messes up. No player wishes to have a bad touch, give away a penalty, or miss an opportunity to score. No player will intentionally set out to lose. All too often, however, players are treated as though they have. They are vilified, often publicly, for poor performances. I have lost track of how many times I have witnessed coaches openly shame a player by either threatening them with substitution, making a comment as a player leaves the pitch (usually, "that's the fastest you've moved all day"[4]), or openly slating them in front of the whole group.

Never make players' mistakes 'personal'. If their poor performance is traced back to a lifestyle issue (e.g., an older teenager spending too much time in the pub or a player who trades physical well-being for junk food), then, of course, this may be addressed – but sensitively. Distinguish clearly between the player and what he is capable of – and the person. Insulting a player's personality, dreams, ambitions, and more, breeds little else other than contempt. When we make mistakes in any field, we want the people in our corner to have our back. We *want* a Mandela to show us that everything will be ok.

Owning Mistakes

Johan Cruyff, the king of inspiring and nail-on-the-head quotes, once said that football is "a game of mistakes." Although he goes on to suggest that teams who make the fewest mistakes win, which may not be necessarily true (John Wooden, another master of the quote, conversely said that the team that 'makes the most mistakes will win'), he did land on something powerful. If we acknowledge that football is a game where mistakes are common, maybe we can more readily accept them. They are part of the course, meaning that all players (and coaches) need to be able to control our reactions to them – they are expected, respected, inspected and, ultimately, can be corrected.

---

[4] My personal favourite though, if that is the right word, is an opposition coach shouting at his goalkeeper: "I hope you are not catching the train home today … you would probably miss that too."

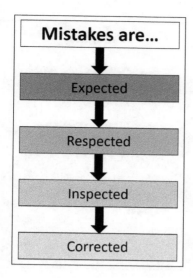

Mistakes are… poster, used in many growth mindset classrooms

This is lesson number one when it comes to managing player mistakes. Players need to realise that, although we aim to be successful in everything we do, these things happen. They can be very useful when the error is 'owned'.

Owning and taking responsibility for mistakes is both empowering and positive, if not fun initially. By owning them, we can control them. It is a habit that can be learned, as a life skill as well as in a football environment. In fact, if you own and 'respect' your own mistakes from the outset, they become less painful when someone else points them out. You control it now and are in a position of power, rather than pain.

I once had a player so entrenched in a fight to show he never made mistakes that he would come laden with some of the most fantastic excuses. He, at *18-years-old*, so not exactly a child, once suggested that he purposely missed an early penalty, so the opposition would under-estimate him for the rest of the game! The chances are that either growing up, or in a previous environment, he was taught (subconsciously or otherwise) that failure was to be avoided at all costs, and it is quite likely that he spent a lot of time in a blame-culture atmosphere.

Owning mistakes is different to dwelling on them. If we spend too long in their company, we lose confidence, we stress, our emotions become negative, and we play safe. Owning mistakes is the first step in the diagram above – acceptance. The eventual 'correcting' comes from this start point. If we own them, they cannot hurt us, and we gain a lot by addressing them head-on.

Our relationship with mistakes is the driver behind dealing with them. In an article for *Believe Perform, Why Mistakes are Brilliant*, psychologist and academy coach James Barraclough (@sportspsychjimbo), uses the acronym T.E.A. Time:

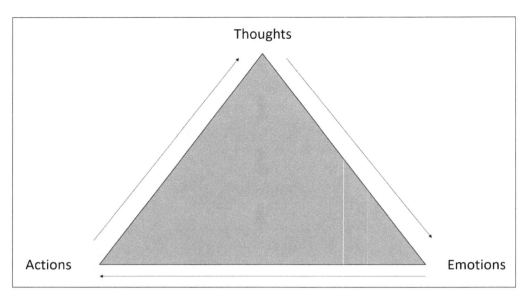

How our thoughts can affect our performance

If our thoughts are negative, they will lead to negative emotions, then ultimately negative actions – e.g., a player's performance. We then enter a vicious cycle that is very difficult to break. If we can get players to own their mistakes at the thought stage, and self-correct where possible, we will have a positive impact on their performance.

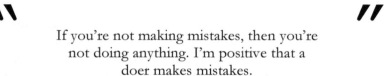

If you're not making mistakes, then you're
not doing anything. I'm positive that a
doer makes mistakes.

John Wooden

Self-Correcting and Skilful Neglect

Sometimes, as coaches, we are quick to jump in with corrections once we see an error. This may be physically stepping into a session and correcting performance, or during matchday when the players receive a comment from the touchline or at half-time. We spot a player doing something wrong and immediately rush in to address the failing.

This, traditionally, is what coaching was – finding mistakes and correcting them. Sometimes, however, the quest to find mistakes is unnecessary and quite energy-sapping for all involved. Not only do *overused interventions* around mistakes cause hostility, they reduce the all-important ball-rolling time in our sessions. Instruction and correction is still a huge part of coaching, but we also need to recognise that all mistakes do not need to be 'coached' the second they are made.

Most of us are familiar with *The Coaching Continuum* and the various types of coaching interventions we can use. The visual below may be familiar to readers of *Making the Ball Roll*.

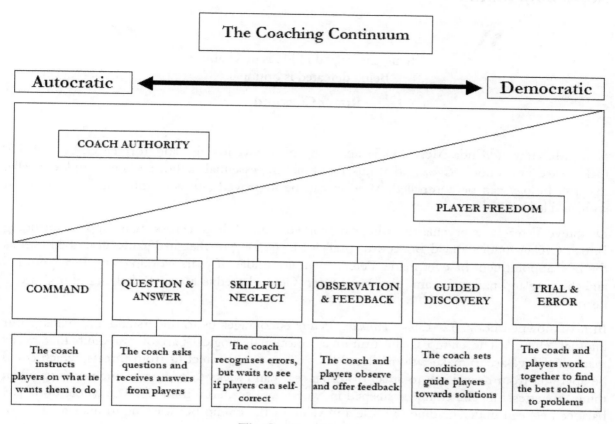

The Coaching Continuum

While we are familiar with interventions that use a command style ("This is what I want you to do…"), Questions and Answers ("What is the best thing to do at this moment?) and guided discovery (literally setting up a practice that spits out certain returns for the players), we may not be over-familiar with the term 'Skillful Neglect,' which is slowly making its way into football coaching vocabulary.

Giving players the time and opportunity to rectify mistakes themselves is being encouraged more and more in coaching. If mistakes can be taken by the player as immediate feedback, he can use this strategy to improve, without the assistance of anyone else. From a learning point of view, this is powerful. If there is an opportunity to self-correct, in any walk of life, we take it and do not require external feedback.

Skillful neglect is both knowing when to intervene, and when to say nothing and stay away. Stand back, note the mistake, and *at least* give players the opportunity to self-correct in the first instance. This is not 'doing nothing' nor is it avoiding coaching; it is skilfully managing the situation.

If the same error is recurring, however, or you don't believe that self-correction will take place (sometimes players will not know the reason for their mistakes, or maybe they do not understand that a mistake has been made at all), then the coach's intervention becomes necessary. Furthermore, by allowing time and seeing a player attempt to solve the problem several times, you also have the opportunity to build a bigger picture of the situation, rather than judging the player for one action only. It also gives you the opportunity to discuss the mistake discreetly, rather than it being highlighted in a group setting.

Reframing failure

"
"

Being challenged in life is inevitable.
Being defeated is optional.

Roger Crawford

Enda McNulty (@Enda_McNulty) is an Irish sport psychologist and former GAA star. He makes clear in his book, *Commit*, that mistakes build the essential skill of resilience, and, critically, that psychology can be controlled. Mindset can be improved and isn't something we are born with, and left with.

Dr. Steve Peters is a psychiatrist who has worked with athletes across many sports, including British Cycling under David Brailsford. Brailsford, the king of marginal gains, described him as the best appointment he ever made. Peters spent a number of years working with Liverpool FC and the England national team. Notably, Steven Gerrard credits him with helping him improve his mindset.

In his renowned book, *The Chimp Paradox*, Peters encourages us to understand and manage our internal 'chimp'. The chimp is the primitive, emotional, illogical part of our brain that needs managing if we are to make rational decisions. He exists to protect us from threats, which could be anything from near-death to small disturbances – and seeks to take over our reactions when things are stressful. The chimp is steeped in 'worst-case scenario' thinking. The whole book is a balance between understanding the role and value of the chimp but learning to manage it – not every negative event is a disaster.

Unlike our chimp, we can recognise and reframe setbacks as an opportunity, a learning curve. Gaining perspective of failure helps us shed our fear of it and helps us to reach our potential. This, however, usually takes time and conscious management experience. A young player will, therefore, need time and support to put short-term setbacks into perspective. They, and their chimp, need to be "nursed" through it.

Any failure or setback should not be seen as critical and/or permanent. Players need to understand that mistakes are short-term, and should be treated as such. It is through these failures that we succeed. Even when players do fail, it doesn't make them a permanent failure.

Failing	Being a Failure
Temporary	Permanent
A setback / disappointment	A mindset
Shows you are stretching yourself and pushing limits	Shows you have given up
Part of the journey	End of the journey
Opportunity to learn and grow	Turning your back on learning and growth

Viewing failure as short-term

Rituals

Mistakes are powerful – they can help you improve – or implode! Implosion comes when you dwell on mistakes and allow them to affect your emotions and actions, and therefore your performance. Improvement comes in the realisation that carrying your mistakes around is the biggest mistake of all. They are no longer short-term bumps in the road, but a long-term traffic jam.

To assist athletes to let go of mistakes, many coaches and sport psychologists will use 'mistake rituals'. These are usually physical procedures that players engage in immediately after a mistake is made and are designed to banish the error, allowing the player to move on. Although different in football, compared to individual sports like tennis or golf where there are more natural breaks in play, rituals can be useful for both expelling the mistake, and also accepting it in the first place.

Rituals need to be short, simple, concise, and subtle. Some of them are listed below:

Once a mistake is made…

A player symbolically takes a piece of grass (which represents the mistake) and lets it blow away in the wind

A player motions 'dirt off my shoulder'

A goalkeeper leaves the pitch via one side of the goal, and re-enters the pitch on the other

Players vocally reply to the mistake with "I'm Learning!" (Andrew DuBos Beyer, via Dan Abrahams)

Players focus their eyesight on the opponent's crossbar (this physically keeps their head up, rather than defeated body language of looking to the ground)

Have a teammate clap you

The next thing you do is positive – track back, next pass is simple, etc.

Practical 'rituals' to help players manage mistakes

These rituals should be reserved for significant mistakes, and not used for *every single error*. Missing a good goal-scoring opportunity, a mistake that led to a goal against you, or the same *recurring* mistake, are ideal opportunities to use this kind of ritual. The last thing anyone needs is a young player throwing grass around the place throughout the game.

Solution-Focused

For players' attitudes to mistakes to change, coaches can help by changing the focus to the solution. In the same article mentioned above, Barraclough suggests a very simple question to use – "What can you do next time to reduce the chances of making the same mistake?" This switches the focus from the problem to the solution. Note also the use of the word "reduce". As referenced earlier, mistakes *will* be made, regardless of any intervention, so expecting a player *never* to make the same mistake again is ironically setting them up to fail. Another question I hear used a lot along the coaching journey is, "If you could do that all over again, what would you do differently?" Both questions are open, solution-based, and reframe a negative to a positive.

"

You have to give players courage so that they
aren't afraid to fail.

Sven-Göran Eriksson

Making Mistakes as a Coach

A lot of the same outcomes we spoke about above, can also be applied to coaches. As coaches, we make mistakes too! Mistakes are often more difficult for adults to take, especially adults who are put in a position of being all-knowing and the one with all the answers. We may preach that we should use errors as ways to improve, to motivate ourselves, and that we need to 'own' failures… but applying these things is often difficult for many. If we are honest, when we mess up, our ego takes a hit.

When a coach does not recognise his or her mistakes, it can lead to victim-blaming – or player-blaming. The wonderful passing exercise you devised keeps breaking down in training, so the players are at fault. A game tactic that proved to be wrong, or which results in a poor defeat, may be blamed on a referee, the opposition, or, yet again, the players. If you find that setbacks in your coaching environment are always the fault of someone, or something else, it may be best to change tack.

In the final chapter of *Making The Ball Roll*, I encouraged coaches to "look in the mirror first" – i.e., to look inwardly first, especially when things have gone wrong. There are certain things that coaches can control – the 'controllables' – but significantly there are elements that you cannot. These include the opposition, the weather, the journey to an away game, and the referee.

The treatment of referees is more important than you may know. First of all, they are human and are making honest decisions, even when they go against your team. I cannot imagine anyone getting up early every weekend to facilitate the playing of youth football, to actively go out and cheat a bunch of kids out of a result. Like you and your players, they will make mistakes, so give them a break.

If you focus your post-game debrief on the performance of a referee – however bad it may have been – you are disowning and allowing players to disown their mistakes or roles in the game. This is a particularly bad habit to embed in young players. Debrief the game from a performance point of view, and if the ref was that bad, then teach players how to deal with adversity, things going against them, and keeping discipline and focus in the midst of perceived injustice. This will help them long-term. Using the referee as an excuse for things going wrong may make players feel better in the short term, but has no real value.

Inducing Mistakes

"

The interesting thing about coaching is that
you have to trouble the comfortable,
and comfort the troubled.

**Ric Charlesworth,
Australian multi-sport coach**

Sometimes, a coach or coach educator comes along and hits the nail on the head. In that way, the quote above from Ric Charlesworth does exactly that. It is one of those sentences that resonates immediately.

Comforting the 'troubled', the ones lacking in confidence or that are having a tough time, is the obvious part of his viewpoint. We, as coaches, spend a lot of time identifying when and why players are struggling, behaviours have changed, or their performance has suffered. We look to help them find their mojo.

"Troubling the comfortable," however, seems counter-intuitive, but is still relevant. When failure and mistakes occur, we can manage situations and help players to manage them. When it's too easy, 'troubling' them may also be necessary.

Troubling players may be as simple as challenging them more in your training environment. We want to offer them problems that need solving. It may be upping the ante in terms of their development – little challenges and improvements to keep them on their toes. It is ensuring players are comfortably uncomfortable from a development point of view.

"

Mistakes are part of the learning process.
If you have a session that's clean and has no
mistakes, you've probably pitched it below the
level of the group.

Michael Beale

Results and the Problem with Not Failing

If your team is winning games and leagues comfortably, it will feel great. We see this so often across youth leagues across the world. "X Football Club is undefeated in two years," "Team A beat Team B 13 – 0," etc. I recently saw an Under-13 league table where the winners had won 18 of 18 games, scoring over 150 goals in the process, and conceded only six! In half those games, they hit double figures, and never scored less than five. This is a sort of utopian environment that will eventually turn dystopian.

With *even the best* professional teams winning around 66% of games, it is vital that young players, at least semi-regularly, experience the feeling of defeat. If players become used to a disproportionate and unrealistic amount of success, the moment they are ultimately defeated will hurt badly. All sense of rationale about losing will be lost. Complacency becomes inherent in them – a fixed mindset well and truly sets in.

As a coach of this type of team, you may ask, "What can I do? My team is good, coached well and wins. I am producing good football players who are better than their rivals – what am I supposed to do?"

In this case, there are several non-negotiable answers to this 'problem'. First of all, it is important that you are winning games in a technical/tactical way, not just relying on the physical players to overrun teams. All players involved should be rotated and given equal game-time, and you should be entered into a league that is appropriate for the level of the team (I have seen unbeaten teams choose to remain in B leagues rather than accept promotion to 'up' the challenge for players).

Regardless of the level of your team, there will broadly be three tiers of player – strivers, copers, and strugglers – a 'top' 'middle' and 'bottom' in terms of *current* ability. Chances are if your team is winning comprehensively over and over again, your players, and certainly the strivers will need challenging. If they are playing at the highest level they can, then it is the coach's duty (not a suggestion) to move them higher up the levels. This may be promoting them to the next age-group, allowing them to move to a club playing at a higher level, etc. This may leave you aghast at first, but if your child was cruising through his or her maths class, you would want and expect the teacher to increase the challenge, and allow him or her to grow and progress in a more stimulating, less easy environment.

In 2017, a local club in Spain hit the headlines worldwide. A Valencia-based Under-11 coach was removed from his position, having overseen his team beat a fellow team 25-0. Club directors felt that is was against the spirit of the game. The defeated side had played 30 league games, losing all of them, and conceding 247 goals.

Conclusion

Failure and mistakes happen from time to time. In fact, they happen all the time. Coaches have bad sessions, lose games, and make poor decisions. Lionel Messi misses penalties. Sergio Ramos gets sent-off at an incredible frequency. Big international teams lose in disgrace. In fact, you could list the greatest teams and players ever to grace the game, and pinpoint a moment of spectacular failure very quickly. This is football. How we deal with this is critical.

Summary

- Even the best teams in the world will only win around 66% of the time. They will lose, or not win, one-third of the games that they play. Losing is a part of the game.

- Germany turned their failings at Euro 2000 and Euro 2004 into a positive that allowed them to drastically improve their long-term performance.

- Youth players and young coaches were integral to the improvement in the German development system.

- Out of failure can come great success, if that failure is acknowledged and actioned.

- In as much as possible, coaches or football organisations should make decisions with long-term consequences in mind.

- Hoffenheim Academy focuses on player development, age-appropriate coaching, values, and developing the person as well as the player.

- As seen in the practical version of the footbonaut, a real skill in coaching is using a session you have seen elsewhere, and adequately adapting it to meet the needs of one's group.

- If players fear failure, they will play safe and struggle to hit peak performance.

- How coaches behave when players make mistakes is important – we all need a Mandela!

- Encourage an environment where mistakes are accepted, respected, inspected, and corrected.

- Our thoughts influence our emotions which, in turn, influence our actions.

- Allow players to self-correct where possible, using the 'skillful neglect' coaching style.

- Failing is short-term; being a failure is permanent. Ensure players treat mistakes as something to learn from, but are short-term. Using 'mistake rituals' can help.

- Coaches should reframe players' mistakes as opportunities to learn and should be solution-focused.

- Coaches can induce mistakes or certainly challenge players to ensure that the 'comfortable are troubled.'

- If your team is winning games consistently with high scores and winning leagues at a canter, the players are not being challenged enough. Cruising players should be promoted and challenged at higher levels.

It's Your Game #1

Making a Point

Anonymous

We are all familiar with the FA Cup. Although in recent years this competition has been deprioritised by many in favour of the Premier League and Champions League, its Under-18 version, the FA Youth Cup, is as strong as ever. The bigger clubs still dominate when it comes to taking the trophy, but the journey for smaller clubs and their players remains one to be savoured.

During one of the early rounds of the competition, I was working as assistant to a very experienced coach. During the first half, a player was injured and received several minutes of treatment on the pitch. His replacement, as is common, was sent to warm-up under the proviso of taking his place in the game.

Once medical attention was complete, the substitute was not quite ready, however. He was organising himself in slow motion – still putting his shin guards on, taping up his socks, and spent what felt like an eternity trying to find his match shirt. The usual behaviour of a coach in this situation would be to stall the referee, hasten the substitute, and get him on the pitch as soon as possible. However, he didn't. He motioned to the referee to carry on with the game, and briefly reorganised the team now playing with ten men, and re-sent the player for a warm-up.

Those of you who have been assistants to experienced coaches will understand the looks and questions asked of you by others. "What's going on?" "He's ready, why isn't the 'gaffer' putting him on?" "Are we missing something here?" These looks, gestures, and quietly-worded questions came from the pitch, the bench, and even from spectators in the stadium. Even the linesman quietly asked me what was happening. For once, as a buffer between the ideas of the head coach and anyone who didn't understand them, I was speechless and could do no more than shrug. It took a full ten minutes before the substitution was finally made.

At half-time, however, all was made clear. In the biggest game of the season for most of us, at the highest stage we could play on at that moment, it was all a lesson. The substitute was berated for being unprofessional and not being ready in the first place, then for warming-up poorly, and then for taking an eternity to equip himself. This was not just a message for the player though; it was a message for everyone. Tidy up the small things, be ready, and behave appropriately – otherwise the team will struggle.

Looking back ten years now, I remember little else of the game – even the final score. The learning outcome, though, I've never forgotten.

<u>**It's Your Game #2**</u>

Jamie

Tony Mee • @CoachTonyMee

Academy Coach

When Ray approached me about contributing an experience from my coaching journey, we discussed several options before one really resonated. While discussing failure and resilience, and the guidance required to help players fulfil their potential, one 16-year-old sprang instantly to mind…

At the end of his Under-16 season, Jamie was released from his hometown professional Academy after not being offered a scholarship. This is a significant point in the timeline of a young English Academy player, and it meant that he would not transfer from being a part-time to a full-time player. Much of the story of his release focused on his physical size at the time, but there was a lot more going on when you scratched the surface.

At the time, I worked in a local college, which ran a football development programme along with a classroom-based sports education programme for 16-19-year-olds. These are often the programmes that ex-Academy players, like Jamie, would find themselves on, having been released from their elite environments.

Jamie clearly had some potential, but he also had some issues! At that stage of his development, I can confidently say that he was not the best player I'd ever worked with at his age. He was 'decent' but not brilliant and with some significant flaws. During his time with us, he went for trials to represent England at college level but didn't do enough to get selected.

Jamie was a poor student, regularly missing work deadlines, and also found himself in trouble away from the classroom too. Such were his decisions at that time, that after the first year of a two-year course, Jamie was asked to leave college – a decision I fully supported. His next step football-wise was to play local non-league football whilst working in a factory. For a period of time, he had to be substituted in the second half of evening games to comply with a court-inspired curfew!

Fast-forward to his mid-twenties, and Jamie is a regular international for England, played in a World Cup, and beat the record held by Ruud van Nistelrooy for the most goals scored in consecutive games in the Premier League, a competition he has also won. If ever there was a tale of overcoming early disappointments, failure and poor life choices, it's … Jamie Vardy!

Chapter 6
Building a Player

" You build a player like you build a house. The basement of the player is the technique. The first floor is the physical talent of the player. The second floor is the tactical aspect – does he understand the game? The final floor – the roof – how much do I want to be successful [psychological]? "

Arsène Wenger

I like to think that most ambitious coaches go through a naïve stage. Assuming that a certain amount of naivety *is* a widespread trait of young, striving coaches makes me feel better considering some of the well-intentioned but off-the-cuff things I have done throughout the years.

One such example was when I was in my very early twenties before I had any sort of coaching qualification. I had been reading a book about the scouting and talent identification of players, where the author had claimed that you needed to watch a player three times before getting a good, overall picture of his capability (today, this time-scale is vastly up for debate!).

As someone who was desperate to carve out a career in football, I decided that I would watch a player the magical three times, document his traits and send it to as many relevant clubs as I could find the contact details for – which I did. The ambition was to work in football, and I thought player scouting was an accessible way of getting into the professional system.

Although I no longer have a copy of that particular report, I do remember being very proud of it. It was organised, seven pages in length and contained information about both his game, and any other titbits I could find about his personality and lifestyle away from the pitch (the same book told me that this was often a vital factor in the eventual signing of players).

None of the information I sent was desperately wrong, and my concluding opinion on the player in question was not too wide of the mark. When you look back on his career, he played mostly in the English Championship, with forays into the lower end of the Premier League with various clubs. For the record, one chief scout that I sent the report to later signed the player when he became a manager, although I humbly do not consider my report to have been a swaying factor in this.

However, *there is a difference between not being wrong, and being thorough and holistically accurate*. Looking back, the layout was exactly what you would expect from someone new to the game – from an amateur. Headings included passing, ball control and position-specific information – details you would expect from such a document. However, the gaps and the structure needed to evaluate a player thoroughly were wildly amiss. I needed to *organise* my thoughts. Something modern coaching has adopted extensively.

PPSTT

When being thorough in analysing and working with players, we use five categories, four of which were mentioned by Wenger above. The rest of this chapter will look at these five areas and will serve as a preface for the following chapters. Although we divide them, here, for the purposes of achieving a greater understanding, we must fully understand that the player himself is a mis-mash of all five characteristics.

The five areas to look at are Physical, Psychological, Social, Technical and Tactical (PPSTT).

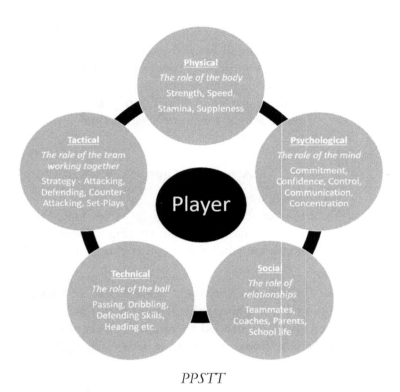

PPSTT

Many football and indeed sports development organisations will use these five measures, but an interesting study from across Europe came from England's Leeds Beckett University (LBU). In 2013-2014, the university was commissioned by UEFA to investigate good practice across youth football in Europe. Development systems from seven of the top European countries – Belgium, England, France, Germany, Italy, the Netherlands and Spain – were studied. The purpose of the project was to "inform" player development and coaching.[1]

The authors highlighted how the elite game looks, when pitted against PPSTT:

---

[1] Full report title: *The Identification of Good Practice Principles to Inform Player Development and Coaching in European Youth Football* – available online.

Physical / Physiological
<ul><li>Has 'high' and 'very high' levels of physical intensity</li><li>Has high levels of physical fitness and endurance</li></ul>
Psychological
<ul><li>Can deal with a game that is mentally intense, highly pressurised and competitive</li><li>Requires players to have a number of highly developed psychological characteristics in learning/development and in performing</li></ul>
Social Lifestyle
<ul><li>Involves high levels of personal scrutiny of players in terms of performance and conduct</li><li>Players are members of a community, club, team and dressing room and need to fit their image and abide by their rules</li><li>High levels of expectation around player conduct and lifestyle</li></ul>
Technical
<ul><li>Although players have varying technical profiles, there is a consensus around particular characteristics and competencies</li><li>Need for highly technically skilled players</li></ul>
Tactical
<ul><li>Teams win using a variety of approaches and formations</li><li>Game is moving towards a possession or counter-attacking-based approach</li><li>Players need to have excellent game understanding and make quick, effective decisions</li></ul>

Player Characteristics – What the Elite Game is Like, LBU Study

We are all very used to simplistic opinions of players from colleagues, rivals or even TV pundits – "He's quick, strong but needs work on his finishing", "He's quiet, but his ball control is excellent. Can drift in and out of games, but scores goals", "He reads the game well, defends strongly, but has discipline issues" – statements that could be applied to James, John and Jim at a local grassroots club, or we could indeed be referring to Raheem Sterling, Leo Messi and Sergio Ramos! How much better would our feedback be if we looked to analyse players from across these five characteristics, rather than just a jumble of the first three or four things that come to mind? In addition, it shows that we understand the player beyond their obvious traits and have a more comprehensive knowledge of their game.

All players in your team will have a different make-up when measured against PPSTT. Even the elite player will have a balance of strengths and weaknesses across different areas. Poor psychological skills may be counterweighed by excellent technique, for example. You can witness players with average technique playing in the top leagues all over the world. They often have strong game understanding (tactical), an exemplary attitude and mentality (psychological) and/or are reliable members of the squad (social). Furthermore, players may have strengths and weaknesses within one area. A striker may be confident, but lack commitment (psychology). A midfielder may be excellent in possession, but poor in transition (tactical).

"

There is no pretence that any elite player will share all these characteristics (a kind of football 'superman') ... weaknesses in some areas are compensated by strengths in other areas.

"

**Leeds Beckett University
Youth Development Report**

The 'Four Corner' Model

Technical / Tactical Corner	Psychological Corner
Physical Corner	Social Corner

The traditional model used in football, and the one you may be most familiar with, is the Four Corner Model, as above. You will notice that PPSTT has become PPST&T, where we see the merging of technical and tactical elements. Not for the first time, it sparks the question about the relationship between technical and tactical training,[2] and indeed the interconnecting relationship between all five components, which we will look at as this chapter, and indeed as this book, progresses.

Using the Four Corner Model

This model can be used in many ways and is used considerably more than it was a decade ago, even though its premise was well established within coach education the world over. Overall, it allows coaches to give structure to the performance and development needs of a player, rather than the first set of criteria that comes to mind. Using this model when working with players allows coaches to be far more comprehensive in their work with individuals.

---

[2] We will look more closely at the relationship between technical and tactical training in an upcoming chapter.

Age-Appropriate Modelling

The first question to consider when working with these characteristics is *what do these four/five corners look like with the age-group I coach?*

In *Making The Ball Roll*, chapter seven goes into great detail about the traits of players in each of the four corners (or the five of PPSTT), depending on their age. The book detailed how tactics with younger players means something entirely different in comparison to those in their late teens. The book referenced how the physical corner needs to be based on more than just size and strength, especially for youngsters who are pre-pubescent. We noted that the psych-social make-up of young people changes as they get older.

The concept of age-appropriate coaching is still something that I believe needs a lot of attention, and, in this respect, I have spent the last number of years delivering coach development seminars to clubs and coaches about how their work needs to start from the age-appropriate characteristics of players.

It was while researching for one such weekend-long Club Coach Development Programme that I came across the wonderful work of Matt Jones (@Matt_Jones7), FA County Coach Developer for Shropshire. Recognising that both coaches and players may not fully understand the model, he devised a child-friendly version, with associated questions for each corner. With Matt's permission, this is shared below.

The Ball & Your Game

Q. What skills have you used today?

Q. How many different playing positions did you try?

Q. What areas of the pitch did you play in?

Q. Did you learn anything about playing football today?

Your Mind & Thinking

Q. How did you feel when playing today? What made you feel that way?

Q. What decisions did you make on & off the pitch?

Q. Have you tried anything new today? Why?

Your Body & Movement

Q. How many different ways have you moved with & without the ball today?

Q. Did you change direction when moving? Why?

Q. How fast did you travel? Did your speed change for any reason?

Your Friends & Squad-mates

Q. How many of your squad-mates have you listened & spoken to today?

Q. Who have you helped on & off the football pitch? How?

Q. What have you learnt about your squad-mates today that can help on match day?

Child-friendly Four Corner Model (@Matt_Jones7)

I find this type of work quite inspiring. While we often spend our time talking about being age-appropriate and working in a player-centred manner, here's a coach going that extra mile to improve and promote *real understanding* of the game in a way that players will understand.

If you are interested in more detail and specifics around age-specific trends, see Chapter 7 of *Making The Ball Roll*.

PPSTT / Four Corner Model in Action

Thinking back to that scouting report I created all those years ago, the use of PPSTT or PPST&T would have been *extremely* beneficial. The report would have been clearer, more organised, and inevitably more thorough. PPSTT is, however, also beneficial in a number of other ways and has been used far more extensively by coaches in recent years. In Academy environments, even the players themselves have a greater understanding of PPSTT than before, with coaches and administrators referring to them frequently. Below, we will analyse several ways in which coaches use this model practically.

1. Development Plans

Below is a slightly edited version of the Four Corner Model used by New Zealand Football in their *Player Development Framework* document. Most development plans of this kind, whether from a professional club or national association, will contain similar models. It simply, yet succinctly, outlines the type of player that they are looking to produce, using each corner to guide them.

	Technical & Tactical		**Mental**
1	We will develop / perfect technique of all players in all positions.	1	We will develop players with outstanding leadership skills.
2	We need flexible players who can adapt technique to achieve the desired outcome in situations under immense pressure and in confined spaces.	2	We will produce self-confident players with a proactive, risk-taking mindset.
3	We will play attractive football with a results-orientated approach.	3	We will present ourselves as passionate, determined and disciplined.
4	We will promote National playing models with concrete assignments for each position, for groups and the whole team, across the four moments of the game.	4	We will develop players who can cope effectively with pressure.
5	We will follow a clear playing philosophy!		

Football Fitness	Social / Emotional
1 We will develop specific football fitness as this will form the basis for high-quality football.	**1** We promote and develop leaders.
2 We have the physical qualities needed for a pace-orientated game, in all positions and throughout the duration of the 90+ minutes.	**2** We are a unified football family – everyone helps one another.
3 We can meet the football-specific aerobic demands in every position at the highest levels.	**3** We promote a 'grow' culture where players and staff continually look for and take opportunities for individual and team growth.
	4 We will develop well-rounded players who have the skills to succeed in all aspects of their life.

National Player Development Framework, New Zealand Football

Here we have an overall look, or a snapshot, of what type of player that development should focus on in New Zealand. We are looking at it with a wide lens, but it is also possible and routine to zoom in and drill down into more specifics and more detail, by player profiling.

2. Player Profiling

First of all, when we talk about position-specific training in football, we must consider age. At pre-puberty ages, your focus as a coach will not, or should not, be based on playing positions – there are a lot of years and development stages to navigate before we have any idea what position or positions a player will ultimately operate in.

The information above from *New Zealand Football*, and the information below from a very well-established academy in the UK (EPPP Category 2[3]), looks at the position-specific skills that players will focus on throughout their time within the academy programme. This 'player profile' is the academy's vision of what their players will look like.

Technical	
In Possession	*Out of Possession*
1. Receiving techniques from and in all areas of the field	1. 1v1 defending – closing down / pressuring
2. 1v1 attacking – going past players	2. 1v1 defending – dictating play / forcing opposition one direction
3. Crossing techniques	3. Intercepting
4. Passing techniques into space behind opposition defenders	4. Tackling / Stealing – all types with appropriate foot
5. Passing techniques into forwards feet	

---

[3] As clubs are very protective of their development programmes, I chose not to name the club or the 'authors' of the document. I do however wish to privately reference and thank them anyway.

6. Running with the ball 7. Turning to change direction 8. Finishing techniques 9. Passing techniques into midfield 10. Passing techniques into defenders 11. Use of 'other' foot 12. Heading 13. Set-play techniques	5. 1v1 defending – blocking crosses 6. 1v1 defending from behind 7. Heading 8. Clearances 9. Blocking space / opposition runs with body

Tactical	
1. Taking good start positions in relation to the ball 2. Decision making in possession – appraisal of risk v reward and being as positive as possible in relation to it 3. Spatial awareness – movements in relation to the ball to receive the ball 4. Spatial awareness – movements in relation to the ball to create space for others 5. Reaction to transitions 6. Managing the game	1. Start positions relevant to ball and man (ball side / distance) 2. Covering / balancing positions (where and distance) 3. When to press / hold / drop 4. Reaction to transitions (team gives the ball away) – recovery runs 5. When to mark space / man

Physical
1. Speed – initial acceleration 0-5m 2. Agility/Mobility 3. Speed – acceleration phase (when moving) 5–30m 4. Anaerobic Endurance 5. Speed – top speed 30m upwards 6. Aerobic Endurance 7. Power

Psychological – CONTROL	Psychological – CONFIDENCE
The wide player does not let the player he is directly playing against cause him to lose control. Ideally, he will force that opposition player, through fair means, to lose control instead	Looks to be as positive as possible particularly in the final third, is not scared to fail

Psychological – COMMITMENT	Psychological - CONCENTRATION
This is an area that all players are expected to be excellent in without exception and what is expected is generic across the playing positions. What follows are examples of what this might include for this position: • Fully committed to get on the ball and beat the opponent	• Remaining focussed throughout the game on his specific jobs (e.g. not allowing control issues to effect this) • Concentrating on recovery run when that player has passed the ball NOT concentrating just on the ball • Concentrating to stay in the game, not to be a peripheral figure

Psychological - COMMUNICATION
Players in this position should mainly be communicating with: 1. Full back on your side (listening) 2. Forward player in front 3. Central Midfielders

Social
• Set a positive example to others • Offer positive, constructive criticism to teammates • Offer leadership at certain times • Be yourself!

Player Profile – Wide Player Characteristics, Category "2" English Academy

It is very important that coaches reading this understand that the players in this particular academy, or those that play football in New Zealand, are not simply born with these traits. These skills are focused on and are a part of the development process. Above is what a winger will *ideally* look like when they leave the particular academy programme. They will hone in on these skills along their journey.

Remember, also, that all players won't have *all* these traits even at the end of the process – they will be stronger in some areas than others. Some of a player's very strong skills will make up for their less developed ones. You will also have individual variations between players. For example, one winger could have better defensive instincts than another. One could be more of a goal scorer, and the other more of a creator. One could be exceptionally quick and direct, the other slower but cleverer in finding space.

Regardless of profiling and development plans, players are still ultimately individuals with varying skillsets, preferences, and abilities across all corners. Having a road map like the ones above remain very useful for coaches.

In generations gone by, coaching would have focused, in the main, on the technical, tactical and physical elements, and there would be a focus on quite a narrow section of these elements. For example, physical training would have been largely about stamina, or technical aspects such as passing and crossing and finishing. PPSTT has therefore had a great impact on coaching sessions, and the planning of them.

3. Session Planning

We are all familiar with session planning, although many of us vary in the methods we use. In *Making The Ball Roll*, we looked at 'laddered' sessions, 'carousel' sessions, and introduced the concept of 'Whole-Part-Whole'. *Predominantly*, these sessions focused on the technical / tactical aspects, and indeed they still do, but now we are seeing more and more elements of coaches planning in terms of the psychological and social corners.

Modern-day sessions, although still weighted heavily towards technical, tactical and physical outcomes, now involve elements from all four (or five) corners. Below is a session plan from the Academy at Sunderland AFC, one of just 24 academies that are considered 'Category One' by the Premier League's EPPP categorisation. Other academies at this level include powerhouse clubs

Chapter 6 – Building a Player

like Arsenal, Chelsea, Liverpool and Manchester City, plus serial youth-development experts, like West Ham United, Everton and Southampton.

I have included the session itself, run with the Under-16 team in August 2016. You will note that much more consideration, when planning, is paid to all four corners:

Technical	<ul><li>Passing & receiving</li><li>Short passing with the inside of both feet</li><li>Receiving skills with the inside of both feet</li><li>Long passing</li><li>Timing of pass & movement</li></ul>
Tactical	Defending Principles:<ul><li>Pressing from the front</li><li>Making play predictable (show outside)</li><li>Game management</li><li>Second balls</li><li>Set-plays</li></ul>
Physical	<ul><li>Very light session due to game tomorrow</li><li>Natural football-related movements</li><li>Elements of warming-up and cooling down</li></ul>
Psychological	<ul><li>Concentration – taking information on board</li><li>Communication skills between players</li></ul>
Social	<ul><li>Communication skills between players</li><li>Knowing your teammates and working off their cues and movements</li></ul>

Activity 1 – 'Boxes' (Rondos) 4v2	Duration: 20 mins
Coaching Notes: • Passing & receiving with both feet • Angles to receive the ball • Decision-making in possession • Working as a pair to regain possession • Talking and communicating with each other	
Activity 2 – Passing Drill	**Duration: 20 mins**
Passing drill working with both feet around passing and receiving. Coaching Notes: • Quality and weight of pass • Body position to receive • Check shoulder before receiving • Execution of pass Progress to step inside, opening out, sets and 1-2's	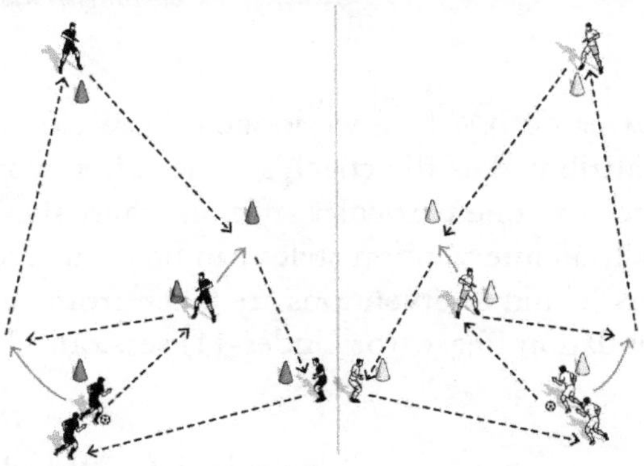
Activity 3 – 11v11 Pressing from Front	**Duration: 50 mins**
The attacking players take up a position to encourage the opponent to play the ball out. The first attacker will close down, and the rest of the team take up a position to do the same. Coaching Notes: • Team shape (out of possession) • Set-plays for and against • Press high, get down line of ball and shuffle across	

4. Coaching Styles and Interventions

When sessions are planned with multiple objectives in mind, it is therefore necessary to involve them within the sessions themselves. One of the most obvious ways to do this is through the use of 'interventions', as per the diagram below.

Coaching Styles Intervention Wheel

In *Making the Ball Roll*, we looked more closely at the above intervention techniques. These are often attributed as the coach's 'style' when working with players. Although most coaches will say that they use one particular style, in reality they probably will use a cross-section of interventions. Critically all intervention styles can be used across all four corners. The concept of using the Four Corners within interventions are taken from an FA presentation on coaching interventions within a 'Foundation Phase' (or Under-11) session. The session focused on 'staying on the ball'.

	Technical / Tactical	Psychological	Physical	Social
Command	*Receive with the foot furthest from the defender*	*You are good enough to keep the ball – demand it whenever possible*	When you beat a player, accelerate away	*When X is outnumbered, move where they can see your feet*
Observation & Feedback	*Watch how X uses different first touches to move away from his defender(s)*	*Count how many times X demands the ball, even when outnumbered*	*Watch when X steps across their defender to prevent them intercepting*	Watch how X supports his teammates when they dribble
Skillful Neglect	A player tries to dribble, but he is unsuccessful, but you let him carry on without intervention. Will he self-correct?	A player reacts emotionally to giving the ball away. Is it a one-off or are such reactions normal for him?	Due to size, maybe a player does have the power to accelerate and 'get away' from the defender – yet!	One of the popular, better players backs his teammates when they dribble – even when it goes wrong – does this rub off on the others?
Question & Answer	*How can you manipulate the ball to retain possession?*	*How will you transfer your success into your next game?*	*Why might you use your arms to help retain possession?*	How can you support the efforts of your teammates when they take risks?

	Technical / Tactical	Psychological	Physical	Social
Guided Discovery	Show me how many touches you would take in crowded areas, versus when you are running into space	*Show me when it's best to retain or release the ball*	*Show me how to use your body to protect the ball*	*Show me how to react positively if you lose possession*
Trial & Error	*Try out[4] how to take your first touch away from pressure*	*Try out how to support in front or behind the ball*	*Try out how to lower your centre of gravity when you are shielding the ball*	Try out how you can praise your teammate when he successfully executes an action – he may return the favour

Use of the Four Corners During Coaching Interventions
The interventions written in italics are taken from this presentation (slightly amended), those in regular font have been added to provide a more comprehensive overview. I have also added a section on 'Skillful Neglect', which was not included in the presentation.

5. Player Reviews

A number of years ago, my mind boggled. I was running a performance programme that recruited players who, in the main, had been released by elite clubs post-16, plus the best from local clubs who may have been late developers or 'missed' by the professional clubs. The concept was that they would play and train full-time, while endeavouring to step back/into the professional game.

Most players are released from English Academies between Christmas and May each year. In the case of Under-16 players, this can happen earlier, as they are either offered full-time opportunities at the club, or released altogether. Today, once players are released, clubs and coaches are now duty-bound to provide an appraisal for them, a bit like an employer's reference or a reference from a school to a university. The concept is to assist players in finding new clubs or opportunities post-release, during what can be an exceptionally traumatic time for young players. I contacted a club with an interest in a player, and asked for his appraisal, which I have included below, word-for-word:

Technical	Technically neat & tidy. Still needs to improve this area of his game
Tactical	Has good tactical understanding
Physical	Good level of strength and power

---

[4] The term 'try out' rather than simply 'try' was added by Dutch language expert, Joost van der Leij (@JoostvanderLeij). Using the term 'try' alone suggests that there is only one single solution to a problem. If this solution fails then it fails completely. 'Try out' however allows players to try and explore different options, with failure in one area encouraging them to explore other solutions.

Chapter 6 – Building a Player

Psychological	Has a commitment to improve
Social	He interacts well with all players and staff
Educational	Doing well in school

The player above had been at this particular academy for *seven* years! Now, rarely do I openly criticise many systems, but the above is not an appraisal – it is a copy and paste job. This level of information, or lack thereof, is not sufficient. To use this, after seven years in a development system, is disgraceful. Based on the information above, we really have no idea what the player is like. We may have a picture in our mind of what a "neat and tidy" 16-year-old football player looks like, but there is still an element of pure guess-work. We can assume he is not a goalkeeper but have no further idea what tactical or positional experience he has had. A "good" level of physicality could mean anything – in elite terms 'good' is the new 'average'. It looks positive but is, in fact, quite middle of the road between excellent and poor. His social and educational comments make him seem like a nice young man, though most academy players are quite compliant when in these environments.

If you send your child to swimming, rock-climbing or tennis sessions, you would expect a certain level of feedback from the coach. In fact, you would insist upon it, or certainly insist on some formal feedback. Football, in my opinion, is no different. This feedback or appraisal will come in different forms depending on the level and age of the players, and indeed the purpose of their football programme. You would expect a greater level of detail in an academy review than you would of a programme targeting kids to keep them out of trouble, for example. You would also expect a different level of review for a short-term trialist than you would for a player playing in a system for seven years! In development programmes, from grassroots to elite, I am convinced that coaches are duty-bound to offer *significant* feedback to players, at regular, pre-planned intervals.

Below, are two further examples of player reviews – both of anonymous players from anonymous clubs. The first is an objective-setting review for an Under-14, as part of a process where objectives are revisited every six weeks. There are objectives set across PPSTT, and an additional one to ensure players are progressing and focused academically. The second is a detail-laden mid-season review for an Under-17 centre-back, using the Four Corner Model.

The detail of the latter two reviews clearly trumps our first example, based on six weeks and half a season's work respectively, rather than several years.

Technical	1. Work on receiving skills; in particular, open body shape. 2. Play off fewer touches; take as many as you need, no more. 3. Try to play forward when you can. 4. Try to combine with others to advance forward.
Tactical	1. Understand defending principles in the midfield unit – pressure, cover, balance, distance. 2. Understand positional responsibilities when the ball is with back 4. 3. Try and get high and wide when we have the ball.
Physical	1. Engage fully in the physical programme which starts in September.
Psychological	1. Try to be positive in matches and training. 2. Make a conscious effort to communicate more with teammates.

| **Social** | 1. Set a positive example to your peer group in training and games.
2. Work on praising and constructive criticism of your teammates. |
| **Educational** | 1. You need to pay attention to your progress and performance at school. Keeping up to date with your coursework and homework is very important to your academic progress. Your performance at school will be reviewed in six weeks time. |

Additional Comments

> Keep working hard to achieve all your goals set above.
> We will review these in 6 weeks to see your progress in them.

Meso (6 week) Objectives for next period

And here is the feedback for a second player (the Under-17 centre-back referenced).

Technical / Tactical
Your in-possession skills are the main strengths of your game, and we have spent most of this year looking to improve them. The best players work on their strengths as well as their weaknesses. You have a better range of passing than when we started and have added extras to it – disguise etc. I love when I see you being brave enough to step out from the back with the ball. Remember, these situations should involve running into space, rather than dribbling. Any resistance I see as a mental one, not a technical / tactical one. If nervous, use DCM to protect the space you leave.
Out of possession, your individual defending has improved greatly – especially the desire to defend in and around the box. This critical defending is so important. Although nervous, you have made good improvements when reading the game and defending bigger areas. Try to improve your reading of the game to stop you from going to ground.
Although we focus on certain aspects of your game, there are still another 100 things that need to be done in a game of football – ensure these are done to the highest standards possible.
Looking forward, I see you as a centre-back. As you have played some games as left-back for the national team, embrace this too (your challenge to step out from the back and to defend big areas will help with this). You may have some intermittent game time in midfield.
Psychological
<u>Commitment</u> – Your commitment levels have been absolutely excellent. You have trained more than any player at the academy, missing sessions only through a slight injury. The doctor points to your mental strength as you (other than when you were injured) have never sought attention from him. I love seeing you practising before and after training.
<u>Communication</u> – At the start of the season, you told us how you wanted to be a leader, but felt you were quiet on the pitch. Today, you are one of the main organisers in the group. When you speak, you say very little, but it is concise and teammates react to your instructions. At times, it is easy to tell from your body language when you are not happy. Be positive, even when challenged.
<u>Concentration</u> – You have a tendency to watch the game as a fan when not directly involved. The best CBs use this time to organise and reduce the chances of the defence being breached. You are a good listener in training and look to implement suggestions immediately.

Control – Very pleased with your reactions to negativity and provocation. I don't think I have ever seen you overly emotional.
Confidence – Generally, you show lots of confidence. I want you to see challenges as opportunities, rather than a threat to what is good in your game.
Physical
Injuries – small niggle in back (resolved). We suspect this may be a one-off.
Part of defending big areas is that you are required to use your body more. As a physically strong young man (although often playing against much older opponents) this should be something you are good at. This same strength is what makes you hard to dispossess when in-possession. Really engage in the core stability and flexibility work done by coaches.
Sometimes there is a fear of playing high due to pace. Learn to understand and read the game to help you conquer this.
Stamina-wise, you are excellent. I have seen you involved in some physical tussles and just carry on with the same energy and enthusiasm. It is a joy to watch.
If you have any nutrition problems, please consult the doctor.
Social
You are loved by your teammates and are a good team player. Nine months ago, you were an individual who just played football. Today you have leadership skills, communicate well, and use your skills for the benefit of the team.
You know my biggest worry for you is what happens outside of the academy. There is a suspicion that your back injury was due to an altercation in your neighbourhood. Be very careful and make good decisions for your future when at home and at school.

Academy Mid-Season Review, based on Four Corner Model[5]

Now, I understand that most coaches outside the professional game may struggle to be as comprehensive as this, when most coaches will be balancing life, work and family also. What is important is that if you do not give formal feedback to players, you should start, in whatever way you think it appropriate. Players and parents will be grateful for it. Your coaching knowledge will improve, as will your ability to analyse players. If the feedback you give is currently more formative than summative, then use the Four Corner Model to help you provide players with useable, reliable feedback.

Pulling It All Together

"　　　　　　　　　　　　　　　　　　　　　　　　　**"**

If players weren't human,
I would never lose.

Marcelo Bielsa

---

[5] Further to the PPST&T detail was how many sessions they attended, how many games they played, a tracking of their height and weight, a note of injuries, and the tracking of their performance against goals that had been set from them previously.

The quote above from Marcelo Bielsa offers us a great insight as to why he's nicknamed 'El Loco' and a clue to his obsessive tactical mind. It also recognises that players are indeed, human. They make human decisions, have human relationships, and make human errors. You can be an expert in the technical, tactical and physical aspects of the game, but working with the psychological and social elements are integral too.

Below is a slide from a recent presentation I delivered to a group of coaches at a particular club – one of the biggest youth football clubs in the country. I asked them to divide the listed attributes into each 'corner'. Feel free to attempt this yourself in the supporting box accompanying it.

Put these attributes under one of the Long-Term Player Development Headings

Passing	Communication	Agility	Game understanding
Family Issues	Emotional control	Confidence	Solving problems together
Defending	Shooting	Long Passing	
Commitment	Balance	Speed	Flexibility
Teamwork	Making friends	Strength / Power	Sharing
Dribbling	Ego-centric	Independence	Concentration
Turning			

Technical / Tactical Corner	Psychological Corner
Physical Corner	Social Corner

From the outset, this task is quite straightforward. Of the 24 'attributes' listed, you simply need to assign them to the 'correct' corner. Many of the 24 will indeed sit neatly into one box. 'Defending' and 'shooting', for example, will sit directly in the Technical / Tactical segment, while 'making friends' and 'solving problems together' will sit in the Social section. Several others, however, start to spark some thought and debate, when the fit isn't quite so neat. Can you pass consistently well without confidence? Can you dribble effectively without agility and flexibility? Does effective teamwork and group problem-solving occur independently of game understanding?

In coach development terms, this is a guided discovery type exercise – put a problem out there, notice if they recognise it, and see if it sparks further, more in-depth learning. The learning outcome was not who could score 24 points. In fact, the more that people got answers 'wrong', the more learning that took place. One group put flexibility, for example, in the psychological corner, sighting 'mental flexibility' as justification. Communication was added to the social box by others. While I stood back and let them argue the point, the following slide was to follow:

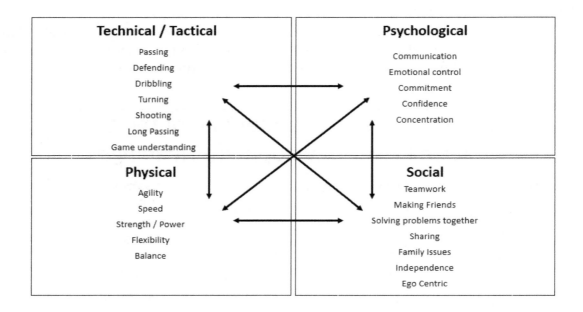

Cornering and Firing Off

Although the model gives us structure to our thoughts, we must also note that each corner is not a completely separate identity. Each corner will impact and 'fire off' into the other three. For example, a player who presents as being technically excellent may have confidence (psychological) to get on the ball and express himself, the suppleness (physical) to control his body while in possession of the ball, and the social skills of recognising his role within the team. A player who is having a rough time at home or at school (social) may struggle to commit to football (psychological), have reduced stamina (physical) due to lack of training and lethargy, and therefore may not be equipped to play certain positions (tactical) or be confident (psychological) enough to try new techniques.

So, while dividing these aspects is very, very useful in getting a broader picture of the player, it is important to understand that the player in front of you will be a complete mishmash of each corner – with each aspect affecting the other.

Imagine a painter using four colours. Rather than using a separate colour to paint 25% of the picture in a boxed off way, he would instead throw and splash the paint against the canvas. The messy canvas, rather than the neat, blocked one, is the player himself.

"   **"**

This game is inclusive, as when you are playing you need your perception skills to recognise what is going on, your cognitive skills to make decisions and solve the game situations, your technique skills to execute the decisions made, the physical and bioenergetics structure to support and enable you to execute the actions, and also the psychological and emotional structure.

Eric Tenllado

Conclusion

"

> In a perfect world, I would have filled every
> team-sheet with 11 men who had as much
> determination as talent. But life is not like that,
> and if I had to choose between someone who
> had great talent but was short on grit and
> desire, and another player who was good but
> had great determination and drive, I would
> always prefer the latter.

"

Sir Alex Ferguson

Most expert coaches are now using PPSTT across the entirety of their work, whether that is within session planning, player reviews, or in their interventions on the pitch. Although the Four Corner Model has been in existence around coach education programmes for a long time, there is now a noticeable, comprehensive use of it across football. Traditionally, coaches could survive based on technical/tactical expertise and physical drills, but now, expert coaches and development academies understand the impact of the psychological and social corners too. They make up the entirety of the player.

Summary

- When reviewing and working with players, coaches need to organise their thoughts, using PPSTT – Physical, Psychological, Social, Technical and Tactical.

- Leeds Beckett University, as part of a UEFA-approved study, looked at PPSTT across seven prominent European systems, noting the need for high levels of skill across all five areas.

- Players will, however, not be expert across all areas ("a football superman") but will have weaknesses in some areas which are compensated for with strengths in others.

- The traditional model is known as the Four Corner Model but still works with PPSTT.

- The first question to consider when working within these characteristics is 'what do these four/five corners look like with the age-group I coach'? All corners will look a lot different at 8, 12, 15 and 18 years old.

- Expert coaches, and expert development systems, use PPSTT when creating development plans, player profiling, session planning, and when using coaching interventions and reviewing players.

- Each corner will impact and 'fire off' into the other three. For example, a player who presents at being technically excellent may have the confidence (psychological) to get on the ball and express himself, the suppleness (physical) to control his body while in possession of the ball, and the social skill of recognising his role within the team.

- Players are a mishmash of all four/five characteristics – each player will be different, with different strengths, weaknesses and preferences. It is a messy canvas rather than a neatly boxed off picture.

> ## It's Your Game #1
>
> # The World's Best Boys Club
>
> ## Nick Cox
>
> ## Academy Operations Manager, Manchester United

Twenty seasons ago, I proudly took charge of my first Academy group, Watford's Under-9s. Back then, I meticulously planned training sessions with technical and tactical objectives, and addressed the group as a whole using next week's game as a focus, and last week's game as a point of reference. I remember the players vividly. Joe, the star player, took up a lot of my thoughts.

Two decades on, I have finally come to some conclusions as to how I could have helped those players more. I've realised the subtle shift is that coaching the sport – the X's and O's – is not as important as coaching the person.

Why? Well, let me take you back to Joe. I had the honour of being able to shape 20 per cent of his waking life (inclusive of training time, travel, games, trips, etc.). What I offered him was a coach-led technical and tactical programme to help his team perform better in the short term. Nothing wrong with any of those approaches but what more could I have done? Heartbreakingly, Joe died aged 14. Could I have spent time differently? Maybe let the players design some of their own learning, put the individual ahead of team performance, build some life-changing positive experiences, concentrate on developing some life skills that could be used in other walks of life, engage in social events, engage the players in free play? As well as all the stuff I was doing, too. The challenge, as I see it, is not to create mini professionals ahead of their time but, instead, to attempt to create 'The World's Best Boys Club'.

As for the weakest player in that group, the one that was released at the end of his first season? He is now playing in the Premier League. If I had let him express himself, would I have seen what was hidden away by taking the alternative approach?

People regularly tell me that this approach is 'fluffy' and that, instead, we need to 'focus on being world-class' and 'players need to make sacrifices in order to succeed'. However, I am confident that the alternate approach will produce better players.

I still don't consider myself an expert. But giving boys time, space, and freedom to express themselves, making sure every child has a champion, and truly making a personal connection, is a healthy set of ingredients for success.

It's Your Game #2

Master the Person, the Ball & then the Game

Anonymous

Youth Coach, England

I was introduced to the Four Corner Model over a decade ago when I started to complete my coaching awards. Before taking formal qualifications, I had been coaching for some time. I had doubted the necessity of qualifications as I had played the game for 20+ years, and I had coached for a further 10. How wrong I was.

To me, I always felt the Four Corner Model was just a soft, academic inclusion that was inserted in courses by someone in an office on a laptop. We all really knew that the technical/tactical and physical corners were the ones that mattered. The social corner was just about teamwork and team spirit, and psychology was whether you should kick a player up the backside after a mistake or put your arm around him.

When I revisited some courses, and joined the newer youth-based ones, all this gradually changed. I began to 'get' it. On day one of a particular course, we had a task. We had to share stories with our group of other coaches. One by one, we told of how either a psychological or social factor had had consequences for our players. The first guy told of how a kid's parents had split up, how his grades had slipped, and his eating and sleeping patterns were poorer. This resulted in the lad becoming more challenging, aggressive, and less disciplined in games. "Sounds like Joe" I thought in my head – he had described a player of mine almost to a tee.

The next story I thought – "sounds like John" – a player whose confidence had increased overnight once he changed position. As these stories went around the table, all of them were resonating somehow – and having a direct impact on the holy grails of the technical/tactical and physical corners. My attitude was challenged, and I was compelled to rethink my views on the game.

Psychology wasn't about lying players down on a sofa and talking about their problems – it impacted all facets of their game. The impact of relationships in the group, school, work, family and 'real life' brought the social corner into focus.

I still don't believe I am an expert in these areas, but I am certainly more open-minded. I now listen more. I pay attention to players. I look at who is happy, whose body language is off. I'm careful about what I say or what banter I have at the expense of some lads. 'Master the person, master the ball, then master the game' is my new mantra.

Chapter 7
Psychology in Action

"

"

If I tell players what I don't want them to do,
I'm a critic. My role is that of a service provider
– I'm here to support the player.

Thomas Tuchel

In the previous chapter, we looked at the Four Corner Model and how coaches work with players through PPSTT – Physically, Psychologically, Socially, Technically, and Tactically. We noted that players are made up of interweaving elements of each category – like the random splash of colours from a painter's brush. Interestingly, however, there is a raging debate amongst experts from each field as to which category is most important.

Technical coaches will say that work with the ball is the most important facet of player development. Those focused on tactics (we looked at a very famous quote from Marcelo Bielsa in the last chapter) will refer everything back to strategy and decision-making. Fitness coaches believe that the physical corner is the platform for everything else. Such is the competitiveness of this argument, it can frequently become very territorial and very petty. I had a technical coach who specialises in ball mastery bemoan that the acronym 'PPSTT' began with the 'P's rather than the 'T's. A strength and conditioning expert who worked at an old club of mine conversely celebrated it. Ultimately, as so eloquently put by Thomas Tuchel, coaches are there to support the player – and our focus in this chapter is looking at how we support and develop players mentally.

Rethinking the Model

Dan Abrahams (@DanAbrahams77) is a very prominent sports psychologist who consults with professional players, professional clubs and other sports organisations. He is both engaging and a frequent sharer of some very good information across his social media platforms and is the author of *Soccer Brain* and *Soccer Tough*, amongst other books. Dan very kindly allowed me to use a story of his from his time working with English Championship/Premier League player, Yannick Bolasie, later in the book.

Abrahams offers us a rethink of the Four Corner Model or PPSTT. Instead of all elements being equal and boxed off, he suggests that it is the psychological and social factors that drive all other parts of the game.

His *Psych-Social Model of Coaching* model (below) suggests a constant "to-ing and fro-ing process" between psychology and the technical, tactical, and physical elements of coaching. He maintains that we, as coaches, first need to be "world-class" in the psych-social areas of coaching, before being an expert in any other aspect.

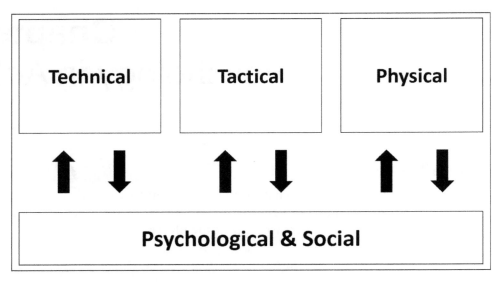

'Psych-Social Model of Coaching' Dan Abrahams

When I think of a psych-social coach, I often think of former Tottenham, West Ham, and Portsmouth manager, Harry Redknapp. Without doing a disservice to the former FA Cup winner, comments from those closest to him suggest that tactics (and alike) were rarely worked on in any great detail – or "close to nothing" as described by Raphael van der Vaart. No "boring speeches" or set-play routines – and the Dutch midfielder loved it. Redknapp would focus on keeping training and the general environment relaxed, heaping praise on his players whenever possible, most notably in post-match press conferences where there were plenty of "terrifics" and "outstandings" to be heard.

The Power and Problem of Psychology for Coaches

In *The Culture Code*, Daniel Coyle highlights the subtle power that psychology has on all of us – from dealing with football hooliganism by focusing on positive relationships between police and supporters (rather than the traditional baton-wielding, riot-gear clad officers), to dealing with how leaders can even unwittingly support and develop those in their charge.

Way back in 1965, Robert Rosenthal, a psychologist based at the famous Harvard University, carried out a study in a California-based elementary school. *The Harvard Test of Inflected Acquisition* was administered to all students in the school, in an attempt to predict which students would excel academically – almost a crystal ball gaze into their academic future. Although the results of the test were not shared with the children involved, the names of the 20% of the student body who had tested as being "special" and "destined to succeed" were shared with the teachers.

A year later, Rosenthal revisited the school to track the performance of this special group and, sure enough, they had indeed excelled.

The catch here, however, is that the named students had not tested well at all – their names were simply selected at random and offered to the teachers. It was the mindset of the educators that were being put to the test, not the students. Rosenthal had replaced one narrative – that these selected kids were average – with a new, more hopeful one – that these children were special and had "unusual potential for intellectual growth." This new narrative resulted in the teachers treating and behaving differently towards the children in question. They were kinder, more attentive, provided them with extra learning material, called on those students more often, listened more carefully and provided more and better-quality feedback. The better grades were essentially a result of better teaching.

"

"

> When you treat man as he is, we make him
> worse than he is. When we treat him as if he
> already was what he potentially could be, we
> make him what he should be.

**Johann Wolfgang von Goethe,
German writer**

If we translate Rosenthal's study from a classroom environment, with students and exam results, to a football environment with players and development signposts, we certainly have parallels. If coaches can view young players as those with "unusual potential for *football* growth" rather than limitations, and if we can provide them with heavier doses of attention, kindness, feedback and listening, there is a sure chance that these players, like the students above, will improve exponentially as a result.

Similarly, in *Making the Ball Roll*, I gave you a great "power of the mind" story from Susan Jeffers' *Feel the Fear and Do It Anyway*, where a small dose of positive feedback brought about huge improvement in physical performance (and similarly small doses of negative feedback brought about huge decline). With this, in addition to the Rosenthal experiment above, it is difficult to deny the power and hugely important role of the mental aspects of football.

For many, however, psychology still remains a bit of a minefield – from those who think that it is the ability to read minds, to those that get completely swamped by the endless number of attributes linked to the discipline.

In the previous chapter, I referred to the UEFA-commissioned study from Leeds Beckett University. The study liaised with dozens of different individuals across seven of Europe's most developed football countries. When *summarising* their findings around psychology, *fifty-six* individual characteristics were listed, leaving the average amateur-psychologist lost in a dictionary-style maze of 'where do I start?' For those who are intrigued, those 56 elements are listed below:

• Ability to adapt and progress	• Dedication	• Problem-solving
• Ability to learn	• Desire	• Resilience
• Ability to reflect	• Determination	• Responsibility
• Adaptability	• Educated	• Sacrifice
• Aggressive but fair	• Effortful	• Self-aware / aware of impact on others
• Always trying their best	• Enjoys challenge	• Self-fulfilment / development
• Ambition	• Fearless / mentally strong in possession	• Self-initiative
• Appetite for learning and seeking out new learning opportunities	• Good attitude	• Self-organisation, for example, football-life balance
• Appetite for personal improvement	• Grounded	• Self-regulation
• Attacking mentality, creative, incisive and driven	• Hard work	• Self-reliance
• Balanced character	• In the present	• Shows initiative
• Chasing every ball	• Independent decision-makers	• Solution-focused
• Commitment	• Insightful	• Speed of mind
• Competitive drive / spirit / will to win	• Intelligence / speed of thought	• Team worker
• Confidence	• Intelligent	• Tough
• Conscious / deliberate self-improvement	• Leadership	• Understands expectations
• Critical thinking	• Mentally tough	• Very intelligent
	• Motivation	• Wanting to be the best
	• Personality / character	• Winning mentality
	• Players that make things happen for themselves	

Commonly cited psychological characteristics (LBU Study)

In addition to this list, one could probably add a further 56 without breaking a sweat – knowledge of the sport, game-understanding and decision-making, belief, engagement, using imagery, self-control, coping strategies, visualisation, etc.

Psychology can, to some, feel more like a vocabulary lesson at an advanced ESOL class. But thankfully, there is a way to organise our work with players, and it's a method used by many leading academies.

The Five Cs

Psychology, as we have seen, is a huge field. Sometimes we can be very good at categorising people from a mental point of view. Most coaches would say they would feel comfortable evaluating which players they felt were confident, communicated well, or had high levels of concentration. However, this discipline can often be very subtle and often very discreet. Judging someone's state of mind or their very personal characteristics is difficult and can be open to interpretation. We must also be open to being entirely wrong!

Players, and indeed people in general, actually have wonderful ways of hiding their insecurities through their behaviour – whether they consciously realise it or not. For example, Cristiano Ronaldo, the poster boy for confident poses, words, and actions (he has been quite happy throughout his career to announce himself as being the best player in the world) has had this dismissed by journalist and biographer, Guillem Balague (@GuillemBalague). He maintains that his ferocious work ethic, desire to improve, and confident outlook, is actually down to a heavy load of self-doubt, rather than unhinging confidence.

The key then to working with players and navigating a review of their mental characteristics is to speak to players, get to know them, and seek out support information from parents, teachers, or other coaches who have worked with them.

Despite the unending vocabulary involved, and the complicated nature of evaluating players, there are methods by which coaches can organise their psychological work with their players. During the previous chapter, we looked at a player profile from an English Academy. The psychology section contained five headings – Commitment, Communication, Concentration, Control, and Confidence. This 5C model was devised by Chris Harwood (@chrishphd) and Richard Anderson in an attempt to develop a way of working with youth football players that is practical and useable for coaches. Their book, *Coaching Psychological Skills in Youth Football* and their related website are very useful, practical resources.

> The 5Cs is a program aimed at increasing your awareness of psychological and social skills that can be introduced to your players through the medium of your coaching.

the5cs.co.uk

The 5Cs model organises mental traits into these five discernible groups. The visual below shows "player behaviour and responses shown in training and/or match play [that] can be grouped together based on their relation to commitment, communication, concentration, control or confidence."

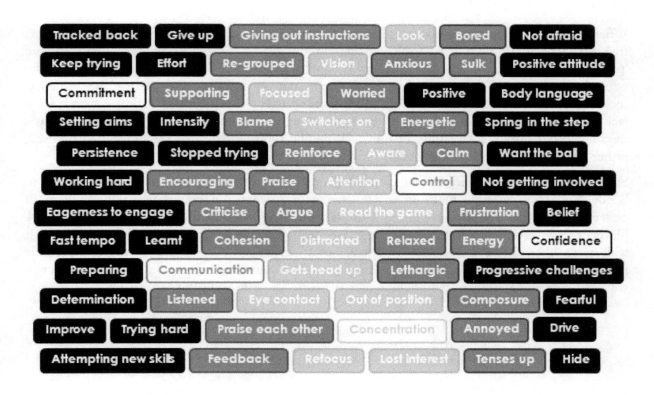

Chapter 7 – Psychology in Action

To help us bring the 5Cs to life and display *Psychology in Action* with players, the *It's Your Game* section of this chapter is longer than usual. We will hear from several coaches and former players about experiences they had, under the 5C headings. We will also hear from an Academy 'Head of Coaching' who details the way his club uses the programme in their academy environment. Before that, let us get an understanding of each 'C', and an overview of working with players mentally.

Over and Over and Over Again

"

> Mental fitness is making decisions properly
> under pressure, over and over and over again.

"

Enda McNulty, Performance Coach

Mental skills can be improved and developed like any other aspect of the game. This may be quite easy to forget as we can quickly pigeon-hole players into categories. "He is confident; he is not." "She has good concentration; she does not." Etc.

"

> It's all about being brave. I love that word in
> English. We must display bravery at all times
> and, since mental preparation is crucial
> nowadays, we send daily messages to this effect
> in different formats and packaging.

"

Mauricio Pochettino

When we read psychological material, I assume most coaches will think about individual players that they coach, or who they have coached in the past – and possibly those with certain 'problems' – the hothead, the one with low confidence, the complete introvert who communicates poorly. When working with them, the tendency is to look for the sentence, technique, or action that will improve a player immediately – a single hit that flips a switch from lack of confidence to confidence, lack of commitment to fully committed, or out of control to a disciplined performer. Like a muscle, however, mental skills get stronger the more they are used, rather than after just one gym workout.

Some traits may be very deep-rooted, and players may have certain habits that are very difficult to break. You may certainly make improvements with players, but completely ridding them of certain habits is difficult, as we will see with Steven Gerrard later in the chapter. The more work players receive from a mental point of view, the stronger their physiological skills will become. It will more likely be a succession of small, subtle messages to a player – rather than one intervention – that will improve a player long-term. The mental techniques and examples that you will read here and elsewhere require longevity of work – a 'little and often' approach.

Commitment

"

"

I made sacrifices by leaving Argentina, leaving
my family to start a new life. Everything I did, I
did for football, to achieve my dream.

Lionel Messi

Commitment is the centrepiece of the 5Cs model – the one that drives the other four. In turn, psychologists advocate, these mental skills go on to drive improvement in other parts of the game (technical, tactical, and physical).

Harwood and Anderson consider "effort, engagement, self-challenge and persistence" to be the "core attributes of the committed player," before considering the traits of both a player with excellent commitment and poor commitment. For example, committed players will be punctual, will close opposition players down effectively, and play through the pain or fatigue barrier, amongst others. Players with poor commitment, however, may have poor pre-match preparation, may sulk and tend to pass any blame on to others. A player displaying high levels of commitment will master skills quicker and more effectively.

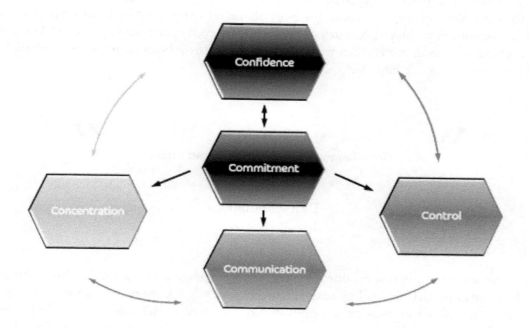

Communication

In *Making The Ball Roll*, we dedicated a chapter to the art of communication, relating a significant portion to the communication skills of the coach. In this case, however, we are exclusively looking at developing players' skills.

Players can be taught how to improve across all areas of communication – both verbally and non-verbally. The acronym HELPA is used to assist with this. A player with good communication is one who:

Chapter 7 – Psychology in Action

- Helps
- Encourages
- Listens
- Praises and
- Acknowledges others

We can often think about communication as *just* talking – it isn't. It is about both verbal elements (including tone, volume, and tempo) and non-verbal communication. HELPA refers to both verbal *and* non-verbal.

Subconscious body language screams at us, and often leaves us in little doubt as to what the person means – inside and outside the football domain. We make instant judgements about people based on their actions, expressions, and behaviours. Body language evidence has caught people lying, sent others to prison, and won political elections. Dan Abrahams, mentioned earlier in this chapter, is a big advocate of the power of conscious body language amongst players – improving it consciously will improve it unconsciously.

Children, youths, and adults are very good at picking up on body language. On a football pitch, that can be anything from direct pieces of communication (pointing and other hand gestures), to less obvious ones like body shape (think of the body shape of a striker who is about to make a darting forward run – everything about his body shape tells you what he is about to do) and eye contact (those who have played football or team sports, even recreationally, will understand that moment where you make eye contact with a teammate and you both know, almost telepathically, how you are going to work together).

"
Body language is not so much an effect,
but more a cause.
"

Dan Abrahams

The quote above is an interesting one. We see body language and we predict how someone is feeling. If a striker gesticulates wildly after missing a shot at goal, we may interpret these gestures to him being frustrated at missing an opportunity to score – the miss comes first, then the negative body language. Abrahams, however, is at pains to put body language first. In other words, good body language can be a precursor to positive performance, not just a result of the performance. Consciously altering negative body language, to a more positive one, works to lift your game. Those who study the wider discipline of positive psychology, some of whom we will meet later in this chapter, also flip this around. Happiness and positivity, they insist, comes before success, not after it.

Verbally, many teams will have their 'own language' – key phases or buzzwords that are unique to them. Often, a new player or visiting coach will spend some time deciphering the code of a team that has formed and performs well together. As a coach, it is vital to ensure that all players speak the same football language – the simpler the better. Later in the chapter, much-travelled coach Blaine McKenna will show us how he used buzzwords when working with a team in Thailand.

Whilst coaches focus heavily on verbal skills (99% of coaches I have ever met believe that their players do not talk enough, or loud enough, and every opponent does this better than them!), we must also understand that some players are simply not 'talkers'. If we had a squad full of the talkers that coaches love so much, there is more likely to be chaos than clarity!

Concentration

Football is a very fluid and variable game. Although the ball will spend around a third of the time 'dead' or out of play, it doesn't remain so for very long. Something is always happening. Teammates are moving, opponents are adjusting their positions, and the ball (or any player) can legitimately travel to all sections of the pitch within seconds. Teammates or opponents can appear to our right, left, in front, or from behind us. Teaching players how to retain their focus and deal with this 'chaos' is very important. Remember, however, a focused eight-year-old will look nothing like a focused 18-year-old! He will, in general, be more open to distraction, so noting that concentration, like the other 'Cs', is something that can be developed – rather than something that you have or don't have – is important.

In Chapter 11, we look at Yannick Bolasie's 'match script', used to keep him focused during games, even when he, or his team, does not have a lot of the ball. This 'script', containing four short, sharp reminders, allows him to 'self-talk' and refocus when he feels it necessary. I would highly recommend that players have small goals – whether they be psychological ones, or technical, tactical, social, or physical ones – that help them focus on their development during games and training sessions, even within the chaos of the game.

If you ever watch professional games live, or from a wide-angle camera view, let your eyes drift away from the ball and hone in on the players who you consider to be 'focused'. I remember watching Fabio Cannavaro live from behind an Italian goal, and he spent all of Italy's attacks organising his teammates and sniffing out any potential danger.

Players with good concentration skills will concern themselves only with the things they can control – their preparation, their decisions, their reactions to opponents, etc. They spend very little time worrying about the weather, supporters, or any other distractions. If you cannot control it, leave it.

Control what you can control.

Control

Skills that centre around 'control' relate to players managing and regulating their emotions. This involves players being in a state of readiness *before* performance, maintaining a positive, proactive state *during* games, and responding well to occurrences *after* the game is over.

Those who are quick to anger, that are overly critical of themselves or others, and who dwell on the negative aspects of performance are examples of those with poor emotional control. I once had a player go ballistic after an honest 50-50 challenge with an opponent. We were 4-0 up and were firmly in control of the game. It wasn't tight, tense, or particularly competitive, but he reacted physically to the opponent and verbally to the referee – and was subsequently sent off. If you had told me (or him) 60 seconds before this incident what was about to happen, you would not believe or predict it. This reaction can typically be a response to the stress that is associated with games that are closely fought, or ones that are going against you. If a player is reacting like this when things are going well, you know you have a problem that needs addressing.

Often, players who are susceptible to this kind of behaviour find it very difficult to explain why this red mist comes down so suddenly – and certainly in the moment they don't want to talk it through with anyone. It is important to teach such players self-awareness – so that they can identify the feelings and sensations that send them from 'in control' to 'out of control'. With the player mentioned above, we came to an arrangement where he would communicate directly to me when he felt the red mist coming, and I would substitute him. This was almost to save him from himself, and take the focus of everyone else off him. He had the option of going straight to the changing room for some alone time if that is what he felt he needed. We had a plan to stop it happening, but also a plan if it did happen.

Confidence

"

You don't get to be the best at anything without blistering confidence and an impenetrable shell. You get there by taking huge risks that others won't take, because you rely on your instincts to know which risks aren't risks at all. When you're standing at the edge of the Zone, it's your dark side that drives its seductive finger into your back and whispers, "Go."

"

Tim S. Grover, Relentless

This 'C' is arguably the most talked-about trait when it comes to a player's mental state. Pundits and coaches will refer to a player "lacking in confidence," "giving the rest of the team confidence," or that "a confident player would have done X, Y or Z."

If Commitment *underpins* a player from a psychological point of view, Communication, Concentration, and Control will regulate it. It is the fifth C – Confidence – that drives his performance to the highest level. Confident players believe in themselves, will take risks where others won't, and confront difficult situations positively. Those with good confidence will show improvement across the other Cs.

Confidence, like the other Cs, can be situational as well as a defined trait of a player. A player with excellent commitment will be late once in a while or will pull out of a tackle unexpectedly. A player with poor emotional control, will not behave like a raging bull 24/7. A player with generally good body language will show signs of disappointment, frustration, or anxiety from time to time. A confident striker may not believe in himself when defending corners. A defender who lacks confidence playing in tight areas, may be very confident in 1v1 duels.

Equally, players can go through spells of supreme confidence, followed by periods where they lack it. Goalscorers are a convenient example of this. When goals follow goals, they will feel like they can go out and score in every game. When goals turn to misses, they may take fewer risks, pass when normally they would go for goal, or shy away from taking a penalty, for example.

The better your previous experience in a certain situation, the greater the likelihood of confidence when facing the same situation. This is why visualisation skills – vividly imagining yourself practicing or being successful – allow you to rehearse success and provide you with a confidence 'hit'.

Studies have shown that by practising imagery like this, the brain and relevant muscles often fire as if it were actually happening. The brain doesn't know what is real, and what is not, so mental rehearsal is a very useful way of preparing for competitive action. Guang Yue, an exercise psychologist, found that a group who conducted mental weight training had a 13.5% muscle increase, despite never attending a gym. Equally, players who imagine and focus on losing or missing a penalty, for example, put themselves at a huge disadvantage. Coaches can be a great help and a great catalyst in 'anchoring' players' mindsets to the good (and the bad) things they have done in the past. Reminding them of goals they score, games where they played well, or the direct opponent they subdued in previous meetings, are great ways of placing players in a confident frame of mind.

" Brain studies now reveal that thoughts produce the same mental instructions as actions. So the brain is getting trained for actual performance during visualisation. It's been found that mental practices can enhance motivation, increase confidence and self-efficacy, improve motor performance, prime your brain for success, and increase states of flow. **"**

Angie LeVann, *Psychology Today*

According to Harwood and Anderson, a confident player demands the ball from teammates (even when under pressure), maintains positive body language, and remains positive with others. They perform actions without the fear of negative results. A player with poor confidence will let their head drop easily, 'hide' when things get difficult, and play safe to avoid risks, amongst other things.

The 5Cs Model – In Action

Now that we understand each element of the 5C Model, let's have a look at it in action. Nothing brings theory to life more than stories from actual coaches working with actual players – the very essence of the *It's Your Game* segment in this book.

During my many interviews for this book, some contributors are happy to be named and have their name in lights. Others, however, prefer to keep their name, their club's name, and anyone connected to their stories, anonymous. The contribution below comes from a 'Head of Coaching' at a Category '2' Academy in the English Premier League. He wavered a couple of times when I asked him to put his name to the piece, but ultimately, safeguarding considerations won out, so the piece remains anonymous, but its value to coaches should not be understated. He also provides us with the *It's Your Game* piece relating to commitment at the end of the chapter.

What I like about the way this Academy uses the 5C model is its simplicity. The account below brings the process 'to life' and I am certain this can be adapted by coaches at any level – to the benefit of coaches, players, and parents.

> ## It's Your Game
> # The 5Cs in Action
> ## EPL Category 2 Academy

The 5Cs Model has been very helpful for the academy in three ways. First of all, the model allows us to organise the psychological support that we give to players. That was the hardest part when we first looked at developing a programme. Psychology can be a bit of a maze so using this has helped us greatly, to a point where we feel we are genuinely helping to develop players' mental skills.

Secondly, the players receive targeted work in a mental capacity. Before, we would judge a player's commitment, confidence, etc. on a bit of a whim. We would judge them very quickly on something that is very complex and never truly work with them to improve it. For example, we tracked a player's in-season and end-of-season reviews from Under-11 to Under-14. Over those three years, his confidence was rated as below average by a succession of coaches – but we never actually did anything to improve it. He and his parents would just read – several times per season – that he did not believe in himself. That is so powerful in such a negative way. If his passing, defending, or tactical understanding, for example, was consistently considered below average, we would have had him in a specific programme long before we reached our fourth season with him.

Thirdly, using the 5Cs model within our programme has helped the coaches. Over the last ten years or so, academy environments have moved wholesale from 'coach what you want, when you want' to structured training. We have a technical syllabus, but we relied on coaches' 'instincts' to work with players mentally. What we got were amateur outcomes in many ways – we could judge the player but couldn't *really* improve him mentally. Telling a player to "be more confident" is not good enough. It is like telling a player "to be taller." Our previous method could be regarded as a bit of a 'butterfly' process – one game a player showed great desire, in the next game that was missing. He was considered to be committed during week one, but uncommitted the next. Coaches may speak to a player about his emotional control after a game, but never refer back to it – there was no process to connect the dots. Now we have one.

Our season is divided into seven blocks, all six weeks in length. Blocks 2, 3, 4, 5, and 6 focus on one of the 5Cs. Blocks 1 and 7 'bookend' the process where we introduce the 5Cs – or the most important aspects of the programme – from the outset, then we use Block 7 to reinforce anything that came up throughout the season.

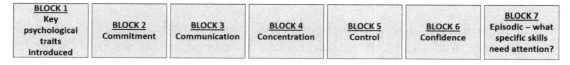

Academy Mental Programme – Season Layout

During Block 1, we focus on the following attributes that we feel need addressing straight away, and are the core of our psychological outlook:

Commitment	Attending all sessions and being punctual
	Players completing their 'homework' and adding their self-analysis to the online data system
Communication	Listening
	Providing feedback to coaches and teammates
	Maintaining positive body language
	Outlining the key "buzzwords" our academy uses
Concentration	Staying focused
	Understanding the roles of their teammates
Control	Remaining disciplined
	Understanding the things we can control and what we cannot
	Controlling emotions even when things are not going well
Confidence	Wanting the ball
	Dealing positively with the mistakes that inevitably lie ahead during the season

Key psychological traits of the Academy player

By doing this at the beginning of the season, players, parents, and coaches understand exactly what we are looking for during the year – and it offers a reminder of what happened during the previous season. However, we didn't always do this during Block 1, but now that we have, we would never go back. This 'hit' of essential information, right from the outset, lets everyone know what is expected from them and allows us to catch any issues before they get too embedded during the season.

We then ringfence one of the 5Cs from Blocks 2 to 6. Block 2, for example, would be related to Commitment. (It is important that we also acknowledge that we are never *not* working with all of the 5Cs – we just make time to focus on each one. For example, if a player is having a confidence issue during Block 3, we will still deal with it). With our long-term thinking hats on, however, by focusing on each trait in an organised way, we assign enough time for them to develop these skills, rather than our previous tendency to butterfly around.

During each block, every age group or phase (groups of age groups) would have at least one classroom-based lecture, normally at the beginning. We ask two coaches from across the academy to lead these workshops, allowing them to develop, as well as the players. By the end of the season, all coaches will have led these sessions at least once, but normally twice, which has been brilliant for their development also.

"

The best way to learn is to teach.

Latin Principle

The centrepiece of these workshops is very simple, and intentionally so. They are designed to allow as much information to come directly from the players, who would be guided by the coaches. We create 'mental role models' for them to look up to – often professional players from our own club, but often other well-renowned players too.

We use four questions for each 'C' during our workshops. The examples below are from a confidence workshop:

1. What does a confident player look like?

2. What does a player lacking in confidence look like?

3. Who is your confidence role model?

4. What can I do to improve my confidence? How can my parents/coaches help?

We also ask the parents' committee to have a representative at each of these workshops, ensuring parents understand what is happening is very important for our process.

On the pitch, during *every* session, the coaches will plan certain psychological outcomes for players, as well as the usual technical/tactical and physical ones. These outcomes are dependent on what the focus is during that particular block, any issues that may be specific to that group, or specific to individuals within that group.

We also try to be creative with how we conduct 'mental training'. For example, during the block where we focus on Control, we have asked coaches to make incorrect 'referee' decisions within small-sided games. We have even gone as far as working with matchday referees to make poor decisions to analyse and teach players how to deal with adversity and unfairness.[1]

Conclusion – Positive Psychology

If psychology still remains a bit of an enigma with you, then I would suggest following one simple rule: *Be positive*. Be positive with people and players. Be positive when games, results, or sessions do not go the way you wanted them too. I referred to Harry Redknapp earlier in this chapter. Harry's son, Jamie, former Liverpool, Tottenham, and England international, summed it up while offering punditry on Sky Sports – "Everyone wants to leave the pitch and to be told 'well done'."

In *The Happiness Advantage*, Shawn Achor (@shawnachor) presents lots of research detailing the power of positivity. Similar research is presented in Mihaly Csikszentmihalyi's *Flow* and Emma Seppälä's (@emmaseppala) *The Happiness Track*.

As recently as 1998, there was a 17:1 negative to positive ratio in the field of psychology. Happiness and positivity were not studied in any great detail – instead, "disorder and depression" were the focus. It was then that Martin Seligman, President of the American Psychological Association, gave birth to "positive psychology".

Since then, research has found huge benefits to back up the use of positivity in everyday life, professional life, in school, and in sport. Even in challenging fields like the military, where training and command structures have a stereotypical reputation for being brutal, negative, and almost designed to 'break' recruits, they found that annual prizes were far more likely to be awarded to squadrons who were led by officers who were openly encouraging. Those led by negative commanders tended to receive the lowest marks. This extends to doctors, salespeople, and students preparing for exams – the more positive their outlook, the better the results in

---

[1] The interviewee was eager to point out that the opposition club were fully aware of the situation.

terms of diagnosis, sales, and results. Even short, quick bursts of positivity can lead to an improvement in mood, which leads to greater output from players.

"

Studies of sports teams have found not only that one happy player was enough to infect the mood of the entire team, but also the happier the team was, the better they played.

"

Shawn Anchor, *The Happiness Advantage*

Summary

- Dan Abrahams offers us *The Psych-Social Model of Coaching*, stating a constant to-ing and fro-ing between the psychological and other elements of the game (technical, tactical, and physical).

- Rosenthal's 1965 experiment in a Californian elementary school displays how a teacher/coach's approach to young students/players can improve their performance greatly.

- One of the greatest challenges for coaches is navigating the huge amount of vocabulary linked to psychological performance. The UEFA-commissioned study from Leeds Beckett University referenced over 50 individual traits.

- The 5C Model of Coaching allows coaches to organise their mental work with players.

- Working with players psychologically is like working with a muscle – the more work you put in, the stronger it becomes. It is more likely that continuous work, rather than a single intervention, will improve players long-term.

- Commitment skills underpin the rest of psychological performance and, in turn, psychological performance drives technical, tactical, and physical improvement.

- Communication, Concentration, and Control help players to regulate performance.

- Confidence, finally, optimises player performance and drives improvement across the other Cs.

- A Head of Coaching at a Premier League Academy is clear that using the 5C model has organised their mental programme, and improved players and coaches.

- If working psychologically with players still intimidates coaches, remember one thing – be positive!

> ## It's Your Game - COMMITMENT
>
> ## Changing Buses
>
> ### Anonymous
>
> ### Academy 'Head of Coaching'

We had just started to introduce the 5Cs into our Academy programme and, to begin with at least, it was quite amateur. We would rate players according to each 'C', but we needed to do more to actually identify and improve these skills.

After a management meeting, we decided that we would use Block 1 of our coaching programme to introduce what we considered to be the most important mental aspects of being a player at our club. If we were going to judge players on something, the least they deserved was to know the criteria they were being judged on.

We decided, along with representatives from the players, that being 'committed' meant three things: you were punctual, had excellent attendance, and that you completed your online data entry away from the club. This extended to the first team also. Many of the senior players played at international level, so there was greater expectation that the younger players follow suit – if the 'big boys' are doing it, there is no reason why *you* shouldn't.

It was here where we identified boys who we felt were struggling under each heading. We used to hammer one particular boy for his lack of commitment – he would miss at least one session a week and was late for most of the others. On matchday at the weekend, however, he would be on time and far more 'motivated'. We labelled his attitude as being a poor trainer but that he came alive on game day – a trait that historically grates on coaches. Looking back, I feel a huge sense of shame for my part in this.

In reality, the lad wasn't a poor trainer and matches were not his only goal. During the week, he was actually getting multiple buses directly from school to make training, hence his frequent tardiness. He came from a single-parent family, where his mum had no means of transport and worked in shifts that were unreliable – but he was too embarrassed to tell us, fearing for his place in the academy. Conversely, rather than banish him, as he feared, we were able to come up with a plan to engage him better. We simply arranged transport with another parent! The lad changed overnight. He no longer had coaches getting on his back for being late; he was not arriving at training stressed and could get on with playing. Psychology in action.

It's Your Game - COMMUNICATION

Football – A Universal Language

Blaine McKenna • @BlaineMcKenna77

Academy Director

When arriving mid-season to coach an Under-17 Thai youth league team, I inherited a team who were struggling badly. After watching them, it was clear the style of play had to change, the players needed to develop a deeper understanding of the game, and we needed to find ways to encourage communication. The biggest issue facing me with these goals was that not one of the players spoke English and my translator, who was not always available, didn't understand 'football language'.

A solution to overcome this was the development of trigger words stemming from our principles of play, which we could use during sessions and games. I'd introduce the word to my translator, with a clear definition, and he would then transfer it to the players. The quality of translation is always a big worry, but monitoring the players' reactions made it clear whether it had been understood. The trigger words introduced each time would depend on the session objective, with practices being set up to encourage the right moment and area of the pitch for each trigger word to be used appropriately. This greatly helped the players' communication with one another as, when one word was said, everyone reacted accordingly.

It was also a great way to simplify our style of play, with each principle having a trigger word associated with it. I'd previously used trigger words as it improves communication amongst those who speak the same language too, when one word triggers a reaction rather than having to explain in depth each time.

I was without a translator on a few occasions, which meant I had to be creative in getting my ideas across. During such sessions, demonstrations in specific positions and pitch areas, and utilising my body language – and recognising theirs – would be the key modes of communication, coupled with the use of trigger words.

In the changing rooms before games, I'd put cones on the floor and move them around to show what we wanted. This would stimulate conversation, as the leaders would explain it to the rest of the group. The information would relate to what we had been working on in training, which helped facilitate understanding. The more we worked on our principles of play as the season progressed, the easier communication became, which greatly improved our performances, both individually and collectively. At the end of the season, we were still unable to have a basic conversation off the pitch but, on the pitch, we shared a football language.

It's Your Game - CONCENTRATION

Gary Neville's Preparation Cycle

David Horrocks • @SoccerLtd

Sport Psychologist & Owner of *Sensible Soccer*

Gary Neville accumulated 602 professional appearances over two decades. His playing career became synonymous with unparalleled success for his team, Manchester United. In total, Neville played in teams that won eight Premier Leagues, three FA Cups, one Champions League, an Intercontinental Cup, a FIFA Club World Cup. and one League Cup. Beyond his success at club level, Neville was first-choice right-back for England for more than ten years. Sir Alex Ferguson described him as 'the best English right-back of his generation.'

For Gary to regularly perform in the stadiums of Manchester, Milan, and Madrid, it required an enormous amount of thought, organisation, concentration, planning, and general cognitive processing.

I define 'elite' as serial winners who are repeatedly winning at the highest level. He admitted that he was not the best player, so to be among the elite of his generation, he paid very close attention to his preparation, which is summarised below:

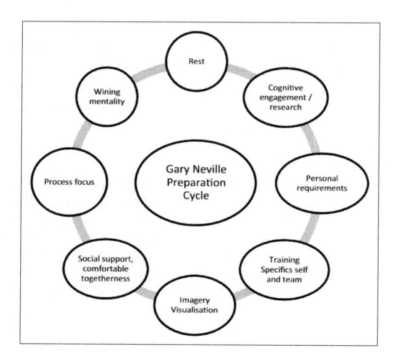

During my work with Gary as part of my Ph.D. (which is published in its entirety in *International Journal of Sports Science & Coaching* 2016, Vol. 11(5) 673–682) he told me:

> "Concentration, I don't believe, should ever change for a sportsperson. The minute I got on the plane on a Tuesday morning for an away game in Europe (Wednesday night) I would switch on, that is where game time begins for me 36 hours before you go in, everything must be right, preparation, for me, is key.

It's not just who I'm playing directly against, or the man I'm facing. Who serves him the ball? Is it a straight pass? Can they play it 60 yards over your head? Can things be stopped at source? Can our midfielder get tighter? Will it be a physical battle? Is he quick and jinky? Can I talk them off their game?

What do I need to do in this training session tonight? Is he quick and jinky? So I'll get somebody to run to me quick and jinky. Is he physical? So I practice my heading."

As a football academic, he left no stone unturned. All possible knowledge was gained of both his own role and of his opponents.

"I would [want to] understand what I needed to do to defeat an opponent. I would ask for a video. I never liked watching selected clips of teams by a coach. I have always liked to see the first half an hour of a match. You can see a player dribbling at somebody three times, but I'm not really interested in that, to be honest. That's probably the most obvious thing to look at. I'm looking at who gives him the ball, when do they give him the ball, what movements does he make to get on the ball, what weaknesses does he have, is he lazy, does he follow you back? If he was quicker than me, I had to stop him in another way. I knew if I had to be aggressive. I knew if I had to be nice because some players you didn't want to wind up.

Ultimately, Neville's preparation and concentration improved his mindset, which he believed facilitated better, and quicker, on-pitch decision making and reaction times. This type of preparation forged a perceived advantage for impending high-pressure football matches; this may distinguish success from failure where the physical development of most competing players is at, or close to, optimum.

"I would say preparation for a match has been the key to my career. If any element of it is wrong, I'm in trouble. My routine and preparation for matches were critical to me. If I didn't do that, I couldn't play."

> ## It's Your Game - CONTROL
> # A Teenage Steven Gerrard
> ## Bill Beswick
> ## Sports Psychologist

Bill Beswick, ex-England, Manchester United, and Middlesbrough sport psychologist tells a great story about working with a teenage Steven Gerrard. The former Liverpool captain was rated highly by the Academy staff at the club, but had issues around emotional control. He would play hard, but often overstep the line – something that intermittently raised its head throughout his career. This included being sent off against rivals Everton following a reckless foul on Kevin Campbell, and later in his career against Manchester United.

In the latter incident, he entered the game as a half-time substitute, before being shown a red card within 40 seconds for a stamp on Ander Herrera. He later admitted to feeling like a "caged animal" that day having been dropped to the substitutes bench, and the team were performing poorly. "We had stood off United in the first half and made very few tackles. It went against everything built into my DNA. Tackling and collisions mattered against Manchester United."[2]

"Tackles and collisions" are a part of the game, but, on occasion, as an adult professional, these spilled over into indiscipline. These moments were far more frequent when Gerrard was a teenager. As a 16-year-old, Beswick took him under his wing in an attempt to improve this aspect of his psychology. Hughie McAuley, then a coach at Liverpool, noted – "Steven didn't like himself at the time. He was going in to win the ball but also to 'leave a bit' on his opponent". As we have just noted, ridding players of certain habits and behaviours is difficult, but persistently working and sending the right messages gives improvement a chance. Beswick worked with Gerrard on recognising the signs when he was losing his temper and feeling the blood of the "caged tiger" boil.

Beswick introduced Gerrard to a 'traffic light' system. When Steven was in the green, all was good, he was 'in the zone' and performing to his highest level. When he hit the red zone, however, it was already too late. Gerrard was challenged to identify when he hit the amber zone – to feel the triggers and emotions when he was starting to lose control), and work to travel back to green. This increase in self-awareness can be the first step to regaining it.

---

[2] *My Story*, autobiography, Steven Gerrard

It's Your Game - CONFIDENCE

If I give up on you now, what sort of man am I?

Paul Ifill • @PaulIfill

Former Professional Footballer

Mark McGhee arrived at Millwall in 2000. As a player with confidence issues, I became stressed about what will happen with a new man in charge. However, in the end, Mark was somebody that would have an amazing effect on me as a player!

In me, he found somebody who wasn't sure they belonged in the world of professional football. I was very eager to improve but was also low on confidence. He often said that I was hard to read, but he always did his best to understand me.

In the 2000-2001 season, we found ourselves battling for promotion to the Championship. I was still playing but was having a poor time in a very good team – I felt like the weakest link. I would speak to Mark, and he would always make me feel better, with frequent words of encouragement. He felt like I could do it – even when I didn't. I was training well but seemed to freeze under the spotlight on game day!

Mark told me that my first action in a game usually told him what was about to occur. If it was a good start, I would go on to play well; if it was bad, I was probably going to have a bad day. On one occasion, I remember pleading with him to drop me as I felt I was letting people down and what he told me literally changed the path of my career. He said, "Listen, you train the house down regularly and it is a matter of time before it transfers over to the games. *I am convinced you can and will actually go on to play at an even higher level.* I give up on you now, what sort of man am I?"

I went away from our meeting feeling energised. I wanted to prove that Mark was right for believing in me. Two weeks later, I scored my first ever professional hat-trick – in an away win that all but secured us promotion. Upon entering the changing room, I received a standing ovation from the boys and a hug from Mark, who whispered: "I told you it would come!"

Mark was right. I could and did play at a higher level, but I honestly believe that a coach that didn't have the man-management skills at that time in my career could have been disastrous for me. Now, as I embark on my own coaching career, I certainly look back and use the many lessons I learnt as a player.

Chapter 8
Football Fitness

It is funny what you remember about coaching courses. A number of years ago, I attended a coach education event which was the first of its kind. Slide #1, on morning one, introduced us to *The Kubler-Ross Change Curve*. The *Kubler-Ross* model suggests that when we are faced with change, or are challenged with new ideas, our initial reaction can be negative. Emotions can range from disbelief to anger and a rejection of the information provided. By including this early, the tutor challenged us to race through (or even past) these initial reactions and settle quickly into more positive emotions of open-mindedness and learning.

This chapter may indeed require you to challenge long-standing ideas around your training – and in particular, the way 'fitness' is approached.

Football Fitness

Coach Carter is one of my favourite movies. For those who haven't seen it, Samuel L. Jackson plays a high-school basketball coach who takes on the seemingly impossible job of turning around a dysfunctional inner-city school basketball team. Indiscipline, gang culture, and poor academic achievement were amongst the challenges faced by Carter and his players. By the end, however, the main characters had not only become better players, better people, and better students, they came together and became a better team. Most achieved the grades required to earn basketball scholarships at various universities. These players, based on a true story, went from low-aspiring kids to degree-achieving young men.

99% of the movie appealed to the holistic coach in me (on one occasion, the coach locked the gym and forced the players into the library when grades weren't being achieved, cancelling games which ended an extended winning streak). One percent, however, did not.

Football coaches are among the best and most reoffending thieves out there. We see, we steal, we copy, and we borrow – and we roll it out to players on our training pitches.

Chapter 8 – Football Fitness

Usually, being called a 'thief' would be seen as quite disparaging, but in this case, it is not meant in a negative way at all. Provided the training material and ideas we 'steal' are appropriate, come from a well-placed source, and have a purpose beyond "X club does this," then I have no issue with it, nor seemingly does Pep Guardiola below! I would suggest that any material you do 'appropriate' – session plans, set-plays routines, tactical nuances, etc. – are developed further by you *for your team* rather than literally being a copy and paste job.

"　　　　　　　　　　　　　　　　　　　　　　　　　　　**"**

I am not an innovator –
I am an 'ideas thief'!

Pep Guardiola

"To the baseline," "suicides," and "push-ups" were frequent instructions from Carter to the teenage basketball players at Richmond High School. On day one, Carter insisted that he could not teach them the game until their conditioning was up to standard. My issue is not with the concept of physical conditioning playing a vital role in improving players and teams; it is – rather – the message this sends the coaching fraternity. As thieves, we tend to copy things that spark our imagination.

Copying a rondo, skill practice, or small-sided game from the internet is one thing, but copying 'fitness' sessions ad hoc is quite another. Whilst lifting a technical session from a coaching book will do no physical harm, lifting 'fitness' sessions and copying them verbatim may well.

We see professional clubs run their players through streets and up hills and make our Under-8s do the same. We see a newspaper headline involving players running an equivalent of a marathon every three days (true story from a Premier League manager, although the headline sounds much worse than it was), so we do the same with our Under-12s. We remember that archaic workout drill that our youth coach did when we were kids and throw that into our Under-15 schedule. We run suicides and push-ups with our Under-18s because Coach Carter was able to discipline and improve the conditioning of his team in this way. It is this type of copying and thieving that needs to stop, especially if there is a complete absence of science behind it.

Isolated Fitness Training

"　　　　　　　　　　　　　　　　　　　　　　　　　　　**"**

With young and novice players, any work
without the ball should focus on general
mobility and coordination exercises, which
could form part of a warm-up or cool-down …
The players' ability to cope with the demands
of small-sided games and practices will
be developed through involvement
in the activities.

FA Education (England)

Just writing a sub-heading dealing with isolated fitness in football sends me sweating. Not only does it challenge the 'we-have-done-it-this-way-for-years' brigade, it also sparks arguments with sports scientists the world over.

We use the term 'isolated fitness' to refer to *fitness-only sessions that contain no other element of the game*. We extract only the fitness elements (or what we perceive as the 'fitness elements') from the game and work them independently from the game. There will be no football played. Isolated fitness sessions will include things like players running laps, completing sprints, using agility equipment, etc. and will more than likely look similar to a training session that you may find at an athletics club.

How Simple Can It Be?

The traditional, widespread use of isolated fitness training, however, has come under scrutiny, particularly over the past decade. The central argument is that all fitness components that are relevant to the game *can be developed whilst playing the game*. The arguments against isolated training are largely five-fold, all of which we will explore further below:

1. It does not replicate the game

2. It is demotivating for young players

3. It is wasting valuable time that could be used developing footballers

4. It plays a part in inducing injury and fatigue

5. It does not contain any of the other football-related elements that are required to develop players holistically

1. Replicating the Game

I don't need too much encouragement to share the table below. If you have read *Making the Ball Roll*, you will be familiar with the statistics. If you haven't, then some of the numbers may surprise you. The table (Source: Sport Dimensions *How to Develop Soccer Players – Soccer Speed* presentation), displays the percentage of time that certain physical actions are undertaken by top-level players during a 90-minute match. Although taken from the top level of the game, statistics from youth football will not vary wildly.

Action Performed	Percentage of Game
Standing	18%
Walking Forward and Backward	36%
Jumping	2%
Jogging	16%
Low-Speed Running	15%
Moderate-Speed Running	10%
High-Speed Running	2%
Sprinting	1%

During a 90-minute game, players will complete around 1,400 changes of direction

Chapter 8 – Football Fitness

There is something in our human nature that steers us towards the extremes when looking at statistics. When presented with a list of values, we first look at the biggest and the smallest numbers – much in the same way we look for the A's and F's when a school report comes through the door – and here is no different.

Even if you have spent a lifetime absorbed in the game, you would be forgiven for assuming that players "run for 90 minutes". Many who are still involved in the game still believe this to be true. The truth, however, as the data tells us, is, they don't – and far from it.

The set of data that occupies the middle of the chart (jogging, low, and moderate-speed running) was not a great surprise, nor was a lowly 2% of the time spent jumping. However, the data at the top and bottom of the chart was certainly surprising. The highest numbers that represent 'standing still' or 'walking' make up over half of the physical actions performed by a player in a game! At first glance, this is a dumbfounding figure, but a completely logical once you let it sink in. At the other end of the data set, a lowly 3% of actions will involve sprinting or high-speed running – about 2 minutes in total.

This data, however, first of all, needs to be interpreted correctly. A number of years ago, I posted these stats on social media and was abruptly confronted by a youth coach working at quite a high level of the game in England. He sarcastically quipped that his 'drills' will now be "54% walking or standing around". Another mockingly suggested incorporating Michael Jackson's 'Moonwalk' into their "fitness drills" to ensure players practice walking backwards. For some with such active, quippy creativity on social media, they completely missed the point.

> Some people suggest that players should do isolated running because 98% of the time during the game, players have to run without the ball. These people should understand that games of 11v11 – 8v8, players also have to run without the ball 98% of the time.
> Problem solved.

Raymond Verheijen

Top-level football players can cover around 10-13 kilometres during a 90-minute game. On the face of it, it may be easy to assume that we ought to produce players that can comfortably run this distance, and therefore coaches need to have this at the foundation of their physical work. This assumption, however, is highly dangerous and highly misleading. *Sending your players on a 12-kilometre run will not make them football fit.*

First of all, the distance covered during a game is not completed by running at the same speed in the same direction, like a middle or long-distance athlete would. It involves moving forwards, backwards, and laterally – and in some cases a mixture of two of the three – and all at varying speeds and in random patterns! Football is, after all, an explosive, 360-degree, multi-directional sport, not a consistent, straight-line one.

Added to that, we will see players running while arching their bodies (think again of that striker making a forward run into space. He is travelling forward but may have his hips turned facing the direction of the passer), running while falling over or out of balance. Strides can be long, short, or require interchanging feet positions depending on the football decision involved. If I am running with the ball into space, my touches will be 'bigger' and, therefore, my strides longer.

Alternatively, if I am moving quickly through a crowded area, my touches will be smaller and my strides shorter.

Players will also skip, jump, slide, balance, fall over, have to burst back onto their feet, or change direction – and all within a competitive environment where opposition players provide physical and football-related interference. Opponents need to be blocked, raced against, predicted, and held off.

The learning outcome of the stats above is not to rearrange your fitness practices so that over half of the time is spent doing nothing. It is *to completely rethink what fitness training is for football*. Why would we even think about devising practices to match this when the beautiful game of football already does it for us?

2. Demotivating

Raymond Verheijen, (@raymondverheije), Dutch football coach, football fitness expert, and author of several books, including the eye-opening *How Simple Can It Be?* is the most vociferous proponent of football fitness and is hugely opposed to isolated fitness work with players.

In an interview with the *Just Kickin' It* podcast, Verheijen uses a lion analogy to highlight his thoughts. One of the arguments he deals with is coaches who claim that isolated sprinting, for example, is the only way to get players to actually sprint at 100% full speed. Verheijen then asks whether this player would sprint faster if a lion was chasing them, leaving us with the inevitable answer – yes! He likens game-related/ball-related practices to encouraging a football lion. The ball motivates us to sprint at top speed. The opponent motivates us to sprint at top speed – while incorporating all those variable movements that we mentioned above, rather than in straight lines. Players train and try harder when exercises are football-based, and all the conditioning that is required to play the game effectively can be done in football-related practices.

There remains a major argument in certain quarters that mental toughness is built using gruelling isolated physical fitness sessions. If players are put through these tough physical sessions, they will become more resilient. This is where team spirit begins as players are "all in it together." This may be one way that resilience and togetherness are built, but it is certainly not the only way, nor is it a sure-fire way to create any positive psychological or social outcome. If you want to build togetherness, and make it really work, I strongly suggest you read *Togetherness* by Dr. Matt Slater (@DrMattSlater).

Using means other than isolated training to improve players' conditioning, namely by simply playing the game or at least incorporating the ball within practices, will not make players 'soft', nor does it make the coach 'soft'. Are we that unimaginative that we, as coaches, cannot find better ways of developing resilience and team spirit in players other than running them until they vomit?

In football, and indeed sport in general, we are losing. Studies and figures from all corners of the Earth are showing devastating drop-out rates from sport. We saw, in the early part of this book, the number of those who will progress to the top of the professional game is minuscule, so we, as coaches, are catering for the masses, not just those with a shot at the top. For those who are unconcerned with developing professional players at all, then you have no reason to be so worried about their fitness stats. If you are desperate to produce top players, then the reality is that if we continue to lose players at the entry-levels of the game, and at the younger ages, we will then produce fewer 'top' players.

Young players are inspired by heroes – those that they see in real life or on TV. Any of us who are sport-orientated will probably have had this feeling as young boys or girls. I remember donning a pair of boxing gloves, having watched Michael Carruth win an Olympic gold medal in 1992. I remember running out to the back garden with a football when Ireland over-achieved by reaching the quarter-finals of the 1990 World Cup. This link between the uptake of sport and the success of those that young people relate to, is undeniable, as we spoke about earlier in the book.

I would like you to dig into your imagination for 30 seconds. You are 10-years-old, and you have just witnessed your country win the World Cup. They beat Spain or France or Brazil in a glorious final. Your whole neighbourhood is joyous and is smothered in the nation's colours. *You* want to be the next World Cup hero so you pester your parents to let you join the local team, which, of course, they oblige.

You arrive for your first training session full of enthusiasm. Then, you are sent jogging around the pitch for the first 10 minutes, followed by some static stretches. You glance at the big bag of footballs in the corner – unopened and underused. The coach then lines you up, and you sprint back and forth, touching cones. At last, the bag is opened, and one ball comes out. You find yourself in a long queue waiting for your turn to pass, shoot, or head. If you are good during this time, and you pay attention, you might even have a game at the end, the coach says.

Now imagine you arrive, and you are given a ball to dribble with, immediately – and all your new friends have a ball too. You warm-up trying to replicate the dribbles and turns you saw during the World Cup. You see one of your teammates do a turn or trick and decide to copy it (you can't do it, but you will go home and practise it for next week!). Quickly after this, teams are picked, and you play games – lots of games with all sorts of little, ever-changing rules. Sometimes your team has an extra player; sometimes you play with one less. You score a goal like your World Cup hero and you go home, now pestering mum and dad for a ball of your own.

Which experience would a 10-year-old you choose?

Now imagine you are 40-years-old, or whatever age you currently are. You dust off your playing gear and head to the local hire-a-pitch facility to play with your workmates. Which session of the above would you choose now? I bet the answer is the same at 40 as it was at 10.

How can you build resilience before you've been inspired? How can you develop team spirit before you've fallen in love with the game? Yet, this is what is witnessed on parks and playing fields the world over. "And this is what is killing sport," according to coach educator, Wayne Goldsmith (@waynegoldcoach). This is the scenario that Goldsmith – who has worked with New Zealand and Australia rugby, with teams in the AFL and with Michael Phelps as part of the US swimming team – finds in all sports, all over the world.

In an eye-opening and shame-inducing article for the *Irish Examiner* newspaper, Goldsmith offers coaches some real home truths. He lambasts the ever-prevailing culture of coaching, where physical-based sessions hold too much weight. He appreciates that there may be some backing for isolated physical training in the world of sports science, but he also notes that the ones who are not there (the drop-outs) are the ones not getting 'fit' at all.

Whilst working with some coaches, Goldsmith heard frequent complaints about the videogame, *Fortnite*. This game was engaging kids and, like other technological-based entertainment that young people indulge in, was steering kids away from the sports pitches and onto games consoles, tablets, and smartphones. Goldsmith flipped this complaint on its head. It is coaches who need to be more creative, imaginative, and inspiring. It is coaches who need to appeal to young people, or at the very least, ensure that the game they came to play is appealing to them. A planet full of kids dropping out of sport cannot be wrong.

"

The kids are not there to do drills or to do speedwork. They are there to have fun and play the game. And if you don't give them that, eventually it'll add up and they'll stop coming.

"

Wayne Goldsmith

3. Wasting Time

"

In Holland, they do not waste a minute on physical training until players are 16 or 17-years-old. A well thought and deliberate choice is made to use the precious time of younger development age groups for technical, tactical, and personal development.

"

Mark Wotte

As a *football* coach, I prefer to spend my time coaching the game – and the limited time that youth players have to train (in most cases) learning to play *football*.

By this, I don't necessarily mean playing games *all the time*, but certainly using activities that involve players and the ball most of, if not, all of the time. Coaches have a relatively small window to improve players technically, tactically and psychologically, and I would prefer if that limited time wasn't spent with players running laps of the pitch, doing punishing shuttle-runs, or hill climbs. What amuses me sometimes is that coaches will isolate their fitness work with players (as these players need to get 'fit' – and fast!), but then spend most of the rest of the session standing players in very low-active straight lines waiting to kick a ball. As a time management exercise, this is a monumentally flawed methodology.

"

It is important to emphasise that the priority of coaches working with young players (aged 6-14) is the development of skills and techniques, not fitness.

"

FA Education (England)

The quote above from the English FA highlights the prioritisation of football development over physical development for those Under-14, and Mark Wotte shares similar thoughts from the

KNVB (Dutch FA) of players younger than 16 or 17 years old. It is important to note that many others are starting to take this thinking into adult football, too, training the physical requirements of the game within their tactical and technical work.

Football fitness allows us, as youth coaches, to maximise our valuable time with players. If you believe that a non-football warm-up followed by some isolated fitness work in every session is not that much of a concession, then let us do the math! If we spend 20 minutes doing this, these minutes add up. Over a 46-week season, with two sessions per week, the minutes run into hours.

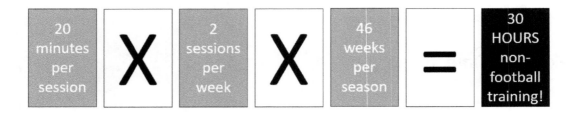

" With this approach [*football* fitness], your team will be as fit as any other team and look even fitter as no accumulation of fatigue. And more importantly, you will have significantly less injuries so you can train and play more often with the best players to develop the strongest team. The result is players with more explosive runs for longer periods throughout the games, faster recovery, less tendency to fatigue and less injuries – and more enjoyment for the player. "

Raymond Verheijen

4. Fitness, Freshness & Fatigue

"We concede late goals."

"We don't seem to run as hard as the opponent."

"We are second to every ball."

"We lose from winning positions."

"Late in games, we look tired."

"We are not fit enough."

These quotes are common in football circles. When we speak to coaches whose teams are struggling, the reason is typically reduced to one specific thing, and often this is around fitness. Frequently, even at the top level of the game, a new head coach would join a new team and they speak first about fitness.

At the end of March 2019, an article was published in the *Mirror* newspaper detailing the distance covered by every Premier League team, and the number of sprints each team completed. At the time, Liverpool and Manchester City were jousting for top spot.

A whole 11 teams ran further than eventual league-winners Manchester City, whose team is commended and celebrated for their work-rate. Bournemouth, who finished in 14th place, topped the distance-covered list, and come second in terms of sprints. Cardiff City, who we found were bottom of the running distance list, were indeed relegated, but their relegation counterparts Fulham sat in the middle of the pack, and Huddersfield, who finished rock bottom, had similar running distances to 97-point Liverpool, and European qualifiers Arsenal. The team with the lowest number of sprints, Burnley, finished almost 30 points ahead of bottom-team Huddersfield.

Final League Position	*Total Distance (rank)	*Number of Sprints (rank)
Manchester City	3,363 (12th)	3,470 (5th)
Liverpool	3,491.7km (5th)	3,794 (1st)
Chelsea	3,402.4 (10th)	3,224 (10th)
Tottenham	3,428.1 (8th)	3,294 (8th)
Arsenal	3,451.5 (7th)	3,469 (6th)
Manchester United	3,240.6 (18th)	3,096 (14th)
Wolves	3,332.2 (14th)	2,934 (17th)
Everton	3,509 (4th)	3,538 (4th)
Leicester City	3,389.5 (11th)	3,454 (7th)
West Ham	3,329.5 (15th)	3,172 (13th)
Watford	3,308.5 (17th)	3,084 (15th)
Crystal Palace	3,359.8 (13th)	2,893 (18th)
Newcastle United	3,532.1 (2nd)	3,285 (9th)
Bournemouth	3,539.5 (1st)	3,749 (2nd)
Burnley	3,523.1 (3rd)	2,722 (20th)
Southampton	3,326.5 (16th)	3,213 (11th)
Brighton	3,176.7 (19th)	2,846 (19th)
Cardiff City (relegated)	3,134.4 (20th)	3,176 (12th)
Fulham (relegated)	3,441,4 (9th)	2,973 (16th)
Huddersfield (relegated)	3,466.2 (6th)	3,592 (3rd)

*as of 25th March 2019

The narrative around fitness needs to change, starting with those who offer punditry on games and ending with coaches working on pitches with kids. The table above finds *little* correlation between distanced covered, or sprints completed, and league position, but we still use these measures to make sense of the game. An irresponsible 'eyeball' look at the data could suggest that more sprints equals success because of Liverpool, but the evidence from the rest of the teams suggests no correlation. We are creating false causation.

Although informative, the *Mirror* article itself was actually a slight on Manchester United, given the turbulent season that they had had, by their standards. The narrative was that the reason for their poor form was that the team was not fit enough (they were 18th in terms of kilometres covered). All the other variables of the game were ignored, and the authors zoomed in on the physical corner simply because it fitted the narrative. If we were to use these stats alone as a precursor for league position, Bournemouth would have run away with the Premier League!

At youth level, the result of this thinking can often be detrimental. It means that we recruit physically bigger players. We recruit runners and athletes that will cover ground and sprint more and quicker. All too often, it means that we add extra 'fitness' sessions. If your team is losing, not playing well, or something doesn't seem quite right in their performances, do not be so quick to jump to a fitness-only based solution. Chances are, if they are suffering mentally, extra isolated fitness will only demotivate them further, and they will associate these types of sessions with failure and punishment.

One of the most common errors is mistaking fatigue for a lack of fitness. A key part of being 'football fit' is being 'football fresh'. In the *It's Your Game* segment, at the end of this chapter, Brian Shrum (@JustKickinItPod) applies this concept to his own team, whose league schedule demands that they play a game every Friday and every Sunday, with only one rest/recovery day in-between. The rule of thumb around having players fit and fresh to play to their maximum potential is to have three clear days between fixtures as signs of muscle damage from a football match can still be evident after 72 hours. In fact, a study[1] based on 14 years of games and over 130,000 match observations suggests that muscle injuries are only significantly reduced when games are preceded by six clear days.

This is why English clubs bemoan the heavy Christmas/New Year schedule, and why Champions League coaches argue against the Wednesday-first-leg Tuesday-second-leg scheduling of the latter stages of the competition, as most will also play a league game in-between – at a time when the league is approaching its end and where every point counts. It is why coaches like Jürgen Klopp have been vocal opponents of the scheduling of the newly-formatted 'Nations League' international competition. We want players to play often, but not to the detriment of their physical well-being. We want them to play often – and to be able to play to their best.

"

If we don't learn to deal with our players in a better way, competition-wise, then it's the only chance to kill this wonderful game. Because without the players, it is not a good one.

"

Jürgen Klopp

At youth level, the intensity is, of course, different to that of the Premier League, Champions League, or Nations League, but the risk of injury from playing too often over short periods remains real. The risk of players being incapable of playing to their maximum potential due to fatigue is also real. Many of us will be familiar with weekend competitions that may involve playing a game every day for three days, for example. Muscle injuries can come in the form of minor aches to major tears and pulls. Muscle injuries can be the most common and also the most avoidable injuries in the game. When we add in muscle damage, or wear and tear, from training, we may well see fatigue rather than a lack of fitness is evident.

---

[1] Study: Muscle injury rate in professional football is higher in matches played within 5 days since the previous match: a 14-year prospective study with more than 130,000 match observations

5. Other Football-Related Elements

The quote at the beginning of this chapter came from a presentation completed by *Football Federation Australia*. Their issues with the game – Down Under – will not be too dissimilar to the game in many other parts of the world. The presentation bemoaned the view of physical fitness as *"the* decisive factor in football," like in rugby or the Australian Football League. Conditioning was becoming a "national obsession." To highlight their central point that *football skill is actually the decisive factor in games*, they highlighted eight teams from the 2010 World Cup – the four that reached the semi-finals (Spain, Holland, Germany and Uruguay) – and four, including Australia, who were eliminated in the Group Stage.

The physical output scores of the four semi-finalists were generally not any better than the scores of those who were eliminated earlier. In fact, some stats from the Australian team were better in terms of distance covered and high intensity running, although they were eliminated earlier. We see the same outcome from the Premier League 'table' above. The FFA concluded that "it's not about how far you run or how fast you run: it's about where you run, when you run, and what you do when you get there." The physical component, therefore, links directly to the tactical component – so training these together would be the logical thing to do.

You may have heard or read that long-distance running sessions for footballers are being frowned upon more and more, but never really understood why. The traditional theory is that distance running provides players with base-level fitness to which you build football-fitness on top. However, rather than being a physically consistent sport, football is a physically explosive one. You go from low to high output quickly and frequently.

There are two types of muscle fibres in the body – 'fast-twitch' and 'slow-twitch'. When we engage in long-distance running, it is the slow-twitch fibres that are activated. When we engage in explosive sports like football, however, the fast-twitch fibres are quickly activated, taking over as the slow-twitch fibres tire. As physically 'fit' as your favourite long-distance runner may be, it is likely that he would not physically excel in an intense, physically-explosive football game, where developed fast-twitch fibres are required. Similarly, your 'fittest' football player may not have the type of stamina required to complete a long-distance running event with any glory (some, of course, may have).

If your football training sessions, therefore, involve the training of slow-twitch muscles only (e.g., long-distance runs), you are actually neglecting the development and activation of the fast-twitch fibres necessary to perform successfully on the football pitch. You are training players to rely exclusively on their aerobic energy systems, when in reality, footballers need a combination of aerobic *and* anaerobic fitness.

Many coaches at both youth and senior level are now questioning the gruelling pre-season physical conditioning that has traditionally underpinned a campaign. These weeks of physical-only sessions have been replaced with a focus on technical-tactical elements. Instead of weeks of isolated 'fitness' training, coaches use the time to introduce and perfect their technical-tactical 'game model' instead, *in parallel* with a focus on improving player conditioning.

Tactical Periodisation

The league position of all those teams above, and any groups of teams from any league in the world, will be a melting pot of variables – only one of which will relate to fitness. Omitting wins, losses, and draws, others would include – and the list is virtually endless – goals scored, goals conceded, percentage possession, expected goals for, expected goals against, individual player errors, outstanding individual moments, proficiency or otherwise from set-plays – and team tactics.

At the time of the publication of the above table, Manchester City were insistent on dominating the ball, meaning that they ran less than the majority of their competitors. The same for Chelsea.

Chapter 8 – Football Fitness

Liverpool utilised a high-pressure game when out of possession and to counter-attack, so they completed more sprints. Brighton utilised a low defensive block, so covered less ground and produced fewer sprints. Huddersfield ran further and sprinted harder, but lacked quality in front of goal, amongst other weaknesses at that level. Bournemouth were punching way above their weight in the Premier League, so dominating statistics like these is a necessary marginal gain to ensure their survival at the top end of English football.

"

A great pianist doesn't run around the piano or do push-ups with his fingers. To be great, he plays the piano. Being a footballer is not about running, push-ups or physical work generally. The best way to be great footballer is to play.

"

José Mourinho

The concept of *Tactical Periodisation* (TP) was first brought into the spotlight by José Mourinho; however, its origin can be credited to Vítor Frade, a university lecturer at the University of Porto. The method has gained a significant following throughout the game, prompted by the success of Mourinho, but also the success of other Portuguese coaches like André Villas-Boas, Marco Silva and Nuno Espírito Santo.

When the first edition of *Making The Ball Roll* went to print in 2014, there were very few English-language based books or articles around TP. Today, however, these resources are far more plentiful, including the translation of *What is Tactical Periodization?* by Xavier Tamarit (@XTamarit) and several articles by the brilliant website and Twitter account, Training Ground Guru (@ground-guru) that help to simplify what sounds like a very complex subject. In an interview for the site, TP expert and 'Football Fitness' Coach[2] at the Aspire Academy in Qatar and author on the topic (*Tactical Periodisation: A Proven Successful Training Model*), Alberto Mendez-Villanueva, introduces us to the concept.

The concept is firstly concerned with the team's tactical 'Game Model', based around the Four Phases of the Game, which are displayed below.

---

[2] Note the job title being *'Football* Fitness Coach', not just 'Fitness Coach'.

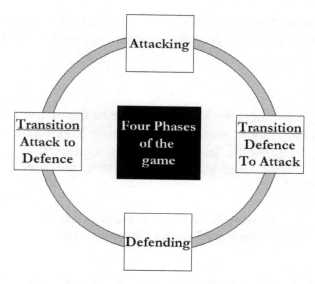

The Four Phases of the Game

On professional training grounds, each day will have a particular tactical *and* physical target, which include rest and recovery days, strength, endurance and speed days, and finally the 'activation' day – the day before the game. All of these physical concepts are worked, not through isolated running, but *through the use of football-related practices*. These are designed in collaboration between the 'football' and the 'fitness' coaches, thus assimilating both aspects of the game.

The below *Weekly Physical Training Pattern* diagram is taken from an article by Luis Delgado-Bordonau and the aforementioned Mendez-Villanueva, *Tactical Periodization; Mourinho's Best-Kept Secret?*, one of the first English-language documentations on TP. It details the physical aspects of a weekly training schedule using the TP model.

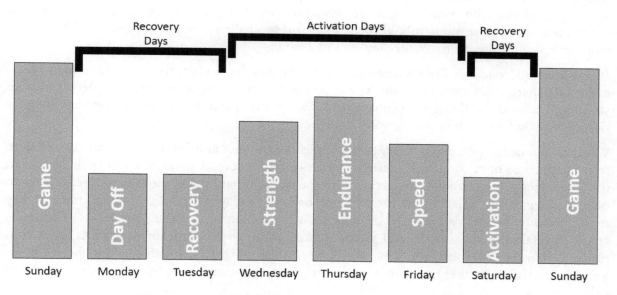

Typical Weekly Physical Pattern of Tactical Periodisation Model

The intense physical output of game day is followed by two 'rest days' – one that is completely free (around this topic, there is some disagreement within the sports science world. Those with physical 'ideologies' normally want the following day to be a 'recovery day' and Tuesday to be a free day. Others, like Mourinho, believe that physiological recovery from game day is paramount and therefore choose Monday as the 'day off'). Wednesday, Thursday, and Friday are reserved for higher intensity work around strength, endurance, and speed respectively. Saturday is about activating players' bodies to perform optimally on game day – and the cycle repeats.

"

The fitness level and adaptation of the players is superior to more isolated training. You will be sure that the fitness provided to the players will transfer better and more directly to the game.

"

Alberto Mendez-Villanueva, Aspire Academy Football Fitness Coach

Relating Tactical Periodisation to the Grassroots Coach

While looking at the training schedules of the world's top coaches is interesting and beneficial to the wider coaching fraternity, we must consider whether if (or how) we might apply this concept in our own, unique settings. Those coaching below the professional game, and even some who are coaching in certain academy environments, will typically have two sessions per week with their teams. Some of you may only have one.

It is arguably even more important and necessary for the grassroots coach to *embed* physical training within his football training sessions. If the contact time available to you and your players is low – let's say for an hour, once a week – players' attendance at your session will be social rather than seriously competitive. If they are sporty, they will probably play other sports on other nights. Stealing some of their time away from playing football to complete isolated fitness work simply does not make sense – it doesn't match their expectations or the role of a football team who train only once per week. Whatever learning can be achieved in this brief time needs to be learned by playing the game. For those who train twice a week, there remains considerable justification that our sessions should focus solely on football, where players can develop 'fitness' inherently from whatever practices they are involved in.

If you want to coach all Four Phases of the Game simultaneously, there is one golden rule – make sure there is always a goal (this could be a goal/goals, a zone, or line) for players to both attack and defend. By doing so, you can *implicitly* hardwire game transitions in the players' game simply by including them in your session design.

When coaching any defending topic, for example, the traditional habit would be for the coach to stop the practice once the attack finishes – often once the defenders win the ball back. However, this is counter-productive when we apply it to the game. What do you want your defenders to do once they regain the ball? Stop playing? Put the ball out of play? Or play to counter-attack (if they cannot counter-attack, can they retain and build possession?). The third option – to counter-attack or retain the ball – is the real game. Similarly, you would not want your attackers to stop playing once they lost the ball! You would want them to react immediately and positively to losing possession, whether that is to counter-press, stop a forward pass, or to recover quickly into defensive shape.

This is a concept that I looked at heavily during *Deliberate Soccer Practice – 50 Defending Practices to Improve Decision Making*. Below are two examples of a defending practice that include all Four Phases of the Game. By including goals for both teams to attack, you are also inducing 'critical moments' into your sessions. These moments are what win and lose games – moments where a goal *must* be scored or *must* be defended. These principles can be included in your sessions, whether you are working 1v1, or with players outnumbered, small-sided games, or tactical games.

8: Critical One v One

PURPOSE OF SESSION:

For defenders to be constantly aware of 1 v 1 threats around them.

INITIAL SET-UP:

- Playing area with eight orange gates placed randomly throughout the inside, each defended by one White player (alter numbers to suit).

- All Black attackers have a ball each.

- Blue-gated goals are also set up around the perimeter of the area

INSTRUCTIONS:

- Each White defender defends one of the internal orange, gated goals as they play 1 v 1 against a Black attacker.

- Defenders must stop the attackers dribbling through the gate. Attackers can attempt to dribble through any orange gate.

- **TRANSITION:** If the Whites regain possession, they can break out and counter-attack through any of the blue gates around the perimeter. Blacks must track the run and look to regain the ball if possible, and start another quick attack.

21: Centre-Backs Defending Box | Screening Forward Passes

PURPOSE OF SESSION:

For a centre-back pairing to defend effectively in and around the penalty area.

INITIAL SET-UP:

- Two centre-backs and goalkeeper versus two strikers in the penalty box.
- Four feeders playing with the attacking team.
- Four gated goals set up around the edge of the box.

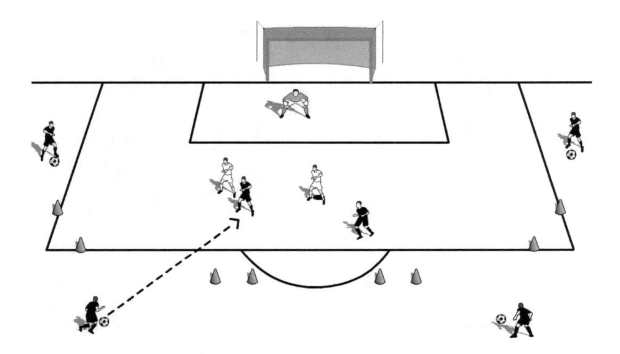

INSTRUCTIONS:

- Feeders take it in turns to pass balls into strikers for them to score a goal. Defenders and the goalkeeper look to stop strikers scoring.
- **TRANSITION:** Once defenders regain possession, they must dribble through any of the gated goals. They must then recover quickly as the Blacks mount another attack.

Using the sessions above as an example, can you list the inherent football actions that we discussed as part of the *Replicate the Game* section above?

Players will jog, run, and sprint forwards, backwards, laterally and change direction frequently. They will also walk and have moments when they are standing still. They will jump, sprint, and arc their bodies when moving, with elements of Agility, Balance and Coordination. They will compete physically against others – hold opposition players off, race against them, look to get their body in front of them, etc. They will fall over (or have to stop themselves from falling over) and get back to their feet quickly. They will use the opponent to make decisions about physical actions – chase, change direction, use body feints and movements to throw opponents off. They will foul or resist being fouled. The list is, in fact, almost endless – and, critically, *the ball is rolling* for the duration.

The Need for Speed?

The game of football is getting more physical – and it is getting quicker. The bodies, (physically and physiologically), of high-level players who make a living from the game, are becoming more finely tuned. Diet, training load, and discipline dominate the off-the-pitch lives of modern players.

It is now relatively normal to have a checkbox on a youth scouting report that refers to a player's speed or pace. At some clubs, having speed is enough to get you in the door – everything else can be taught, according to those involved. Such is the value of speed, youth coaches and recruitment officers can often now be found wandering the athletic clubs and 100m tracks of their vicinity. Upon retirement from athletics, world-record sprinter Usain Bolt, well into his 30s, received offers from all over the world to play professional football (although this may have had as much to do with media exposure, and 'brand', than gaining a football player).

Ironically, though, there lies a juxtaposition. As we enter an era where the boundaries of pace and power are being surpassed in the game, we are seeing 'non-physical' players making a huge mark. In 2018, the diminutive Luka Modric won the Ballon d'Or as the best player in the world. He was both an essential cog in the machine that took the Croatian National Team all the way to the World Cup Final, and the focal point for his club team, Real Madrid, as they triumphed in three consecutive Champions League Finals, winning four of the five available titles between 2014 and 2018.

The central point here is that while the game is becoming quicker, and the need for players who can hold-up in this physical environment is important, it is not just the big and quick ones who will shine through. The intelligent ones will too, as we will see later in the book.

Remember also that speed can be a product of size and physical power too, which can, in your youth teams, be down to relative age (more on that in the next chapter). The quickest player in your current Under-12 team may not be the quickest by the time that group of players reaches adulthood. As we previously noted with size and strength, speed is relative to one's peers and to the individual development phase of them all. If we are constantly looking to tick the 'speed' checkbox when reviewing a player's ability, our focus is far too narrow.

With the need for speed being at the forefront of many coaches and parents' wish-lists, there can be a tendency to put players on a speed-programme, designed purely to increase a player's speed, in much the same way as a sprinter would train.

However, sprinters train to be as quick as possible over, say, 100 metres, or whatever their centrepiece event may be, and then they rest until they are recharged and ready to go again. In football, sprint distances will vary in length, and will be multi-directional rather than straight-line and require continuous acceleration, and critically, deceleration. Rest-and-recovery times vary in football, in comparison to sprint events and the opportunity for perfect form and technique is severely hampered by opposition players, the ball, changing direction, running one way but facing the other, etc.

You become good at what you train at, and any variation from that set of circumstances will impact negatively on performances. If you train heavily to sprint in straight lines for 40 metres, for example, that is what you will master. However, the game is not *just* about going from point A to point B as quickly as possible. It is about speed of thought, recognising what may develop, and any tactical or game-related cues that may be present. There is no point in being able to run 100mph if you cannot time your runs based on the cues that the game gives us. Sprinting in football is more *than just sprinting from a pistol crack to a ticker-tape!*

Likewise, if players spend their time running laps of the pitch at one tempo, they will improve at exactly that – running around the pitch at one tempo.

Conclusion

The vast majority of the best-known coaches and teams that you see play or train will use isolated fitness sessions with their players. But there is a growing trend away from them, especially with youth players who are still developing. It is worth noting, also, that these coaches and teams will be supported by some of the most qualified sport scientists in the game.

Whilst using the concept of football fitness, as described in this chapter, it is important to note that the physical corner is not simply omitted. The physical development of players at all ages remains very important – but it has to be age-appropriate. We simply should not copy the Coach Carters of this world and base our fitness sessions simply on putting duress on players' bodies. The key takeaway message is that fitness and the physical corner *is embedded in the process*. It is not simply forgotten about – it is simply put into a football context.

Summary

- Football coaches are thieves, stealing and copying sessions and ideas from other coaches. Whilst copying technical practices is one thing, copying physical exercises without basis is dangerous.

- We use the term 'isolated fitness' to refer to fitness-only sessions that contain no other element of the game. The physical actions completed by players during a game do not match the content of isolated fitness sessions.

- Isolated fitness work is not the only way to build team spirit or resilience.

- Sport is losing players due to drop-out. Using football sessions to engage and inspire is necessary to save our game.

- Both the English FA and Dutch FA are keen to point out that fitness training is not a priority under the age of 14-16/17.

- Even doing 20 minutes of non-football exercises per session can lead to players missing out on hours of football over the course of a season.

- If teams are struggling, their fitness is often blamed, although the correlation between distance run and sprints and success is negligible.

- Be aware of whether your players are not fit, or whether they are fatigued.

- The concept of Tactical Periodisation looks to incorporate physical exercises within football training.

- All sessions under TP will have both a physical and tactical element, relating to the Four Phases of the Game.

- Although TP is designed for full-time teams, the lessons can be incorporated into our part-time environments.

- Including transitions and practices, where players are not standing still in straight lines, gives us clear tactical and physical outcomes.

- Football is becoming quicker, meaning that the speed of players is becoming prioritised, often to the detriment of other playing qualities.

- This results in teams recruiting directly from athletics clubs and players being sent for athletics-type speed training, which does not incorporate the multi-directional movements required for football.

It's Your Game #1

Rethinking Conditioning

Brian Shrum • @JustKickinItPod

Coach & Presenter of the *Just Kickin' It* Podcast

During the run-up to the 2014 playoffs, we were in contention for a spot to represent our school in the conference tournament. However, most of our key players were sitting on the bench during training or haggled by some minor injury.

We found that four to five days into the preseason, many players began suffering from muscle strains. We were trying to get through a competitive season with less than optimal performance from the players. It was like trying to drive across the United States as fast as possible in a Corvette, except the vehicle had two spare tyres on the rear-drive axle.

Why were we picking up so many injuries when we did plenty of fitness training? Why were they breaking down so early and so often? Why couldn't they last a season without getting a soft tissue injury? We could have said, "bad luck," but that would not be taking responsibility as a coach.

The answer for us, at that time, was to change pragmatically. A typical week of training consisted of Monday, day off; Tuesday, isolated fitness training followed by a training session; Wednesday and Thursday team training; Friday game; Saturday recovery training; and Sunday game. We had to work around the Friday/Sunday game format. Furthermore, all training sessions lasted, on average, 90-120 minutes.

In the days that followed our Tuesday training, the players seemed to not play at the speed to which we would face in the upcoming games. The connection finally hit me – they were exhausted! Too much training load equals a decrease in the speed in performance.

Our answer was to train *less*, but make sure that we were training at top speed. We traded quantity for quality. We mapped out a new week that consisted of Monday, off day; Tuesday, 50-60 minute session with bigger games to reduce the actions per minute; Wednesday, 75-90 minute session consisting of bigger games to push the fitness boundaries specifically in maintaining actions per minute; Thursday, a 50-60 minute session with smaller numbers to increase the tempo of the game and replicate the speed of decision making.

The new format worked. Feedback from the players was that they felt fresher for games. *Soft tissue injuries were completely eliminated during the 2015 and 2016 seasons.* We did not experience one soft tissue injury for two years! Furthermore, the 2015 season marked the first conference championship ever in school history.

It's Your Game #2

Let's Pick Two Teams

Shane Smith • @ShaneSmith197

Fitness Expert & Author

"You're clearly not fit, that other team was far fitter than you girls. We need to do more running. I will see you all on Tuesday at 7.30pm for the beep test."

The above outburst was from an Under-11 coach following a defeat. First of all, it's important to recognise the wonderful work carried out by volunteers in ensuring children get to train and play on a regular basis. I have no doubt that this was a very well-meaning coach who simply channelled his frustration in the wrong way. On reflection, I am sure that he regretted his outburst. However, blaming fitness for the loss of a game is a very easy conclusion, but often the issue is deeper.

There are a variety of reasons why an Under-11 team lost a game, and fitness is certainly not one. Coaching takes many, many forms, and it's not all about the player. It's about the person. For 11-year-old girls, we should consider this. Having written two theses on gender differences in exercise, I can categorically say that children play sport for two main reasons. One is to meet friends, and two is to have fun. Now, if we know this, I am not sure a fitness test will meet their needs.

As coaches, we must continue to reflect on our practices. In preparing children for games, our role as coaches is not to get them fit, but rather to develop the technical aspects in a fun environment to maximise enjoyment. Our role, as coaches, is to develop a lifelong love of the game where participation matters more than winning. There is nothing enjoyable for an 11-year-old about fitness tests. Every day is an opportunity to learn from mistakes and even failures. Every day is a school day.

One of the first questions we should ask ourselves after every training session is, did the players make a minimum of 300 ball contacts? And if not, why not? There is often a traditional, deep-rooted fascination with fitness and running. When, in fact, the fascination should be on skills and match situations. By this, I mean ensuring every player trains as they play – with the ball! Here are a few magic words that players love to hear at training, "Let's pick two teams and play a match."

Chapter 9
Age & Development

"

No correlation exists between the average
height of teams and results achieved.

CIES Football Observatory

Scotland failed to qualify for the 2018 World Cup. Then Head Coach, Gordon Strachan, himself a diminutive former midfielder, grumbled that Scottish players were "genetically behind" other nations, and offered their lack of height and physicality as *the* major reason for their shortcomings. During qualifying, the Scots were the second smallest team. Unfortunately for Strachan, the shortest group was the magnificent Spain!

In the same year, CIES Football Observatory conducted a test spanning 36 European leagues, analysing the average height of each team. As the quote above bluntly outlines, they found *no correlation between the height of a team and their results at adult, first-team level.* A team's height was more a reflection of the style used by teams, according to CIES, with 'giants' Manchester City and Barcelona amongst the shortest, and Roma and Schalke amongst the tallest.

Unfortunately, in kid's football, *there is* – or at least there is a perceived – correlation between the results of a team and the size of its players – and the younger they are, the more pronounced this can be. This is why coaches who put winning before all else veer towards the physically more developed players – the so-called "early developers". If you want to give your pre-pubescent team the greatest chance of winning *now*, then you pick the big kids.

Even for the more honest coaches amongst us, judging players based on size is common, if not intentional, and leads us to one of football's, and sport's greatest phenomena – birth bias.

Relative Age Effect

"

Pre-maturation Talent ID is a myth. It is also
immoral and, quite possibly, illegal.

**Stuart Armstrong,
The Talent Equation (@stu_arm)**

I see tweets now on a weekly basis, offering trials and talent ID camps to pre-pubescent kids. The tweets are either from clubs or coaches offering trials, or from others who are bemoaning the practice. Amongst the advertising and the blowback from the practice, there is very little evidence that supports the early identification of players. In fact, trialling and judging players *too young* merely weakens our whole football system. Long term, we significantly lose copious numbers of talent by selecting so early.

Prior to the 2018 World Cup, Belgian youth coach and administrator, Bob Browaeys, suggested that the country is losing a quarter of its potential pool of players due to a continued preference for players born in the early part of the selection year.

Several times in this book, we have looked at the pitfalls of an over-focus on physical traits too early in the young footballer's journey. At younger ages, the most effective players are often the ones who are maturing earlier than others in the group. To the untrained eye, player X is better, when really all he is doing is relying on pace, power, and strength to overcome opponents.

I have seen both sessions and games – at grassroots *and* academy level – where a physically dominant player is able to recover his poor technical play by simply leaning into and often knocking over his compatriots. The player with longer limbs can stretch and recover their poor touch before it becomes detrimental to his team or his performance. By consistently having this advantage, he (ironically) is not in an environment to improve and he may potentially enter adult football with poor technique and diminishing physical advantages to help him recover. This size advantage will level out in time meaning, in the long run, he may not be the 'best' player in that group, although he helps his team to win matches as a kid.

The central premise of Relative Age Effect (RAE), therefore, is that coaches and selectors, often *unintentionally,* select players that were born in the early parts of the selection year.[1] What you then find, over time, is that squads end up filled with players born in the first quarter or half year.

Example 1 – U17 European Championships

In the summer of 2019, the European Under-17 Championships were held in Ireland, of which 16 teams competed to be crowned Champions of Europe for those born in 2002 and beyond. Laura Finnegan (@finnegan_laura), an expert on RAE and talent development in sport, dug deep into the birth dates of those competing, and unearthed some astonishing numbers:

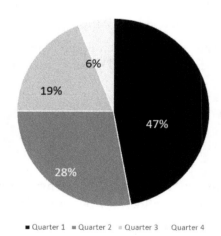

■ Quarter 1 ■ Quarter 2 ▨ Quarter 3   Quarter 4

Of the 344[2] players who had played more than two games in qualifying for the tournament, 47% were born in the first quarter of the year (January – March) and only 6% in the fourth quarter (October – December).

---

[1] In most of the world, football age groups are run along the calendar year (January – December). In England, these age groups are run along school year lines (September – August).
[2] 330 of the players were born in 2002, with 14 born in 2003.

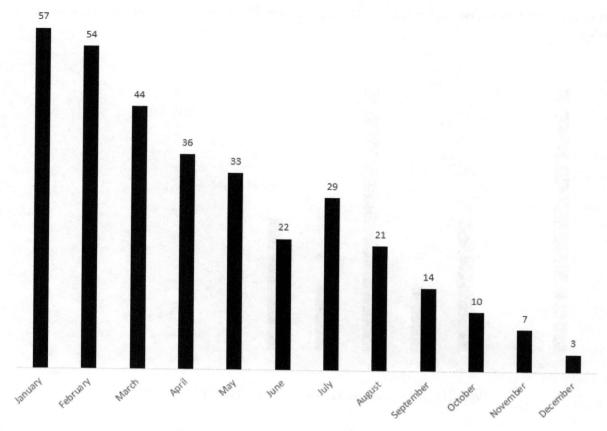

57 were born in January, while only three were December-born

Other birth-related statistics identified by Finnegan[3] included:

- The number of fourth quarter birthdays were the lowest in all 16 squads.

- Over 85% of Portugal's squad was born in the first half of the selection year, whereas over 60% of the Netherland's title-winning squad was born in quarter one.

- Only one of Italy's 24-man squad and one of Belgium's 23-man squad was born October – December. The 20-man Russian squad did not contain a single player from quarter four. These three, along with four other nations, had no 2003 representatives at all.

- When all 344 players were grouped by playing position, all positions were found to have a birth bias towards quarter one born players.

- Only Hungary had any sort of balance with 11 players born in the first half of the year, and 12 in the second (although their quarter four was still the least represented. Quarter three was their most represented).

Example 2 – Chelsea Under-18s

In July 2018, an unaffiliated Chelsea FC social media account (@chelseayouth) released a short montage video of the club's new scholarship intake (In England, at 16, players that make the step from part-time players attending school, to full-time players training within the club, are often known as 'scholars' due to the education element of the programme). There are 14 players in this

---

[3] For further detail, statistics and diagrams in relation to Relative Age Effect at this tournament, go to talentdevelopmentinirishfootball.com

montage, born between September 2001 and August 2002; their birth months spread out as below:

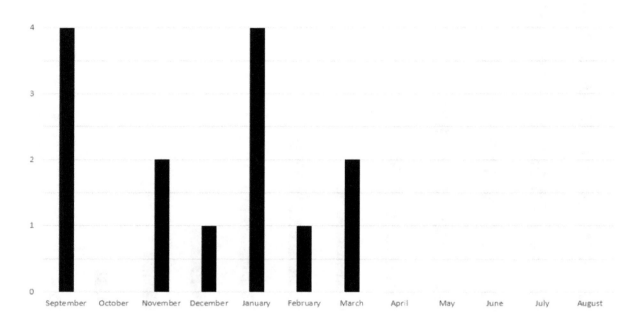

Birth Month Distribution, Chelsea FC First Year 'Scholars', 2018

The first thing that jumps out from the graph is that none of the 14 were born in the final five months of the English selection year. Seven of them (half the group) have birthdays between September and December (the oldest in their year group in England). However, further reinforcing the heavy presence of birth bias in this instance, five of the seven that were born January–March were brought up in a football system where the year runs from January to December (Germany, France, Holland, Northern Ireland, and the USA). In total, over 85% of this group were born in the first four months of their respective selection year(s).

Evidence from the Professional Game

In a further study of the top 1,000 players playing in elite football (based on transfer value[4]), the legacy of RAE remains evident. In a random sample of a group of 100 people, you would expect a 25%+/- spread across the four quarters of the year. Of the top 100 most valuable players in this study, 59 were born in the first half of the year, rather than 50, and only 15 born in the final quarter, rather than 25. Only five were born in December (there were *no* August-born English players on the list) – Karim Benzema, Gonzalo Higuaín, Alexis Sánchez, Santi Cazorla and Seydou Doumbia – way below average. There were 12 born in January, significantly above average.

Inspired by Malcolm Gladwell's *Outliers*, data analyst Mohammed Hemayed (@mhmdhmydsd) investigated Relative Age Effect across ten of the top footballing nations in the world. Although England's September–August selection year skewed his data, he found strong evidence of RAE across all nations. The birth distribution of professional footballers from Argentina, Spain, Germany, France, the Netherlands, Portugal and Belgium showed a bias towards first quarter born (around a third of their players, rather than a quarter which 'should' be the average).

---

[4] Full title of study: *Relative Age Effect in Elite Soccer: More Early-Born Players, but no Better Valued, and no Paragon Clubs or Countries,* by John R. Doyle and Paul A. Bottomley. Available online.

Professional players from Brazil, however, displayed a massive 68% of their professional footballers who were born between January and March – an outlier in itself, but no less shocking.[5]

> "
>
> The problem is that youth coaches are too focused on winning rather than developing players. That has to change.
>
> Look at the birth dates of players in the youth teams here in Belgium. There are still too many born in the first few months of the year. We are still missing talent and I am convinced it still remains as much as 25%.
>
> "
>
> **Bob Browaeys, Belgian FA**

This problem, however, does not *start* with European Under-17 teams, with Chelsea at Under-18, or at the top level of the game in Brazil, France, or Argentina – the problem simply *manifests itself there*. It does, in fact, start much earlier. From the earliest ages, clubs and coaches at all levels (but not *all* clubs and coaches), including both grassroots and academy structures, gravitate towards the 'older' players in the selection year. By the time they reach the age where selection for elite or representative squads is being made, the 'older' players will have played more, trained more, and – once selected for further, 'better' squads – will have received better coaching, are coached more often, and are pitted against better players. All this contributes to aggregated developmental advantages over time. While the older players are on an upward curve, a lot of the younger ones are spending more time on the bench, playing in 'B' squads, or dropping out of the game altogether.

The Underdog

Amongst all these early-born players, however, are the late-born underdogs. Mesut Özil is October-born, Marco Verratti and Philipp Lahm were born in November, and Iker Muniain in December. Alex Oxlade-Chamberlain has an August birthday (the last month of the English system). Later-born players *do survive*. Although RAE is widely evident, it does not mean that later-born players simply do not exist, just like not *all* early-born players will become elite; and not all players with January birthdays grow up dwarfing their teammates (David Silva, Eden Hazard, Luis Suárez and Toni Kroos, are four such examples).

The silver lining for those born in the latter part of the year often goes unnoticed. If you are a player born in the last quarter, and you manage to persevere in the system, it can provide advantages. First of all, you learn to fight. You learn to 'mix it' with older players and are required to solve problems technically and tactically and through clever, intelligent play, rather than by brute force. By the time adulthood comes around, at a stage when physical differences are less pronounced, these players will be able to compete physically but will have excellent technique and game understanding too. Lots of professional players, especially those from generations where street football proved popular, credit a huge part of their development to playing and competing (and struggling) against their older brother/sisters and his or her mates. We saw in an

---

[5] https://public.tableau.com/profile/mohammed.hemayed~!/vizhome/TheStoryofSuccess/TheStoryofSuccess

earlier chapter how struggle can be a factor in attaining glory. Players develop grit and excel because of it. This is known as the "underdog hypothesis".

"

"

In our cul-de-sac, I pretended to be exactly like [John] Barnes – skilful and unplayable, a dribbling machine and a scorer of wonder goals against my big brother Paul and his mates who were between three and fives years older than me. They tackled hard and sometimes brought me down, making my knees bleed. I just got up, refusing to cry, and became John Barnes all over again.

Steven Gerrard

Harry Kane

As the 2018 World Cup drew to a close in Russia, standing atop the goal-scorer charts was 'young'[6] English striker, Harry Kane. At the time, he had scored over 100 goals for Tottenham Hotspur. A few weeks after the World Cup ended – on 28th July – Kane turned 25. He is one of the hottest properties in global football – even with a 'late' birthday. Kane's rise to the top, however, was far from conventional; you could say he battled RAE all the way there.

Before puberty, Kane had been trialled and released from Arsenal, Tottenham, and Watford, with physical reasons cited on more than one occasion. Even when he did make the breakthrough and signed formally for Tottenham, the club's ex-Academy Director, Alex Inglethorpe, now in the same position at Liverpool, commented that even at 13, Kane was still "playing catch-up from a physical perspective" and at 14, he felt that Kane was "middle of the group" – i.e. he was not one of the best players, or one of the worst. Tottenham, however, saw his long-term potential and stood by him.

Kane's predecessor in the main striker's role, for the England team, was Wayne Rooney. The former Everton frontman made his debut in the Premier League at 16, his England debut at 17, and secured a multi-million-pound transfer to Manchester United shortly before turning 19. Conversely, in his late teens and early twenties, Kane was sent on various loans to teams in the lower divisions. He scored a mere 14 goals spanning 56 appearances for four different clubs. There is a wonderful photo of both Kane and Jamie Vardy, soon to be two of the hottest strikers in the Premier League, sitting on Leicester City's bench as they entertained Watford in a 2013 play-off just to gain promotion to the Premier League.

With physical issues to the forefront, Kane had to rely on what he is now famous for (beyond his goalscoring) – his work rate and the ability to get shots away quickly to avoid physical contact where possible. He anticipates well and is comfortable dropping to find space, again, away from crowded areas.

There are the Rooneys of this world who burst onto the scene early, and the Kanes of this world who need time, understanding, nurturing, and … patience.

---

[6] Although Kane was approaching 25 at the World Cup, the public still views him as 'young' due to his late appearance on the highest stage, in a similar way to Manchester United's Jesse Lingard.

While the stats around relative age are pretty damning, we must also acknowledge that amongst the physical differences between kids born in the early part of the year compared to the late-borns, there are also individual cases of bias. Just because you are a quarter four player, it doesn't mean you are underdeveloped. You may still be amongst the physically biggest in the group. And just because you are quarter one born, it won't make you a physical giant.

" **"**

I went to Spurs when I was 11. It wasn't like it took off straight from then; I still had to work hard. There were highs and lows along the way. As I got older, I caught up to the rest of the players my age and went from there.

Harry Kane

Antoine Griezmann

At the time of writing, March-born Antoine Griezmann is the sixth most valuable player in the world, according to the highly-rated 'market value' section of transfermarkt.co.uk. He is the highest-ranked French player, just ahead of Ousmane Dembélé (ninth), N'goglo Kanté (eleventh), and Paul Pogba (eighteenth). He is, at 28, considered the best French player in a squad that had just won the World Cup – the best player in the best national team in the world.

However, rewind back to Griezmann's teenage years, and things did not look so rosy. He was used sparingly in the French youth system and was 23 before making his senior debut for *Les Bleus*. As a kid, while playing for his hometown club, he had trials with several French-based academies, but was frequently turned away, with coaches highlighting his lightweight frame as one, if not *the* main, reason. Auxerre, Lyon, Montpellier, Saint-Etienne, and Sochaux were among those who turned down his signature before his 14th birthday.

A freak opportunity, however, was to present itself in the form of the Basque region which straddles France and its southern neighbours, Spain. A scout from La Liga club Real Sociedad saw him playing in a trial game for Montpellier against Paris Saint-Germain and took him across the border. Eric Olhats, the scout in question, allegedly took 10 minutes to decide that he was worth taking to San Sebastian, telling CNN: "The first time I saw him my attention was drawn to the technique he had, the fluidity of his technique. He was very short, but his technique was marvellous." Olhats saw beyond the obvious. *He identified talent.*

" **"**

It was very difficult for Antoine – a little short-ass who wasn't very fast. It must have hurt him too when they [the rejecting clubs] said he was too small.

**Alain Griezmann,
Antoine Griezmann's dad**

Like Kane, the struggle (in the long term) can be seen as doing Griezmann good, although during his early teens the experience was far from easy, as can be seen by the tone and tears of both the French international and his father during the Netflix documentary *Antoine Griezmann: The Making of a Legend*. The diminutive forward is so comfortable in possession, yet so comfortable out of possession, and was both a worker and a quality component in an Atletico Madrid team that's based on its organisation and fighting spirit (before his move to Barcelona). He calmly took and scored a vital penalty for France against Germany during the 2016 European Championships, despite missing a penalty in the Champions League Final weeks earlier. This was a big moment in the match for the French as Germany had the upper hand. Arsène Wenger credits him with having the 'hardness' that Academy-produced forwards tend to lack. We are given further clues to this spirit, mental toughness, and 'bounce-back-ability' throughout the Netflix film.

The underdog spirit of both Kane and Griezmann is certainly a lesson for young players, but more so for coaches and those working in football. How many Kanes do we force out of the game due to size? How many Griezmanns are not given a chance despite their easily acknowledged technique?

"

Many youth academies claim to be great talent identifiers and point to the results of a foundation all-star team as proof. Yet they aren't talent identifiers. They are talent selectors. The difference couldn't be more striking, or maybe, more damaging.

**Jorg van der Breggen
(@JvanderB78), KNVB**

"

People will forever argue over the 'ground zero' location of RAE. Some lambast academies for it; others insist it begins at grassroots. Some would say that RAE goes to work as soon as kids begin formal play. The challenge for all of us, however, is to become talent identifiers, rather than talent selectors. We need to give time and patience to players whether they are late-born like Kane, or just physically late-developing, like Griezmann. Amongst this great concern for the little, late-maturing boys and girls, we must also show some concern for those early-maturers who are rampaging around pitches winning us games throughout their childhood and early teens.

Up and Down

The 'best' players, when I was a kid, played up an age group, or they played with both their age-group and the one directly older than them. They could handle it technically, tactically, psychologically and, more often than not, physically. If you are a frequent reader of biographies of former high-level professional players, there is usually a reference to playing 'up' in formal clubs or playing with and against their older siblings or older, and bigger neighbours when they play in the street, like Steven Gerrard outlines above.

The impact of playing players with, and against, older youngsters can help drive the 'Underdog Theory'. When playing with and against older ones, there is struggle. It can build a strong mentality, a strong body, and it requires players to adapt technically to their environments. While the big one has the luxury of being able to recover from poor technique, the little one doesn't. He is forced to be technically on-point. The little one playing street football will need to find space and move the ball quicker so he is not physically overpowered. He will implicitly work on his ABCs (Agility, Balance, Coordination, Speed) as avoiding physical contact, slaloming tackles, and ensuring you don't come crashing to the ground frequently becomes essential.

In *The Sports Gene*, author David Epstein provides us with research that younger siblings are disproportionately the ones who become the best in the sports arena. In one study, conducted by the United States Soccer Federation, they found that 95% of their national female players aged 13-23 had siblings (national average is 75-80%) and that 75% of those had older siblings.

Younger siblings have a childhood of pushing themselves to match the physical power of their older brothers or sisters, while the older ones are essentially spending years playing 'below' themselves when competing with their younger siblings. Competitiveness becomes the norm. The younger one's body and mindset are constantly pushed to the limits through deliberate play, becoming conditioned and attuned to a high level of performance and competition. Those of you who witness older and younger siblings 'play-fighting' will no-doubt note the familiar facial expression on the younger one's face – pure determination, struggle, challenge, and a willingness to get one over the older brother or sister! It has also been suggested that later-born children become more competitive in school and in sport to win favour from parents and teachers.

"

Competing is about matching one's talent, intelligence and skill against a *worthy* opponent. That opponent is not the enemy, but an ally in the learning journey.

"

Todd Beane

To Move or Not to Move

Playing a player 'up' an age-group can accelerate their development in many ways, so long as they can handle it appropriately and it is the *best decision for the player*. Paul McGuiness (@Paulmcg8), who we will meet again later, describes how a 12-year-old Marcus Rashford would train with 18-year-old Paul Pogba and Jesse Lingard. Too often, however, players are blocked from playing up because their coach wants to keep 'their' best players in 'their' team, normally to win more matches. As we have discussed earlier, this attitude towards winning is a flawed one. I would whole-heartedly encourage coaches to freely allow players to make this move, even if it threatens your result without him or her on game day. Having a good, working relationship with the coaches above and below you should allow a reasonable amount of flow through your football system.

It may be the best thing for Player A to move to a higher age-group entirely. I personally had a player in Africa who we *had* to move up. He was 14 at the time, would play anywhere in the front four positions (striker, number 10, both wings, and often floating around this area). This team was winning games where he would score freely – often in threes and fours. There were games where he fell below his general all-round level but would still score twice! I was trying to speak to him about improving his game and he was looking at me thinking "I've scored a million goals this season – what do you want from me!?!"

His teammates, although apart of a winning team, were actually suffering too. They soon realised that even if they gave him a bad pass, he could make something of it. Midfielders, instead of being precise, would just pass in his general direction, knowing that eventually he would win the battle and find the net. Defenders and goalkeepers, if they felt pressure when building from the back, would launch the ball in his direction, satisfied that something could come from it. By the time the clock hit 60 minutes, most games were over as a contest, so the opposition's motivation would decrease and the game became too easy. The game he was playing, and the game the others were playing, was too easy, and ultimately not of any great benefit to anyone. By moving him up an age-group (in fact, it was a double age-group due to our structure) he benefitted from a greater challenge, even though his goal count decreased, *and* the players in his natural age-group also had a greater challenge of solving match-related problems without their safety-net.

For Player B, however, moving *temporarily* from one age-group to the other might be better. It is all about finding that 'sweet-spot' where players are comfortable, but uncomfortable; content, but stressed. He may be exceptional in his own age-group but take time to find his feet playing with, and against, older ones. This may be a technical, tactical, psychological, physical – or social reason. One player that comes to mind (he played in the same team as Player A) played up every few weeks. Although physically he was very dominant in his own age-group, socially he was not ready to play in a team that was two years older. He was very easily influenced, and, as you know, 16-year-old conversations are very different to 14-year-old ones![7]

Player C, who will probably be most of your age-group, will be the one that is challenged and finds benefit in playing in his natural age-group. It is imperative that these decisions are made on an individual basis, with all elements of PPSTT in mind.

I speak to coaches frequently on this matter, and many problems around playing up are pointed out. On top of the issues that over-zealous, territorial coaches can cause around letting go of the player, it is often complained that the player is not the same once he plays back at his natural age-group – he loses motivation when he plays down again. Parents and other players wonder why A is playing up, but C is not, and start to complain and put pressure on the coach. In the US, especially, the headline of their child playing up could lead to favourable college offers, etc. A coach with a lot of good players cannot send five or six up, and the coach above cannot take five or six as he has players there, already. The older coach may not want younger players disrupting *his* winning season. It can create friction in all manner of ways, but there are some solutions.

First of all, a club understanding of this issue, long-term player development, PPSTT, and a good working relationship between coaches is important. But arguably the most important one is communication between the club/coach and the player/parent. "We are moving Player A up permanently as he needs to be challenged more technically because... tactically because... physically because... etc. We would expect, however, that should he fall back into his natural age-group that he brings back with him his quality, learning, and maturity." "We want Player B to play most of his football for his natural age-group but move him up to the older boys for X period or Y number of games. His main team will be his natural age-group, but we would like to see how he fares with and against older players." And, finally, *always be willing to reverse a decision*, but for the right reasons.

″　　　　　　　　　　　　　　　　　　**″**

I was 5ft 5in until I was 16, when I grew six inches. I was quite small, quite petite. I think the way I have done it [become a professional player] has made me who I am because when I was young I had to play with men. That made me quite strong and quite physical.

Michail Antonio

Former Manchester United player and coach, and current National Coach Educator with the FA, Paul McGuinness, is a major advocate of mixing age-groups. Earlier in this book, we looked at

---

[7] He went on to be signed by a club who drafted him straight to under-19s as a 15-year-old. What ensued were major problems with behaviour, application, and motivation.

Marginal Gains, although McGuiness believes that mixing age-groups is a "massive gain", outlining some major positives for it below:

Benefits for Younger Players
• Allows them to collaborate with more skilled players within their *Zone of Proximal Development*
• Introduces them to skills that are too complex or difficult to do with players of the same age
• Older, more skilled players provide 'scaffolds' that raise the levels of the younger children's play
• Provides them with 'models' to copy
• They are 'privileged spectators' – watching from the pitch
• Perceptual learning by "osmosis" is automatic and self-correcting – learning without thinking
• Provides them with additional care, protection, and emotional support
• Creates a 'Band of Brothers' theme
Benefits for Older Players
• Older players can expand their understanding through teaching
• Develops their leadership skills
• Develops their capacity to protect and nurture young players
• Allows more opportunity for experimentation and creativity

Benefits of Age Mixing for Younger and Older Players, Paul McGuiness

Playing Down

" Look after the late developers. "

Kris Van Der Haegen, Belgian FA

If navigating the playing up terrain looks difficult, let us present something that is even more fraught with the possibilities of disagreement and disgruntlement – players playing *down* an age group.

Establishing a policy where the relevant players can play down is, and will always be, a tough sell. There is huge potential for players and parents to take a suggestion like this very badly, and even the mention of it could decrease confidence, motivation and even personal relationships between the coach and the player/parent – and there are also league rules to navigate, too!

Once again, a decision like this should be done for the right reasons and communicated clearly to all those involved. If the physical struggle is manageable for them at their own age-group, even though they may not be a 'top' performer, leave them be. Don't rob them of their underdog development, but make sure their game-time is sufficient to drive this. If they are really struggling, however, and you can see spots of potential that just need the opportunity to be showcased, then the option to move them down an age-group may be the best decision for their long-term development – although remaining a tough sell to player and parent!

The best cases I have seen of this working effectively is when all parties understand and are on board. My first experience of this was when I took over an Under-16 Academy team. During the warm-up of my first session, my assistant took me to one side and asked who I felt was standing out. The wry smile on his face suggested he knew my answer. One player immediately stuck out in terms of technique but, most of all, desire. Everything he did with the ball, and everything he did off the ball, was done with full focus, full effort, and full enthusiasm. This was his first session back with his natural age-group, having spent the previous season playing with the Under-14s rather than the Under-15 group. He was physically small – a late developer – but had the "heart of a lion" my assistant proclaimed. Not only did this boy go on to earn a two-year youth contract, he went on to sign professionally for the club.

As my first experience of this, it gave me a little shock. How must the player have reacted? How did he take what could be viewed as a setback by many, and come out the better for it? At the end of the season, I asked him just that. His mature response was that it was "the best thing for me" – a reply which complemented his attitude, but also what must have been excellent and careful communication from the club and its coaches.

It is my view that all youth leagues should have a system where older players can play down, even if this is restricted to two or three in any one match squad. This system will no doubt be abused by the 'win at all costs' guys, who draft in older players to win games, but the rest of us can use it effectively. Those guys will get their little thrill from abusing the system, but we will claim the moral high-ground and be proud of using the concept of playing down for the long-term development of players.

This allows late-born or physically under-developed players the chance to compete at a physical level that is more ideal for them. It allows them to showcase their ability that is hidden behind a wall of difficulty. Remember, if someone is a late-born (say, December) she will be closer in age to many of the age-group below her than her current team. If RAE is prevalent, she will be closer in age to the January to April cohort of the age-group below, than the January to April cohort of her own group. The reality, however, sees us judge her earlier and against different standards than by which we judge everyone else.[8]

If the thought of pulling a parent and player to one side and suggesting he or she play down an age-group is enough to fill you with dread, it is good to have a trailblazer illuminate the path – someone who you know, they know, and who came out the other side of it stronger.

Jesse Lingard

If you search Google or social media for pictures of Jesse Lingard, you will come across the 15-year-old playing for Manchester United's Academy against Italian giants, Roma. In the picture, taken during the *Nike Cup*, there are three Italian opponents surrounding the Englishman, and it certainly does seem like the land of the giants. He was dwarfed by their size and physique, although all of them were 15 at the time. It was men against boy.

---

[8] RAE expert Steve Lawrence (@SteveLawrence) showed a brilliant visual example in a presentation for Soccerex's Global Convention, a presentation that can be found on YouTube. He shows a picture of a baby who is a couple of weeks old, 'stuck' in the foetal position, versus a 10 or 11-month-old toddler who is starting to find his feet. Both will end up in the same selection year for sport and school!

Lingard joined the Academy at Man Utd as a young boy, but by the time he was an Under-18, he still was physically very much behind his peers, although with a December birthday, relative age had nothing to do with it. He was simply a small one! Instead of playing with the Under-18s, the club made the decision that he would play with the Under-16s instead. Although Lingard is often seen smiling, dancing, and generally enjoying himself (something he makes no apologies for), you can imagine the impact this may have had on him – or any teenager of that age. The 16-18-year age band is a very big one socially. As you approach 18, you are let off the leash more by your parents; you are preparing to drive, vote, and leave second-level education. And here he was… being sent back to play with the 'kids'.

Crucially, however, he did so with the entire backing of the coaching staff at the club – even from Sir Alex Ferguson. Patience was preached by Ferguson and the whole United staff to both the player and his family. It is believed that even as a pre-teen, skill coach René Mulensteen would reserve some extra time after training to speak to his family to ensure that they understood a) how much the club believed in him, and b) the need for patience.

"

Honestly, I don't think I'd be here if it weren't for Sir Alex. If it weren't for the main man. One day he had a meeting with me and my family. He sat us down in his office and he said: "It's going to take a while for you, Jesse. We believe in you. But you're going to have to be patient. You're not going to be ready for the first team until you're 22 or 23."

"

Jesse Lingard

Like Kane and Griezmann above, Lingard was well into his twenties before he made his breakthrough with the Manchester United first team. If a club of the size and resources of Manchester United – who can cherry-pick the best players in England, Europe, and even further afield – can invest time and trust in a skinny kid who was the smallest boy on most pitches, then I am sure that modest grassroots or community clubs in London, Denver, Sydney, Beijing, or Johannesburg could do the same.

Bio-Banding

Playing individual players up or down may be something that works for certain individuals, in certain circumstances, but what more can be done, systematically, to help combat players being selected based on size, maturity, or Relative Age Effect?

One potential way that has been proposed is the use of 'bio-banding'. In its most basic premise, players are grouped in terms of their 'biological age', rather than their 'chronological age', as is the staple for youth development. Biology then, rather than date of birth, becomes the separation tool we use to group players. Here, we analyse all the players and re-group all of them as necessary, rather than as individuals moving here or there.

There is, however, a common misunderstanding around bio-banding that first needs to be clarified. Without fully understanding or scrutinising the concept, one could believe that it is about grouping players around their current size. However, *players are not grouped by current height alone*. It is not a case of lining players up and putting the bottom of the line in a little person's game, and the top of the line in a big person's game. With the long-term development of players in mind, as always, this simplistic version simply creates a falseness. No matter what, players will *always* have to deal with some sort of physical mismatch, even in the adult game, so eliminating it completely is counter-productive.

From a social point of view, grouping players on current size alone, could create problems. A 16-year-old may end up banded with a group of 13-year-olds which would have a negative impact on his social and psychological skills, and likewise younger players placed with a group several years older than them might suffer. The maturation that we consider is related to the whole player, not just their physical attributes. We mentioned in an earlier chapter that the categories that we consider when player profiling (PPSTT) are all interlinked, and need to be viewed as a whole, not just in isolation.

Secondly, bio-banding does not completely replace teams based on age-groups – it is designed to work alongside it. In some Premier League programmes, for example, one-off bio-banding competitions have been used, but only in parallel to their regular, chronological age competition. An Academy Manager put it succinctly in a recent chat. "We can group players however we want, but it will probably always gravitate back to age-defined competitions. In *our* system, we want to see every player in situations where he is the oldest in the group, and also the youngest, so we are quite happy to manipulate the age-boundaries. Due to busy schedules, this may just be for a few games, certain training sessions or blocks of sessions, but we always find it informative. By doing this, we can judge a player's potential on a range of criteria. Viewing players like this always gives you a surprise – the physically strong kid who is tested so, so hard technically, and the little one who suddenly thrives without the big brutes around him! The lad you think of as 'middle of the pack' suddenly bosses certain games and sessions where he is one of the older ones."

Predicted Adult Height

In a 2016 edition of a Premier League bio-banding tournament, players aged 12-15 from four clubs took part, with the players banded according to their *Predicted Adult Height* – using the *Khamis-Roche* method. Rather than measuring skeletal markers, like using x-rays, for example, this method takes the child's current age, height and weight, and the height of his mother and father to estimate the child's height come adulthood (other factors – nutrition, genetics, health, etc. can lead to inaccuracies – although the average error of the method is less than one inch from childhood to adulthood).

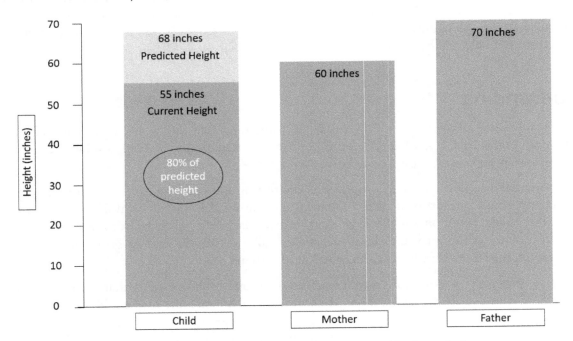

Example result of Khamis-Roche Predicted Adult Height method

Players were grouped into teams where they currently stood at 91-97%, 86-91% and 80-85% of their predicted height. The child above, for example (chart adapted from https://www.infantchart.com/heightpredictor.php) is at 80% of his Predicted Adult Height, so would be grouped in the 80-85% band for that competition.

By using predicted height, rather than current size, there remains a size differential between players, but it is certainly less pronounced, reducing what Sean Cumming, leading international expert on growth and maturation, called "David v Goliath scenarios". The predicted height method then includes size variations amongst players that will still benefit them long-term, but reduce what James Bunce, former Head of Sports Science at Southampton FC and current US Soccer Performance Director, termed the "violent swings of maturity difference within the chronological system."

Benefits

"

Early developers forced to play more technical.
Late developers given the opportunity to show
true ability.

US Soccer

There are obvious benefits of bio-banding for all players. Early developers, or those who are physically 'big' for their age, can no longer rely on sheer power and need to call on their technical and tactical skills to a greater extent. Late developers (or players who just happen to be physically small, like Lingard) can now play in an environment where their lack of size and power is not a hindrance to their performance. They can showcase their skills, their true potential, and not be judged against a biased set of circumstances; potentially, their coaches can see strengths in these players, that might have gone unseen.

There is also the opportunity to develop players socially. Players who are young in their natural age-group may become the oldest and therefore take the initiative around leadership, communication, and teaching the young players about the game.

Flaws

It is worth noting, however, that bio-banding is not the single solution to RAE and physical bias – it has its flaws. In an interview for *Training Ground Guru* (@ground_guru), Dr Sean Cumming pointed out two of them:

"

If a player falls within a specific maturity band
but lacks the technical or emotional maturity to
thrive, he or she would not be encouraged to
play up a level; and if a late developer is already
excelling within their age group, there may be
limited benefit to them playing down.

Sean Cumming, University of Bath

You could add further that the little guy could be getting stressed (in a good way) and improving *because* of the physical struggles within his age-group (provided it is challenging, not impossibly difficult). Also, we have noted the 'Underdog Theory' – that those late-born players who do make it through can be stronger for it. Coaches are therefore encouraged to keep the big picture in mind when re-grouping players, or when identifying, judging, and predicting 'talent'. Patience may be the most important thing, as highlighted above by the plight of Jesse Lingard at Manchester United, something that not many late developers are provided with. Bio-banding is a tool, but not a one-size-fits-all solution. Maybe more patience with players would negate the need for bio-banding – or any other type of banding – altogether.

Conclusion

Once, we thought the age-grouping of our players was so simple; now, it has become so very complex. In previous generations, kids playing street football had the advantage of playing with both older and younger players. Today, however, with this type of street football becoming more and more uncommon in the developed world, it may come down to the work of coaches to promote this type of intrinsic development. This may involve the complicated policies of playing players up, or down, with whatever regularity is seen to work for individual players.

We, as coaches, have to become better identifiers of talent, rather than simply selecting the best players for now. What would all of your players look like if they were amongst the oldest players in a group, and amongst the youngest? What do you see when you watch a skinny mini-Griezmann run around your training pitch?

The drive to build winning teams at the earliest opportunity, and to trial and select players younger and younger, has led to an international bottle-necking of players who were born earlier in the year. Can you imagine how much talent has been cast aside before puberty because children were not effective right away? Even Belgium's system for catching late-developers, which was established in 2008, still misses what Bob Browaeys estimates as 25% of their potential talent pool – a massive number.

There is a growing campaign that any type of talent identification should be dropped until players are at least beyond puberty, in a bid to reduce or diminish the phenomenon of Relative Age Effect. Two of the countries involved in the Under-17 European Championships research earlier in this chapter (and there are most likely other initiatives, too, in other countries) are taking the lead in combatting this. Head of Coach Education at the Belgian FA, Kris Van Der Haegen (@KrisVDHaegen), told me that they have created 'Future Teams' in the country, which caters for late maturers, allowing the late-developers to be integrated at Under-19 level. In Sweden, coach educator Mark O'Sullivan (@markstkhlm) details a growing policy in the country of keeping the system as open for players as long as possible: "As many as possible, as long as possible, as good as possible."

The various football associations around the world can implement as many programmes and policies as they want. However, if you are coaching a youth football team, the solution starts with you.

Summary

- In the adult, professional game, there is no correlation between the height of players and the team's results. Unfortunately, in youth football, there is – and this becomes more pronounced the younger you get.

- There is a bias in football and in many other sports – Relative Age Effect – where those born in the early part of the year are selected above those born in the later part. This will be for maturation reasons, namely physical, but also psychological ones.

- Examples of RAE are present everywhere, but the effect really manifests itself higher up the system – for example during the European Under-17 Championships, with Chelsea FC's Under-18 squad, and within the professional, adult game.

- This bias does not start at the highest level – it starts as soon as we, as coaches, start selecting, trialling, and judging players. The earlier this starts, the greater the opportunity for RAE to fester.

- The silver lining for those born in the latter part of the year often goes unnoticed. If you are a player born in the last quarter (Kane) or you are simply physically under-developed as a kid (Griezmann), and you manage to persevere in the system, it can provide advantages grouped under the *Underdog Theory*.

- Individual players develop at different stages. Kane was well into his twenties before he made an impression at the highest level. His England predecessor, Wayne Rooney was just 16.

- Antoine Griezmann suffered huge rejection as a kid until a scout was prepared to look beyond the now – identifying potential talent, rather than selecting talent for the now.

- Playing able players up an age-group has many advantages, allowing the better/bigger ones to develop their game through "osmosis". There is further evidence of this in sport where those who are successful in the sports arena are disproportionately a second-born in (or later) their family.

- Playing players down is also an option if it is for their long-term benefit. Jesse Lingard at Manchester United was one such example.

- Bio-banding can be seen as one way to help combat RAE and other physical disparities between youth players, using *Predicted Adult Height* as a method of grouping youth players.

It's Your Game #1

Thinking Differently

Nick Levett • @nlevett

Head of Talent & Performance, UK Coaching

It was during a 'working break' on a coaching course a few years ago that the conversation drifted from technique and tactics to a phenomenon in football, and indeed sport as a whole – 'Birth Bias' or Relative Age Effect.

The first interesting thing was that half the room was completely attuned to it, but half the room have never heard of it before!

Even more mind-boggling, however, was that a coach in his thirties, whose wife was pregnant, was animatedly worried about the birth date of his impending child. His wife was due at the very end of August, and he joked about delaying her labour for a few days so that the baby would be September-born rather than August-born!

My thoughts went to my son – a May-born, a fact that made many in the room visibly wince. At the time, only 14% of Premier League football academy players were born between May and August, the latter third of the selection year.

The world of football scouts selects their children from grassroots – from local leagues that play up and down the country. These leagues are often biased already, due to a coach making the 'first selection' of players and deciding who plays and who doesn't. Evidence suggests that it doesn't always mean that quarter 3 and 4 born children don't get to play; it means they might be in teams in lower divisions rather than the top teams. Where do scouts look? Primarily at the top.

However, I'm going to give an alternative view from my own experiences.

Being the smallest or youngest sometimes isn't a disadvantage – it can be really helpful – if you get *in* the system. And that's the challenge. Getting in. However, once you are in the accelerated learning experience, it can be advantageous. My son will be challenged more frequently. He will learn to look after himself physically and learn to overcome older boys by using technique and agility.

Once my son starts playing, I hope the coaches think differently. Will they allow him to develop a mix of skills by giving players the opportunity to play up, or, possibly in my son's case, the opportunity to play down? I want the coach to have patience with my son. This patience is key to it all. Give every kid the same opportunity, not just because they are shaped in a particular way today. I want the coaches to see beyond what is in front of them now, because the long term will look very different.

It's Your Game #2

'Wee' John McGinn

Graeme Mathie • @gmathie82

Head of Player ID & Recruitment, Hibernian FC, SPL

I was in the office at Celtic about 15 years ago when Willie McStay was the Under-18 coach. He came in, holding a pile of team sheets – probably not long after the registration year in Scotland changed from August to January. He made a comment that most of the players in his team used to be born August-October, with very few in the summer. Now, most were born January-March, with very few born in winter.

There was no discussion about Relative Age Effect, but there was an understanding of a shift in the make-up of 'elite' youth squads, and a recognition that there was an enormity of players potentially lost, because they were born in the 'wrong' month.

When I got the opportunity to lead Talent ID & Player Recruitment at Hibs, I wanted to look into this more closely. We exist in a relatively small 'market' in Scotland with some big competitors. If we want to be able to operate effectively, we need to be prepared to do things differently. Within a year, we ran our first '4th Quarter Kids' assessment day. It gave an opportunity for fourth quarter players to come to the Centre, be involved in some testing with the sport science department, take part in sessions with Academy coaches, and play small-sided matches with players closer in age than they were used to.

It was fascinating, and highlighted that RAE isn't just about earlier born players being 'bigger', as there were still many instances of a physical disparity. It allowed us the chance to assess the results against players in the year group down, and to judge whether the players could handle playing with the Academy team a year younger. We invited six players to train and play with the Academy team a year younger for three months, and now most have migrated back to their chronological age level.

We signed John McGinn as a first team player from St Mirren. He was already an established professional, but he tells a great story about his development, sharing it with all the late physical developers and '4th quarter kids' in our Academy when he was here. He was a 4th quarter birthday and also – interestingly – the youngest of three brothers who all played professionally. He talked about the challenges of competing against players in his own age group but who were up to 11 months older. He used to be called 'wee McGinn' by opponents – something he detested. I have no doubt that these experiences are factors in the type of aggression, desire and determination he shows in every game in the Premier League now.

Chapter 10
Football Intelligence

" "

Behind every kick of the ball
there has to be a thought.

Dennis Bergkamp

We all know what an 'intelligent' player looks like, don't we? We use the term frequently to describe players with high levels of game understanding, and who have the technical skills to carry out what they are thinking.

Many club and national association development documents refer to the desire to produce "intelligent" players, as well as those with technique, plus athletic and psychological capability. The famous Ajax TIPS model places a huge emphasis on "Insight". The England DNA document aims for their teams to be "intelligent across all Four Phases of the Game – in possession, out of possession, and during both transitions, further including phrases like "selecting the right moments," "consideration of the state of the game," "sense changing moments in the game," and doing these things "instinctively."

'Intelligence', though, as a term, is extremely broad. Traditionally, someone who was intelligent meant that they produced high-level academic work or were 'clever' in a scholastic sense. They would have degrees, and work in jobs that involve problem-solving and being creative.

Just like we have separated 'football fitness' from generic fitness, we can also separate football intelligence from what we generally interpret as 'intelligence'. In *Making The Ball Roll*, we looked at the concept of *Multiple Intelligences*. This was first proposed by Howard Gardner back in 1983 who advocated a wider use of the term, rather than the traditional view where either linguistic or logical skills were deemed intelligent.[1]

---

[1] In 2009, a ninth 'intelligence' was added – 'Existential' (moral) intelligence

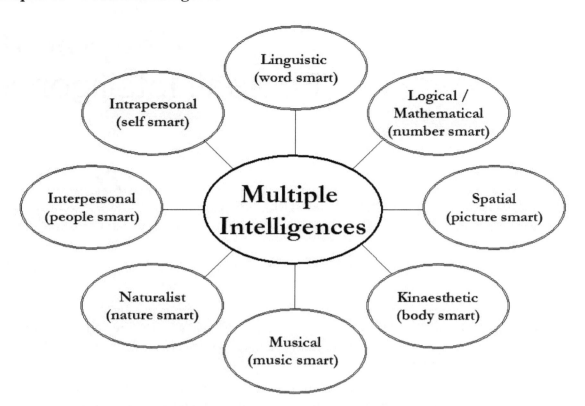

Howard Gardner's 1983 Theory of Multiple Intelligences

Instinctive Intelligence

It is not our job as youth coaches, however, to define and pigeon-hole which of our players is intelligent and who is not – in fact, this is both a dangerous and entirely inaccurate practice. Whether you apply all eight (or nine) of Gardner's intelligences to players is largely irrelevant. The main learning point here is that intelligence is much, much broader and more complicated to define. Some of your players may display poor academic achievement, but have an instinct around the game, developed by playing throughout their childhood and youth.

How intelligence Displays Itself in Football

Three of the most interesting football autobiographies, in my opinion, come from three of the most revered players when it comes to football intelligence – Dennis Bergkamp's *Stillness and Speed*, Andrea Pirlo's *I Think Therefore I Play* and Andreas Iniesta's *The Artist*. Even the book titles suggest that their games are seen on a much more intellectual level than others.

What struck me most about these books was their reasoning behind everything. Pirlo speaks about his search for a space as if speaking to a religious congregation – "A few square metres to be myself. A space where I can continue to profess my creed: take the ball, give it to a team-mate, team-mate scores." Iniesta refers to having almost supernatural powers of seeing what is going to happen in the game – the day before it is played.

One of Bergkamp's career-defining moments was his wonder-goal in the 1998 World Cup against Argentina. If you are not familiar with it, open YouTube, have a look and appreciate. Added to the high technical level of the goal was the state of the game at that moment – it was 1-1 at the quarter-final stage, with little more than seconds remaining in the match. In fact, further highlighting his thoughtfulness about the game in general, he speaks more about his first touch to control the long pass, than the next two touches that allow the ball to end up in the Argentine net.

Bergkamp first refers to his eye contact with Frank de Boer. "There's contact. You're watching him. He's looking at you. You know his body language. He's going to give the ball. So then: full sprint away." After escaping his defender, he goes on to describe the intricacies of what happened next, the continuing use of small sentences adding to the methodological process involved:

"

The ball is coming over my shoulder. I know where it's going. But you know, as well, that you are running in a straight line, and that's the line you want to take to go to the goal, the line where you have a chance of scoring. If you go a little bit wider it's gone. The ball is coming here and you have two options. One: let it bounce and control it on the floor. That will be easier, but by then you are at the corner flag. So you have to jump to meet the ball and at the same time control the ball. Control it dead … You have to take it inside because the defender is storming [the other] way. He's running with you and as soon as the ball changes direction, and you change direction as well, then he's gone, which gives you an open chance.

"

Dennis Bergkamp, *Stillness & Speed*

Bergkamp goes on to describe the rest of the goal, talking about balancing and "standing still" in the air, why he controlled it with the top of his foot, rather than the side, how he judged the wind, and much more. This, remember, is computed in seconds or milliseconds.

Every player you coach will have the potential for football intelligence – whether he or she can articulate it or not. This is why pigeon-holing them as intelligent or unintelligent is dangerous and frankly, wrong. Pirlo or Bergkamp-level descriptions or articulations, or Iniesta-style fortune-telling will not be inside everyone, nor is it necessary.

Often it is perfectly acceptable that players will not or cannot verbalise their thought process. Their game understanding may be inherent, honed from a lifetime of playing and watching the game. I frequently asked a high-level youth player I coached *why* he did certain things, and I cannot remember him ever being able to tell me. I don't even remember him answering a question in a group setting. *He just knew,* and this is a concept that comes up over and over again. I call this *Instinctive Intelligence.* If you feel that your players lack this aspect, or have poor game understanding, the first step is to expose them to the game more. They need to play, of course, but also to watch and analyse.

"

I train to play without thinking.

"

**Marc Roca, Espanyol & Spain U21
midfielder**

Scanning

Geir Jordet is a Norwegian psychologist who carried out much research on the topics of perception and anticipation in football. After watching Frank Lampard playing for Chelsea in a Premier League game, he had the opportunity to ask the midfielder why he scanned or "searched" so much in the moments before he received the ball. Lampard's answer – "I guess I was born with it" – is a characteristically automatic answer that is not untypical of an elite performer, indicating how players often cannot tell you the why behind what they do. It has become instinctive.

Jordet did not pick Frank Lampard at random. In his Masters and Ph.D. studies of the behaviour of players in the moments before they received the ball, he found that Lampard averaged 0.62 'scans' every second – the highest "Visual Exploratory Frequency" in the Premier League at that time (a "very high" score, according to Jordet, is 0.5). Scanning is the term used when we talk about players looking away from the ball to check their surroundings.[2]

"

Very good players scan six to eight times in the 10 seconds before getting the ball, and normal ones three to four times. This is a major step for improvement.

"

Arsène Wenger

The importance of having the most relevant football information available to players before they receive the ball is something that coaches will promote relentlessly. Scanning is the physical means of taking in as much *relevant* information as possible to make the best decision possible.

Jordet split the 250 or so players he researched, using an individual player-cam type analysis, into three groups – low, medium, and high-frequency scanners. His findings showed that players who were high-frequency scanners completed more of their subsequent passes and, drilling deeper, more of their forward passes. Visuals of his findings were presented by Ben Lyttleton (@benlyt) in his excellent book on football leadership, *Edge:*

---

[2] Incidentally, there is a wonderful video of Lampard feverously scanning his surroundings in a 2009 fixture against Blackburn Rovers – ten times in just seven seconds – before receiving the ball, a great and widely used example when showing players.

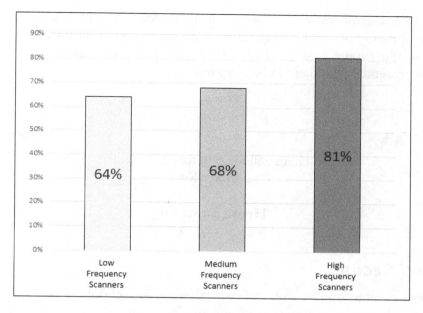

Passes Completed

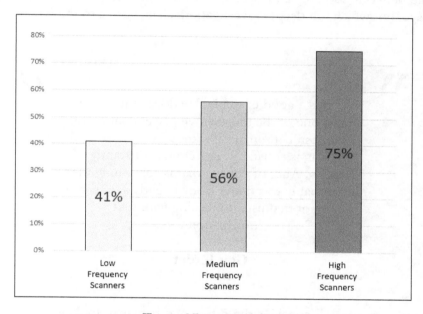

Forward Passes Completed

Furthermore, Jordet's work found that the correlation between scanning and successful *forward passes in the opposition's half* (where the game tends to be 'busier' and, therefore, forward passes are more difficult due to the high stakes nature of the pitch) was pronounced. Low-frequency scanners had a 44% success rate, medium scanners 55%, and high-frequency ones 77%. These statistics, and others that were derived from Jordet's studies, are – according to the man himself – consistent "across situations, across leagues and across levels." The ends justify the means.

From the study, top of the research charts was, unsurprisingly, ex-Barcelona midfielder and game controller, Xavi Hernandez, with a scan average of 0.83 scans per second. Wayne Harrison, who we will meet again later in the *It's Your Game* segment at the end of the chapter, uses further statistics from Xavi as part of his *Soccer Awareness* method. He reveals that the Catalan midfielder looks away from the ball 841 times during a 90-minute game. As is well documented, Xavi was not big, strong, and quick, but was considered 'intelligent' with good positioning, movement to receive the ball, and technique. His style and success with this approach can be seen as having changed the modern game from a physical one to a technical one. Such was his reliance on scanning for information before he received the ball that, if there were occasions where he could not 'scan', he would simply pass the ball back to where it came from. You could argue that scanning was the essential ingredient in Xavi's game.

"　　　　　　　　　　　　　　　　　　　　　　　　　　　　**"**

There will be a 'Before Xavi' and
an 'After Xavi'.

Hristo Stoichkov

Looking and Seeing

One of the most common quips from teachers throughout school, to both my classmates and me, was that "you heard me, but you were not *listening* to me!" It was a statement that sounded contradictory, but one where you knew exactly what was meant. This is the same when we look at the difference between 'looking' and 'seeing' – words that are pretty much interchangeable in everyday language, but which, on deeper investigation, challenge us to think deeper.

"　　　　　　　　　　　　　　　　　　　　　　　　　　　　**"**

Xavi is a good example. He doesn't just look,
he is one of the most active players out there;
he doesn't automatically know what is around
him, is constantly searching, constantly
looking. And, of course, that is something that
he probably was doing from an early age so he's
gotten used to dealing with that
information too.

Geir Jordet

For our purposes here, we will consider the difference between 'looking' and 'seeing' along the same lines as www.differencebetween.net – "looking is turning one's eyes to a certain object, while *seeing is the perception of an object or how a person determines what he is looking at.*"

It is therefore extremely important that footballers are encouraged not just to look, but to see, and to *interpret what they are looking at.*

Players can spend day and night looking around themselves, 'checking their shoulders' and 'playing with rear-view mirrors', but what are they seeing? To further the driving analogy, it is insufficient, and very dangerous, for a motorway driver to just look at his mirrors. If he wants to switch lanes at 100mph, he must decipher whether it is safe to do so. He must calculate the time and distance of the vehicles behind him, and in the other lanes, but also the vehicles in front of him and in the same lane. If the driver does not interpret what he is seeing, he is a risk on the road. For those of us who drive, we can compute these calculations pretty quickly – almost instinctively.

In researching for this particular segment of this book, I did a simple Google search of "scanning sessions in football" and came across a pretty clear problem – they encourage looking, but not seeing. They encourage the physical act of turning your head or eyes away from the ball, but often lack the perception elements. Scanning is also misinterpreted as looking for something behind you. This will, of course, be where major blind spots are, but the scanning is not just something that is reserved for checking what is behind you. Think of a centre-back receiving a backwards pass from a full-back. The most relevant information (Where is the opposition pressure coming from? Can I play a first-time pass to a free player? Where do we overload the opposition? Who is making himself available? Is there space to carry the ball forward?) is most likely in front of him.

The most common session I found was a 'drill' and something I have seen in coach education circles for a number of years, but which has always perplexed me. Three players are placed in a line, maybe ten metres apart. The central player must receive a pass from one outer player, control it, and pass to the other. This continues for a number of minutes. The outer players are then given three different coloured cones or bibs and are asked to hold one of them high before the central player receives the ball. The central player must look behind him and shout the relevant colour aloud, before the ball reaches him. This does, indeed, force the player to scan, and it certainly allows coaches to offer guidance on the most efficient body-shape needed to complete the task with more guile; but you could argue that what they are searching for is irrelevant.

I also came across a small-sided game that asked players to both play a normal game, and to throw another object (a small bean bag) between their teammates simultaneously. So, players who were without the ball had to constantly scan and search for teammates to both throw the bean bag to, and to catch the bean bag from. Like the drill, it is missing arguably the most important element – information that is actually relevant to improving or making better game decisions.

Imagine learning to drive on the motorway, and your instructor asked you to scan your mirrors for birds flying overhead, to check the colour of the van somewhere in the background, or to count the number of trucks you can see. He is asking you to analyse the things that are not relevant to your driving. Sure, he gets you to pay attention to your mirrors and your environment, but the content and the context is insufficient. This is similar to both sessions above. The colour of a cone or the whereabouts of a beanbag is not getting players to *see and analyse* the information they really need – the spaces (both free and crowded), the position and movements of other players (both from your team and the opposition's) as well as other key information markers like the goals, the defence's offside line, and the touchline boundaries. This context is crucial – we want players to see and analyse, not just look.

In the video of Frank Lampard, mentioned earlier, he clearly looks over his shoulder and detects the pretty blatant oncoming presence of the defender. This requires little, but also essential, analytical skills. These "pictures", as Lampard was schooled in by his father, change considerably and quickly in football, hence the amount of scans necessary to gain the most information possible. The striker who is onside now, may be offside in one second. He may be marked, then away from his marker in a flash. Being able to predict these moments comes with practice and developing good habits as we learn the game. To improve them, and make them instinctive, we have to experience the game and all its randomness over and over again. We have to 'see' the game over and over again.

Search – Decide – Execute

"

The problem in football is that you learn to play
the wrong way around – first execution, then
decision-making, and perception last.

Arsène Wenger

It would be fair to say that those players who we consider to be 'intelligent' footballers have a mix of game understanding *and* the technical ability to act on it. Individuals with high levels of game understanding, but who do not have the requisite technical skills to put what they are thinking into action, are at a distinct disadvantage. It is, therefore, a huge plus if we can coach both game understanding and technique together.

Back in Chapter 6, we looked at 'perception-action coupling', but maybe a more understandable, straightforward way of understanding football thought processing is through the action of search, decide, and execute.

In the quote above, Arsène Wenger bemoans the sequence in which traditional coaching has looked to develop players. Most of our work focuses *first* on the execution of certain skills and omits the process in which that execution comes about. The whole concept of my own *Deliberate Soccer Practice* book series was to engrain this idea in our coaching – to work with the execution *and* the precursory elements involved – to work both technique and elements of game understanding. So, rather than passing in straight lines from cone to cone, for example, we use more variable practices in our sessions. The *execution* of certain skills remains hugely important, but is wrapped up with elements of searching and deciding too.

Compromise and Justify

"

Practice is a rehearsal and any rehearsal should
be a 'word for word' run-through of the event.
Football practices should therefore replicate the
things that are likely to happen in a match or
the techniques / skills that are going
to be needed.

FA, *Module 2:*
Developing the Practice course

Any practice that you put on for your players that is anything less than an unrestricted 11v11 game will contain elements of *compromise* with the 'real game'. That does not mean that it is simply enough to play 11v11 games within your practice sessions. To produce technically excellent players, our practices need to involve players having many more frequent contacts with the ball than an 11v11 game allows. Your practice sessions, therefore, require two things – players regularly playing with a ball, and in situations where these contacts are as game realistic as possible. We want more ball contacts and we want more decisions.

Regardless of the type of practices you use in your sessions, it is important to be able to *justify* them. In certain circumstances, you could easily justify the use of any session types, but *recognising and being comfortable with the inherent compromise is essential.* If your sessions are compromising the game too much, too often, are you really coaching football at all?

Over the last number of years, we have seen practice types being broken down into three categories – constant, variable, and random. Within them, there will always be an element of compromise – although some will contain a larger 'trade-off' than others, and will all have an impact on what you are asking players from a football intelligence point of view.

'Constant' Practices

Constant-type practices are ones where players practice the *same technical movements repeatedly.* These moves will generally be practiced over the same distance and conditions, and the exercise will be unopposed. These practices are extremely common, and arguably far more common than they are worth. Because the emphasis is on the repetition of a specific technique, constant practices are best used to help players learn a new technique or develop a specific technique further. Often, these practices are called 'blocked practices' or more disparagingly 'line drills' or 'cone-to-cone' practices given the static nature of their content.

They focus heavily on the *execution* aspect of football, but display very little in terms of searching and deciding. The nature of the practice means that players are told specifically where to pass, move, shoot, etc. They are told where the ball is coming from, and where it needs to go. They don't have to search for any other information and the decision is already made for them by the exercise. The variability of the game is missing, although the repetition of a technique is present.

The sample constant practice below, known as the *Celtic Shooting Drill* due to its origins on the Glasgow club's training ground, and the subsequent variable and random examples will be based around shooting for the sake of convenient comparison.

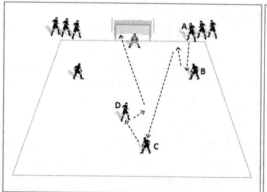

Practice Setup

Ball start with the players to the goalkeeper's left.

Player A plays a one-two with Player B before playing a long pass to Player C.

Player C plays a one-two with Player D before shooting at goal.

All players follow their pass to the next position.

Celtic Shooting Drill – example of a constant practice

In this practice, along with other constant-type practices, there is a huge compromise with the 'real game'. There is no opposition, and there is nothing to influence the players' decisions with regards to what to do with the ball. All players have to pass, move, and shoot from prescribed positions and distances. Player A cannot choose to dribble or move to an open space. He must pass and follow his pass. He is not required to think to any great degree.

The player shooting on goal will be influenced by the goalkeeper's behaviour and start position – to an extent. He or she will decide on their shooting technique based only on what the keeper is doing. In reality, if a player is aiming to score a goal in this situation, with no defenders or the potential for recovering defenders, he would most likely dribble closer to goal and the goalkeeper before making his decision and executing. He is making a decision based on the goalkeeper, but the setup means this is a fake decision.

'Variable' Practices

Unlike constant practices, variable ones start to introduce more searching, decision-making, and become more closely related to the game. There may be a focus on one particular technique, like above, but other techniques will also be required to solve the problems set by the coach. There is the repetition of techniques, but without the repetition of the exact same conditions (we will look at this 'repetition, without repetition' again later). In football, the real game presents players with similar situations, but the game is too random for these situations to be exactly the same. The moves are not as pre-defined as they are in constant practices, allowing for more decisions to be made, whilst there is more information required by players to complete the exercise.

Variable practices may contain interference[3] or opposition. In the case of the exercise below, from Chelsea's Development Centre, there is opposition.

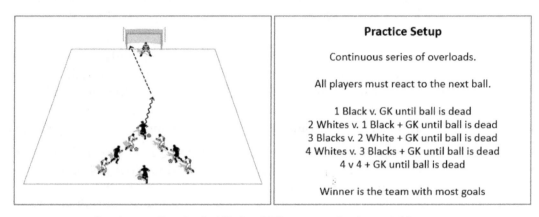

Practice Setup

Continuous series of overloads.

All players must react to the next ball.

1 Black v. GK until ball is dead
2 Whites v. 1 Black + GK until ball is dead
3 Blacks v. 2 White + GK until ball is dead
4 Whites v. 3 Blacks + GK until ball is dead
4 v 4 + GK until ball is dead

Winner is the team with most goals

Continuous Overloads (Chelsea FC) – example of a variable practice
(produced by Michael Beale (@MichaelBeale)

This shooting session moves the needle closer to the real game – there are defenders, and the player with the ball has to search and decide before executing, based on what is happening around him/her. It still, however, contains large elements of compromise.

In the original document from Chelsea, there is a note that says, "play at match speed." If you are running sessions where you have to stipulate match speed or realism, the session inherently contains high levels of compromise. Some examples, in this case, are that those shooting for goal outnumber the defenders (excluding the goalkeeper and until it arrives at 4 v 4); elements of transition are included (the attacking players must defend straightaway), but the defenders do not have a way of counter-attacking should they win the ball back. In effect, we are teaching defenders to win the ball back and then do nothing with it, when in reality, we would want them to search for a possible counter-attack, and decide whether to counter, retain possession, or indeed, make a defensive clearance.

---

[3] 'Interference' differs from 'opposition' in that rather than the players directly competing against each other, they will instead hinder what players are trying to do. Interference adds an extra layer to the practice as it will require players to search and decide before executing their technique. An example of variable practice that include interference rather than direct opposition was detailed in *Making The Ball Roll*.

'Random' Practices

Random practices start to mimic the game more closely than variable practices, and a lot more than constant ones. Random practices will generally be in the form of game-based exercises, and will involve players playing against opponents. The set-up and opposition add more interference and make the practices more game-realistic. There is the inherent need for players to scan and make decisions based on what is happening around them. The chaos of the real game is present.

The sample random practice, below, is taken from a document produced by the academy management at Leicester City, which is particularly focused on foundation phase players.

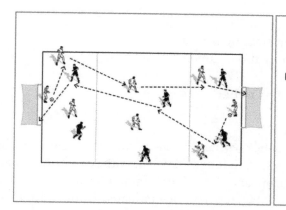

Practice Setup

Play 2 v 2 in all three zones.

Play with two footballs to create more randomness and goalscoring opportunities.

Progression 1:
Goals can only be scored from the middle third.
Forwards can score from a rebound

Progression 2:
Players are no longer confined to their zones.
3 points if they score from a header

Leicester City Shooting SSG – example of random practice

This session develops from players being locked into zones, before being free to play a full 7 v 7 small-sided game. Even-sided small-sided games are the closest coaches will get to the 'real game' in our training sessions, but still contain compromise in terms of the size of the pitch, size of goals, the positions players take up, etc. In this case, there are two balls, to begin with, to increase scoring opportunities, which will definitely affect the ebb and flow of the natural game. Also, at no point in the game will players get extra points for scoring a header or will it be stipulated that you can only score from certain zones.

The key here, as with the other practices, is whether you are happy with the inherent compromises and can justify them. The SSG from Leicester wants to focus on shooting, but zoom in on long shots, strikers scoring from rebounds (an essential part of the game) and heading, so they can and will justify it. It is worth getting into the habit of justifying your football sessions – are you happy with the compromise involved? As mentioned above, if you are using exercises with too much compromise, too often, your players are not experiencing the real game enough.

Creativity

In the sample variable practice above, from Chelsea, we noted that, for the majority of the time, the attackers outnumbered the defenders. This continuous overload is designed to make the strikers play quickly while they have the numerical advantage. However, the majority of the time, in the real game, defenders will outnumber the attackers. Are we, therefore, by making training sessions easier than the game itself, truly helping players deal with the game with all its complications?

Coaches will often veer to the 'easier' exercises. The notion being that players need something easy to begin with, or they need immediate success to draw confidence. We, therefore, dumb down our sessions and end up running 'line-drills' that look and seem very organised and intricate, but deny players the exposure to the real variability of the game. Constant practices are too common around our training pitches – often, I have seen them taking up the majority of sessions. If we were to coach anything that mimics the 80/20 Principle (that 80% of the time you work on the things that are the most important), then the constant stream of constant practices takes us to a poor place. We are compromising the game too much, dumbing down the game further and more often than necessary; We are not putting players in enough random, chaotic situations that they will meet in the game. The new-found confidence of your striker after scoring frequently in a 3v1 situation, for example, won't last long when the opposition surrounds him on matchday.

> The idea is that training is more
> complicated than the game.

Thomas Tuchel

One of the most thoughtful, exciting young coaches working in the professional game, adding to a plethora of other German coaches in this mould, is Thomas Tuchel. Although only in his early 40s, Tuchel has been the Head Coach at European giants Paris Saint Germain and Borussia Dortmund, having started his coaching career at Mainz, where he graduated from youth to senior coach at the age of just 35.

Tuchel, inspired by the work of Wolfgang Schöllhorn in the field of physical development, uses a method called *Differential Training*. This involves developing practices that force players to think and find new ways of solving problems; and to develop as many solutions for problems as possible. However, rather than simplify the training, Tuchel actually aims to make it more complicated.

This struggle, he believes, leads to enhanced performance and helps players to become more creative, even if his sessions are considered unconventional in some quarters. He sees his role of coach as a position where he can get the best out of his players by constantly challenging them. Players admitted to initially thinking it was strange – until it started to improve them.

> At first, we wondered what these things had to
> do with football, but we realised quickly that
> they worked.

Neven Subotić

For example, to stop defenders grappling the opposition when defending, he made them train with tennis balls in their hands. They trained on slippery surfaces to challenge and therefore enhance their balance and control. They would play on extremely narrow and also extremely wide pitches. In one exercise, players were only allowed to control the ball with their knees! When coaching diagonal forward runs, he changed the shape of the pitch, to the one below. Tuchel's Differential Training methods include manipulating the task, the player, and/or the environment to make sessions more difficult, a method known as Constraints-Based Coaching.

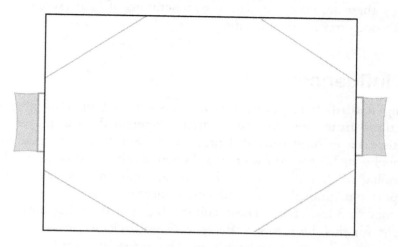

Tuchel's adapted training pitch

Players are required to become more creative and adaptable when faced with *real* problems, bringing back a memory of when Johan Cruyff debuted his famous 'Cryuff Turn' at the 1974 World Cup against Sweden. When asked when or why he 'invented' this turn, he simply answered that it was not a trick, just a way of solving a problem that the game provided. Tuchel aims to create an environment where players are forced to explore as many solutions to problems as possible, rather than the "pass there, move here" style from constant practices. Players learn to discover new and creative ways to solve a problem and adapt to unpredictable circumstances – when competition comes around, the challenges faced seem easier.

Portuguese researcher on creativity in football, Sara Santos (@SaraDLSantos), put this concept to the test with 40 youth players from Under-13 and Under-15 squads. Players were divided into two groups of 20 and spent five months playing small-sided games in training. The first group were engaged in traditional SSGs, whereas the second played differential learning games. The creativity of all groups was measured before and after the study using the "Creative Behaviour Assessment in Team Sports" template. The results found that the differential group displayed increased originality and versatility of actions, made fewer errors, and became better in terms of positional sense. The more they were challenged, the more their creativity and game understanding improved.

Repetition, Without Repetition

The key feature of *Differential Training* was repetition, without repetition, as described above. Schöllhorn believes that repetition, constant correction, and criticism (the cornerstone of much of the coaching landscape for a very long time) leads to players being self-critical and therefore taking fewer risks which, in turn, dampens creativity. If we just give players the answers to problems, how would we ever expect them to be creative? He believes that in the same way that all players have different physical mechanics, they will also have different technical mechanics and different ways of executing the same skill, making the 'coaching manual' learning of techniques defunct.

Tuchel's sessions, therefore, include a huge amount of variation. As every player learns differently and at different rates there cannot be a "one-size-fits-all" approach to training exercises. Not all players require the passing drill you want to run, for example. This variation means that even when sessions lasted 2.5 hours, the players never felt the time go, as they were engaged as the sessions flowed and changed constantly. Similarly, at La Masia, the famed academy at Barcelona, (whose methodology has been largely influenced by Paco Seirul·lo Vargas, an advocate of

Differential Training), there are no more than three repetitions of each exercise – keeping the game and the training sessions fresh and stimulating.

The Wider Influence

When researching football intelligence, I found a somewhat obvious geographical disparity. Bloggers and writers from the US and Australia bemoaned their players' lack of football intelligence. There was a jealously towards European and South American countries where young players were brought up playing *and* watching the game. Sheer exposure to the game breeds a deeper understanding of it. I noticed that in Africa, while there was a brilliant, fervent, and festival-type support and atmosphere around games, there was a lack of analysis coming from the crowd that you may find elsewhere. These cultural facets make a big impact. There may be a number of reasons for this, be it time difference issues, lack of access to high-level games, or other sports dominating the sporting landscape. The extremely detailed analysis of football in Italy, for example, feeds their desire for high-level thought on the game and produces players with high levels of football intelligence, as the constant debate and open confrontation around football philosophies does in the Netherlands.

How the game is reported can also make a real difference to both players and coaches. If those involved in football are exposed to deep, meaningful analysis, you foster a deeper understanding of the game in the viewer's living room. If this is basic, lazy, or substandard, our resulting opinions can be affected. I watched some shows around the 2018 World Cup and the 2019 Women's World Cup that seemed to concentrate on the decisions of the Video Assistant Referee (VAR), rather than the *how* and *why* of the game. Previously, we saw how a greater level of football thought, exposure, and analysis helped lift Germany from their slump in the early 2000s.

The level of analysis to which players and coaches are exposed to is bound to raise (or lower) the bar. It sparks thought, debate, and conjecture about 'real' footballing detail – and gets the wheels of the football nation turning. Players are very good at mimicking their heroes on the grass. How many of us, as kids, would have watched a game, then gone straight outside to practise the move for the winning goal? I wanted to play in a 'free role' as a 10-year-old, as Steve McManaman did for Liverpool. In the mid-nineties, this was my first exposure to such a term. Playing 3-5-2 allowed McManaman "to roam and affect the game," the TV pundit told me. I wanted to do that. We see a further fantastic example of this from Kelly in our *It's Your Game* segment below.

There is no reason why we, as coaches, with all the access we have to video clips and analysis in the Western World, cannot help to expose the top-level game to the youth players that we work with.

Conclusion

It seems fitting to go full circle in this chapter by coming back to another goal by Dennis Bergkamp. In the 1992 European Championships, the Netherlands were pitted against old footballing foes and neighbours Germany. The third goal in a 3-1 wins sums up both individual and collective football intelligence. With Dutch winger Aron Winter in possession on the right-hand side, and preparing to cross, accomplished striker, Marco van Basten, made a darting run towards the near-post area. This is a typical move by strikers looking to attack a cross. However, en route, van Basten can be seen pointing behind him. Rather than making a run for himself to score, van Basten was very aware that he was dragging defenders with him, allowing space for Bergkamp behind him. Winter got the message and placed an inch-perfect cross onto the head of the second striker who found the net. Van Basten didn't touch the ball, but his movement and intelligence, as well as the movement of his teammates, personified both individual and collective football intelligence.

In the next chapter, we will zone in on individual development within a team environment, and also how these individuals connect as a team.

Summary

- Developing players with *Football Intelligence* has become an integral part of youth development.

- It is dangerous to pigeon-hole players as 'unintelligent' or as having certain types of intelligence. Often, players will not be able to articulate why they do something, but they do it instinctively from a lifetime of playing, watching, and analysing the game.

- Geir Jordet found that players who scan for information more often before receiving the ball produce better technical actions after receiving it.

- Scanning is not simply looking around, and not just looking behind you. It is 'seeing' relevant information and being able to interpret it. Traditional football sessions around scanning ask players to look around, but not to 'see'.

- Sessions that require players to search for information, and make decisions for themselves, before executing the football decision are more optimal in developing *Football Intelligence*.

- Any practice that you put on for your players that is anything less than an unrestricted 11v11 game will contain elements of *compromise* with the 'real game'. Coaches need to understand the compromise, and be able to justify it. The more dramatic our compromises, and how often we make them, will affect player development.

- We divide our practices into three categories – constant, variable, and random. Compromise with the real game lessens as we move through these categories.

- If we want to develop creative players, we need to give them decisions to make and ask them to solve problems. Thomas Tuchel makes sessions more difficult than competitive games to encourage players to explore more solutions to problems, allowing them to become more creative.

- Tuchel's Differential Training methods include manipulating the task, the player, and/or the environment to make sessions more difficult (Constraints-Based Coaching).

- He constantly changes and progresses sessions to keep them fresh and stimulating for players.

- The level of football, and the level of football analysis that players are exposed to, will also help to develop their Football Intelligence.

It's Your Game #1

New Ball Please

Wayne Harrison • @WayneHarrison9

Author; Founder of *Soccer Awareness*

In the early 1980s, I was a young professional footballer at Blackpool FC. At the time, football in England was characterised by a very physical, non-technical style of play. However, a former World Cup winner was to arrive and change my outlook on the game forever.

Alan Ball – a member of England's 1966 World Cup-winning team – became our player-manager in 1980. One of his catchphrases was that he only needed to use "half a touch" when in possession. Of course, the concept is not real but it neatly summed up the speed of his thinking. His mind was so quick that he knew what he was going to do with the ball before he received it.

At 21, I was one of the youngest players in the squad. However much I wanted to learn, or however much I tried to emulate his "half a touch" approach, I couldn't get anywhere close to his level. I was open-minded but never made the headway that was going to take this part of my game any further.

When I started coaching, however, it was always on my mind to focus on the thinking that 'Bally' introduced me to as a player. If it worked for him, I felt, it could work for most players – *if* they were introduced to it early enough.

At 21, I think I was a bit too late to absorb the aspects required to match the level that I was exposed to. My footballing habits were hardwired following more than a decade as a youth player, where I was not exposed to this. Over time, and with my coach mentality to the fore, I have narrowed the concept down to what I call a 'one-touch mentality'. I encourage players not just to be able to play using just one touch (this inherently makes them think quicker anyway) but to start to think 'one-touch'. It is about players absorbing enough information from around them so that they know what they want to achieve once they receive the ball.

My goal is to develop behaviour that is automatic and subconscious, and to develop great habits at a very young age. The focus is to teach the one-touch mentality, although this does not only mean always playing one-touch football. "How often do you look over your shoulder before you receive the ball?" "Have you scanned the field to discover your best options?" I want to give the kids I come into contact with the footballing education that I was too late to soak up.

It's Your Game #2
Live, Full Speed, Dramatic
Anonymous
Father (Coach) & Daughter (Player)

My teenage daughter is a much better player than I am a coach. In fact, the more she plays, the more she teaches me. Every weekend, we go to a game. It has taken us to all levels of the professional game in the UK. One such weekend, she had a game in the North-West, which coincided with Liverpool v Tottenham. Tickets proved difficult to come by, so we ended up separated. I was behind the goal; Kelly was in the main stand. We were disappointed, but it ended up being a blessing in disguise.

For Liverpool, the match was a must-win. With the score at 1–1 late in the game, Tottenham counter-attacked and found themselves in a 2v1 situation heading towards goal. Virgil van Dijk was the defender, Moussa Sissoko was the ball-carrier, and Son Heung-min was offering support. We had the pleasure of witnessing this live, but from different angles, allowing us to pick up details the other didn't.

While defending in a 2v1 situation, the coaching manual would tell you to position yourself in a 'V' shape between both attackers – let them pass to each other to slow the game down to allow for your teammates to recover. I was certain that Tottenham were going to score and it seemed that 50,000 others, and Kelly, did too.

Van Dijk, however, was computing something entirely different – we were witnessing live, full speed, dramatic football intelligence at work. When back home, we replayed the video footage over and over again, so we could both pick the details apart further.

Instead of allowing passes between the two, van Dijk dared Sissoko to advance, exaggeratingly cutting off the pass to Son. The South Korean, after all, is a much bigger threat in these situations. Van Dijk also kept Sissoko on his left foot – the Frenchman's weaker foot. We are certain, too, that van Dijk was also thinking that with Allison, the ultra-reliable goalkeeper in goal, that he could take the risk of allowing Sissoko to shoot. It is only at the last moment, as Sissoko's body language tells us that he is going to shoot, that the Dutch defender threatens the ball. His lunging presence affected Sissoko further as his frantic shot sailed over the crossbar.

The most impressive thing was that this situation took only a mere matter of seconds. Van Dijk's decision-making was quick, incisive, and allowed him to control a potentially impossible situation. Although sat apart, those seconds brought my daughter and me closer together and share an even deeper passion to learn the game.

> ## It's Your Game #3
> ## A Letter to My Younger Self
> ### Sean O'Driscoll
> ### Former England Youth & First Team Coach, Liverpool FC

A Letter to My Younger Self – Why you coach the way you coach…

"Why don't we start every session with a problem that needs solving, rather than a technical solution that needs to be coached?"

You are 22 and have signed your first professional contract with Fulham in the old second division (now Championship), after two seasons playing semi-professional football in the Midlands for Willenhall Town and Alvechurch. If someone had asked you the above question when you were in your early 20s, you would have smiled and not given it a second thought.

When the same question is posed, 40 years later, at a 'Future of Coaching' Conference, you think 'If I had been coached or taught that way, would I have been a better player? Would I be a different coach? Would I think differently to the way I do now?

You always enjoyed training, but endless drills didn't stimulate you, and at the time you didn't even recognise what you were doing as a 'drill'; you were just following a list of instructions.

"When you receive the ball, get it out of your feet," followed by an instruction as to where the coach wants you to play it. Forward, out wide, switch the play, then run here or go there. You thought it was a list of rules you were required to follow. Asking questions, especially any question starting with 'why?' always seemed to get you into trouble.

Sean, remember this session? You were required to close down five players on your own, but if they completed five passes, you got an extra defender? And if they completed five more, you got another one? What did you do? In your head, you're thinking, 'Why would I go on my own?' You stand there. They get five passes and you got an extra man! So you kept standing still.

'Why would I go with two when they have five?' So another five passes are completed and another defender comes in. Now there were three of you defenders versus the five. You had a chance now.

But instead of being praised for recognising the problem, and manipulating the constraint to your advantage, you get accused of being 'unprofessional' and 'guilty' of ruining the session. You thought 'Sean, just do what the coach says, even though you think it wrong.'

But you swore to yourself then, 'If you ever get the chance to become a coach, don't make the same mistake.' You would ask yourself, what do you want your players to become? Do you want them to be intelligent footballers, capable of making decisions and solving problems, or 'good soldiers' adept at following instructions?

You see the game as complex but not complicated; you either have the ball or you don't. You will ask yourself in every training session what is being asked of your team or you. You don't just listen to the rules; you try to understand them, then apply a strategy to achieve the objective. As a coach, you will try to change behaviours without taking away decision making. You won't tell players what to do, but you will offer advice. You will make a distinction between coaching for learning, coaching for performance, and coaching for competition. You will become fascinated by how players learn, not how to coach. And you will understand – at last – why you start every session with a problem that needs to be solved, rather than a technical solution that needs coaching.

Chapter 11
The 'I' in Team

"

Teams don't learn. Individuals within the team learn. Development is a personal process, even when conducted in a team environment.

"

Johann Cruyff

"There is no 'I' in TEAM" was traditionally the standard-bearing motto for coaches of team sports. The team was the most important thing, and all players were obliged to sacrifice themselves for the group.

This has since moved on to "there is no 'I' in TEAM, but there is 'ME'", highlighting the growing importance of the individual in team sports. In this chapter, we will look at how youth development environments are increasingly looking to systematically develop individual players, rather than building teams and what that means for youth coaches on the whole.

Priorities

Chris Ramsey spent a decade working with the Academy players at Tottenham Hotspur. Since leaving Spurs, he has held several job titles at Queens Park Rangers, namely *Head of Player Development*. He has had a couple of spells working with England youth international teams and is one of the most respected youth coaches in the English game. His focus on the individual means that he works in a way that very few youth coaches do. The title of 'Development Coach' is certainly an easy fit for him. In the *It's Your Game* segment, at the end of the chapter, Ramsey details the unique way that he, and his youth coaches at QPR, approach training and games.[1]

Ramsey acknowledges the importance of winning for the players. Regardless of the age of the participants, winning will be important – but never at the expense of developing the player. It is, for Ramsey, all about developing the individual. As such, in an interview with ESPN, Ramsey presented interviewer Iain MacIntosh with the graphic below:

---

[1] Between 2014 and January 2020, a whopping 18 academy players have played in the QPR team.

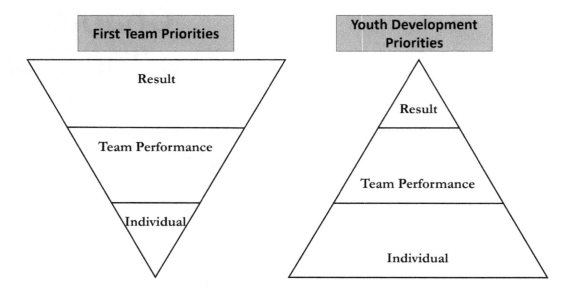

The first pyramid – the inverted one – represents the priorities of senior first-teams. Winning is the main goal. Head coaches are sacked if results are not deemed satisfactory. Team performance comes second on the list of priorities, although some teams will place far more emphasis on this than others. For example, FC Barcelona and the Dutch National Team place great importance on how the team plays – but the result still has to be right. Bottom of the pyramid, and the least important factor in the senior environment, is improving the individual. In fact, in many teams, little or no emphasis is put on this. I once spoke to a 29-year-old striker who had played for his country and in every professional division in England. He claimed that no coach actively helped him become a better player once he turned professional. Fortunately, this is beginning to change.

> When you're in the first team, you have to win. If you play terribly and still win, people will forgive you. But in development, the performance is for the player; the result is for the coach. If I want to win more than I want those players to develop, sure, we might win the youth league. But eventually, those players won't make the grade.

Chris Ramsey

In April 2019, Brentford Football Club advertised for an 'Individual Development Coach' to "accelerate the development of our top prospects" – mainly the players in the Under-23 'reserve' group. As a club focused on marginal gains and getting value for money, there was a focus on developing the players they have, rather than spending vast sums purchasing new players. The key responsibilities of this role included:

- Creating and updating player IDPs (Individual Development Plans – something we will delve into during this chapter), and ensuring they were executed with top quality

- Giving players feedback relating to their IDPs

- Working with heads of departments to ensure that each player's priorities were aligned and that messages to the players were consistent

- Driving a culture where individual focus and (self) training is high priority

Unfortunately, for youth coaches, it is the first-team pyramid that we are exposed to and inspired by, rather than developments at a club like Brentford. We hear things like "the only thing that matters is the three points" from high-profile coaches that we admire on a weekly basis, while Chris Ramsey and other Individual Development Coaches are working unseen in the background. That is also the message that parents hear, and the only tangible thing we have from our coaching is league tables and match scores.

However, as youth development coaches, we have to be willing to flip the first-team pyramid around and *prioritise improving every individual within our group*. Once this is effective and honest, we can then look at team performance and ultimately winning games. The great thing is that if every individual is improving, then the team will improve, and ultimately results get better too. The team is greater than the sum of its parts, as the saying goes, but if we work on improving the parts, we will inevitably improve the team.

Embedding the Individual in Your Programme

"

I have never seen a team make its debut.
Individual players do.

"

Johann Cruyff

Traditionally, our coaching of individual players came in two forms. The first was to narrate and commentate on their performance as they played, whether it is the command-style "do this, do that" or the guided-discovery type Q&A "what could you have done differently there?" Then, after the game or training session, we give a player some advice or comment about their game.

What this amounts to is a series of subjective *formative* pieces of feedback. This is momentary feedback; after game A, you tell a player his passing needs improvement; after game B, it was his defending skills; after game C his body shape. This type of feedback may still have its place *in the moment*. Engaging in it, in the right way, allows you and the player to immediately address good or bad pieces of performance. Its weakness is that this feedback is rarely tracked and is rarely used as a reference point for future performance. Coaches can butterfly from one suggestion to another, rarely tying it all together. Imagine trying to improve at anything if your mentor just lobbed suggestions at you whenever it seemed appropriate.

Feedback, however, can tend to be abused. Coaches may become over-zealous in offering too much feedback, or changing the focus of the feedback from game to game, or session to session. As this feedback is more informal and unrecorded, players, especially younger ones, may not absorb the information fully or correctly – or they may just simply forget! When offering this type of feedback, ensure that it is backed up and *revisited* to give players a measure of their improvement.

What we are seeing more and more today, in development environments, is *summative* feedback. Formative feedback is still used, but is no longer advice given on the side of the pitch and allowed to blow away in the wind. It is tracked and linked to the player's long-term development. English academies are now bound by EPPP criteria, as outlined earlier in this book. Although critics would say it has turned coaches from on-the-field experts to data-inputting, office workers, shackled to desks, those who implemented the process would point to the individual tracking and improvement of players as being one of its great successes. Individual information in relation to player performance is tracked after training sessions, and after every game. These small pieces of feedback help to identify player strengths and weaknesses, which can *both* become a long-term focus.

Know the Person

Above, we looked briefly at Brentford FC's Individual Development Coach's key responsibilities. Along with the football-specific requirements of the position, two aspects stuck out. The first was around culture. The club wants individual development to be a "top priority". The person in charge should "drive" this culture. Ultimately, they want players walking into their environment, not to come to just train, but to come to strategically improve. All staff members that affect this player should also be focused on these specific development foci.

Secondly, and something I did not include above, was "building close relationships to them [the players] to make sure that they develop both as footballers *and as human beings.*" Understanding the person before you can understand the player is a growing theme in modern coaching literature, although I will personally admit to not realising how important it was until a recent experience.

I was conducting my first one-to-one with a 17-year-old player. I had planned to ask him about his best position and talk about improving his out-of-possession skills; in particular, his pressing. We engaged in some small talk beforehand. The small talk became big as he detailed how his early life resembled some of the horrific scenes that you will know from the heart-wrenching movie, *Hotel Rwanda*, and the subsequent impact of this on his personal and family life. Suddenly, his pressing skills were less important. From then on, any targets we spoke about involved making the most of the game he loved and, regardless of what life was throwing at him, we would focus first on him playing football with a smile on his face.

"

Seeing the world through the eyes of your individual players is fundamental if you want to get the very best from them. Each player is unique, with a different profile, personality, and purpose. True empathy unlocks your ability to relate to their tensions, anxieties, frustrations and ambitions. When you understand the person, you get double from the player. We are human beings; we all feel the need to be valued and loved, to contribute, to feel connected.

Tom Bates

Tom Bates is a performance psychologist who formally worked for Aston Villa, Birmingham City, and West Bromwich Albion. In his book, *The Future Coach*, Bates talks about "The Relationship Coach". He challenges us to get to know the person behind the player. A consequence of doing so leads us to get more from them. The personal connection, and a player knowing you care, allows a relationship to form, and the player to trust you. Thus, the player will be more willing to accept your ideas.

This approach to coaching, however, can often be misinterpreted. Coaches complain that this type of relationship-building means that they end up with minimal control. I personally often wondered how someone like Harry Redknapp could keep players in check whilst also spending a lifetime lauding them as "fantastic". In the same book, Bates offers the *Control-Warmth Matrix*, suggesting that the optimal balance around control and being warm (or cold) with players is to adopt a "coach knows, coach cares" approach.

Control – Warmth Matrix, Tom Bates, The Future Coach

People don't care how much you know until
they know how much you care.

Theodore Roosevelt

The young footballer that you see for an hour or two, once, twice or three times a week, has an expansive life away from you and the training pitch. As coaches, we spend a huge amount of money, time, and resources in preparation for these limited encounters. Coaches will have a life away from the pitch too, where often great sacrifices are made for us to indulge in coaching a sport we love. This may include work, family, and other commitments. If you are lucky enough to coach football for a living, we all know there is a trade-off – it is not a 40-hour work week – it is coaching sessions, reviewing players, completing admin, staff meetings, watching potential players, speaking to parents or agents, inputting an endless amount of data into player tracking databases – and the list goes on!

Chapter 11 – The 'I' in Team

The children or teenagers[2] that you meet on these fleeting occasions will also have a whole life that encircles their training sessions with you. Anything could be happening in their experiences away from the pitch – school could be positive or negative – full of pressure or the best days of their lives. Family life could be pleasant or full of heartache – a perfect nuclear family or a nuclear disaster. When they leave your training session, anything could be waiting for them when they reach for their phone – a loving message, a banter-filled group chat, a bullying post on social media, or anything in-between.

"

Each player belongs to the group and the same
rules apply to everybody. But at the same time,
they are different human beings and you have
to study them really well.

José Mourinho

Know Their Game

As team coaches, we spend a lot of time thinking exclusively about the team as a whole. What formation we will play, what sessions we need to put on to improve results and performance, and how best to build team spirit and cohesion. There is nothing wrong with this – we know our teams very well, and the performance of the team is often our main reference point for how 'good' our coaching is.

Along with having team performance goals, it is important to know (or get to know) the strengths, weaknesses, and *capabilities* of each and every one of the players. As you will expect by now, these topics should cover all aspects of PPSTT.

I specifically included the term 'capabilities' above for several reasons. As a coaching fraternity, we are very good at describing what players are good at *now* and what they need to improve. However, if we understand what they are capable of, we will know how to judge them fairly and how far we can push them. Remember, also, that your opinion of what a player is capable of may be subjective, and this may change. Kids, in any part of life, have the uncanny ability to surprise us with their capabilities, so always be willing to change your opinion on players.

Hopefully, the preceding and following chapters will allow you to build a framework around understanding your players' games. Instead of being generic in your assessment, you can drill into the detail. So, instead of a player being psychologically 'strong' or 'weak', they may have good *commitment* or poor *control* (or any of the other 'Cs' as we discussed in Chapter 7).

They Know Their Game

Coaches come in all different shapes and sizes. Like we have seen throughout the book so far, some will focus on X, others on Y. Some will like method A; another will prefer method B. You could start a debate or an argument between coaches just by discussing methodologies. Regardless of style and coaching preferences, every coach is a conduit for the improvement of players.

---

[2] A colleague of mine recently told me to replace the word 'player' with 'child' or 'teenager' every once in a while. It will change the way you speak about them and judge them.

A key trait in this development path is having players *evaluate their own performance* and their own learning goals. The traditional means of a coach telling a player what to do and them simply obliging is slowly being replaced by a more two-way process. Players, like in academic education, are being tasked with taking control of their own learning. They are being empowered to self-assess. We facilitate this by encouraging them to self-reflect and set their own targets. Below is a very simple reflective piece from Marcus Rashford when he was a young player, facilitated by his academy coaches at Manchester United.

Name	Marcus Rashford
Favourite position	Right wing and up front
What are my strengths?	My strengths are my pace and my skill
What do I need to improve?	I need to improve on my left foot
How can I improve?	I can improve by practicing everyday
Who do I think is the best U11 player?	Dev
And why?	Because he's got everything a great player needs

Marcus Rashford Under-11 Self-Review at Manchester United

In this self-review, you see the child rather than the professional player that we are familiar with today. Rashford's analysis is not deep or detailed and is exactly what you would expect from a 10-year-old. He considers his teammate 'Dev' to be the best as he has, non-specifically, "got everything", for example. In this situation, as a coach, we can now help Marcus drill deeper into these titbits. What specific "skills" are you strong at? What precisely is Dev good at? Etc.

In addition to a self-analysis task like this, it is extremely valuable to ask players about their role models – a player who they aspire to be like. Normally, they are current players, and normally they are famous ones. Depending on age, this player can play in the same position or not. It is helpful if they share the same traits. The modern-day Marcus Rashford could be the role model for the skilful attacker in your team (it always helps if they support the team for whom that player plays!). Sometimes, coaches can even suggest players for our youngsters to follow and analyse.

This process allows us to get players to look at the game of a professional, but also self-reflect. What does this player *do* that makes him stand out? What are his strengths and weaknesses? Did you see the way he tracked back in the game at the weekend? Did you see the work-rate involved? Did you notice his or her ingenuity when they used a certain skill? We can use the journey and traits of existing players to help inspire and mould the players we are developing.

Individual Development Plans

" **"**

> Having my own Individual Development Plan
> helps me greatly. I know exactly the parts of my
> game that are good and that I need to improve.
> I know *me* more.

Anonymous Academy Player

Recently, I shadowed some coaches working with top-level 17 and 18-year-old players. Both were good guys and knew the game. For most of the first half, however, they muttered and complained about the technical deficiencies of their right full-back. They were correct. He certainly had a major, specific technical weakness. He was unreliable with the ball and frequently lost possession due to a lack of composure.

I had only one question about this player to the coaches on the bus journey home – "Does *he* know this part of his game is so deficient?" The answer, worryingly, was no – it had never even been discussed with him. Players in a development environment, especially the older they are, should have a clear understanding of where their game is both strong and where it needs to improve. They should also be spending significant time working on both these areas.

Under Premier League EPPP regulations, all clubs should produce and maintain a 'Performance Clock' (IDP) for every player. The players are reviewed regularly and their strengths/weaknesses are collated to aid their progress. This clock is intended to track the development of the player throughout his time at the club, is shared with the player and his parents, and is – if necessary – then passed on to his next club.

The Review Process

In Premier League Academies, Individual Player Reviews are completed every 12 weeks for players in the 'Foundation Phase' (Under-9 to Under-12), and for older players, every six weeks. These are known as 'Meso' Reviews (we looked at Macro – Meso – Micro planning in *Making The Ball Roll*). The reviews are aimed to allow everyone involved in the child's development to be in the loop on how the player is progressing – the player, the parents, immediate coaches, and other support and management staff.

Below, is a very detailed six-week 'Meso' review for a 15-year-old player at a professional club in the UK from 2012. Since then, this player has gone on to play professionally for this club in the Championship, has played in the Premier League, and in the top leagues in other countries. Note that the player is evaluated around each element of PPSTT.

Player Name: _____ **Age Group:** <u>Under-16</u> **Date:** _____

Meso (6 week) Objectives for next period:

<u>Technical / Tactical:</u>

1. You are far too unreliable in possession. This is down to a combination of inconsistent technique and poor decision making. This needs to be addressed through training and games.

2. Out of possession, you have really improved your positional understanding – well done! Aim to maintain and improve on these standards.

3. Your positional understanding when we have the ball has improved when the ball is on your side of the pitch, but needs big improvements on the other side, which we will discuss how to address.

<u>Physical:</u>

1. Work towards fitness targets as set by the conditioning coaches and Sport Science staff

2. Fully engage in the physical programme which starts next week.

<u>Psychological:</u>

1. Work on your Control – in particular to your mistakes, the opposition and the referee. This is severely letting you down. For the next 6-week period you will be substituted every time we have a problem with this.

2. You switch off too early in games, particularly when our team has the ball, you must learn to Concentrate throughout the game.

<u>Social:</u>

1. Set a positive example to your peer group.

2. Work on praising and constructive criticism of your teammates rather than just moaning!

<u>Additional Comments:</u>

It is clear you have the physical attributes to progress. However, while you possess undoubted technical ability, this needs to become more consistent and your tactical understanding of the game has to improve. Finally, it is very important you address the issues you have surrounding self-control and concentration as they directly link into your technical and tactical shortcomings. You can do these things; you just have to be far more reliable! We will review all your goals in 6 weeks to see your progress in them. All the subjective goals we'll review via video footage.

Developing an Individual Development Process

Coaches working within an academy environment will often express frustration with the amount of paperwork involved in their line of work. The constant review of players and tracking of data is considered one of the strengths, but also one of the major drawbacks of the EPPP process. For a part-time, grassroots coach, who is balancing family life, work-life, and the rest of life, he will most likely shirk when he thinks of completing anything like the review above for 15-20 players every six weeks, for which I certainly have some sympathy.

While the review above is detailed and the effort involved in completing it is beneficial, for coaches outside the professional game, this commitment is difficult and the process will most likely fall apart for being too ambitious. There is a strong argument here also that this review, as a 6-week Meso one, contains *too much* information. Sometimes, less is more; players should be allowed to focus on specific aspects, rather than having to memorise everything. I don't believe the player (or even the coach) will remember or have the opportunity to meaningfully work on *all* those aspects. If you have a review at work, you want to be given a handful of targets that you can really home in on, rather than a mass of targets that can potentially become overwhelming. For the grassroots coach, I prefer a much more simplified process.

To help the busy coach review players *regularly and effectively*, I have included a template for a six-week (or 12-week) review below (and also templates for a 'mid-season' and 'end of season' review after the It's Your Game section at the end of the chapter).

Height (+/- from previous review):		Weight (+/- from previous review):		
No. Training Sessions / Total:	No. of Games / Total:		No. of Game Minutes:	
Notable Injuries:				
Individual Learning Plan - Actions (minimum one; maximum four)				
Actions met from prev. review? ✓ Complete ! Carry forward				**1** **2** **3** **4**
1				
2				
3				
4				
Agreed:	Agreed:		Date:	

The reality of grassroots coaching, and life in general, is that some coaches may not be able to commit to completing reviews every six weeks. For me, it does not matter if this process extends to every seven or eight weeks. What *is* important is that the process works for you, the players, and in the context of your environment. Any review process is better than no process at all. Maybe you coach Under-16s but decide to use the Foundation Phase process where players are reviewed every 12 weeks, rather than six. Whilst more frequent reviews are beneficial, a watered-down version is better than abandoning the whole process altogether.

What is very helpful during this process is 'chunking' your season into small, 'meso' blocks. For example, if you have a 36-week season, players can be reviewed during weeks 6, 12, 18, 24, 30 and 36. If you have 42 weeks, it can be done every seven weeks (7, 14, 21, 28, 35 and 42), or every eight weeks if you have a 48-week season.

I recommend starting every season with an individual 'Season Pre-View' for each player. This is the same template as above. Actions that are identified in this review will be assessed again six weeks later, before the coach and player decide they have sufficiently been completed or whether they should be carried forward for the next block. *It is important to note that carrying forward certain actions is not a bad thing,* just a necessary one. Maybe you decide to up-the-ante on a certain element. This process carries on throughout the season and into the next. At the end of the season, players can receive an 'End of Season Review', and for players in the Youth Development Phase (Under-13 onwards), you can use a 'Mid-Season' review.[3]

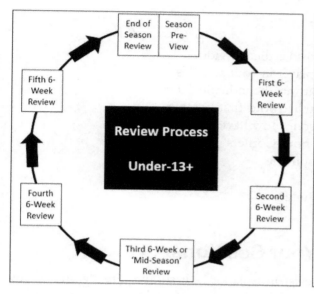
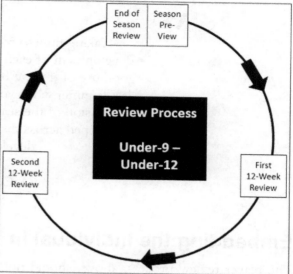

When completing reviews with players, it is important to remember the following:

- Include all aspects of player development (PPSTT) at some point in the process, ideally during every review. A lot of clubs will focus heavily on the technical/tactical corner (like the Leicester City example, below) but elements of PPS may be important in underpinning the player's TT development.

- Any highlighted areas for development should be re-examined during the following review. Actions may be kept to develop them further, or signed off.

- Always get input from the player. *Their* opinions may give *you* something to think about.

- Include player strengths as well as their weaknesses. Strengths can also be developed, thus improving the player further.

- Ensure that the process is about the player improving, not you 'rating' them.

- On occasion, it is possible that a review may include only one action. This particular action may be important and underpin the player's whole development process. For example, if a player suffers from a lack of emotional control, you may feel that she needs to address this exclusively for six weeks. This needs to be improved before any meaningful improvement can be made in any other area of their game.

- Ensure actions are age, ability, and individually appropriate. Tasking a 9-year-old to improve their fitness scores, a C team striker to score 30 goals, or a 16-year-old defender to improve his finishing are a waste of time.

- The inclusion of a player's height and weight is not to measure their current size, but to analyse the physical side of their game. Weight gain (or loss) or growth spurts will impact

---

[3] Mid-Season and End of Season Review templates can be found at the end of the chapter. These reviews are designed to be more detailed and robust than meso reviews.

their performance, so understanding what is happening physically as they grow is important.[4]

" Taking time to consider the individual development of each player in your squad is a good use of time. What was the individual like last summer when you had your first training session of the season? How have they developed across the Four Corners of player development? **"**

FA Education

Embedding the Individual in Your Sessions

The player review process, above, should not exist in isolation – it should directly link to your training and games programme. You cannot agree a development plan with players, then leave it on a piece of paper in a folder to look pretty. In the *It's Your Game* segment at the end of this chapter, Dan Abrahams speaks about using 'match scripts' with Yannick Bolasie, and these IDPs are essentially where his match script comes from. They are taken from paper and brought to life on the pitch. Below are four ways in which coaches can embed individual development practically within a team environment.

Player-Led

It is important that players take responsibility for their own development. The most committed players will independently take charge of their own learning away from the club, and the most invested coaches will encourage players to do so. This may include physically practicing skills, analysing players they see on TV, or working on psychological elements.

In a presentation by Tottenham Hotspur Academy Director, John McDermott, he spoke to an audience about the "10-Minute Rule" that they utilised at the Academy. Players spend 10 minutes at the beginning of every session practicing a part of their game that they are struggling with. This 'little and often' approach empowers players to take control of their own development, be more aware of the own strengths and weaknesses in their IDP, and to work on *their* game practically. These 10 minutes all add up over the course of a season.

Critically, and importantly for coaches that struggle with the idea of planning practical sessions for 15-20 individual players, the concept of Tottenham's 10-Minute Rule allows us to cater for this. Although, let me also offer some other worthwhile alternatives.

Small Group Work

The graphic below is from the Academy at Leicester City that outlines the process for six-week reviews at the club. They put forward a method where one coach works with a targeted group of

---

[4] Significant growth spurts can cause players to temporarily lose aspects of coordination and they may suddenly come across as clumsy – falling over at random times, for example. It can also lead to pains, injury, and a subsequent loss of confidence. Identifying when players have had a growth spurt is important as they are reviewed.

players, while another works with the rest of the players in line with their age-group curriculum. This is a great option if you can link the development areas of players together, where they are working on the same topic. So, for example, if you have a handful of players who need to improve their passing, then these players can work with a coach, separate to the main group. This method requires organising. To do it properly, all players should have the opportunity to work in small groups.

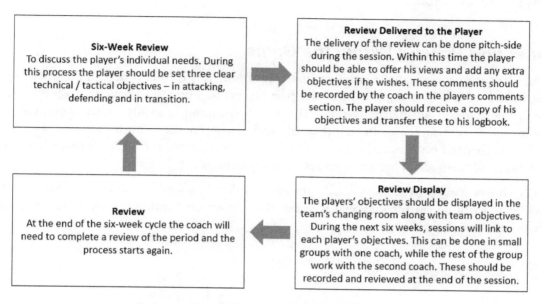

Leicester City Academy Six-Week Review Process

Whole-Group IDP Sessions

In the Small-Sided Game edition of my *Deliberate Soccer Practice* book series, I put forward the session below. When drafting it, for my own purposes, I saved the document on my computer as the "mother of all sessions".

Traditionally when coaches devise conditioned SSGs, the games have one rule. For example, all players can only have two-touches, players can only finish using one-touch, etc. The 7v7 game below, however, has a specific condition, constraint, or focus for all 14 players that relate to their *individual* games. All players are playing the same SSG, but with different outcomes. The focus for every player is generated by their IDP.

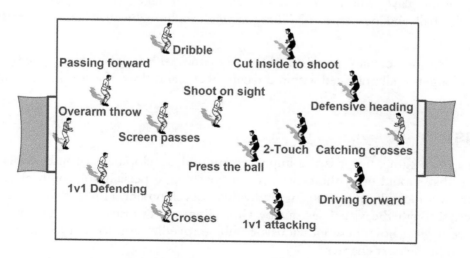

Deliberate Soccer Practice Small-Sided Game Conditioned for Players

Instead of all players playing freely, all players will be constrained or have a 'condition' to their play. This may limit them (the midfielder on the black team who has to play two-touch) or encourage more from them (the white forward who must 'shoot on sight').

We can further adapt this game by giving players one in-possession and one out-of-possession condition (or from transition phases). They could include a physical, psychological, or social outcome. I call this SSG the "mother" of all football practices as it is so busy, but the returns for each player are invaluable.

Connecting Players Within the Game

We can also use progressions that allow us to home in further on certain individuals, or small groups of individuals. For example, we may pair players together who have opposing targets, like the SSG (1) below. One player is focused on 1v1 attacking, and his direct opponent on 1v1 defending. This will increase the number of duels between them both. We see also that one midfielder is focused on forward runs, and the other on recovery runs. One winger is required to cross more, and the goalkeeper has a target to catch crosses.

SSG (2) shows a way of linking small groups of players together from the same team. The midfielder is working on his diagonal passing, the winger on beating the defender 1v1, and the striker on one-touch finishing.

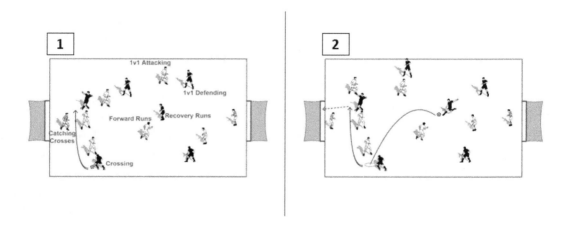

Some of the conditions above are quantifiable – you can tell when the midfielder has taken more than two touches, for example. Many of them, however, you cannot measure. When is it appropriate for the player who must "shoot on sight' not to take a shot at goal? When should the winger get the ball and not cross it? These topics can be subjective and require the coach's discretion.

You are trading off certain parts of the real game with a focus on specific, individual development targets – all practiced within the natural ebb and flow of a small-sided game.

Conclusion

Football is a team game, but it is the improvement and development of individuals within our environment that should be at the centre of our coaching, especially for youth players. Early in the chapter, we looked at prioritising individual development rather than results or team performance, through the visual set out by Chris Ramsey. Prioritising the individual does not mean that we neglect how these individuals combine together and form a team; something that we will look at in the next chapter.

Summary

- The 'There is no I in TEAM' philosophy is changing. The development of individuals within your team environment is important.

- While senior, first-team squads will focus on the result first, youth coaches should prioritise the individual development of every player.

- To aid this, we build an Individual Development Plan (IDP) for each player.

- Before developing the player, we must know the person.

- Coaches must have a deep knowledge of the players' games, but also encourage players to know their own games.

- As part of the IDP process, players can be reviewed every 12 weeks in the Foundation Phase, or every six weeks in the Youth Development Phase. Importantly, this process has to be manageable for the coach. If the process in your context needs to be different (e.g., every eight weeks), then do this. Chunk your season to ensure the process works.

- Any review process is better than none.

- When reviewing players, leaving them with one to four areas to develop is enough. The more you include, the less manageable it will feel for players.

- In reviews, include PPSTT, player strengths as well as weaknesses, and ensure that any action set is revisited during the next review. Ensure actions are appropriate for the player and that the process is about improving the player, not 'rating' them.

- This IDP must not exist in isolation – it must be taken onto the pitch.

- We can take this onto the pitch by encouraging player-led activities, small-group work, or by using the "mother" of all small-sided games.

> ## <u>It's Your Game #1</u>
>
> # For Us, It's Just Common Sense
>
> ## Chris Ramsey
>
> ## Technical Director, Queens Park Rangers FC

At Tottenham, and now QPR, our priority with youth players was always development and always about the individual players – before winning, and before the team's 'success'. We want all players to succeed through a training programme that addresses individual needs and a games programme that allows for maximal opportunities to develop.

First of all, we don't work in traditional age-groups. We assign players to teams using a 'Strength-Based Capability' approach. All factors – technical/tactical, physical, social, and psychological – are considered before that decision is made. If the best thing for the player is to play a couple of years above his birth age, then we do so, or even a year down. It all depends on the individual.

Secondly – and something that is hard for most coaches to do, especially those who just want to win matches – is to manipulate the match to ensure our players are challenged. If we are too comfortable in a game, we may bring a player off, for example.

If our right-back is having a tough afternoon against the left-winger, we don't protect him, like you would see in a first-team situation, where winning is vital. We don't ask our midfielder or winger to double up with him. We don't change shape and add an extra centre-back to ensure we don't concede goals. We 'expose' him to allow him lots of practice defending 1v1. The idea is that the challenge in a match situation will improve him and help him learn more so than any other environment. Of course, if it gets to the point where there is a physical or psychological issue, where the player simply cannot cope, then we adjust accordingly. We would not allow a player who's 5'6" be dominated by one that's 6'2" for example – that doesn't help either player. If it's a purely technical issue though, we will let it run its course.

This philosophy applies throughout our programme, whether you are 10, 15, or 21. If you are a 17-year-old playing in the Under-23s, you will be given more room for error than a 22-year-old whose next step is the first team.

Many consider the above to be enlightened thinking but, for us, it's just common sense. It's all about the individual.

It's Your Game #2

The Master & The Student

Dan Fieldsend • @danfieldsend

Author, *The European Game*

I made my way across the bridge from the Amsterdam ArenA, to *De Toekomst*, the Ajax Academy, which fittingly translates as "The Future". The structure is a metaphor for the journey of the player through the Ajax system – you cross 'the bridge' from the Academy to the Stadium, from youth prospect to professional (the same concept has been borrowed by Manchester City and their academy). Youth players are marched across this bridge on matchday to be further inspired by the journey.

Once there, there was a collection of smaller bridges that crossed a stream that flows through the facility, giving a feeling of tranquillity. I was on my way to catch the Under-18 team, and their coach, former Dutch International, Jaap Stam. Along with a series of individual awards, Stam, an imperious defender, won a collection of leagues and cups in Holland, England, and Italy, as well as the Champions League with Manchester United.

By the time the group came into view, they were finishing up and packing away to get in out of the rain. Whilst the rest of the group made their way to the changing rooms, Stam collared a young defender. He spent ten minutes – one-to-one – demonstrating defensive movement to him. You could imagine him visualising his duels against the great strikers of the 1990s and 2000s in his mind's eye: Ronaldo (the Brazilian), Christian Vieri, and Michael Owen, amongst many others.

The teen stood in the drizzly rain nodding, both of them seemingly oblivious to the fact that they were the only two people left on the field. Just a famous international player and a young wannabe – the master and the student. Stam crouched, gesticulated, moved about, and pointed, explaining to the boy how to shepherd great attackers away from goal. I could not hear a word of what was being said, but I could understand exactly what was happening.

I was inspired just watching it – I am certain the teenage defender was too. Not only was there are serial champion passing on his knowledge, but he was also devoting extra time to improve *him*, and him only.

> ## It's Your Game #3
>
> # Yannick Bolasie and 'Match Scripts'
>
> ## Dan Abrahams • @DanAbrahams77
>
> ## Sport Psychologist

A match script is two or three actions / behaviours that players *can control*. He or she will run onto the pitch and focus on them as they train, and especially, as they play. They can be related to the technical, tactical, physical, or psychological sides of the game.

Too often, players run onto the pitch and they are just trying to 'play well'. *What are you going to do to do that?* What things are going to help you to achieve those things? Rather than having 'performance' goals (e.g., complete my passes) or outcome goals (e.g., be man or woman of the match), we have 'process goals' – things that you can control. This gives players the best chance to perform *towards* their best.

A match script gives the players the opportunity to focus. When they've made a mistake or if it's not going so well – "come back to your match script." It can aid communication between coach and player [and a coach can] empower players to develop their match script – a great way for you to enhance your relationship with a player, to help them become students of *their* game and students of *the* game.

Yannick Bolasie is a winger, and one of the big challenges for a winger at the very top level is patience. You are not always making an impact. At that time, the reality was that Crystal Palace conceded possession to the opposition. At times, he wouldn't see much of the ball. He would say to me, "Dan, I'm getting so frustrated. I'm not getting the ball. I want to make an impact. I want to be the best that I can be." One of his match scripts [to deal with this was]:

1. Be patient
2. Show great body language
3. Stay lively and alert
4. Act Ronaldo! (Ronaldo would always be ready to make an impact)

It was those little things that he had when he ran onto the pitch. No matter how the first half went, or the first 70 minutes, he would keep saying those things to himself to keep himself in the game.

In 2014, Crystal Palace were three-nil down within 70 minutes against Liverpool. He said to me, "If I'd have let that first 70 minutes get to me, it would have sapped my confidence, I would have been distracted." The match script kept talking to him about how he had to stay focused. Crystal Palace ended up recovering to draw 3-3, with Yannick being instrumental and providing a key assist.

Match scripts can work for an Under-8, even if you have just one thing, and it can work at the top end at the biggest leagues in the world.

I have spent a lifetime in football – and have been involved in the game thanks to a wide spectrum of experiences. I played as a schoolboy, an apprentice at a professional club, and ultimately as a fully-fledged pro in England and Scandinavia. I now work in the game through the media, coach at an academy, and mentor some professional managers.

Throughout these experiences, I have worked with, alongside, and had a close-up view of, many different types of coaches within the game.

All of these people know the game. To be honest, at any given level, I have found that not much will separate the knowledge-base of each coach. They understand tactics, systems, and the on-the-pitch stuff. Not all of them, however, understand how to communicate this knowledge or how to get the best out of people. I learned first-hand that it is the interpersonal skills that separate the best from the rest. They know the person first, the player second.

Earlier in this book, Ray spoke about our 'Coaching Lens' – how our experiences in football shape the way we understand, see, and coach the game. I will go one step further by saying that we are all a product of our experiences. We cannot separate football from the rest of life. We, as coaches, bring our life and past to the training pitches, as do the players under our guise.

I didn't always think like this. For four years, prior to taking my UEFA B Licence, I had been a practicing life coach. During the nine months it took me to complete the life coaching programme of study, I found my 'lightbulb moment'. The content actually linked seamlessly to our football environments. I could connect the information from this course directly to my time as a player, and felt it would enable me to be a much better coach.

Much of what we studied was about good questioning, being an excellent listener, and helping people to find the answer. I wondered, at the time, whether football would ever catch up with this way of thinking. Now, I see it is definitely moving in the right direction. If this discipline could help people untangle their lives, then it can certainly enable us to get the best out of players.

Prior to taking my B Licence, I must admit that I felt I could end up out of my depth on the course. To my surprise, however, the conversations were not just around tactics, but around communication skills too. We debated how to get the best out of players from a psychological or social point of view, rather than focusing entirely on the balls, bibs, and cones. Understanding the game was important, of course, but understanding how to help people learn the game was the glue to sticking all this together.

From my youth, as a player, I had a number of coaches. When I think of the one who got on a level with me and facilitated my learning of the game, it is actually my schoolboy coach who springs to mind. Another I can say I learned very, very little from. He did not connect with me and he taught football in a way I could not understand. When he barked tactical instructions, I just couldn't 'see' it. This was not because he didn't know the game – far from it – he just didn't know me.

I would, without hesitation, say that if any coach wants to expand their repertoire, then studying life coaching or Neuro-Linguistic Programming (NLP) will take you to another level. You will have a skillset that many others won't.

Mid-Season Review Template[5]

Height (+/- from Start of Season):		Weight (+/- from Start of Season):	
No. Training Sessions / Total:	No. of Games / Total:		No. of Game Minutes:
Notable Injuries:			

Technical / Tactical	Psychological
Technical / Tactical Review from the Season	Psychological Review from the Season
Physical	**Social**
Physical Review from the Season	Social Review from the Season

Individual Learning Plan - Actions (minimum one; maximum four)					
Actions met from prev. review? √ Complete ! Carry forward		1	2	3	4
1					
2					
3					
4					
Agreed: (Player)	**Agreed:** (Coach)		**Date:**		

---

[5] This template can be used as an End of Season Review for Foundation Phase players.

End of Season Review

Height (+/- from Start of Season):	Weight (+/- from Start of Season):	
Total No. Training Sessions / Total:	Total No. of Games / Total:	Total No. of Game Minutes:
Notable Injuries:		

Technical / Tactical

Technical / Tactical Review from the Season

Psychological

Psychological Review from the Season

Physical
Physical Review from the Season

Social
Social Review from the Season

Individual Learning Plan - Actions (minimum one; maximum four)					
Actions met from prev. review? ✓ Complete ! Carry forward		**1**	**2**	**3**	**4**
1					
2					
3					
4					
Agreed: Player	**Agreed:** Coach		**Date:**		

Chapter 12
The 'We' in Team

"
> The strength of the team is each individual
> member. The strength of each member
> is the team.
"

Phil Jackson, basketball coach

Paradoxically, one of the most important *individual* traits within football is the ability to work within a team.

In the last chapter, we spoke at length about the importance of developing the individual in youth football. Chris Ramsey presented us with his priority triangles, with individual development occupying the most space in the youth development triangle. The development of the team, however, remains an important factor in getting the best out of the players as a group.

"
> Individual commitment to a group effort: that
> is what makes a team work, a company work, a
> society work, a civilisation work.
"

Vince Lombardy, American Football coach

The individual and the team are not mutually exclusive. When we work with players, you work with the individual within the team setting. They co-exist. The contributions of each individual player makes up the functioning of the team. As much as we hear about "one-man teams", no team can function to its maximum capability without the cooperation of everyone involved. Sure, some teams will be dominated by certain individuals, but that is true of most group settings and the social order of any band of people. There will be the introverts, the extroverts, and those in-between. There will be the well-behaved, the poorly-behaved, and those in-between. You are dealing with 12-20 different personalities, all of whom are vying for their social position within the team. If the dominant personalities are difficult to manage, then you may have a problem in establishing authority and behaviour within the group. If the dominant personalities are hard workers and good listeners, the others tend to follow.

Referring back to the *Individual Development Plans* from the last chapter, it is conceivable that an action for any player may be about becoming a better teammate, or working more effectively within a group setting. We note how the two social actions in the Meso, six-week player review example from the last chapter was:

1. To "set a positive example to your peer group" and

2. To "work on praising and constructive criticism of your teammates rather than just moaning!"

Working within a team may be the most important aspect of being a player.

Bringing a Team Together

I always found those corporate team-building days very annoying. You know... the one-off events that are organised for you and your colleagues to build morale and efficiency. I have worked with colleagues to build rafts, win a race while wearing beer goggles, and used paper 'stepping stones' to cross an imaginary, alligator-filled river.

Upon researching *effective* team-bonding, however, I've found that these one-off events are actually very poor at making your team work more effectively together. The first issue is context. The problem of raft-building with my coaching or teaching colleagues was nothing like the actual problems we faced daily. If we want players to come together and to solve problems they will actually face within the team, then this process can only improve by putting them in situations where they have to solve *football problems* together.

Secondly, as stand-alone events, they can only have a very limited long-term effect. It is certainly possible that a succession of events of this nature, *that link to our actual job roles*, may help. In a conversation with Luc Martin (@LucMartin11) (Associate Professor of Sport and Exercise Psychology at Queen's University in Ontario) he used the words "purposeful" and "coherent" So, instead of stand-alone, one-off team building sessions, effective team-building sessions will resemble the real-life situations the team faces, and have a long-term, comprehensive plan – a strategic 'little and often' series of relatable events.

Forming to Performing – A Process

Expecting a group of players who have just come together to act and behave like a fully-functioning team is probably not going to happen. We often expect this to occur straightaway and, worse again, we have the habit of simply telling players to "act like a team", expecting that to be enough. Forming an effective team takes time, and the group will pass through several non-negotiable stages along the way. This is inevitable. You cannot have a group of players on morning one, and then a fully-functional football team by the afternoon. Creating a 'team' takes work. Once you understand these stages, and have a team-building plan, you can help your team get there quicker.

In the mid-sixties, Bruce Tuckman proposed the *Forming-Storming-Norming-Performing* model of team development in an article entitled *Developmental Sequence in Small Groups*. He proposed that these four phases are necessary for the development of any team.

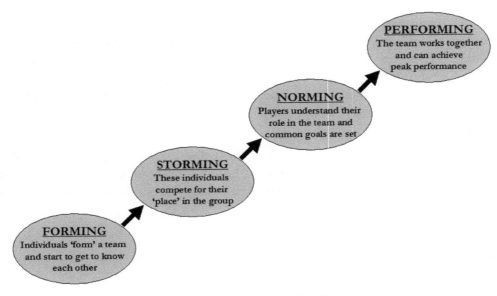

Tuckman's Stages of Team Development

A decade later, Tuckman and his colleagues added a fifth stage – *Adjourning* (or Re-forming). This stage, in a football context, is about managing change. Maybe the players you have leave, or new players join. These changes, depending on how severe they are, may take you back to the forming stage or allow you to re-join later in the process.

There is, therefore, advantages to keeping your team together in the long-term. High-level coaches are often chastised when they do not sign new players, or enough new players. In the last few years, in the Premier League, Liverpool, Pochettino's Tottenham Hotspur, and traditionally Arsène Wenger's Arsenal, have suffered such derision from fans and the media.

"

> Groups both change, and are changed by,
> individuals within them.

Dr Matt Slater, *Togetherness*

Keeping the core of your team together, however, is underestimated in terms of effectiveness. The coaches in charge of the teams above (Jürgen Klopp, Mauricio Pochettino, and Wenger) understand full well the importance of having the right characters within the group. Adding unknown quantities in new players may improve the team from a technical and tactical point of view, but not at the expense of changing the culture of the group. An ineffective team culture may work against the technical/tactical capability of the team. Klopp once quipped that he, "would never sign an asshole just because he's great at football."

It is also why you often see teams who sign an extraordinary number of players, based only on technical/tactical ability, or their existing profile within the game, who fail to 'gel'. A great example of this is Fulham in 2018/19, who signed 12 players upon their return to the Premier League. Despite the quality of those who were recruited, they were promptly relegated that season having completely failed to 'click', despite the new recruits being 'better' on paper that those they replaced.

"

> I think the team has so much potential to do
> some great stuff. There is a lot of talent. But it
> is not only talent; you really have to build a
> team.

**Romelu Lukaku
on Manchester United**

Taking a group of players from 'me' to 'we' is, therefore, a process that takes time. In the following paragraphs, we are going to look at the importance of 'we', and also at strategies to build identity, connectivity, and leadership within your group.

The Power of 'We'

Football fans the world over refer to 'their' team with a "we". "We won," "We lost," "We played well," etc. This is not just supporters that go to the stadium and watch the games live, or who travel across country and continents to watch 'their' team play. This will include supporters from all over the world who may never have even visited the team's city or country, let alone have the opportunity to see the team play in the flesh. They may not even speak the language of the team they follow, but they speak in the club's language – the 'we'.

Big European clubs are very conscious of this and now tour the US and Asia to further promote their clubs – to increase the feeling of 'we' around the world. Although clearly with a marketing and money-focused objective in mind, clubs travel to new and foreign lands in the hope of exporting their brand. In 2019, Juventus exchanged their traditional black and white striped jersey for a half-and-half version as they felt that US supporters associated the former with a referee's uniform, rather than a sports kit. Real Madrid removed the Christian Cross from their crest on branded clothing sold in the Middle East to attract more Muslim followers.

Whilst such actions seem trivial and often *too* money-minded, the impact of symbols like kit and the club crest's (or national emblems) are powerful. The wearer becomes identified as part of a distinct group, making many feel special.

Now, the normal youth coach will have no concern with marketing or exporting their team around the world, but it is certainly worth looking at what makes players in your team identify with the team. One of the most exciting days in pre-season with youth players is when new kit is distributed. There is pride in the badge and pride in being a part of a group. The 'uniform' unifies players with each other and the coaches, naturally promoting a togetherness amongst those who wear the same colours. It gives them a group and social identity, connecting them to each other. The group changes from a me, me, him, and her… to we and us.

"　　　　　　　　　　　　　　　**"**

Boys, I don't want to talk too much. We all know where we are. We all know what we want. We all know how far we have come. We know it in our hearts, in our eyes. I can see it boys, we are concentrated. We cannot forget. Maybe I am repeating myself. We are 90 minutes away from possibly making history. 90 minutes. One match. One match. I don't know how many matches we have played in our careers, but this is one match that changes everything, that changes all of history. There are two teams; there is one trophy. For them, it's the same; they want it. We know we lost a final [Euro 2016]. We know it. We feel it here [points to his heart]. It's still in our heads. Today we are not going to let another team take what is ours. Tonight, I want us to be in the memory of all the French people who are watching us, their kids, their grandkids, even their great-grandkids. I want us to go on the pitch, as warriors, as leaders.

**Paul Pogba, Speech to France teammates
before World Cup Final**

In *Togetherness: How to Build a Winning Team,*[1] Dr. Matt Slater studied the above speech from Paul Pogba. In a speech lasting less than a minute, the French international used the word "we" every four seconds – 16 times in total. He used the "we" in terms of him and his teammates, but also referred to the national "we" – the French people as a whole – and their kids, their grandkids and great-grandkids.

For the youth coach, using language associated with 'we', like Pogba, can give a unifying effect. Many books, blogs, and posts you read surrounding youth sport will tell you that coaching kids is about them, not about the coach. It is quite common for coaches to take credit for successes ('I' told them to do that, they did what 'I' asked, they followed 'my' tactics) and distance themselves from defeat or poor performance ('you' were poor today, 'you' need to improve, 'I' don't run this team for 'you' to play badly). Players, at any age and at any level, need to know that you, the coach – as leader – are with them, not just in the good times, but during difficult ones as well. It builds trust when you stand side-by-side with players regardless of the level of the result or performance. In the *It's Your Game* segment at the end of this chapter, much-travelled coach Matt Ward (@mattwardy1) tells us how he worked to build this trust with a very destitute group of players in Ghana.

Team Identity & Cohesion

The Wales national team, accustomed to not even qualifying for major tournaments, reached the semi-finals of Euro 2016. This included the knock-out defeat of highly fancied Belgium along the way. They are a wonderful example of investing a lot of time and effort in their identity and togetherness.

They heavily used and promoted the concept (and hashtag) of #TogetherStronger. The team itself contained superstar Gareth Bale, and now Juventus midfielder Aaron Ramsey, but below them, the squad was made up of – in the most respectful way –unfashionable players. Striker, Hal Robson-Kanu was even without a club at the moment he swivelled and scored a wonderful goal in their unexpected victory over the Belgians. The nation bought into their #TogetherStronger mindset, the players did, the superstar players did, and the coaching staff did. Wherever the team went, the hashtag followed – and they believed in it.

At the time of writing, three years after their successful European Championship campaign, a quick Twitter search of the #TogetherStronger hashtag, revealed its continued use by Wales Football. There were posts about the country's crest, the traditional dragon and daffodil emblems, and the national team motto 'Gorau Chwarae Cyd Chwarae' (The Best Play is Team Play). It was used when announcing their national Under-15 squad and for the Cardiff Met University Women's team. It is all-encompassing and aims to unify and solidify all members of the game in Wales – the clubs, the players, the superstars, the youth players, the women's teams, the supporters, and the entire country.

Identity is something that is very individual to *your* team, club, or group. You may be coaching at an iconic club where the traditions and history represent it. New players and coaches automatically assimilate to the culture of the club. On the other hand, you may have just started a team with your children and other kids on the street. Or maybe your situation is somewhere in-between. *I* cannot tell you what your identity should be, or could be. That is something for you, as a leader, to investigate or even invent.

---

[1] An excellent practical guide to building togetherness within groups.

Creating a Connection

"　　　　　　　　　　　　　　　　　　　　　　**"**

No significant learning can occur without a
significant relationship.

**Rita Pierson, *Every Child Needs a
Champion*, TED Talk**

One of the main reasons that people join groups and make friends is to get a feeling of belonging. Being cared for by someone not only alleviates loneliness but being wanted and cared about also promotes well-being. Human beings need people close to them to feel valued and connected.

In our football environments, two types of connections are important – first, the connection between you, the coach, and secondly – the connection with the players.

Connecting Coach to Players

Trust is an exceptionally undervalued trait of coaches. Over the last decade or so, 'power', in a leadership sense, has changed. Conventionally, you did what you were told by the person in power. Today, it is about the power of trust. Trust in the coach allows the team to flourish.

Central to trust is integrity. In fact, I am a firm believer that without integrity, you cannot be trusted. On a simple level, if you promise something, or say something, you stick to it. For example, if your policy around playing time is that every player receives equal time, then that *has to happen*, whether the game is a meaningless friendly or an 'important' cup final. If you promise equal playing time, but then waiver on this at the first sign of pressure, it ultimately tells your players you will go back on your word. If you can lie or be deceitful about one thing, you are capable of lying or being deceitful about anything.

"　　　　　　　　　　　　　　　　　　　　　　**"**

A team is not a group of people who work
together. A team is a group of people who trust
each other.

**Simon Sinek,
author and motivational speaker**

Trust is not necessarily simply about making everyone feel good. If players trust you, they will go the extra mile for you. It allows you greater scope to challenge them, or even become stern with them. You can be honest with them, have difficult conversations with them, with all parties knowing it comes from a safe place.

"

> I am going to defend you until the last day of
> my life in the press conference, but inside the
> locker room I am going to tell you the truth.

"

**Pep Guardiola to his
Manchester City players**

Those of you who watch Jürgen Klopp regularly will be well aware of his trademark hug. Every player receives one after the game. This physical connection is not just because the German likes a cuddle – it builds trust. Watching videos of him returning to the Liverpool training ground after the 2019 summer break, saw everyone get the same attention from him. Every player he met, office staff, the football staff, and the ladies who work in the canteen, all got a hug. The power of this display of togetherness has led many youth academies to insist that players shake hands (this may also be a high five or a fist pump, etc.) with the coach and each other before and after the session.

Klopp acknowledges the importance of physical contact – in his case, the hugs – as a way to balance the high-level demands that he asks of the players. Players will go the extra mile for those they feel who care for them. Klopp feels he can get more from everyone by building a connection through physical contact. The roar says he wants intensity; the hug says I love you for it.

"

> I think it makes football much more enjoyable
> when you really feel this togetherness because
> we are often enough alone.

"

Jürgen Klopp

This physical contact, enacted appropriately, of course, is more powerful than you may initially believe. First of all, it allows everyone to connect with one another every time they meet. The handshake, hug, or high-five may just take a moment, but it allows the opportunity to look a player in the eye and ask them questions about their life, their game, or whatever is going on at the time. Adding a smile tells the player that you are interested in them as a person, that they are important to you. They learn to trust you. Physical contact from someone you trust has even been proven to even alleviate human pain. We comfort children with a hug, cradle a baby who is crying, and put our arm around people during moments of grief.

Player Leadership

In *Making the Ball Roll*, we spent an entire chapter looking at the concept of leadership as a coach. You are, however, not the only leader in the team. You may be organiser-in-chief and indeed you play a significant leadership role, but you are not the only one.

Harnessing the leadership skills of the players is important. Ultimately, it is the players who take to the field and will be responsible for what goes on between the white lines. I do not believe the coach is *fully* redundant once a game starts, but there certainly must be ownership and leadership on the field of play. Players should not need to be choreographed and talked through every kick of the ball, or told how to behave in a given circumstance. To facilitate this, training sessions that involve players making decisions and solving problems that will arise in the game are critical.

Chapter 12 – The 'We' in Team

"

Decision making is key. Players have to
experience the ideas in training before they can
fully grasp what they are doing, and it is not
enough to just tell them.

"

Pep Guardiola

In an interview for *FourFourTwo* magazine, former Reading and Leeds United coach, and scout for Arsenal, Brian McDermott, spoke about getting senior players onside. In age-group football, the concept of senior players is different, but you will have a group dynamic where certain players are particularly influential – every group has a certain social hierarchy. Their behaviour and influence may be greater than yours at times, as we will see later in the *It's Your Game* segment. Players are often more inclined to be influenced by peers than by adults. Using this circumstance to get the best out of the team is very valuable as a coach and as a leader.

In his aforementioned book, *Togetherness*, Slater speaks about the *Senior Leadership Team*, a group made up of players who act as a conduit between coach and the team. I have seen this concept work under the format suggested by Slater, but also in different forms and under different names, whether that's a *Leadership Group* or *Skipper's Group*.

The central concept of the group is to form the leadership metronome of the team. In forming this group, I prefer to offer the opportunity for players to join, rather than choose membership on who I think should be involved, as suggested by Slater (although there is merit to offering all players the opportunity to be 'leaders' on a rotational basis – leadership is a skill that we can look to develop in all young people).

This empowerment allows players to have a greater buy-in to the process which they are an integral part of. When managing an academy, with around 80 players, I offered out this opportunity to anyone who thought they had leadership skills, or those who felt they wanted to develop them. Being the best player was not a factor, nor was any perceived seniority.

We used this peer leadership group to help bring the team together (and often to transmit messages from the coach to the group) in many ways. Leaders were tasked with managing the clearing up of equipment, to influence others and improve player behaviour, ensure that the teams were run fairly and any relevant issues were understood by management, and even to get other players back into the classroom. A teammate encouraging a peer to complete assignments on time is a much better sell than a coach, 20+ years his elder, dictating that they *must do their homework*. A strong player-led peer leadership group can deliver your messages in a different and more palatable way than you can.

In many ways, those who wish to join the group are both surprising, and no surprise at all. The dominant voices on the pitch show up as expected, but others, often the quiet members of the group, do so too. Those who are behaviourally sound and mature show up, and so do (more often than you might think) the more difficult members. This is a great opportunity to harness the positive intentions and aspirations of everyone.

Connecting Players with Each Other

In July 2003, the US Army War College carried out a study entitled *Why They Fight*. Authors Wong, Kolditz, Millen, and Potter wanted to understand soldiers' motivation to fight during the Iraq War. It was not (necessarily) for the flag, political reasons, or money (although elements of them will always be present). They found that the soldiers were motivated to carry out their duties primarily out of loyalty to *their colleagues* – they had developed a connection that would motivate them in – literally – life or death situations.

This bond, however, was not forged on the shooting range, with long, gruelling midnight hikes through forests, or in excruciating PT sessions. Their relationships were formed away from these organised settings, during "noncombat time – the hours of nothingness, the shared boredom." It was here "where bonds of trust, friendships and group identity were built."

Steve Magness (@stevemagness), co-author of *The Passion Paradox*, compared this to the leadership of renowned team-bonder and basketball coach, Gregg Popovich. In his article, *Why Team Building Exercises Don't Work... and What Actually Does*, Magness notes the use of social occasions, namely two to three-hour team meals, that drove a deeper level of conversation amongst players from the San Antonio Spurs than in the locker room, or in the gym – just like the unstructured, unorganised downtime soldiers had to build bonds while in the military.

Popovich would strategically set up tables prior to the squad's arrival to ensure that players communicated, interacted, and connected. One player claimed that as a result of the methods of 'Pop' that he became *friends* with every single member of the roster, a rarity in any group that includes over a dozen individuals.

In an interview with the BBC's *Football Focus*, AFC Bournemouth striker Callum Wilson divulged some of the details behind the club's ability to mix with the major Premier League clubs, despite a vast gap in terms of finance and revenue. He cited team spirit as being amongst the key features of the group. This, however, was not conceived while white-water rafting or by abseiling, but in an entirely different way. Bournemouth get personal, allowing players to share their most intimate moments from their life.

"

We have a thing called 'Timeline' and players tell their life story ... There are things people say in their timeline that they are never going to say in the dressing room in general chat.

Callum Wilson

Wilson himself detailed his childhood in foster care and safe houses in his timeline, which intrigued his teammates. They wanted to know more. Their connection was no longer about football, cars, and women (which is the stereotype of most adult, male football dressing rooms), but a deep, personal one. When you go into 'battle' with those who know, understand, and are interested in your deepest moments, and you know his or hers, you *will* fight for each other.

In a youth context, however, we need to be age-appropriate. Sharing vulnerable moments in a shared group meeting, like Wilson's above, may forge confusion, rather than connection, and would probably become a safeguarding issue. In *Team Building in Sport: Linking Theory and Research to Practical Application*, Paradis and Martin would "only recommend it for certain levels of maturity." In the same study, Martin points to research, summed up below:

"

Crace and Hardy (1997) suggested that mutual understanding between team members is the cornerstone of the team building process. Similarly, Orlick (1990) stated that many personal problems that arise in team settings stem from teammates' lack of understanding of each other's needs, motives and feelings. Further, he argued that it is difficult to be responsive to teammates' needs or understand their perspectives if those needs are not known and the perspectives are not understood.

"

Paradis & Martin

Some youth-friendly examples from the same study include getting the players to share a personal story about why they played football, and the reason for their continued participation. Other topics can include non-football info like details about their family, their favorite music/movies/TV shows/websites/games, etc. After these shared meetings, Paradis and Martin detail that players feel closer, have increased collective efficiency, and have a sense of invincibility.

Conclusion – Tactical Connections

Although a major chunk of youth coaching is dedicated to improving individuals, it remains important to develop the team and how these individuals work and behave in a team environment. Along with unifying players through the setting of team goals (as detailed in *Making The Ball Roll*), we find that making connections between all involved is a very strong aspect of team bonding. Changing a group or a bunch of me's to 'we', developing a team identify, and sharing leadership with players, increases the strength and success of your team.

Beyond the social aspects, a facet of team cohesion that is often overlooked, however, is their connection on the pitch – the *physical* way they move and behave in unison.

In chapter 10, when analysing his goal against Argentina, Dennis Bergkamp talks about his eye contact with Frank de Boer, before the long pass which was to assist the winning goal. Later, in the *It's Your Game* segment, author, mathematician and football coach, David Sumpter, shows us how he uses maths and stats to develop tactical team cohesion and communication, even amongst the youngest players.

Raymond Verheijen, who we met extensively in chapter 8, links fitness to this concept of team cohesion. He states that the more players play together, the more this non-verbal communication grows organically. In the context of a professional team, he implores a training method that reduces the likelihood of players being injured. This means that you "play your best team more often," and the team is therefore stronger because its communication is better. He points to the Barcelona-heavy Spanish National Team who won all before them between 2008 and 2012, and the Bayern Munich-centric German National Team that won the 2014 World Cup.

This "communication" he speaks about, however, is not necessarily the type that you would imagine. It is not verbal, but non-verbal – and not just body language. It is about the habits of your teammates. It is about developing an almost unconscious understanding of your teammates around you. You know them and understand what they are going to do next. You know what they are capable of, and what they are not – another positive in not changing the personnel in the group any more than is absolutely necessary.

The youth coach will arguably have a much tougher task in maintaining this than those in the professional environment. If we remember Chris Ramsey's pyramid, we accept that youth coaches will prioritise the development of the individual over the performance of the team. We have to juggle the responsibility of offering all players sufficient game-time, with developing this tactical communication. For example, if you have three centre-backs in your squad, all three should get the opportunity to play with each other and develop this communication. The same goes, of course, for those playing in other positions.

In the following two chapters, we will look at tactics, through individual playing positions and modern tactical trends.

Summary

- One of the most important *individual* traits within football is the ability to work within a team.
- Expecting a group of players who have just come together to act and behave like a fully-functioning team is probably not going to happen. Forming an effective team takes time.
- Bruce Tuckman proposed the *Forming-Storming-Norming-Performing* model of team development. Understanding these stages, and the specific stage your team is at, is important.
- There are clear team-building advantages to keeping your team together long-term. Adding new members, or too many new members, may upset the balance of the team environment.
- 'We' is an important word in football and team building. Paul Pogba used the word 'we' 16 times during a one-minute speech prior to the 2018 World Cup Final.
- The Wales National Team used and continue to use the hashtag and concept of #TogetherStronger to unite supporters, players and staff, uniting everyone in the process.
- Identity is unique to your team. I cannot tell you what your identity should be, but devising some unifying methods is worth it.
- Creating connections between players, and between coach and players, is a vital piece in the team-building process.
- Being trustworthy and showing integrity will encourage players to work harder for you as coach.
- Appropriate physical contact can be used to develop trust and a connection between coach and players, and between the players themselves.
- The coach is not the only leader in the group. Ensure you develop players' decision-making and leadership skills.
- Utilising a leadership group within your environment can be a great tool to help manage your team.
- Gregg Popovich and AFC Bournemouth use strategies to help players interact and communicate on a deeper level than they normally would, thus increasing the bond between members of the team. Similar age-appropriate 'sharing meetings' can be used by the youth coach to help players get to know each other.
- It is important to develop tactical cohesion, as well as social cohesion, in your team. This develops non-verbal communication where players inherently understand each other's game.

> ## It's Your Game #1
>
> # Standing With Us
>
> ## Matt Ward • @Coach_mattward
>
> ## International Coach

After a spell in China, I accepted an offer from a club in Division 1 of Ghana.

On day one, I was waiting outside my office, watching the lads turn up in dribs and drabs. Time was getting closer to the start of training, but players were still slowly arriving, some still getting their boots on. When I got to the pitch, I introduced myself to those who were there, but made it clear with body language, that no pleasantries were going to be made just yet. I stood in silence with the players who were already there. The players who were late started running to join us, some of them still in just their socks.

There was an obvious lack of discipline. I had heard that there was an issue with the players' lack of respect for management as they felt that they were alone, that nobody supported them. It was my first job to quickly create a bond between myself and this group who were an underpaid, underfed, and uncared for group of players.

I had to set rules and expectations, but at the same time I had to connect with them – to show that was one of them, that we were a team and a family. I made it clear that they had a choice to turn up to training on time or be locked out of the stadium and find another job. I didn't drag it on, just a quick, sharp message before we got stuck into training, which was about quality and putting smiles on faces, allowing them to feel my personality.

Away matches were particularly tough to get a result. Logistics were a nightmare; travel times were huge, and clubs didn't have the best resources for hotels, food, and other basic needs. Referees were renowned for favouring home teams. Instead of travelling more comfortably, like previous coaches, I chose to travel on the bus with the players. Everyone was cramped into a tight, hot, minibus, but it was real life. It gave me first-hand experience of what the players went through. We would sing, pray, and chant together

After an away F.A. Cup penalty shoot-out victory, we travelled home with non-stop singing and dancing for hours. When the time for toilet breaks came around, I'd stand on the roadside taking a pee with the lads, all of us in a line. They would laugh so hard, and when I asked them why (expecting a cruder joke!), they said it was because our coach was standing with us "even when taking a toilet"!

We went on to break two club records for away matches and this couldn't have been done, without the players firstly, wanting to play for their coach.

It's Your Game #2

Shapes & Numbers

David Sumpter • @Soccermatics

Professor of Applied Mathematics, Coach & Author

There is no lower age limit for starting to talk about the mathematical patterns underlying teamwork with your players.

For 6-year-olds, who are beginning both their footballing careers and their academic schooling, I talk a lot about triangles and diamonds. I tell them that – when they don't have the ball but a teammate does – they should move so they create a triangle with the player with the ball and another player. This starts to open up space, and they will soon notice that some triangles create better passing opportunities than others. Emphasising triangles is a much more useful and specific instruction than simply shouting "spread out".

As players develop, they can start to understand and visualise the structures they create on the field. One tool I use for this is the passing network. Before the match, I print out a sheet with the diamond we will play. Then, every time a pass is made between two players during a match, I draw a line. Pretty soon, we get a picture of who is passing to who. Discussing these networks at half time can build to a wider discussion: "Why isn't the ball getting out to the left?" or "You know you can use the goalkeeper during build-up?"

Instead of selecting a "best player" at the end of the match, I use the passing network to pick out a "passing pair" – two players for which there are lots of connecting lines on the passing diagram. This is a small change in emphasis that makes a massive difference to how the players perceive their role in the team.

Most of the points I have emphasised here relate to matches, but a philosophy based around presenting simple statistics and talking geometry can be used in every aspect of training sessions, and at all levels. Counting the number of unbroken completed passes in a rondo, awarding points for changing the direction of play during a build-up exercise, stopping play and looking at how many players are standing in a line with each other, are just a few of many ways in which simple 'analytics' can be incorporated into the players' thinking. Statistics set targets and motivate players to complete tasks.

Long tactical monologues are a no-no at any level, but short, engaging discussions about numbers and shapes always have a central part to play in football.

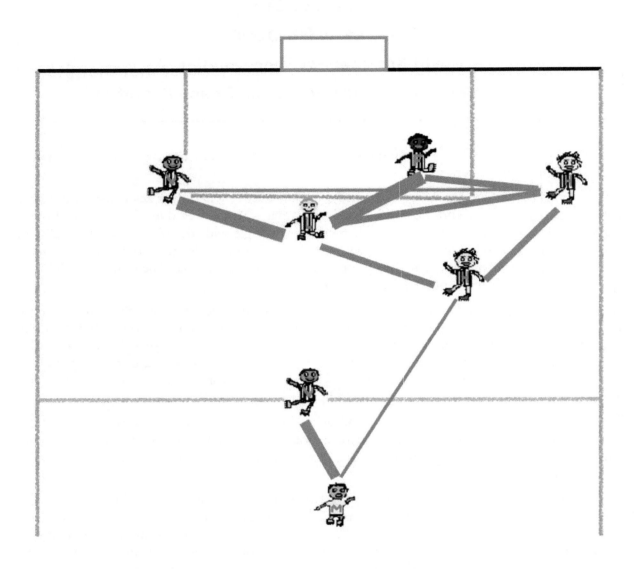

One example of a passing network I made to illustrate build-up for 10-year-olds playing 7-aside.
Thickness of line illustrates number of passes made.

It's Your Game #3

A Tale of an Untucked Shirt

Anonymous

Academy Coach

I once took over a team of Under-19 boys, most of whom were inner-city kids. A number of them had huge problems with authority, and it quickly became a power battle when I made any significant decision. One moment changed that.

Davis (pseudonym) was a striker and admired by everyone in the team. This admiration came, however, from fear. He was a tough kid. He had a colourful history in school and in his neighbourhood, one renowned for gang violence. You got the feeling that all the other players just wanted to be on the right side of him. *His* music played in the locker room always. If he misbehaved, the flock followed suit. If he was late, everyone was late. If he was early, everyone was there.

Davis also possessed elements of Obsessive Compulsive Disorder (OCD). Before playing, his boots and kit had to be neat and clean. His clothes had to be folded and his shoes stowed neatly underneath. His hair always needed to be perfect.

After warming-up one day, he made a really big deal out of his shirt becoming untucked – I mean, the world is going to end type level of hysteria. It was one of very few team rules that he liked, but one that was barely acknowledged due to the dysfunction of the environment. Almost immediately, however, one by one, like lemmings, all the other players tucked their shirts in. I thought, this is my in.

You see Davis had no idea how powerful he was. He had no idea how influential he was within the group – until I pointed it out. I was the coach, but he was undoubtedly the leader of the team. I arranged to meet him away from everybody else. I had to address this with him. He spoke about being kicked out of school, out of home, and how every adult close to him left his life, including the coach I had taken over from. I asked him what he wanted from the team, which were the same outcomes that I had – play well, win games, improve, be hard to beat, score goals, train well, come together, etc. I told him, like the untucked shirt incident, that the group would follow him. If he argued with me, the group would become argumentative. If he trained poorly, the group would see it as a green light to follow.

From then on, Davis and I had a connection. We were from different worlds in every respect, but we found a bond. We were going to lead this team together. I would organise all the coach bits; he would manage the players through his behaviour. The group dynamic and player-coach relationship changed instantly. We were all now pulling in the same direction – with our shirts tucked in.

It's Your Game #4

Bringing People Together

Dr Matt Slater • @DrMattSlater

Author, *Togetherness*

Togetherness, togetherness, togetherness. During my time across various academies in youth football, I am always struck by the transformative effect of bringing people together. There is a magical spell of developing togetherness that truly unlocks the power of the group.

I am drawn to a particular – true – story.

You can picture the scene. The referee blew the final whistle and the team was ecstatic, celebrating on the pitch, after a strong performance and victory. High fives, fist pumps, embraces all round. After some time, the team returned to the changing rooms fully buoyant.

Here, the routine process happened – as it does in all changing rooms after a match – the coaching group debriefed. Specific analytical points were made about players' performances, as well as general points of reflection about the team as a whole. Nothing special there. But, what happened next was special. One of the players, Sarah (17), stood up and spoke: "We, as players, are going to stay behind for a while to think some more about today's game." The players stayed behind after the coaching group had left. At this point in the togetherness journey, the team had shared their VBV (Vision / Behaviour / Values).

Sarah proposed that the team led their own analysis on how well they lived their shared values and behaviours on the pitch (and in preparation for the match).

"Had we lived by our team identity?"

"Had we shown our values and behaviours to the best of our ability?"

This was completely instigated by Sarah. The shared sense of togetherness was so strong at that time that Sarah was empowered to lead by example. And all of the team followed. So, after that match, and every match in the future, the player-led values and behaviours discussion simply became part of what "we" do. Away from matchdays, too, it became a valuable reference point. Perhaps a key and difficult decision had to be made, or a training session hadn't quite gone to plan. The check and challenge player-led discussion was a powerful tool.

This is what togetherness looks like in practice. The strength of the psychological connections between individuals fuels the fire of continual team improvement and high performance. Note too that Sarah led the player-led discussion *following a victory,* not a root and branch analysis of a defeat. Togetherness is where the magic happens.

Chapter 13
Modern Playing Positions

"
As long as humanity exists, something new will
come along – otherwise football dies.
"

Arrigo Sacchi

After the absorbingly entertaining World Cup in Brazil, I published a book, *Soccer Tactics 2014*. The book was designed, not as a commentary on that particular tournament, but using the tournament as a lens to look at modern football tactics, much of which will be presented here.

Nostalgia for a game we once knew often means we overlook change. If we are not abreast of the game, we revert back to what we are comfortable with and what we know. If you grew up in an era of 4-4-2, then that may be your reference point. If you spent a significant part of your lifetime playing or coaching to a certain blueprint, it may have become outdated. Therefore, understanding modern tactical trends, and having a clear idea of the direction the game is going is a necessity for the youth coach in preparing young players for what is to come.

Trends and Counter-Trends

Just when you think you have a firm handle on the topic of football tactics, something else pops up that changes the landscape. There is a constant tactical ebb and flow, trend and counter-trend. As soon as one style begins to dominate, its antidote is being concocted. Over the last decade, we have seen a punch-up between possession-based, attacking football and the counter-attacking game, for example.

In a positional sense, this trend and counter-trend is also evident. No sooner had two striker formations faded towards extinction, with experts predicting a future where teams would more likely play with no strikers at all, than we have seen a resurgence in the strike partnership in recent years. The increase in defensive midfielders to combat assist areas (Zone 14), has led to a decrease in specialist number 10s. We could go on, and will go on, as the chapter develops.

Pigeon-Holing Youth Players

One of the great debates within youth football is around playing positions. When does a kid become a centre-back, a midfielder, a striker, etc.?

The general consensus is that young players should begin specialising positionally around 15 or 16-years-old (although this point of view has its detractors too). They certainly may have 'secondary' positions also, but, with a few years before they enter adult football, becoming an expert in a certain position is certainly an option. 'Positions' today, however, are a lot more fluid than they once were, as we will learn as we read on.

In 2010, I was lucky enough to have a long conversation with Nick Cox, then Academy Manager at Watford FC (now at Manchester United and the contributor to the *It's Your Game* segment in Chapter 6). Watford's academy, at the time, was run along very different lines than it is today. In fact, it was arguably the most dynamic, forward-thinking programme in England. Their players all schooled together, they had a robust (and documented) development programme, and an enviable record of producing professional footballers.

Their approach to specialising, in terms of playing positions, was well-formed. From the age of 14, 80% of the 'work' players did in training and games would be based on 'their' position. So centre-backs would rarely get involved in crossing and finishing sessions (unless they were defending them) and strikers would rarely get involved in defending exercises that did not relate to their role in the team. It was a narrow view (it was supposed to be). Watford were particularly strict on this – it was their way of producing expert players, their way of giving their academy players an edge. They believed the best chance of getting players into the professional game (we know how hard that is from chapter 2) was to develop positional experts.

The policy was designed to allow players to understand one role fully, whilst also making allowances for change. Players *did* have secondary positions, the concept being 'one up/down, one over, or opposite side'. For example, a right full-back will also learn to play right-wing (one up), right centre-back (one over) or left full-back (opposite side). Ashley Young is a good example of this. He came through Watford's Academy at this time as a left-winger, but played full-back for Manchester United in his 30s (one down). While not an exact science, the policy allows players to specialise, but also allows a certain amount of versatility, something the modern game demands.

Versatility in Youth Football

Being positionally versatile is important for younger players before any positional specialisation occurs. Certainly, up to the age of puberty, players should experience playing multiple positions. This may not necessarily mean playing them as a defender for 10 minutes, a midfielder for 10, and a striker for 15. It would be much more robust if this involved rotating players' positions every few weeks. This will give them significant playing experience in all areas, and allow them to foster an open-mind for where they play when they are older.

I have lost count of the number of conversations I have been involved with players, parents, spectators, and other coaches who will say that a pre-pubescent is a "natural goal-scorer" or a "born centre-back". The absolute truth in these situations is that we simply do not know what a player will become as they, and their game, evolve through their teens and into adulthood.

Jamie Carragher was a striker with Liverpool up until he became a professional, when he dropped back to midfield, full-back, and ultimately, centre-back. Ashley Cole and Rio Ferdinand also notably played as attackers before spending their senior careers in 'defence'. None became goal-scoring defenders in any way despite that being their forte at youth level. These high-level youth attackers settled into the game as high-level adult defenders.

Facilitating the rotation of positions allows each player to experience different roles, different responsibilities, and to see the pitch from a different viewpoint. They have to use their weaker feet, play in areas where space is open, and where it is at a premium. It allows all players to appreciate both attacking and defending phases (and therefore transition phases also). We want to develop their conscious football ability, but also develop their instincts by exposing them to multiple playing positions.

I once had a discussion with a very highly-rated player when he was 16. His instincts were, overwhelmingly, attacking ones, and at this age he would play in the attacking positions, whether as a central striker or as a wide attacker (more on this later). His defensive instincts, however, were largely non-existent. I never believed that it was through laziness or a bad attitude; he just did not know how to defend. If the ball was there, he would challenge for it, but positioning or sensing danger when out of possession was underdeveloped.

At the time of our discussion, he was about to secure a move to a Premier League club who, at the time, had just recruited a Head Coach who was very pragmatic. He expected his attack-minded players to contribute to defensive situations, much like how someone like Roy Hodgson would do today. His teams were more organised than open, more defensive than attacking, more cautious than thrill-seeking. The player never did play in this first team, or for that particular manager, partly due to age, but something tells me that a defensive string to his bow may have made a big impact on his career (he has gone on to have a respectable career in the game). You would not take any of his attacking instincts away, just add elements of defensive ones.

As a kid, all his coaches played him in attack. What he did, with the ball, was on another level to most others. However, long-term, I always feel that he suffered because he never experienced *having* to defend. The same goes for the big kid who plays all his youth days at centre-back, and is suddenly asked to carry the ball forward, play out from the back, or offer support to a teammate in possession. A balance, however imbalanced, between defensive and attacking nous is essential for any player.

This is one of the strongest reasons why small-sided game formats (3v3/4v4) are important for the youngest players. The pitches are so small that you are a couple of seconds away from being in a defensive position and an attacking one. The number of players is so small that all have to take part in both attacking and defensive phases of the game. 'Strikers' cannot stand on the half-way line and watch as everyone else defends, and likewise a 'defender' cannot take a back seat when their team is attacking or in possession.

Once players have a reasonable experience of positions all over the pitch, and a good grasp of both defensive and attacking responsibilities, then specialising in one position (with secondary options) becomes more palatable as they get older.

With this, and the tactical ebb and flow in mind, we will look at the game that we are preparing players for, from a positional sense.

Positions

At the time of writing, in 2020, we are seeing an increasing change in how traditional playing positions are viewed, and even how they are grouped. There is a movement, albeit slight, away from traditional – Goalkeepers, Defenders, Midfielders and Attackers – categories of players. In the run-up to Euro 2016, Antonio Conte's Italy squad used the categories of Goalkeepers, Defenders, *Wide Players*, Midfielders and Strikers. Their emphasis on 'Wide Players' was largely due to the fact that they played with three centre-backs and wing-backs, rather than full-backs and wingers. In a similar vein, Germany often use 'Attackers' to group both attacking midfielders and strikers as their squads usually only carried one traditional number 9. In a further reorganisation of the way we traditionally think about playing positions, Thiago Motta, then a youth coach at Paris Saint-Germain, put forward a puzzling 2-7-2 formation in an interview, with the goalkeeper as a 'midfielder'. Initially, the football world scratched its head,[1] until realising that Motta was reading a 4-3-3 formation horizontally, rather than vertically as is the norm (see below).

---

[1] This notion, when first released even prompted some writers to believe that the goalkeeper would actually play in midfield ahead of two centre-backs. As dynamic as football may become in the future, I am highly sceptical that something like this would be successful in any way.

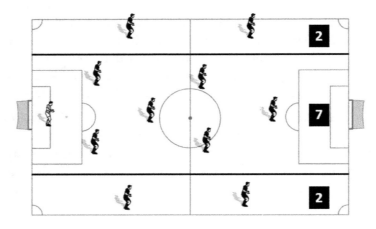

Thiago Motta's "2-7-2" Formation

For the sake of organising the remainder of this chapter, however, we will use the traditional Goalkeeper-Defenders-Midfielders-Forwards grouping, all the while recognising that *all player in all positions will have duties that cross those labels.* Along the way, we will come across many grey areas.

From here on, we will take a look at how the evolution of football tactics has changed the roles and responsibilities of the players who play within them. We will analyse – position by position – the main trends that have altered the way we look at (and stereotype) players positionally, whilst relating them back to the youth players that you coach.

Goalkeepers

"

When we have the ball, we want the goalkeeper to be an additional outfield player – the eleventh player.

"

Martin Thomas / Tim Dittmer, England National Team Goalkeeper Coaches

We demand a lot from the modern goalkeeper. It is no longer sufficient for any keeper to simply stand on his line, make saves, and distribute the ball as far down the pitch as possible. Although he or she still needs to make match-winning saves, he needs to have the passing, receiving, and distribution skills to rival his outfield teammates. The modern goalkeeper now uses his feet seven times more than he did in the early 1990s, and there is a roughly 3:1 ratio in using his feet compared to his hands. A study by Calvary FC goalkeeper coach, Jordan Santiago (@jordansantiag0), found that the club's "goalkeepers distributed the ball with their feet 933% more than shots they faced in the 2019 season."

Nowadays, being a goalkeeper is an all-inclusive role, crucial in both classic and modern ways. Shot-stopping and reflexes remain as important ever, but new dynamics such as distribution, sweeping up, aggressive positioning, and improved athleticism, are necessities too.

In *The Evolution of the Goalkeeper: What Makes the Perfect Modern-Day No. 1?* an article from *The Bleacher Report,* their consulting goalkeeper (former Premier League stopper Asmir Begovic) identified eight traits to being a modern goalkeeper:

Shot-Stopping	Regardless of the newer skillset that is required of a goalkeeper, stopping goal-bound shots remains the fundamental base of the keeper's duties.
Handling	Beyond shot-stopping, 'handling' requires catching, parrying, punching, dealing with crosses, and even 'batting' the ball away.
Reflexes	This requires the goalkeeper to react quickly both physically and mentally to balls that may be coming at them (or at goal) fast, from a short distance, awkward angles, or having taken a deflection.
Aerial Command	The professional goalkeeper tends to have a bigger reach than most other players. They can reach the ball at a higher point due to the permitted use of their hands and extended arms. Being able to handle high balls is important, as is their judgement as to whether to come for high balls, or not.
Big-Game Ability	Goalkeeping has a unique pressure – any mistake can result in a goal, so handling this pressure is vital. Successful goalkeepers tend to thrive in this environment. The more important the game, the more they come to the fore.
Penalty-Saving	The taking of a penalty is a unique situation in football, with odds stacked against the goalkeeper as the taker has a big target and a relatively short distance to shoot. Rules (e.g. keepers penalised for stepping off the goal-line) disfavour the shot-stopper further. Shot-stopping, reflexes, reading/out-psyching the opponent and even luck are involved.
Distribution (hands and feet)	Goalkeepers are now considered the starter of attacks as well as the last line of defence. Their ability to distribute short and long, with hands and feet, to teammates and then become a passing option for them are skills that are highly sought-after in possession teams, but also quick, accurate passes are required from those who play in counter-attacking ones.

In *Making The Ball Roll*, we looked at the turning point for goalkeepers in the modern game, and ironically this came from the rather dour World Cup in 1990:

"　　　　　　　　　　　　　　　　　　　　　　**"**

In 1992, the "back-pass" rule was introduced into the Laws of Association Football. For those young enough not to remember football pre-1992, it was perfectly acceptable for a goalkeeper to pick up a pass from his teammate. This was often used as the ultimate means to time-waste, legally, and often led to dull games, which came to a head at the Italia 1990 World Cup.

One game springs to mind from that tournament. England were leading Egypt 1-0 in Cagliari, and in the meantime – 400km away in Palermo – the Republic of Ireland and Holland merely needed a draw for both to qualify from Group F. With the scores level at 1-1, the game petered out in the closing stages leading to the Irish goalkeeper, Pat Bonner, constantly rolling the ball out to his defenders, before happily collecting the back pass to kill the game. Against Egypt in the same tournament, Bonner allegedly had the ball in his possession for a total of six minutes!

Making the Ball Roll

Bonner himself confessed that this new law changed the role of the goalkeeper forever – and noted that those who could not cope with the new technical demands of the goalkeeper's game, quickly faded away. Nearly three decades later, we now have goalkeepers that are more than capable of using their feet as well as their hands, *and* arguably as well as their outfield team-mates.

Out of possession, modern goalkeepers are quick to leave their goal line to 'sweep' up behind their defenders. Against Algeria in the 2014 World Cup, Germany and Bayern Munich goalkeeper Manuel Neuer had a phenomenal 17 touches of the ball outside his penalty area. For Germany to play their modern brand of attacking football (at the time), and to maintain a high defensive line, they needed Neuer to play this type of game. There was even a joke that in the run-up to Germany's quarter-final versus France, Neuer and his French counterpart, Hugo Lloris, would clash for possession in midfield, given their propensities for leaving their boxes!

"　　　　　　　　　　　　　　　　　　　　　　**"**

A goalkeeper is a part of the team, not apart from the team

FA Learning

For us coaches, then, it is imperative that we adapt our coaching to involve the goalkeeper in team training sessions. Traditionally we would see goalkeepers trudge off to the corner with a specialist coach and join in with the rest of the team when required. They are a part of the team, not apart from it! If we are to produce goalkeepers who are as competent with their feet as outfield players, we need to involve them in 'outfield' technical/tactical sessions. It is extremely difficult to get to a technical level without taking part in opposed, pressured practices, and just relying on unopposed passes to a goalkeeper coach.

Defenders

I am almost certain that if football was invented today, and played in its current form, and we had to come up with the terms we would use for playing positions, the word 'defender' probably wouldn't be used for either centre-backs and certainly not for full-backs.

"

[John] Stones, Luke Shaw, Nathaniel Clyne, Calum Chambers ... they are not just defenders. They can play. Look at Stones: what a delightful, lovely footballer. I still hear people go: "Yeah, but he makes the odd mistake, he shouldn't be messing about with the ball". No, let him; he'll learn when's right and when's wrong.

"

Gary Lineker, from *Fifty Years of Hurt*

Centre-Backs

In times gone by, we looked at centre-backs as defenders *only*. They tended to be big and strong and were often described as being "no-nonsense". When dealing with opposition strikers, coaches would instruct these defenders to "let them know you are there" which is basically code for an over-aggressive approach to the duel.

Centre-backs have, however, evolved. Sure, for the most part, they are still big, strong, and can be aggressive – they are, after all, the last line of defence in front of the goalkeeper, will often take physical charge at set-plays, and they need to defend vigorously against direct play. France's Mamadou Sakho, for example, has the physique and traits of a traditional centre-back, yet his biggest criticism is that he is not technical enough and liable to make mistakes when in possession. Conversely, Manchester City's John Stones is considered to be the opposite – excellent in possession, but poor defensively. The modern centre-back needs to be effective when out of possession, and an excellent footballer in possession.

Rather than simply being responsible for launching the ball from back to front, centre-backs now regularly have possession statistics comparable to midfield players, if not better. Frequently, we now see defenders amongst the players with the highest pass completion rates across leagues and tournaments (we must acknowledge, however, that the passes defenders are required to make are considerably less likely to be intercepted than, say, an attacking midfielder trying to play a complicated through ball).

"

"

The two players that see the ball the most amount of time, with possibilities to choose the pass they are going to give throughout the entire game, is always the two central defenders.

That's why, when I choose my central defenders, they have to be able to defend, be aggressive, be able to recover the ball, but they have to be good on the ball, so the build-up from the back is more fluid.

Marcelo Bielsa

More is now demanded of centre-backs as footballers. Not only are they defenders, they are the starters of attacks; they have licence to forage forward and influence important games with their forward play.

Overlapping

At the end of the 2018/19 season, Sheffield United gained promotion from the Championship to the Premier League under Head Coach, Chris Wilder. Despite being among the favourites to be relegated, they started the 2019/20 season well, and were lodged in the top half of the league throughout. Against a deep-lying defending Crystal Palace, their tactic of using *overlapping centre-backs*, brought them their first victory, and set tails wagging amongst football tacticians. By the time midfielder John Lundstram put the ball in the net to record a 1-0 win, the left-sided centre-back (Jack O'Connell) was positioned on the left-wing, their left wing-back (Enda Stevens) had moved into a central attacking position, and striker David McGoldrick (whose positioning cued all of this to happen) was closer to the half-way line than the goal.

Critical to this strategy is their formation, which contains three centre-backs. When playing a back four, any over-lapping duties from 'defenders' tend to fall to the full-backs. By playing with three, Wilder allows for the outside centre-backs to join in attacks in this way instead.[2] It is a prime example of a coach being innovative and pushing the boundaries of what we consider to be tactically 'normal' in football.

The strategy was born from the need to give the team a tactical edge, particularly when they began using it two seasons earlier, prior to their Premier League arrival, when the club was in League One (two levels below the Premier League). As one of the most notable teams in that division, assistant coach Alan Knill felt that they needed something extra to confuse opponents and create overloads when playing against teams who would invariably defend in a deep and organised manner against them.

Opponents will often have a defensive strategy to track and defend against an overlapping full-back, but not so much when a centre-back is doing it. Teams could but, in general, don't ask their strikers to chase centre-backs back into their defensive third. This style of overlapping often

---

[2] For clarity, *both* outside centre-backs are not required to abandon their half in favour of these long, forward runs *at the same time*. If the left centre-back overlaps the left wing-back, for example, then the right centre-back adjusts his position to narrow closer to the central defender, thus organising the team against opposition counter-attacks.

resulted in time, space, and an overload of players in the wide areas; it added to the confusion generated in the opposition by their movement.

In an interview for the *Telegraph* newspaper, Knill admits that not all centre-backs will have the tools to do this but, in time, this may become a tool that is required when developing young 'defenders'.

Defenders, Defending

One of the biggest criticisms about the rise and necessity for technical players to operate as defenders is the lack of focus that goes into *actual* defending. For some centre-backs, online bookmakers offer odds of around 1/1 (evens) for them to make even one successful tackle during a 90-minute match! In their view, defenders are as likely to make zero tackles as they are to make just one!

"

With old-school coaches, 60-70 per cent of your training ground work would be defensive.

I started off with a high defensive base. Players now are starting out with a high technical grounding and learn the defending later.

"

Gary Neville

While players in Gary Neville's era would do specific defensive work three times a week, the former Valencia Head Coach estimates that, today, 80% of their training regime is now attacking work, with only 20% reserved for defensive duties.

Another former Premier League defender I spoke to, was Craig Short, now Under-23 coach at Derby County in the Championship. As a defensive defender of some note, Short worries for those under his tutelage. In the *It's Your Game* segment at the end of this chapter, Short describes a game where the opposition played with two strikers – and his central defenders could not handle it, from a technical, tactical, physical or, mostly, psychologically point of view.

Most youth development experts firmly believe that the "technical grounding" that Neville describes is the right way of developing young players, so much so that the diagram below has proved very popular in youth coaching circles. There, however, does need to be a place in youth development for defending. It is, after all, a major piece of the football jigsaw.

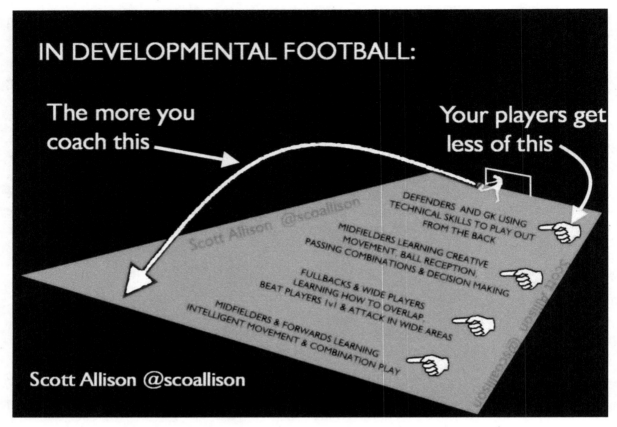

Benefits of playing out from the back in youth football development.
Used with permission from Scott Allison (@scoallison)

With the propensity of youth teams playing out from the goalkeeper using short passes, youth games can often seem a little sterile – we pass for a bit, then you pass for a bit. The long-term problem, as noted by Short, is not necessarily with *your* team playing out from the back, but it is when *every* opponent you face does so too. At what point during these experiences do players experience playing against opponents who play 'direct', using long balls for quick/big strikers to compete with – something they will face time and time again throughout their careers.

As a result of defenders at the top level being largely unused to playing against two strikers, will we see a further increase in teams who do just that? Another way of evolving to get an 'edge'. Will we then see a return of traditional wingers, playing on their 'strong side' (left-footers on the left, right-footers on the right) providing crosses for two strikers? As we noted at the beginning of the chapter, the game is active and reactive. Trend and counter-trend. Technical defenders who are, at a minimum, competent on the ball is a modern necessity, but upskilling them defensively might be what sets them apart from others in the future.

Full-Backs (Wing-Backs)

> **"**
>
> He joins in attacks without neglecting
> his defensive duties.
> **"**
>
> **Gérard Houllier upon signing**
> **full-back, Steve Finnan**

When I wrote about attacking full-backs in 2014, I stated that their role as essential attackers in the team was a "growing one". Today, attacking is as much – if not more – a non-negotiable positional trait than defending. In previous generations, we looked at Brazil, with Roberto Carlos and Cafu both powering into attacking areas, as being the exception. Now, almost every team will use their full-backs as offensive as well as defensive players. Most full-backs could legitimately now be described as wing-backs, and this reason is why I have included both terms in the title.

Traditionally, those selected to play in full-back positions were small and often technically limited. Their main job was to mark the opposition winger, stop crosses and protect/cover their centre-backs. Their attacking threat was generally about feeding the ball to their winger, or directly into the strikers. Crossing the halfway line was a suggestion, and if one did so, the opposite full-back would certainly not advance at the same time. Today, however, we frequently see teams attacking simultaneously with two advanced full-backs, with the responsibility of defending counter-attacks left to the centre-backs, 'holding' midfielder, and goalkeeper.

In the 2018/19 season, Liverpool full-back duo Trent Alexander-Arnold and Andy Robertson provided the team with 12 and 11 Premier League goal assists respectively – both in the top five assist-providers in the league. They were in the same company as attacking players Eden Hazard, Ryan Fraser and Christian Eriksen, followed closely behind by Manchester City rivals, Leroy Sané and Raheem Sterling. Full-backs now have the skillset of a traditional winger, but while Alexander-Arnold and Robertson were powering forward, it was Guardiola's City that were using full-backs in an entirely different way.

Inverted Full-Backs

There was rarely a more magnificent sight in 21st century football than Dani Alves racing to join attacks for Barcelona. He was, like we discussed above, the ultimate attacking wing-back, certainly more of an attacker than a defender. This sight is synonymous with the tenure of Guardiola at the Camp Nou.

When the Catalan coach finally left Barça for Bayern Munich (via a season of rest), many thought he would lift his template from Spain to Germany, and that Philip Lahm and David Alaba would be tasked with emulating the likes of Alves in bombing forward at every opportunity. In the end, however, we saw a very different concept, and something he followed up at Manchester City – the 'inverted' full-back.

With Bayern boasting wingers like Arjen Robben and Franck Ribéry, Guardiola preferred to keep them both in wide positions to create 1v1 situations against opposition full-backs, and also to allow them to attack the back post when the ball was on the other side. They would stay wide until the time came to enter central areas and look to make assists or score goals. They were not inside forwards like Messi, Pedro, or Villa; they were 'proper' wingers with a start position as wide as possible.

So, rather than overlapping when the team attacked, these full-backs would (often, not always) tuck infield, closer to the defensive midfielder. As a result of this, Guardiola is quite happy to use natural midfielder players in those positions – Alaba, Fabian Delph, and Oleksandr Zinchenko, for example – and also to convert the previously rampaging wing-back Kyle Walker into this hybrid full-back/midfielder role. When these players did venture forward, it allowed them to exploit the 'half-space',[3] as opposed to the wider areas.

---

[3] The term 'Half Space' is taken from the German word 'Halbraum', which is why you may see the English version spelled as one word also. More on this area of the pitch in the following chapter.

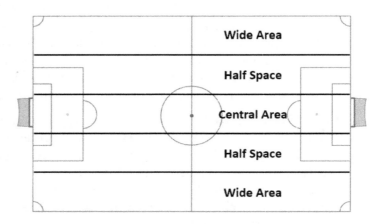

The 'Half Space'

In a sense, Guardiola was keeping the full-backs out of the way of their own wingers. Their support for Robben et al. was to offer a backwards pass if they couldn't achieve success 1v1, whilst also positioned to stop the counter-attack – a very common, prolific tactic of the German domestic game. Guardiola being Guardiola also wanted them to help the team dominate possession in midfield.

Midfielders

Midfield is often seen as where the game is won or lost. Whichever team dominates midfield, will dominate and control the game. Players in this area of the pitch are expected to be exceptionally technical, and have high levels of game understanding and stamina to dominate the game. Midfielders, too, can be divided into those who behave primarily defensively, those who behave primarily offensively, and those who are required to do it all.

When I was growing up learning the game, often in a 4-4-2 with two central midfielders, coach after coach would instruct us that "when one goes, one stays". In other words, if one midfielder joined the attack, the other must retain a defensive position. Today, however, we see these roles are largely divided up with specialised players – defensive or 'deep-lying' midfielders who both start attacks and quash opposition advances, and attacking midfielders who are duty-bound to join into attacks.

Deep-Lying Midfielders

"

Holding midfielders have such an important
role as they give the team balance, allowing you
to release both full-backs at the same time.

Carlos Alberto Parreira, *FIFA World Cup*
2018 Technical Report

One of modern tactic's greatest trends has been the introduction and specialisation of the deep-lying midfield player (often referred to as a 'holding' midfielder as he holds his position in a disciplined way, or, simply, a 'defensive midfielder'). By definition, these are players that will command a holding position in the central midfield areas. Arguably, France's Claude Makélélé popularised the position, although maybe his particular set of attributes suited the defensive role required in formations such as 4-3-3 and 4-2-3-1 once teams had routinely sacrificed a striker in a 4-4-2 for a more defensive midfield player.

José Mourinho, discussing the role of the Frenchman in his Chelsea team, stated:

"

If I have a triangle in midfield – Claude
Makélélé behind and two others just in front – I
will always have an advantage against a pure 4-
4-2 where the central midfielders are side by
side. That's because I will always have an extra
man. It starts with Makélélé, who is between
the lines. If nobody comes to him, he can see
the whole pitch and has time. If he gets closed
down, it means one of the two other central
midfielders is open. If they are closed down and
the other team's wingers come inside to help, it
means there is space now for us on the flank,
either for our own wingers or for our full-
backs. There is nothing a pure 4-4-2 can do to
stop things.

José Mourinho

The 'Makélélé Role', as the position affectionately became known, has evolved as quickly as it was established, though. There are few "Makélélés" left – players that are purely defensive and with a focus on destruction rather than construction in a football sense. The 'defensive midfielder' is now a technical, deep-lying midfielder – football's version of American Football's 'quarter-back' – a player that looks to control games *with* the ball, start attacks, and set the tempo for the game.

More and more technical players are now placed in these positions, rather than the 'destroyers' that were previously deployed in these roles. Spain's Sergio Busquets and Brazil's Fabinho are often described in disparaging terms for their destructiveness, and although both are renowned for their tackling and defensive positioning, they are both technically excellent. Let us not pretend that the defensive qualities of these players are suddenly unimportant – they are. However, intercepting the ball rather than making crunching tackles are the order of the day now, and their positioning when out-of-possession remains vital for the smooth running of their teams.

When their teams are in possession, we see these deep-lying midfielders often lying even deeper, dropping into central defensive positions to allow centre-backs to step forward with the ball, and kill teams who tried to press them.

Over the last decade or so, this destructive player has either been replaced, or become accompanied by, a more technical midfield partner. The 4-2-3-1 has become the order of the day. Using two deep-lying midfield players was a reaction to the rise of number 10s and goals typically being created from 'Zone 14', the area in the central area outside the penalty box (see *Making The Ball Roll* for more detail here).

Along with technical central midfield quarter-backs like Xavi Alonso and Michael Carrick, the new breed of technical deep-lying midfielders often made their names as *diminutive* number 10's – Luka Modrić and Ivan Rakitić played together as the deep-lying double-pivot for Croatia for example.

8s and Free '8s'

In August 2016, distinguished tactics writer Jonathan Wilson (@jonawils) posed a question early in Guardiola's rule at Manchester City – "Can De Bruyne and Silva prosper in their 'Free No8' roles?" Three years on, at the time of writing, we can unanimously say their use in these positions has been a huge success.

Wilson posed the question off the back of Manchester City's first game of the 2016/17 season – a 2-1 win over Sunderland. At this time, a lot of doubts surrounded Guardiola's ability to translate his ultra-possession-based game into the Premier League, a league in a country known for teams being victorious due to physical prowess rather than technical qualities. Indeed, I vividly remember his first line up – two wingers in Nolito and Sterling, and also two number 10s – David Silva and Kevin De Bruyne. A rare combination of individuals and styles.

> **"**
> It's a different role. I play not as a
> number 10 but as a free 8 with a lot of
> movement everywhere.
> **"**
>
> **Kevin De Bruyne**

The term 'Free 8', certainly publicly, was coined by De Bruyne when describing the new role that he and Silva had in common, playing either side of one deep-lying midfielder. Both, traditionally, and indeed when they started their careers, were considered as number 10s who would play in the pocket of space behind a striker (this pocket of space, so prevalent in a 4-4-2, now rarely exists with teams playing with one and then two defensive midfielders). Now, they are tasked with operating and creating from the 'half spaces'. They became a hybrid of an 8, a 10, and a winger, looking to create goals from an area of the pitch now associated with high levels of assists – the spaces either side of the opponent's defensive midfielders.

Attackers

In an interview with a German publication, Thomas Müller was asked about his unique skillset and role with both Bayern Munich and the country's national team. Müller, arguably more than any other player, is very difficult to pigeon-hole. Former German international Mehmet Scholl even described him as a "Wild 13" (Müller's national team squad number) given his propensity for popping up almost anywhere. He plays most of his football as a wide player, but few classify him as a winger. He spends time playing as a striker, but few would categorise him as one. He has played some time as a number 10 or midfielder, but nobody would brand him as either. Müller's reply was that he was a *Raumdeuter* – a space finder.

This term, and the evolving attitude to how forward players are being classified, is widespread across the attacking areas of the pitch. Attacking players, en masse, are arguably more positionally 'fluid' than ever before. Wingers staying wide and providing crosses for strikers, as their *primary duty*, is conceptually out-dated. 'Pure' number 10's – players that operate *exclusively* in the 'pocket' between midfielders and strikers – are becoming increasingly rare. Those who play in the most forward positions are not necessarily goalscoring strikers. More attacking players are becoming 'space-finding' multi-purpose attackers.

Multi-Purpose Attackers

In 2001, Roberto Mancini, a former *trequartista* (number 10) himself, wrote his thesis for his coaching badge with the Italian FA. He noted that the number 10 had "a scarce presence in the defensive phase" – how much this has changed in two decades. The evolution of some traditional number 10's into more deep-lying positions can be seen as a direct result of the change in the style and requirements of the *trequartista*.

Traditionally, a team's number 10 would look to exploit the space on the edge of the opposition's penalty area – known as 'zone 14'. With the large-scale presence of one, if not two, deep-lying midfielders reducing the space in these central areas, these players have had to evolve, adapt, and go elsewhere to cause opposition defences damage. The 10 is no longer simply "a player who positions himself in the central zone between the midfielders' line and the attackers' line", as noted by Mancini. Those who cannot adapt have started to drift out of the game.

The 10 must now have the traits of a winger (we are increasingly seeing number 10s being called "inside wingers") – he must be able to dribble, run with the ball, play centrally or out wide in either left or right areas – and crucially, he will be asked to contribute to the defensive phase of the game. Others like Philippe Coutinho and Angel Di Maria even became central midfielders in the 'free 8' role. Others, like the aforementioned Modrić, dropped even deeper into midfield.

> The situation of the playmaker or Number 10 doesn't really exist anymore and hasn't done for a long time.
>
> **Joachim Löw**

Wingers & Wide Forwards

There has been a real blurring of the lines between those who play as number 10s and those who play as wide attackers. Now, natural number 10s have the traits of wingers and wingers have the traditional traits of number 10s – they seek spaces to exploit in crowded central areas, rather than exclusively looking for 1v1 situations out wide, and have more in their technical armoury than simply dribbling and crossing. The blurring of these lines often allows teams to rotate the specific positions of their attacking midfielders, either within one game, or from game to game.

The very best of these attacking players (Hazard, Messi, Ronaldo, Di Maria, Salah, Reus, Sterling – the list can go on and on!) have the ability to appear, and affect games, in various attacking areas of the pitch.

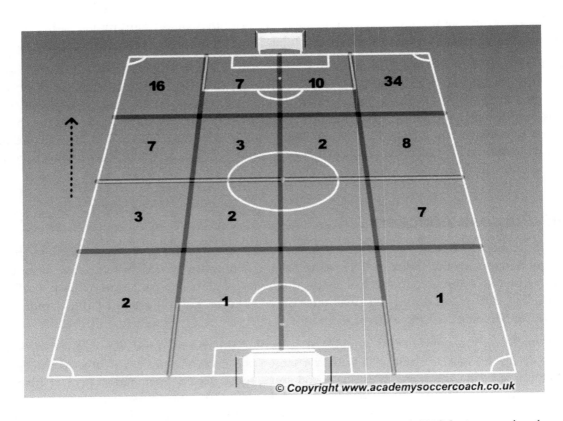

In their quarter-final of the 2014 World Cup against Switzerland, Argentina's Di María was selected to play from the right, although we see from his individual possession chart (via Prozone) that he consistently popped up all over the pitch, particularly in the Swiss half.

Not only are attacking players becoming more fluid, position-wise, we are also seeing a minor yet significant increase in natural wingers playing as central midfielders. With the growing propensity for 'inside wingers', we may well see more natural wide players evolving into central positions. Stereotypical central midfielders would play off two-touches, switching the play and do most of their 'box-to-box' running without the ball. In contrast now, however, there is a growing trend for midfield players who pick the ball up in central areas and drive forward in possession. Natural wide players, like Alex Oxlade-Chamberlain, for example, with these skills already honed, may begin to influence central positions more and more.

We have briefly mentioned some 'natural' wingers such as Robben, Ribéry, and Notlito in the previous section (this is not to say they never played elsewhere). We would normally consider these players as assist-makers, rather than goal-scorers. When the 4-4-2 formation was the predominant one, wingers were most certainly considered as wide midfield players. The Manchester United team of Giggs and Beckham are great examples of this.

In contrast, we now see 'Wide Forwards' whose starting positions are the same as a winger, but their role is much different. They are renowned as goal-scorers, as much as they are providers. Present-day examples are Mo Salah and Sadio Mané at Liverpool, and David Villa and Pedro Rodriguez while at Barcelona.

The False 9

In 1953, Hungary visited Wembley Stadium to take on England. Tactically at that time, football could have been described as a game of 1v1s, with teams playing man-to-man all over the pitch within 'WM' formations.[4] Not only did Hungary stun the English with a 6-3 win, but they also introduced an innovation to football tactics in the shape of number 9, Nándor Hidegkuti. Instead of playing directly against centre-back Harry Johnston, he puzzled the English defender by instead dropping towards midfield. The modern Liverpool and Barcelona teams, mentioned above, both share a common tactical trait with Hidegkuti, one that allowed their wide forwards to impact the game in goal-scoring situations; so-called 'False 9s'.

Although Messi's days of being a False 9 are rarer since the arrival of traditional number nine, Luis Suarez, the trait of his game under Pep Guardiola paved the way for the re-popularisation of the role. Guardiola trialled this in an away game against Real Madrid of all places, and like Johnston et al., above, his movement away from goal caused problems for the Madrid centre-backs and midfielders at the Bernabéu. Nobody quite knew who was responsible for marking or tracking Messi. The goal-scoring success of Liverpool wide-forwards Salah and Mané (both joint Premier League top-scorers in the 2018/19 season) is largely down to the same movement of Firmino. The Brazilian rarely plays as an out-and-out striker and his movement into deeper positions, again causing problems for defences, allows both wide players to capitalise on the confusion and space he vacates.

"

False nine: ancient tactical curveball still retains the power to shock.

Jonathan Wilson

Just like our conundrum of pigeon-holing attacking midfielders, above, it is difficult to bracket the False 9 also. In the simplest terms, they are something of a mix between a striker and attacking midfield player. Their start position may be as a traditional number 9, but they drop off into attacking midfield areas and into wide positions. This leaves a real problem for opposing central defenders, and it becomes a significant challenge for defenders to work out who is responsible for picking them up – and when.

Strikers

When we analyse strikers, the first attribute next to their name is their goal-scoring statistics. Historically, we were told that every team needed a number nine who scored goals and was judged on little else. It did not truly matter whether they worked hard out-of-possession – putting the ball in the back of the net was their job.

The complicated positional nature of attackers, however, makes the out-and-out striker less of a necessity for some teams. Germany won the World Cup in 2014 often playing with no striker when Miroslav Klose was not selected. It was substitute 'false 9' Mario Götze who was to score the winning goal in the final itself.

---

[4] This is where the term "winning your individual battles" was coined, although now somewhat outdated given that players do not simply battle 1v1 for an entire game. Two central defenders will share battles against one striker, wingers will swap sides and cut infield, their marking detail changing as the game develops.

In contrast, however, it was a pure striker who won the World Cup for France in 2018 in the shape of Olivier Giroud. The striker was not in the starting 11 for the opening match of the tournament, but his inclusion thereafter and occupation of opposition defenders, quickly allowed the team to 'click'. Despite not scoring a single goal in Russia, it is arguably a shift away from using a false or multi-purpose attacker in central areas that got the best out of the rest of the team, and which allowed Antoine Griezmann and Kylian Mbappe to both score the goals that won the tournament.

Giroud could be further pigeon-holed as a 'target' striker, in the team to provide a focal point for attacks, challenge central defenders physically, and be a 'wall' for other players to play off. These types of strikers have a very good first touch using all surfaces, are good in the air, and play off very few touches. This is opposed to other types of strikers that we could categorise; those like Leicester City's Jamie Vardy who looks to run into the space behind the defence, or those who come alive in the penalty box, such as Argentine Mauro Icardi, whose impact comes in front of goal rather than outside the penalty box.

Of course, we know the danger of pigeon-holing and limiting *every* striker. The traits of those mentioned above are not their only traits. Jamie Vardy will hold the ball up, Icardi will be involved in the build-up play, and Giroud will score his share of goals. Many, like Sergio Aguero, will be a gentle fusion of all these styles, capable of scoring goals, holding the ball up, dropping deep, and running in behind.

"

All he does is score goals.

"

Football phrase

In the 1980s and 1990s, the above quote was a compliment. Strikers were goal-scorers and goal-scorers only. That was their job and anything else was a bonus. Today, however, attackers and strikers, depending on their size and style, have a range of duties and requirements. In times gone by, a goal-scoring striker was in the team, *always*. Today, the style of the striker and the tactic of the team is what gets strikers selected.

Conclusion

All players, in all positions, have responsibilities in both the attacking and defensive phases. In fact, a document from Tottenham Hotspur's recruitment department, detailing a template for players they want to sign, gives *all* players a percentage in terms of how much they expected them to both attack and defend:

Position	Percentage Defender / Attacker
Goalkeeper	Undefined
Full-back	75% Defender
Centre-Back	80% Defender
Deep-Lying Midfielder	50% Defender
Midfielder Number '8'	50% Defender
Number '10'	30% Defender; 70% Attacker
Wide Player	25% Defender; 75% Attacker
Striker	20% Defender; 80% Attacker

Tottenham Hotspur Player Profile – Defending & Attacking Duties

This chapter is very different to any other in this book, or the previous one. If this chapter was a coaching session, it would fall into the *Guided Discovery* style. The purpose was not to offer you all the tactical answers (which are endless), but to spark some thinking around how the modern game looks from a positional point of view, how the game changes, and what the future player whom you are coaching will need to look like. It challenges you, the youth coach, to consider how you prepare your players for the game that exists today, and also the game that may exist tomorrow.

Summary

- Understanding modern tactical trends, and having a clear idea of the direction the game is going is a necessity for the youth coach in preparing young players for what is to come.
- There is a constant tactical ebb and flow, positional trend and counter-trend. As soon as one style begins to dominate, its antidote is being concocted.
- The age at which youth players should specialise, positionally, is hotly debated. General consensus says that this should happen around 15 or 16, while pre-pubescent players should experience playing in lots of positions.
- The rotation of positions allows each player to experience different roles, different responsibilities, and to see the pitch from a different viewpoint. They have to use their weaker foot, play in areas where space is open, and where it is at a premium. It allows all players to appreciate both attacking and defending (and transition) phases.
- Modern football is starting to move away (slowly) from how positions are grouped. Players now do not neatly sit in one position; there are a lot of grey areas and shared roles.
- Goalkeepers need to have the skillset of traditional shot-stoppers, but also the modern footballing traits of an outfield player.
- Centre-backs used to be defenders only, something they may struggle with in today's game, given the emphasis on the development of their technical skills.
- Full-backs now are responsible for attacking as much as defending. They have the skillset of wingers (wing backs) and central midfielders (inverted full-back).
- In the 1990s, midfielders shared attacking and defending duties; now we see specialists and those who are fluid positionally.
- Deep-lying midfielders evolved from being exclusively defensive before being joined or replaced by 'quarter-back' style technicians.

Chapter 13 – Modern Playing Positions

- Box-to-box 'number 8' midfielders, who affect the game going forward and backwards, still exist, although 'free 8's (a mixture of an 8, a 10, and a winger) are becoming more popular.
- More attacking players are becoming 'space-finding' multi-purpose attackers, as the role of the number 10 has diminished.
- False 9s allow their wide forward teammates to get into more goalscoring positions, dragging and confusing defenders and midfielders in the process.
- Strikers, regardless of type, are now more than 'just' goal-scorers.

It's Your Game #1

The Other Team Doesn't Score

Craig Short

Former Premier League Player; Coach, Derby County

Last season (2018/19), I took a group of young professionals for a league game against Brighton and Hove Albion. The day ended with my Derby County players encountering a problem they never had before – despite a lifetime in the game.

You see, I was a centre-back since I can remember. As I was physically big, loved defending, and could play, my coaches tended to put me there. Always.

When I was learning the game, defenders were defenders. Our job was to mark, be aggressive, win duels, and defend the box. How I contributed to attacks was up to me, but crossing the halfway line in open-play was not pre-approved or frequent! That day in Brighton, however, the two central defenders struggled with the very thing I was brought up doing every week – playing directly against two strikers!

Today's young defenders spend so long being taught how to 'play' – taking the ball from the goalkeeper, passing through midfield, advancing forward to launch attacks – that sometimes being able to defend takes a back seat. Now, I'm not against technical defenders, whatsoever, but balancing these 'modern' skills with the traditional, vital defensive ones is key for me. That doesn't mean being 'anti-football', kicking opponents or being brutal, but the 'Virgil van Dijk' way – can defend 1v1, can dominate opponents in aerial and ground duels, can read the game, sense danger, and can communicate effectively with others *to ensure the team doesn't concede a goal*. One, without the other, doesn't make sense.

That day at Brighton was an eye-opener for us all. The centre-backs looked shocked at even the thought of facing off against two out-and-out strikers. Brighton's 'get the ball forward quickly' style also unsettled them greatly. They had no idea how to pull a full-back around and just accepted they would be two v. two, even though they couldn't handle it. When one striker went short, he dragged his marking centre-back with him time and time again, which allowed his strike partner to freely run in behind. Neither recognised when to go with the striker and hold their position.

As a development coach, I have to prepare players to play at the highest levels of the professional game, or the reality, for many of them, at non-league level, where this type of game is far more frequent than they would believe. Am I doing my job if players spend 10 years+ in a development environment but leave unable to play the game at a level that suits them?

<u>It's Your Game #2</u>

Multi-Purpose

Gary Taylor-Fletcher • @GTF_12

Ex-Professional Player, Non-League – Premier League

When I was young, I was a quick and small winger. It wasn't until I was about 15 that I started to grow and was moved to being a central striker.

At 18, when I first started at Northwich Victoria in the English Football Conference, I was an out-and-out central striker playing in a two.

When I went to Lincoln City, we played a 5-2-3 formation where the front three had licence to roam anywhere we wanted. I was mainly the middle man, who dropped deep to link up play. We were, however, all very hard working and would fill in as long as the three positions were filled upon losing the ball.

When I signed for Huddersfield, in my mid-twenties, I was considered an out-and-out front man. I was initially third choice striker, but always seemed to score as substitute. I was on the bench during an away game against Tranmere, and watched the team go 2-0 down inside 20 minutes – then our right midfielder got injured.

The manager, Peter Jackson, said that I would go on to replace him, but he wanted me to be more of an attacker than midfielder. We drew the game 2-2, and I scored both of our goals! From then on, for the rest of the season, and most of my time at Huddersfield, I played either right or left midfield. With it not being my natural game, people always asked if I was bothered with playing "out of position". My main aim, however, was to play every game whatever position that may be in.

By the time I moved to Blackpool (and we ended up in the Premier League), I was known as an attacking winger. For the first two seasons, I was a right midfield workhorse (in a 4-4-2), getting forward into the box and then back to help my fullback. Physically, it was relentless. It was only when Ian Holloway came in and we changed to a 4-3-3 that I was moved into a more attacking role.

We played very similarly, as a front three, to how we did it at Lincoln, so it was natural. The biggest difference was that Holloway didn't want us to defend if the ball was on the other side. He wanted his wingers to stay high to give us an outlet and have a so-called 'cat and mouse' scenario, often pinning the full-back back.

Little did I know that my versatile positional experiences from 15 to my mid-twenties was preparing me for some of the most exhilarating experiences – and to dine at the top table of English football.

Chapter 14
Modern Team Tactics

" The first task is to get to know the players really well – watching them as individuals in training and in match play to see what is good in their natural game. Then, and only then, can we begin to outline the general tactics. **"**

Helenio Herrera

In *Making The Ball Roll*, we looked at the subject of tactics through the eyes of youth players. We also noted, frequently, that age-appropriate considerations have to be put to the forefront of matters when discussing tactics. Both of these topics, I feel, are necessary to address *again*, before we get into the guts of looking at modern football tactics.

It is all well and good being a tactical mastermind, but it is of little use if a coach cannot apply this knowledge relevantly to the group in front of him or her. That is probably the same for any knowledge. If we ask a university mathematics professor to teach six-year-olds all he knows, we would not be surprised if they were unsuccessful! Conversely, the skill that the specialist primary/elementary school teacher has is keeping back certain knowledge until they feel that the child is ready and equipped to absorb it; skillfully pushing their boundaries as required.

" Meet them where they are – and take them from there. **"**

**Kim Poulsen, Danish Coach &
FIFA Instructor**

When you look back at your time in coaching, there will be certain moments that stand out. If ever there was a moment of learning and clarity that I go back to, time and time again, it is the quote above from friend and former colleague, Kim Poulsen. Its simplicity does not do justice to its power. It can be translated into any field that involves teaching, mentoring, advising, or leadership. In a football sense, it is particularly useful when you are coaching a new team. If we drill deeper and apply it when working with players tactically, it becomes a mantra.

One of the primary bad habits possessed by the coaching fraternity is that we teach an adult game to young players *too* early. We enforce concepts on players, and often in a language that they are not yet able to understand. If you find that players are frequently "not doing what you told them" then they probably simply do not understand.

With this in mind, the European Club Association (ECA) examined tactics and age in their *Report on Youth Academies in Europe*, the details of when tactics are introduced to players are summarised below:

Club	Age
Ajax	12
Arsenal	14
Barcelona	8 (individual tactics)
	12 (team tactics)
Bayern Munich	11
Inter Milan	8 (individual tactics)
	13/14 (team tactics)
FC Levadia Tallinn	16
Dinamo Zagreb	13
Racing Club Lens	12
Standard Liege	14
Sporting Lisbon	12

When players begin learning tactics at renowned academies. Source: ECA

Removing the outliers (Bayern Munich, 11 and FC Levadia Tallinn, 16), most youth development experts start to focus on team tactics between the ages of 12 and 14.

While we now have a *guide* in terms of age and the coaching of team tactics, we must appreciate that the table above is not the complete answer. This 'data' needs to be translated to the players you coach. Some would say that 12 is too young, others delve straight in at 11, others wait until 16. The key skill here is the coach evaluating *their* players in *their* context. The concept is to be able to hit the sweet-spot between developing players' game understanding, whilst not underdoing or overdoing it.

Formations – A Starting Point

"

Formations are just telephone numbers.

"

Pep Guardiola

It always worries me slightly when I see an article, book, or coaching video, with a title like *'How to Coach 4-2-3-1'* or *'How to Defend Against a 4-3-3'*. These resources may well be useful, but we must acknowledge that formations are just the starting point when it comes to tactics. This starting point is important, but the details of the game are more plentiful and more important.

For example, how you defend against a 4-3-3 will be different depending on the unique style and skillset of the players involved. How you combat the movement of a False 9 like Roberto Firmino, versus the Jamie Vardy 'run-in-behind' type striker, would be exceptionally different.

"
> I can't work out why in football they're always
> talking about formations, because when I watch
> the game, I don't see formations. I see them
> trying to get space and keep some sort of shape.
"

Eddie Jones, International Rugby Coach

Your formation is not your tactics. The stated formation of any team is not their 'tactics'. What they do provide is simply a starting point and a positional guide for players to return to when they become organised.

Every team is a mix and match of different individual styles that feed into the overall team style. A team's formation may remain the same, but the addition of even one different player can change that. As mentioned in the previous chapter, although France has a plentiful number of talented attacking players, the use of the less-talented Oliver Giroud, was *arguably* the individual tactical change that won France the 2018 World Cup.

If you are a coach with experience of coaching a number of teams, you will have noted that each team you have coached will interpret the same tactics differently, stamping their own identity onto them, simply by bringing their natural game to the table. You may work in the same way, ask the same things of the team, and use the same organisation, but you will most likely see at least a slightly different product on the pitch.

One Formation or Multi-Formations?

Some outstanding youth development environments build their development programmes around one formation, or the blending of more than one. Youth development juggernauts Ajax and Barcelona, for example, build players around a 4-3-3 formation, something that is laid out from their first team, right down to the youngest academy players. Playing from the same template is important, and it is often credited with why academy players are so successful once they reach the first team. They understand the club's game, starting from its formation, implicitly.

For a Club or For the Game?

Earlier in this book, I introduced you to Chris Ramsay, the ex-Tottenham and now QPR player-developer. During the same conversation in which we discussed the prioritisation of the individual above the team, he also asked a probing question – in youth environments, are we preparing players for the club? Or are we preparing them for the wider game? What may seem like semantics, at first, soon became completely relevant.

Twelve years after joining Ajax as an 11-year-old, Denis Bergkamp left Amsterdam to join Italian giants, Inter Milan. Although the club's style of play was an important part of Bergkamp's decision in making the move, the inherent football culture in Italy became a challenge he could not overcome. A world-class number 10 that was brought up in the Ajax style, he struggled in Italy where Inter would not play as 'openly' as Ajax, and Italian club opponents tended to be far more defensively organised and disciplined. You could argue that Bergkamp spent so much time playing *in one tactical manner*, that change for him was very difficult. It was only when he left Italy for England, and Arsenal, that he came into his own in Arsène Wenger's possession-based style.

In *Making The Ball Roll*, I shared the visual below, which details how a club may work through the ages around one formation (in this case, a 4-2-3-1).

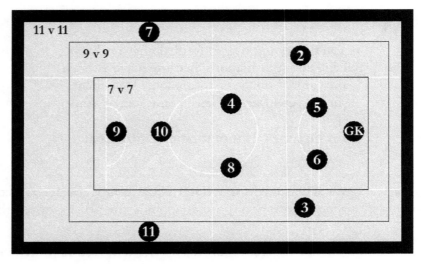

The 4-2-3-1 formation at 7v7, 9v9 and 11v11

So, whether it is the oldest players playing 11-a-side, the youngest playing 7v7 or intermediately at 9v9, all the players will learn the same system both implicitly and explicitly. By the time these players come through the club's youth development process, they will have had significant experience playing the same way, in the same formation. This, in theory, allows players to be experts in this, by the time they play in the club's first team.

The issue here, however, as we know, is how many players will a) make it into the first team from the youth academy of any club, or b) how many do we really think will be asked to play in the same way for their entire careers. We are, after all, in a youth setting, preparing players for the future game, whether they become professional or not.

In the previous chapter, Derby County's Craig Short admitted concerns about his young centre-backs. If all he does is produce technical, ball-playing centre-backs, will they be capable of having a career in the hustle-bustle of the lower or non-league competitions in England? In a similar way, here, we may find that a tactical or formational focus that is too narrow, may hinder the rounded tactical development of players.

Let's continue to look at our centre-backs, for example. Let's say he spends 10 years playing 4-2-3-1 in a youth environment, always with two midfield players protecting the defence. What happens when he graduates to a different environment, let's say one that plays with three central defenders, and only one midfielder protecting? In this case, he is essentially required to learn 'on the job', attempting to figure it out whilst in the limelight of results-driven senior football, much like Bergkamp in Italy.

"

We in our club have to take care, in my opinion, that we don't put the system over the talent and over the individual talent and skills of the youth players… If I have an excellent number 10… it is necessary that we put him there and we develop him there, no matter if the first team plays at this time with a number 10 or not.

Thomas Tuchel

This was the centrepiece of Ramsay's question. If you prepare players just for the club, this may end up debilitating them. If you develop them for the game, we will see players who are tactically and formationally more versatile.

On this topic, I spoke to another youth development expert who was not permitted to use his or the club's name in the publication. They focus their formational development on producing players who are positionally expert, but able to cope with different formations. From Under-13 on, instead of focusing on one formation, academy teams focus on three across one year, spending 12 – 16 weeks embedded in each one. These three formations were 4-3-3, 4-2-3-1, and 3-5-2. When explaining the rationale, the coach noted the following:

- Goalkeepers play behind a back two, three, four, and five at various times.

- Full-backs will learn to play in a 'traditional' four at the back, but also learn to play as an outside centre-back and a wing-back.

- Centre-backs learn to play in a back three, back four, and back five (when the 3-5-2 changes naturally to a defensive 5-3-2). They also learn to play as a 'sweeper'-type central defender and as outside centre-backs, learning to both read the game from the deepest position, and as tight markers.

- Deep-lying midfielders have the opportunity to play there alone, and also with a partner.

- Natural number 8s learn to play in a midfield two and three, with responsibility to play in an attacking role, and also learn to play in a deep midfield position.

- Those who play in attacking midfield areas can experience playing as wingers and number 10s.

- Strikers learn to play upfront alone, in a two, and both with and without the support of number 10s.

The combination of formations used can be different, of course, but this rotation allows players to experience a much more diverse version of their own game, preparing them for a tactical future that is unknown in terms of tactical trends, but also the future requirements of each individual.

Critical to this process is not just to play these formations on an ad hoc basis, but to play them for a significant period to allow meaningful learning and experience to take place. Changing formation from week to week, for example, will not allow players to achieve momentum in their learning. The next year, all teams go back to the start and rotate through the process once more. Over five years, before players enter adult football, one-third of each year is spent embedded in a formation.

The coach added: "At the beginning, all teams played the same formation at the same time. The thought was that if players needed to step up (or down) an age-group, then they could seamlessly fit in. After a couple of years, however, we changed it to allow each coach to decide in what order these formations were played. So, when we would play in-house games, players play in and against different formations, too.

He added: "Up until Under-12, we move players around positionally so that they experience the whole game. From Under-13 to Under-18, we rotate formations. By the end, we want players to be as well-rounded positionally as possible. We do, however, also recognise that a formation is not necessarily tactics. You could play 4-3-3 in many different ways, defending deep or pressing high, for example. For this, we ask the individual age-group coaches to play whatever style is necessary from game to game. It is not perfect, but we feel that this method gives them the best chance."

Game Model

" "

All members of the team have a responsibility
to participate in all four key moments of the
game. All practice must centre around/prepare
players to be successful in these four key
moments of the game.

**Wolverhampton Wanderers, Club Football
Philosophy**

We have referred to the *Four Phases of the Game* on a number of occasions throughout this book, and will largely base the rest of the chapter around this.

The concept of a 'Game Model' is about tying these four phases together, which will ultimately become the tactics for your team. Importantly, within each of these phases, there will be team, positional, and individual tasks.

One of the most obvious, consistent, and unquestionable game models is arguably that of Pep Guardiola. Other teams and coaches will, of course, have a strong, unique game model too, but the blatant consistency of Guardiola's, with its added success, make it pertinent to look at here[1].

---

[1] As special note here to thank Lee Scott (@FMAnalysis), author of *Mastering the Premier League*, for his input here!

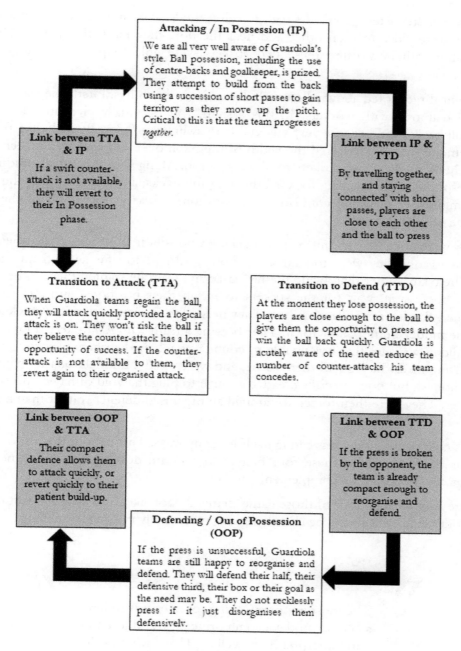

Attacking / In Possession (IP)

We are all very well aware of Guardiola's style. Ball possession, including the use of centre-backs and goalkeeper, is prized. They attempt to build from the back using a succession of short passes to gain territory as they move up the pitch. Critical to this is that the team progresses *together*.

Link between TTA & IP

If a swift counter-attack is not available, they will revert to their In Possession phase.

Link between IP & TTD

By travelling together, and staying 'connected' with short passes, players are close to each other and the ball to press

Transition to Attack (TTA)

When Guardiola teams regain the ball, they will attack quickly provided a logical attack is on. They won't risk the ball if they believe the counter-attack has a low opportunity of success. If the counter-attack is not available to them, they revert again to their organised attack.

Transition to Defend (TTD)

At the moment they lose possession, the players are close enough to the ball to give them the opportunity to press and win the ball back quickly. Guardiola is acutely aware of the need reduce the number of counter-attacks his team concedes.

Link between OOP & TTA

Their compact defence allows them to attack quickly, or revert quickly to their patient build-up.

Link between TTD & OOP

If the press is broken by the opponent, the team is already compact enough to reorganise and defend.

Defending / Out of Possession (OOP)

If the press is unsuccessful, Guardiola teams are still happy to reorganise and defend. They will defend their half, their defensive third, their box or their goal as the need may be. They do not recklessly press if it just disorganises them defensively.

Guardiola 'Game Model'

At times, however, a coach's game model can work against itself. For example, I worked reasonably closely with a coach who played a 4-4-2 formation with a diamond midfield. When devising his game plan, he wanted to do four things:

1. Play with two strikers as he felt it would cause most opponents a lot of problems (as discussed in the previous chapter).

2. Play a system other than the traditional 'flat' 4-4-2.

3. Be able to attack teams quickly and isolate the two strikers against the two centre-backs.

4. Ensure that by adding an 'extra' striker, the team would remain stable when in the defensive phase.

His approach in the attacking phase was to get the ball forward early to both strikers as they had the physical and technical skills to cause defenders problems. They were both direct, quick, and willing runners. After a few games, I began to call it the 'sledgehammer' way of attacking. When both strikers were close to each other and near the box, they ramraided teams. The problem, however, came with how often these two strikers were able to play 'close together' in the attacking phase.

To solve point three, noted above, the coach decided on two things. Firstly, he was going to pack his midfield diamond with workers. In this system, you essentially give up a lot of space to opponent full-backs, and become very vulnerable to switches of play. By including four workers, he could demand that they covered the width of the pitch over and over again. Secondly, out of possession, he wanted the two strikers to play a part too. Along with the outside midfielders, they were also responsible for tracking forward-thinking full-backs, and also stopping the opponent's deep-lying midfielder receiving comfortable possession. It was at this point of the four-phase cycle that the problems began.

The strikers were spending so much time tracking opposition full-backs that, when their team regained possession, they were too far away from goal and too far away from each other to 'ramraid'. The team, rather than being the fast-attacking team he wanted them to be, had to slow down, keep possession, wait for the strikers to regain their positions, and *then* try to use the sledgehammer. But it was too late by then. They needed to be a team that was quick in transition, but the game model did not allow for it. They became a team who *had* to keep a lot of possession when they didn't want to, that was unable to counter-attack, had strikers playing too far apart to be the attacking threat he wanted them to be, and which had a midfield quartet who were high-energy and honest, but not especially creative enough to plug the void of having no strikers in the game at times. They were then forced to ramraid an organised defence, rather than a disorganised one.

The coach's own game model was eating itself in many ways. Throughout the rest of the chapter, we will look more closely at these four phases. If you are developing your game model, ask yourself logically if each phase complements the others.

Until you are sure what all four of those game elements look like, or what you want them to look like, then your tactics will always be slightly flawed, or certainly missing something.

"

The most important thing for a team is to have
a certain model, certain principles, and to know
and interpret them well … That's what I call
the 'Organisation of the Game'.

"

José Mourinho

YOUR Game Model

Each of the four phases can further be broken down into individual segments. In his *Tactical Teacher* online course, Stevie Grieve (@Steviegrieve) presents it in the form of a figure of eight *Match Cycle*, further highlighting the constant links and cyclical behaviours between all moments of the game.

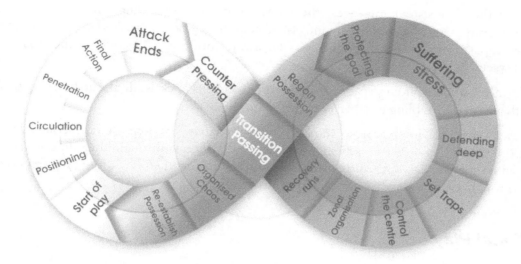

Tactical Teacher 'Match Cycle'

More commonly, each phase can be divided into three distinct phases, which often correlate to the position on the pitch, although these lines can be quite blurred.

In Possession	**Out of Possession**
Building & Retaining	Press
Progressing & Penetrating	Delay, Deny, Dictate
Creating & Scoring	Emergency Defending & Goal Protection

In Possession

Generally, your own half is the area used to build and retain possession, and to look for opportunities to play through the opposition towards attacking areas. The final third of the pitch is clearly reserved for creating chances and ultimately scoring goals. The intervening segment of the pitch, from around halfway until the final third, is used to progress possession up the pitch and penetrate into areas to create and score.

Playing Out From The Back

It is commonly accepted in youth development circles that the optimal way of developing players is to 'play out' or 'build' from the back. This, as a starting point, involves the goalkeeper and defenders playing short passes from their defensive third. The diagram produced by Scott Allison in the last chapter displays some of the long-term benefits of this style for players.

When I was learning to play the game, staple comments were often "get rid" of the ball, and "if in doubt, put it out" (in other words, if you are under pressure, it is ok just to kick the ball out of play). "Don't pass it across your goal" was also a common message, and I often got a "well done" for kicking it as far as I could. These constant messages have an aggregated effect over time. They tell the player to fear having the ball, and to be cowardly in possession, rather than brave. You tell a child "well done" for anything, and you will get more of it. How can we backup our time spent coaching technical proficiency, then shirk the bravery required to let the players (defenders, goalkeepers, or otherwise) get on the ball and test-drive their technical capabilities?

Because of these persistent messages, the older I got, the less willing and able I was to take possession from the goalkeeper or anyone else. Everything I did was rushed and lacked finesse. If I received a pass, I would sooner send it as far away from goal as I could, rather than look to express myself.

A common misunderstanding is that playing out from the back is all about passing. In fact, it frequently involves dribbling and players 'staying on the ball' too.

In a tactical sense, playing out from the back is about safely 'breaking defensive lines'. Let's say our opponent plays 4-4-2, our job in possession is to break through their lines of pressure, starting with their front two, then their midfield, and ultimately their back four. We can do this by passing through, or by individuals dribbling or driving through.

Positional Play

"   **"**

It's a game of position, not possession! It's about how you place yourself in relation to the others on the field when you have the ball and where you should be so that you can continue pressing when you lose it.

Domènec Torrent

If the *technical* skills around playing out from the back are passing and receiving, dribbling and running with the ball, then the *tactical* skills need to be defined also.

Two misconceptions may exist around possession-based football. Firstly, it is not about how many passes you can make, or what percentage of the game you have. Simply keeping the ball defies the object of football when in possession of the ball – to score goals. How strange would it look to watch a basketball game, but the baskets at either end were removed? In the future, expect to see increasing use of 'packing' statistics, rather than possession ones. Packing, a concept developed in Germany, relates to how many opposition players a player bypasses when he plays forward.[2]

Secondly, if the goalkeeper passes to a defender, and the defender then just launches it downfield, or the style becomes compromised simply because the opposition puts players under pressure, then you cannot profess to using the tactic correctly. We need to encourage all players to play a technical game with an absence of fear. They will make mistakes, and you will concede goals because of it – if you can handle that before a ball is kicked, then – long-term – your players will have a greater chance of success.

If you want your team to advance from the goalkeeper into the final part of the pitch to 'create and score', then it will be the positioning of the players that dictates success or otherwise. Traditionally, the adage of 'possession-based' would be to make the pitch as big as possible when in possession (but as small as possible without the ball). In other words, players position themselves as wide as possible, as deep as possible, and then others position themselves in the spaces (or between the lines that this creates). Today, this has evolved to the point that these teams now position themselves and 'open up' only as much as they need to (this allows them to

---

[2] For further info on packing, check out impect.com and @impect_official on twitter.

both continue moving the ball, and be more effective in defensive transition as they are positioned closer together).

We often see defenders and midfielders play several short passes amongst themselves. This is not as pointless as it looks, nor is it showboating. These passes are designed to tempt the opposition players into a press where they can then be safely played past. The longer your pass is, the less likely it will make it safely to its destination. You may also see defenders keeping the ball on the halfway line in something of a horseshoe shape. Then, unprovoked, they play the ball back 40 metres to the goalkeeper. Instead of the pointless pass that it may look like, it is simply a way of drawing the opposition out, as they could not find sufficient gaps to play forward.

Out of Possession

Later in the chapter, we will look at goal-scoring both in terms of attacking, but also in how we defend and stop goals. Emergency defending and protecting the goal is the final stage of defending and therefore takes place in and around the penalty area. Higher up the pitch, whilst the opponent builds, the defending team looks to prevent these opportunities from arising. They look to 'delay' attacks, 'deny' space and opportunities to enter dangerous areas, and 'dictate' them away from goal.

Pressing

The common interpretation of 'pressing' is putting immediate, intense pressure on the opponent with the ball. It is somewhat 'en vogue' currently, given the success of teams like Spain, Barcelona, Liverpool, and Manchester City; sides who have borne success from it since the late noughties. This 'full-court press' type system, however, is only one form and view of pressing.

One of the most important aspects of pressing is understanding when *not to press*. To help with this, teams will generally have a 'pressing line', along with certain pressing triggers. These lines and triggers help the team to press in a coordinated way, and only when it is appropriate. Teams who are poor at pressing tend to use the tactic in a disorganised and disjointed manner. Triggers to press may include when the ball arrives with a certain opposition player (a centre-back who is not very good with the ball, for example), or a pass that is slow, under-hit, bobbling, lacking in direction, etc.). Teams may also set 'pressing traps' where they encourage opponents to enter certain areas, but have a trap ready where they aggressively aim to regain possession from there.

The negative aspect of a constant, aggressive pressing system is that players can tire quickly. Maintaining a relentless pressing style can lead to player burnout either over the course of a game, or over the course of a season, or both. Historically, teams coached by Jürgen Klopp, Marcelo Bielsa, and Mauricio Pochettino have all suffered from this, and all have worked to adapt their styles to counter this. The 2018/19 (and later) Liverpool team under Klopp, for example, was a significantly different team compared to their 2017/18 one. The result was fewer goals conceded, especially late in games, more games won without the opponent scoring, and a more sustained title-challenge, (compared to a year earlier previously where significant points were dropped late in games, and games were finishing with both teams scoring highly).

Compactness

" "

All the good teams, they defend compact …
The lower block is more defensive, the higher
block is more offensive … but always in a
block. It's just a basic principle; you have to
defend compact.

José Mourinho

A word you frequently hear when talking about defending is the term 'compact'. This essentially means that the defending team is positioned closely together to stop the opposition playing through them. We often associate being defensively compact with a team that is a "defensive team"; however, offensive teams must also be compact when they defend.

Compactness refers to the positions of a side's teammates in relation to each other. This provides resistance against the attacking team from penetrating and advancing into scoring positions. There is a distance between each player in each line that must be as big as possible to cover space, but close enough so the opposition cannot penetrate through them with ease. There must also be compactness between each 'line' of your team. We often hear of the attacking team appearing 'between the lines' which, in general, means a player has got into a position where he is largely unmarked and able to attack the defensive line. Being compact negates the opportunities for the opposition to play through your team.

In general, a team becomes compact by forming a 'block'. Where, on the pitch, this block is positioned will depend on the style of the team, the instructions of the coach, and the state of the game. Blocks may also be situational. Ultimately, even a high pressing team will have to form a low block at some point during a game. Atletico Madrid, who are exceptionally famous for their compact, low block under coach Diego Simeone, will, at times, defend high and press aggressively in the opponent's half – if they think they can regain the ball. If they cannot regain the ball in the first few seconds of the press, they will retreat into their low block.

The 'low block' is often disparagingly known as 'parking the bus'. Any pressure on the ball is reserved for when the opposition enter or get close to the team's defensive third. In general, the opposition will be allowed to keep possession in the other two thirds. They may have the ball, but they will have to break down an organised defence to make full use of it.

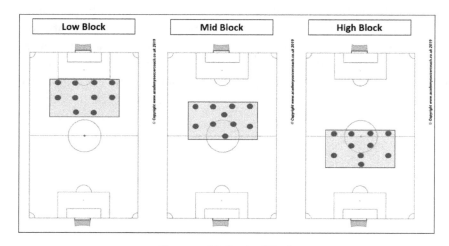

Compact Defensive Blocks

Most professional teams you watch will defend using a mid-block. Given that most goals originate from regains in the middle third of the pitch (more on this below), this is not a great surprise. Teams with a high block will actively look to disrupt the opposition's build-up to a) stop them progressing through the pitch, and b) in an effort to win the ball back nearer to their opponent's goal.

Remembering back to the beginning of the chapter, regarding formations, blocks are a great example of being independent of formations. Defending in a low, mid, or high block is not dependent on a particular formation. In theory, you can defend in any type of block regardless of the formation you employ. Some formations may be more conducive to a particular block (for example, a team with a low block may use five defenders, or a high block team will have three strikers), but there is certainly no hard-and-fast rule.

Critical Moments

While trawling through the game models of many teams and coaches, often there are two aspects that are strangely and commonly omitted. Even more strangely, these moments are exceptionally important ones, the ones that will ultimately win or lose games. They are the final piece of the game – "scoring" and "goal protection", as above. They are the reason we defend as we do, or attack as we do.

Understanding where goals come from is essential, both in terms of scoring them and being able to stop the opposition from scoring them. Regardless of your game model, formation, style, or the level of your team, you will have moments in games where you will have the opportunity to score, or *have to* stop the opposition from scoring. So, where do goals come from?

Goals

These 'critical' moments, the vast majority of the time, take place within only a very small part of the pitch – in the central area of both boxes.

Across leagues and tournaments, around 80-90% of goals come from within the penalty area. If you think of the last ten goals your team has scored, chances are that eight of them will be from inside the box – with players taking only one or two touches to finish. This is not a rule of course, and there will be outliers (maybe your best player is a dribbler who scores bundles of goals for you after long, mazy runs; or maybe your opposition goalkeepers are physically small so concede lots of long-range shots), but when things like this start to level out, and the players you coach move towards the adult game, most games will be won or lost in this way.

The detail below was pulled from *Soccer Tactics 2014* about the World Cup in Brazil, and the goal analysis is a very neat example of goal-scoring trends across the game.

58.9% of the 171 tournament goals came from a one-touch finish. This stat, of course, includes penalty-kicks (12), direct free-kicks (3), and headers (32). Added to this, 20.9% of goals were from a two-touch finish, meaning that almost four of every five goals were scored from a maximum of two-touches.

"

Usually, the attack is in numerical inferiority in
the game ... but the training is not configured
like this.

Pedro Mendonça (@PedMenCoach)

Chapter 14 – Modern Team Tactics

Despite long-range goals often being the most memorable, only 19 of the goals at the 2014 World Cup (11%) came from *outside* the penalty area. Significantly though, almost 90% of goals were scored from *inside* the box, or, more specifically, from the 'Gold Zone' below.

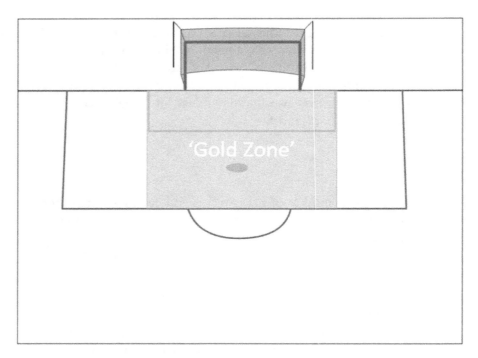

80% of World Cup 2014 goals were scored from the 'Gold Zone' (@Sportspath).

Added to this, further evidence from Colin Trainor (@colintrainor) at *Opta* shows that shots, across major European leagues, are now being taken closer to goal. Add this to the 'touch' statistics, above, and we find that the overwhelming majority of goals come from one or two-touch finishes inside the penalty area, rather than the beloved mazy dribbles and thunderbolt strikes from distance.

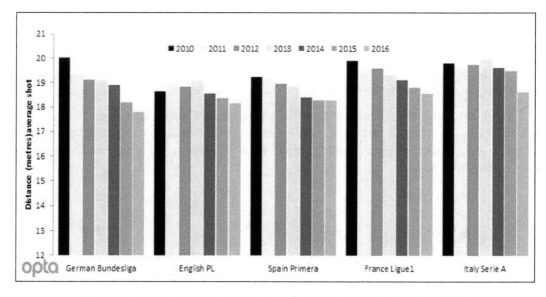

Distance (metres) of average shot (excluding penalties and direct free-kicks)
in 'Big Five' Leagues 2010/11 – 2016/17

"

A speculative shot from 35 yards is not a chance. Shooting from 35 yards out, you always remember the one that screams in. You don't remember the other 99 that end up in Row X or Row Z. That's the truth of it. He (Matthew Benham, analyst and former colleague) would be very frustrated if players shot from 35 yards. Even if he hits the bar. You know the chances of scoring are very slim. There's another pass, to give ourselves a higher probability of scoring.

"

Mark Warburton, in an interview with Jack Pitt-Brooke at _The Athletic_

Assists

If where goals are scored from is important, then so are the positions from where assists come from. In _Making the Ball Roll_ and _Soccer Tactics 2014,_ we referenced the importance of 'Zone 14' – the central area just outside the penalty box, and also mentioned what briefly became known as 'Zone 13.5' (the areas between zone 14 and 13, and 14 and 15). These eventually became known as the 'half-spaces'. The assist zones are now right the way across these three central zones, where most passes that lead to a goal originate.

Direction of Attack

1	4	7	10	13	16
2	5	8	11	Zone 14	17
3	6	9	12	15	18

The stats in the table below are from a selection of teams and tournaments based on the extensive tweets of @HalfSpaceSoccer, highlighting the importance of these central and half-space zones areas in terms of assists. Most of these assists came within about 15 metres from the edge of the penalty area.

2018/19 Season	Wide Left	Left Half Space	Central Area	Right Half Space	Wide Right
Borussia Dortmund	3%	34%	27%	34%	2%
Man City	5%	45%	26%	23%	1%
Barcelona	5%	30%	36%	27%	2%
PSG	3%	34%	32%	29%	2%
Women's World Cup	11%	26%	20%	34%	9%

Areas of the pitch where assists come from (stats from @HalfSpaceSoccer)

Further to my analysis of the 2014 World Cup, Coaching and Performance Analyst, Ron Smith (@Smudger_RS), completed a Ph.D. around goal-scoring patterns for four of these competitions (2002, 2006, 2010, and 2014). In all four tournaments,[3] goals from crosses were the least prevalent, dramatically so in 2006, 2010, and 2014. During these tournaments, the most successful strategy to score goals was passing the ball behind the last defender where the attacker "could take the ball forwards and either shoot or pass to a teammate." In other words – passing to break the last line.

Despite the growth of teams playing possession-based football, and goals today often being scored following long sequences of passes, it may surprise you that most goals still stem from attacks involving five passes or less. This statistic has been around football for a long time, but it needs to be interpreted very carefully. In fact, its misinterpretation led to decades of direct football, particularly in the UK, where the resultant tactics were to get the ball forward fast and early – often using huge, high balls into the opponent's box. Decades of this direct style had a huge impact on the national playing culture that is only now seeing signs of change.

Today, the coaching fraternity uses this statistic to influence their strategies in the attacking transition phase rather than their possession phase. Teams establish defensive blocks with a view to attacking quickly and directly towards goal. The increase in possession allows teams to build and arrive in the opponent's half together and connected. This connection means they can press once the ball is regained. Alternatively, a low block team will still attack with minimal passes by utilising a longer pass when counter-attacking.

When we break down the game of football, scoring goals is largely about getting the ball close to the penalty box to produce an assist, and then into the box to produce a goal – in the minimum amount of time and number of passes that is necessary.

Transitions

"

Include elements of transitions in all practices and sessions, where possible.

"

England DNA

---

[3] Smith also states that trends are virtually the same when extended to the European Championships, the Asian Cups, English Premier League and the Australian 'A' League.

Transitions, for clarity, are the brief moments in the game that the ball changes possession from one team to the other. When you win the ball back, you are in *attacking transition*. When you lose possession, you are in *defensive transition*.

Generally speaking, the higher up the levels you go, the fewer transitions occur. Teams at a high level are capable of retaining the ball for longer periods; waiting for moments to break lines and progress and penetrate into scoring areas. As a result of this, transitions have become even more important, and high-level teams now spend a considerable amount of time working on these 'moments'.

Once possession is lost or regained, The *England DNA* outlines four stages:

1. **Recognise the 'State of the Game'** – e.g., if we are 1-0 up in the last five minutes, we do not have to risk losing the ball by counter-attacking recklessly. If we are 1-0 down, however, taking the risk to counter-attack quickly and directly becomes more important.

2. **Decision Making** – we are 1-0 up, so let's look to retain possession instead.

3. **First Individual Action** – e.g., the player closest to the ball presses immediately.

4. **Unit / Team Reaction** – e.g., the press of the first player cues a press from the rest of the team.

Transition to Attack

Counter-attacking has become a common theme in football strategy and analysis in recent years. In response to a growing focus on teams like Spain and Barcelona dominating and winning through dictating possession, other teams have focused on how to play without the ball, and making optimal use of transitional moments and fast-break attacks.

Quick attacks in these moments allow the team that regained the ball the opportunity to strike a team who are in full attacking shape, and maybe defensively disorganised. Often, attacking teams leave spaces that can be exploited when they lose the ball. Leicester City dramatically won the English Premier League by using a low block when out of possession, then counter-attacking the space behind the opposition, in particular through pacey striker, Jamie Vardy. The Real Madrid team of José Mourinho broke Barcelona's La Liga stranglehold by utilising quick attacks to hurt opponents.

While Leicester formed a low block to force transitions and counter-attacks, many coaches and teams use high block strategies to force transitions to occur nearer to the opponent's goal – the theory being that the closer they win the ball to the opposition's goal, the less distance is needed to travel to score. Liverpool and former Borussia Dortmund coach, Jürgen Klopp, has become the standard-bearer for this 'counter-pressing' tactic. He believes so strongly in this strategy that he stated, "No playmaker in the world can be as good as a good counter-pressing situation."

Transition to Defend

Your team is arguably never as exposed as when it loses the ball. The team may be spread out and focused on going forward. Think of full-backs with attacking intent, midfielders taking up advanced positions, etc. Being 'alive' and positionally correct is, therefore, very important when your team is in defensive transition.

According to the *Wolverhampton Wanderers Playing Philosophy*, they base their defensive transitions on the following:

> On losing control of the ball, our teams should have the following questions:
>
> - Can we press high up the field to successfully regain possession? If yes, we must do so.
>
> - If not, can we delay our pressing of the ball by retreating to a new line of confrontation to win back control of the ball?

Wolverhampton Wanderers Philosophy in Defensive Transition

Teams that are characterised by excellent defensive transitions tend to respond quickly and energetically to losing the ball. There are some very good video clips available of Simeone's Atletico Madrid, and Bielsa's Leeds United recovering to defend once possession is lost.

The Fifth Phase – Set-Pieces

We constantly speak about the variability of the game of football. Even compared to other invasion games like Rugby, American Football, or Basketball, it is distinctly more difficult to plan 'routines' that are not affected by this variability.

Set-pieces give teams the unique opportunity to do this, and top-level coaches will have a playbook of set-pieces for their teams to utilise. Set-pieces include kick-offs, throw-ins, free-kicks, and corner-kicks. Of course, it is necessary for your team to both attack and defend these set-pieces.

Attacking Set-Pieces

Although lots of set-pieces are heavily pre-planned, it is important that, as a coach, we do not script everything. Especially with young players, we need to leave room for players to be inventive in the moment. Coaches often complain about their players being robotic, so encouraging them to play quickly and off-the-cuff when necessary is important. In an interview with Liverpool's Trent Alexander-Arnold, he describes his clever corner-kick that led to the winning goal against Barcelona (2019) – a corner he should not even have taken (Xherdan Shaqiri was the designated taker for that particular one).

The key to any pre-planned set-piece routine, however, I believe, is simplicity. The less moving parts there are in a routine, the greater the likelihood of success and the less variability that will be present to influence it. Simple, defined individual roles, and all players knowing their responsibilities is important. Remember, as soon as the ball moves, our predictable set-piece becomes threatened.

All set-pieces rely on all elements of PPSTT. Players must be physically and technically capable of completing the task. They must be psychologically switched on to what's happening, aware of the state of the game, and have the ability to read cues for what is happening. Socially, they must work together either as a whole group or a small unit of players. These reasons are why working on set-pieces with pre-pubescent players, who are not even playing 11v11 yet, is difficult and probably frowned up.

Defending Set-Plays

Most professional teams will prepare their defensive set-pieces, especially in relation to corner-kicks and free-kicks that threaten the penalty box – but how?

Zonal v. Man-to-Man Marking

If you are reading this in Britain, you probably choke at the thought of zonal marking when defending corner-kicks. I would, however, gently ask you to become far more open-minded.

Pulling, Robins, and Rixon carried out a study of corner-kicks over 50 Premier League matches. They noted that their remains a huge preference for man-marking systems (90%), but also noted that those who defended zonally conceded fewer goals and fewer chances.[4]

Zonal marking[5] at corner-kicks is often chastised as being ineffective, especially by television pundits. Former Liverpool, Napoli and Real Madrid coach, Rafael Benitez, is a firm believer in the tactic, however. Five of the six seasons when 'Rafa' was at Liverpool, the Merseyside club were in the bottom four for conceding from corner-kicks, although every time they did, their zonal system was used by lazy pundits to account for it. Using data from this period on his website, Benitez was clear about the effectiveness of zonal marking, and noted how – like most football tactics – its success depends on the individual actions of the players.

"

It [the data] shows that it should not be the system that is blamed for conceding goals at set-pieces, but it will always depend on the determination, concentration and ability in the air of the players at the moment of delivery of the set-piece. The data certainly does not show that one system will always be better than the other. It is about using the right system for the right players at the right time. In fact, at Liverpool, the zonal marking evolved through the years ... to take into consideration the changes in personnel of the team, but still maintained the high success rate.

Raphael Benitez

I intentionally misled you when I wrote the title of the above section. The heading, "Zonal v. Man-Marking", suggests that there is a conflict between both, or that one way is better than another. This comparison has probably been over-analysed for far too long, when the truth is that the vast majority of teams actually defend corners using a *combination of both*. Designated man-markers, normally those with the best aerial attributes, are designated to mark the biggest, most dangerous opponents. Even man-marking systems place zonal players in high-risk areas, where a body is needed to thwart the chances of a goal being conceded. Most commonly, zonal players in

---

[4] How exactly you define a full man-marking system is difficult. Usually teams who man-mark dangerous players on corners will also have several players who are zonal.

[5] In the *It's Your Game* segment from set-piece expert Stuart Reid (@From_The_Wing), at the end of the chapter, we can see how Swansea City set-up zonally, and how his team, Millwall, exploited it.

man-marking systems will be found in an area screening the near post area, on the edge of the six-yard box, and the edge of the penalty box, as we can see from the set-up below from Leicester City Academy.

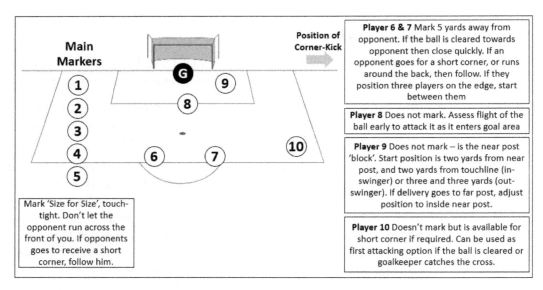

Leicester City Academy Defending Corners (taken from club's 'Our Standards' document)

Traditionally, placing players (usually smaller ones) on each post was also common, designed to clear any efforts on goal that were out of the reach of the goalkeeper. Very few teams now defend corners with a player on each post (as with Leicester above). In the study from Pulling, Robins, and Rixon mentioned above, he found no significant difference between goals conceded whether players marked the posts or not. The reasons for teams using two, one, or zero players in these positions can be wide and varied. They often depend on the philosophy of the coach. Player-centred coaches will also consult their goalkeeper and his preferences. Modern goalkeepers are generally happy to take more responsibility for defending their whole goal line, and indeed their whole goal area.

Teams that defend corners with one or no players marking the posts can use these 'extra' players to compete and stop teams winning the first header. This, in turn, reduces the chance of the opposition getting a shot on goal at all, thus negating the need for players on the posts. Should a team threaten the goal, the players that adopt zonal screening positions near the front post often drop onto the line if the corner goes over their heads. We also see more teams being caught offside once the ball is cleared and quickly re-delivered into the goal area.

Conclusion

While there is a tendency to focus tactical discussions around formations and player roles – which are both important factors – we must understand that tactics are based around *all* Four Phases of the Game. How these phases link together will determine the strength of your 'Game Model'. Although we have split the chapter into defined segments for all four, it is almost impossible to speak about one phase without mentioning another.

I will end the chapter in the same way I began, by pointing out that our work around tactics needs to be age-appropriate. If you work with pre-pubescent players, for example, you will probably lose them if you approached their games like we have above; but like a skilled primary school teacher, we can guide them through this discovery process, holding back what we feel that cannot handle. Having an understanding of what these players will need for the future remains very important.

Summary

- The first and last thing a coach needs to understand about tactics is whether they are age-appropriate, and level-appropriate. Meet players where they are, and take them from there.

- Generally, expert youth development academies begin their team tactics training between 12 and 14-years-old.

- Formations are not tactics – they are simply a starting point.

- Some youth development academies use one formation when producing players. Chris Ramsay, therefore, poses the question about whether we are producing players for one club, or producing them for the game?

- There is a case where we can develop players too narrowly, when a well-rounded tactical education is needed for wider, long-term development.

- A youth development expert outlined using three formations across a season to allow players to implicitly practice all the positional elements they need.

- Your 'Game Model' is based around the Four Phases of the Game (plus set-pieces). Critically, these four moments must inter-link to be effective.

- You can divide the 'In-Possession' phase into three segments – 'Building & Retaining', 'Progressing & Penetrating', and Creating & Scoring'.

- Playing out from the back is the optimal way of developing young players.

- You can also divide the 'Out of Possession' phase into three segments – 'Press', 'Delay, Deny, Dictate', 'Emergency Defending & Goal Protection'.

- Regardless of tactics, the key principle of defending is the compactness of your team.

- 'Critical' moments involve scoring and preventing goals from being scored – understanding where goals and assists come from are an important part of building your In and Out of Possession Game Model.

- Transitions have become a major part of planned football tactics – both when the ball is lost and regained. The England DNA advocates the use of transition moments in all sessions.

- Set-pieces are unique moments and can be considered the 'fifth phase' of the game.

It's Your Game #1

One Tweak, Many Outcomes

Gareth Jennings • @JenningsGareth

FIFA Technical Lead; Ex-Stoke City Academy Manger

Our first team liked to play with intensity, and the then Head Coach, Mark Hughes, challenged us to produce players who would be ready to cope with that intensity.

The traditional response would have been to increase the quantity of 'fitness' sessions, with laps, sprints, and gym work. Instead of changing our physical work, however, we tweaked our sessions in a tactical way, basing them around *transitions*.

We introduced a concept that the ball would never go 'dead' in sessions. This meant that the natural rest periods within practices became shorter. The extent to which we did so varied for each age-group (due to the high physical load), and we generally did more of it with our older players than our younger ones.

In a small-sided game, for example, if the ball went out of play, a new ball was immediately produced. Other practices, even those based around defending or possession or finishing would also always contain immediate moments of transition.

As a result, we found that the intensity of the players' games did go up, along with other tactical returns. In a negative sense, players became 'risk-averse'. They stopped playing the risky passes that were often necessary to create scoring opportunities. This was something our coaches had to manage, in an environment where developing creativity and risk-taking was important.

In a positive sense, some players became *more* creative, taking on the task of being the 'creator' for their team. They were happy to be 'risky' in possession, even if that meant they surrendered the ball more than others. With one player, for example, his teammates would look for him to carry the main creative threat, before then understanding when *not* to pass to him, recognising open spaces elsewhere.

Collectively, our counter-pressing also became stronger. Once a player lost the ball, his immediate reaction was to press his error quickly over 5-10 metres for a couple of seconds, rather than have to chase 20-40 metres back.

As coaches, our greatest learning from this was that even small manipulations to practices can have wide-reaching impacts. A tactical focus does not just change tactics – it affects the technical, physical, mental, and social aspects of the players' game. Emphasising one 'moment' will not just change transitions, but also have an effect on all other moments of the game. One tweak, many outcomes.

It's Your Game #2

Analysing Set-Pieces at The Den

Stuart Reid • @From_The_Wing

Set-Piece Analyst

During the 2018/19 season, I worked with English Championship club Millwall, employed to look at their proficiency from set-pieces.

In early September, we played against Swansea City at our home stadium, *The Den.* Since Swansea were one of the three teams recently relegated from the Premier League, and therefore one of the top teams in the division, it was important for us to seek whatever advantages against them that we could find.

Swansea used a zonal marking system to defend corners (see their set-up below). Their defensive setup usually consisted of three or four 'blockers' (B) that were used to delay runners from reaching the six-yard area. These blockers were then complemented by four or five zonal markers (Z) – one just in front of the near post with the rest along the six-yard line. The final player (C) had a dual purpose: defending the edge of the penalty area whilst also providing the counter-attacking threat for the team as there was no outlet up the pitch due to defending corners with all 11 players back in the penalty area.

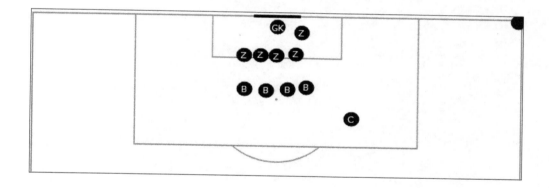

Swansea were physically quite a small side with only four players that started the game being over six feet – the two centre-backs, Leroy Fer in central midfield, and Oli McBurnie upfront. We had seven players that were six feet or over starting the game. This gave us quite the advantage, but we needed to be clever in how we utilised the players. Our tallest player was the centre-back Jake Cooper who at six-foot-four was well-built and is like a juggernaut when he attacks a ball.

Swansea positioned all their height with the zonal markers, and we flagged up that the goalkeeper rarely came off his line (which he rarely needed to do – if everyone did their respective duties correctly, then the zonal markers would be mopping up any deliveries that troubled the 6-yard area). However, one area looked like an interesting area to attack – the back post. With the blockers focusing on protecting the middle of the six-yard area and the zonal markers also focused there, it would allow a relatively unobstructed run-up if Cooper began his run from a deeper angle compared to the rest of the players. The rest of the players would then follow up by attacking the middle of the 6-yard area in case of second balls or to challenge the ball if there were any problems with the delivery (such as being under-hit).

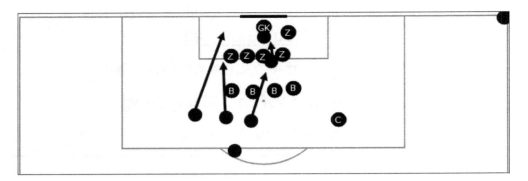

Our first corner of the match was a warning sign for Swansea as Cooper rose highest and headed the ball back across the six-yard area, but Swansea managed to clear. The second corner was a poor delivery that went over Cooper's head (the longer the pass, the more difficult pinpoint accuracy becomes), but the third corner was delivered to perfection.

Cooper rose above the Swansea defence and won the header, as planned, directing the ball into the crowded six-yard box for teammate Murray Wallace to score.

Although Swansea won the game that day, we found this was an effective strategy against a majority of defensive set-ups used, so we used it quite regularly from that point onwards. Jake Cooper ended the season with six goals and six assists (in the league) – a great return for a centre-back!

> ## It's Your Game #3
>
> # What the Game is Telling Us
>
> ## Anonymous
>
> ## National Coach Educator

Five years ago, I read *Soccer Tactics 2014* after a pulsating World Cup. What I thought would be a book simply about the tournament in Brazil ended up sparking huge and significant questions with how I, and the coaches I support, coach players.

My day job is as coach developer for a modest national FA. I spend lots of time with youth coaches from all over the country.

Having read the chapter relating to attacking play, the statistics around goal-scoring and goal-assisting drew me in. The game was telling us something very specific – that an overwhelming number of goals were scored in the box, in front of goal. So much so, that you could almost classify the goals from further out as 'outliers'. Assists also, significantly, came from the zones that form a horseshoe around the box, rather than wide crosses, for example.

I wanted to test-drive whether coaches on the ground a) practiced goal-scoring frequently, b) whether these practices included shots from outside or inside the penalty area, and finally c) whether in sessions that involved a focus on assists, where the focus of these assists lay.

We pulled together a random dozen portfolios that had been submitted over several coaching courses we had operated. Our findings, displayed succinctly, are below:

a) The time given to goal-scoring was minuscule. Arguably the most important part of the game barely registering as a targeted activity.

b) The overwhelming majority (90+%) of finishing-specific practices saw players shooting from outside the penalty area. Players were practicing the 'wrong' skill nine times more than the one that is central to the game.

c) Around 3/4 of the sessions that dealt with assisting were based around crossing – most of the crosses coming from near the touchline. These crosses were generally high, with the ball traveling a long way. Again, the game tells us that assists from crosses come from nearer to the box.

Based on these findings, we ended up revamping the 'creating and scoring' segments of our coaching courses. Out went long, high crosses and shooting from distance. In came the elements of what the game was actually telling us.

Chapter 15
Small-Sided Games

"

The true measure of a technical player is how they resolve a game situation by deciding on a tactical intention and the necessary technique, executing in the correct moment and space, and properly considering all conditional factors.

This requires the game.

David Garcia (@IJaS), *It's Just a Sport*

"

"If you could bring one item onto a desert island, what would it be?" is a hypothetical question to help you figure out what is really important in your life. So, I will ask you a similar question and relate it to coaching – if you could only coach the game of football using one method, what would that be? 'Drills'? Isolated physical training? Shadow play? The answer, I hope, would be clear. The single most important method for players to learn and practice the game ... is the game.

I am pretty certain that no other sport has such a conflict of training ideas that football has. I spend a lot of time with a lot of coaches, and often, there are occasions when I still need to *heavily convince* them to even use the game as a training tool. As we will see throughout this chapter, the lengths that we can go to use the essence of a game to improve players are virtually endless.

Small-Sided Games (SSGs) encourage the exploration of the game and its possibilities, and give players real-time feedback in relation to performance. If a player passes from cone A to cone B in a drill exercise, it doesn't really matter if the pass is too soft, for example – so long as it gets there. In a game situation, however, a pass that is too soft may be intercepted by an opponent. In a game context, players can bank this learning and, hopefully, can self-correct the next time. During the game, the player may think, "I need to pass the ball harder to ensure it gets to its destination," rather than "I need to pass the ball harder, so the coach doesn't find fault with me" (from the drill). We are 'coupling' the pass with what happens in the real game, rather than de-coupling it from the game, and thus providing contextual learning in the process: a promotion of 'guided-discovery' as a teaching and learning technique. Through games, coaches are encouraging decision-making, problem-solving, and the development of thinking players.

Street Football

Although we hear a lot about the 'death' of street football, particularly in Western societies, I am not sure we fully understand the long-term implications. In a recent conversation I had with a member of FIFA's technical staff, he highlighted a street football model that *remains* relied upon in a particular South American country he works with. Largely, the federation there allows the street game to develop the player. It is only when they enter formal youth development, or national team environments in their teens, that they teach the players the tactical game. The streets literally produce the players.

Before the presence of widespread youth football development environments, we still produced players. Before the era when coaches had a library of session plans, Google searches, and animated graphics available to them (and even during eras when youth coaching was not based on what we would now consider to be 'best-practice'), the players had parks, street corners, and urban squares that would hone their skills – generally with only one ball and without bibs, cones, ladders, hurdles or formal goals.

My question is, what if we could recreate the benefits of street football, in addition to all the best-practice and resources now available to coaches?

> **"**
>
> Kids should be allowed to play. They learn most from their own mistakes, so give them space to make mistakes.
>
> **"**
>
> **Johan Cruyff**

The use of SSGs within our training sessions allows us the opportunity to bring the essence of the streets back to life, albeit in a way that is slightly more manufactured than the unfiltered, neighbourhood versions you may have played as a child. For *some* sessions, clubs are now even training in car parks, on beaches, and other unmanicured surfaces. Coaches arrive with equipment only, and let the children get on with organising the game. If teams are unfair, the children alter them. Mixed age-groups play a part, too. As discussed earlier, there is a huge element of playing with and against older players (and younger ones) that contributes to the long-term development of players. This concept is present in the background of many of those who made it to the highest levels of the game.

> **"**
>
> We need to change players from being reliant on structures to have the confidence to play unstructured. You've got to coach the players to play the game, which, in the most part, is chaotic.
>
> **"**
>
> **Eddie Jones, International Rugby Coach**

Can We Have a Game Now?

The term 'Small-Sided Game' can have slightly different meanings depending on who you talk to, or what article or book you read. Here, SSGs are considered as being two teams playing a reduced numbers version of the 11v11 game – from 1v1 onwards. Each team has at least one goal (or target area/target player/gate to score into) and also a goal to defend. Later in the chapter, we will develop this idea by looking at games without even numbers, where you overload or underload the teams.

So, as a reduced version of the 11v11 game, SSGs are the closest we often get to the real game in our training sessions. As a result, their inherent value in teaching young players the game is invaluable.

"

Every exercise should be a simplification of
11v11. Therefore designing and implementing
the exercise in as much of a game-like state as
possible is desirable.

Marcelo Bielsa

If you can do one thing after reading this book, *please stop using the game as a reward for training 'properly'.* So often I hear coaches bribing kids with the game. "Do this drill right, then this drill and this drill, and I'll let you play a game" or "We'll just play a game for the last 10 minutes." The game should not be a reward – it should be the centre-piece or your training regime. That is, quite likely, why the players are there – and this applies right through the ages, from tots to adults, from amateur to professional.

If you find yourself in a constant battle with players about when they can have a game, do yourself a favour and *work with them rather than against them.* You can legitimately use the game as the most frequent method of practice in your training sessions, whether that is through free play, or with some of the constraints, conditions, overloads, and numbers that we will speak about throughout the chapter.

One of the best coaches I ever saw at work was 19 and unqualified. His skill was his intuitiveness about the players in front of him. He used to say, "I smell boredom on them" and tailored his entire training regime to ensure players were fully engaged, all the time. This meant games – and lots of them.

He developed half a dozen 'game boards', as he called them, and would bring one to training every night. One board would be full of 1v1, 2v2, and 3v3 games. Another 4v4 – 6v6. One had overload/underload games, one had several goals with no specific GKs, one had an emphasis on attacking and one on defending.

Now here was his trick. Depending on the outcome he wanted to achieve, he would bring the relevant board with him. So, if his curriculum dictated defensive work, he would bring the defending SSG board. If he wanted ball mastery outcomes, he would bring the 1v1 board. He then empowered the players to choose which games they would play during the session. So very simple, yet so very effective – and there were no arguments about when they could play a game!

Ball Mastery and 1v1s

During the rest of this chapter, I am looking to display a thread that runs from a player's first experience with the ball, through to the 11v11 game that we see on television at the weekends, and spoke extensively about in the last two chapters.

Before speaking about SSGs in detail, it is important to preamble it with a look at *ball mastery* – the foundation of the football player.

"

Nothing good in soccer happens without the
ball, so developing the touch and coordination
to keep it and shoot, pass, or dribble effectively
is a critical skill for every soccer player.

Coerver Coaching

Mastering the ball underpins all football actions. This cannot be emphasised enough. The more time a player spends with the ball at his or her feet, receiving significant touches of the ball, the greater the chance that they will become technically proficient as they grow older. The more technically proficient the players are, the more chance they will have of maximising their ability. Mastering the ball allows players to become comfortable, confident, and creative in the game. If you find, with older age groups, that your players lack this technical proficiency, it is likely due to a lack of experience with the ball in their former years.

Very rarely do I use 'absolute statements' (statements that suggest something is 100% – they usually contain terms like "always", "never" etc.). In this case, however, I will make an exception. If you are coaching pre-pubescent players, including ball mastery segments in *all* your sessions is an absolute requirement.

Ball mastery is not just for attacking players, wingers, or flair players. It is not all tricks, flicks, and circus actions. It does not matter what position the player plays, or will play in years to come. *Ball mastery impacts the technical levels of all players.* By having a solid technical foundation, all players will be able to protect the ball, turn out of trouble, beat players with a dribble, etc. For example, in *Mastering the Premier League*, author Lee Scott (@FMAnalysis) discusses the skills of defensive midfielder, Fernandinho, a player more renowned for positional discipline, playing simple passes and, frequently, the dark arts of tactical fouling. The key technical attributes of the Brazilian, along with the above, are his ability to move, turn, disguise his intentions, protect the ball, 'stay on the ball' (making him resistant to players pressing him), and, often, being able to dribble through opponents to break lines.

There are, however, two problems with a lot of ball mastery sessions that we might find online or elsewhere. Firstly, they are often with a player and coach in one-to-one environments. When we then try to replicate these types of sessions with a group of players, they tend to involve one player working, while a dozen or more stand watching on. Secondly, they can involve long queues of players waiting to take their turn, or players dribbling through static cones, without some of the necessary reference points that players need when manipulating the ball during games.

The most effective ball mastery practices are those in which all players have a ball for the majority of the exercise. This may only be 10-20 minutes per session, but the long-term, aggregated impact of this can and will be noticeable.

Ball Mastery at Home

"

Because your first touch is the most important in football.

"

**Mark Neville & Geraint Twose,
Cardiff City FC Academy**

At the beginning of the chapter, we discussed street football. Along with the demise of kids playing 'pick-up' games in the street, many will not practice at all away from your coaching environment. Owning a football, and practicing alone, is arguably one of the most important things to promote to players. Lone practice, away from the team, is certainly beneficial to players, although many will argue that transference to 'the game' is difficult. Personally, any time spent with a ball at a player's feet is a plus for developing them – be that in terms of their technique, or as a way of enticing them to fall in love with the ball and the game.

Tom Byer is an American coach who spends a lot of time working for clubs and national associations all over the world, particularly in Asia. Byer is best known for his book, *Football Starts at Home*, which advocates ball mastery starting from the moment a child is able to comprehend the idea of manoeuvring a ball with their feet. He advocates leaving round balls around the house and garden, and allowing young children to manipulate them and familiarise themselves with the ball(s).

Mark Neville and Geraint Twose, former coaches at Cardiff City FC, produced a homework document to allow players to practice ball mastery, and specifically their first touch, away from the training environment. One such practice involved "keepy-ups". They designed three programmes to allow players to practice at home:

Cardiff City Keepy-Up Home Practice for Players		
Light Practice (12 mins)	**Medium (22 mins)**	**Intense (30 mins)**
3 minutes keepy-ups whatever you like	3 minutes keepy-ups whatever you like	3 minutes keeps ups whatever you like
1 minute right foot	2 minutes right foot	2 minutes right foot
1 minute left foot	2 minutes left foot	2 minutes left foot
1 minute inside right foot	2 minutes inside right foot	2 minutes inside right foot
1 minute inside left foot	2 minutes inside left foot	2 minutes inside left foot
1 minute outside right foot	2 minutes outside right foot	2 minutes outside right foot
1 minute outside left foot	2 minutes outside left foot	2 minutes outside left foot
1 minute can-can (left/right)	2 minutes can-can (left/right)	2 minutes can-can (left/right)
1 minute 'Maradona 7'[1]	2 minutes 'Maradona 7'	2 minutes 'Maradona 7'
	2 Minutes 'Brazilian 8'[2]	2 Minutes 'Brazilian 8'
		2 minutes Low-Low-High
1 minute as many as you can	1 minute as many as you can	1 minute as many as you can
		3 Minutes – Be creative

Another former coach at the club, Andy Davies, described to me how every Saturday they would have 20 minutes of ball mastery practice that linked to the above and other ball mastery 'homework'. This 20-minute window allowed players to showcase moves before being 'signed-off' by one of the coaches. He describes the players going home to "practice like crazy". Fostering this love of the ball, in such a child-friendly manner, allows players to deliberately practice with the football away from the team coaching environment; it may not resuscitate the street game that we pine for so much, but it is a breath of life.

---

[1] Right foot, left foot, right thigh, left thigh, right shoulder, left shoulder, head.
[2] Laces, inside the foot, laces, outside the foot, then swap to the other foot.

1v1

Ultimately, ball mastery skills need to be transferred into the game – to be 'tested' against opposition. This is where they pick up the 'cues' from opponents, and the game, that allows them to display their technical ability. These situations are not just a winger dribbling against a defender, as we saw with the Fernandinho example above. They involve controlling the ball under pressure, shielding and hiding it, moving it into space, etc. – skills required by players playing in all positions. Paul McGuinness, who we met earlier, calls this "intimidation by skill", as opposed to intimidating an opponent physically. Learning and experiencing how to dominate 1v1 situations – both offensively and defensively, too – is an essential ingredient in learning the game. Below is an example of a 1v1 session (that includes both offensive and defensive elements) from the FA's Technical Lead for the 5-11-year-old age group, Pete Sturgess (@sturge_p):

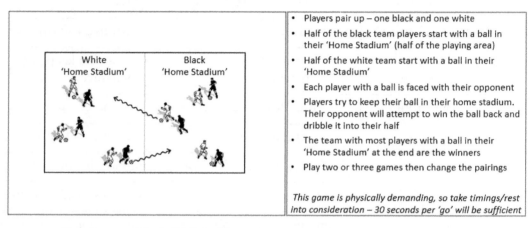

Pete Sturgess, F.A. DNA, 'Home Stadium' 1v1 Game (Foundation Phase)

1v1s – Before, During and After

The tendency for 1v1 exercises is to focus on the 'during' part of the skill – the duel between dribbler and defender, like the exercise above. However, to bring this *further* towards the game, we must consider what happens both *before* and *after* the duel. In a *Boot Room* article, Geoff Noonan looks at ways of planning 1v1s to include the during and after elements, too. He changes the traditional 1v1 (exercise one below) to contain the *before* aspects too – the player's movements to receive and shield the ball, scan to access the position of opponents or space, and the decisions necessary whether the player is marked tightly, loosely, etc. (exercise two). He then further adds the *after* aspect by including a goal – an action at the end of the duel that finishes the move – generally a pass, a cross, or a shot at goal.

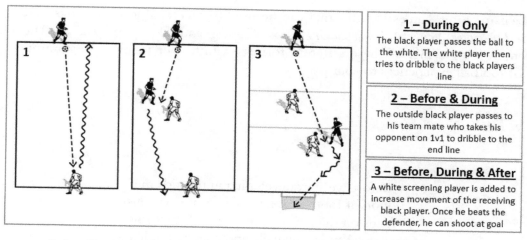

1 – During Only
The black player passes the ball to the white. The white player then tries to dribble to the black players line

2 – Before & During
The outside black player passes to his team mate who takes his opponent on 1v1 to dribble to the end line

3 – Before, During & After
A white screening player is added to increase movement of the receiving black player. Once he beats the defender, he can shoot at goal

Before, During, and After – 1v1 Session Planning (adapted from Geoff Noonan)

Once we start to consider the before, during, and after elements, we find that these 1v1 games expand to involve more players. The three sessions above, for example, have evolved from a basic 'during only' 1v1 to what are essentially 2v2 games. To be fully effective in 1v1 situations, it is important to know what comes before and after. It could be argued that, ultimately, the best dribblers know *when not to dribble* – when the better option is to use the support of a teammate by passing, or to shoot at goal.

Ball mastery and 1v1s are the foundation of the game and the development of the player, so they do not simply go away once we add more players. There are, in fact, over 200 1v1 situations that arise in a typical top-level, 90-minute game. You will note that during the following section on 'smaller' SSGs, we will frequently refer back to the inherent 1v1 situations they produce.

Smaller Small-Sided Games (2v2 – 5v5)

" If you increase the numbers, you reduce each player's 'individual actions' at a time when we need to prioritise this. "

**Pete Sturgess, FA Technical Lead
(Foundation Phase)**

Data, and indeed logic, tells you that the fewer players you have playing in a small-sided game, the more involved each player will be. They will perform more actions, whether they are technical ones like passing, dribbling, and shooting, or tactical actions like defending, attacking, and transitioning. At the same time, the more we reduce the number of players, the more we move away from what the actual game looks like. There is, therefore, a trade-off or compromise that is necessary when we run any training practice, including SSGs.

There are common acknowledgments that are present across studies that advocate the use of *small* SSGs. Players have more touches, score more goals, and complete more dribbles and 1v1s than the larger formats of the game.

Much of what we look at, below, refers to the format of 'competitive' games, but all can be also be used in our sessions. The specific games below are not the only way of utilising each format. For example, in the 3v3 section, we will look at the format advocated by Funiño, but there are also dozens of other games like this that can be used (see Peter Prickett's books based on 3v3 SSGs – *Developing Skill: A Guide to 3v3 Soccer Coaching* and *Developing Skill 2*). The essential ingredient is using a mix of these different formats within your training programme to give a variety of football experiences to your players.

Two v Two

" **"**

Before we start developing in the kids the notion of football as a passing game, we must focus on the development of skills that suit where they are mentally and cognitively, like keeping the ball, running with the ball, and scoring.

**Kris van der Haegen,
Royal Belgian Football Association**

In 2014, the Belgian Football Association created a smaller format of football for players who were playing Under-6 and Under-7. These will be the very first players playing organised football in the country. Instead of sending them straight into 5v5 football, which they felt was still too complex for many, they adopted a 2v2 format with the aim of adding more focus to each individual child. Compared to 5v5 (or 7v7 in many countries), the players experienced the game more, and completed considerably more football actions. Although this received opposition at first, it became accepted once parents and coaches saw the benefits first hand.

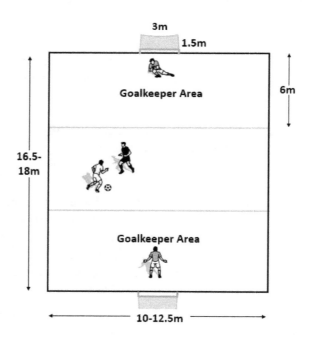

Belgian 2v2 Format

This format includes a 'fly' goalkeeper (who can handle the ball in the goalkeeper area), and players can use dribble-ins instead of throw-ins (the defender must stand at least three metres away), which again increases football actions. There are no corners, which tend to just result in players playing long, high crosses into the goal area. As a result of this format and these rules, Kris van der Haegen (@KrisVDHaegen), calls this "dribblevoetbal" (dribbling football).

Three v Three

In Chapter 5, we looked at Germany and their reaction to their football failures. A major reaction to their early World Cup 2018 exit was a re-emphasis on small-sided games, and in particular a 3v3 format, within their youth development structures from 5 – 9 years old. Players play a series of games in a festival-type format, largely based on the Funiño model (below), where a player is subbed on every time a goal is scored. They also include an option to play with goalkeepers, one bigger goal, and the option to shoot from halfway to ensure that there is a natural development of potential goalkeepers. After each game in the festival, the goalkeeper must be changed. In their research, they found that the goalkeeper had five times more actions in the 3v3 than in the 7v7 equivalent.

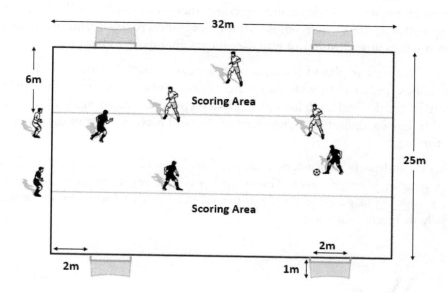

Funiño 3v3 Format

Four v Four

The Dutch have traditionally been considered world leaders in coach and player development. It was the *Oranje* who triumphed the concept of using 4v4 SSGs when developing youth players. In his book *Coaching Soccer*, former Netherlands Women's coach, Bert van Lingen, calls 4v4 "the smallest manifestation of a real match" as "there are options in all directions of play" (players have the ability to play backwards, sideways, or forwards, something that 3v3 and below does not allow).

The *Cologne Study on Small-Sided Games*, researched through the Deutschland Fussball Bund and the University of Cologne, concluded that the use of this type of small-sided football is "a must for technical and basic tactical development," as did the independent *Small-Sided Games Study of Young Football (Soccer) Players in Scotland*, conducted by the University of Abertay, Dundee.

In the mid-2000s, Manchester Metropolitan University and Manchester United carried out a pilot study around the use of 4v4 in their games program.[3] The club based all their Under-9 and Under-10 games on a four-game round-robin of 4v4. Their aim was "to optimise the 'window of opportunity' that exists for skill development." The 4v4 program, compared to the 8v8 equivalent produced the following results:

- 135% more passes
- 260% more scoring attempts
- 500% more goals scored
- 225% more 1 v 1 encounters
- 280% more dribbling skills (tricks)

Five v Five & Futsal

The 5v5 format is often the means by which players are introduced to the game. It was the traditional go-to format when players trained, even in the adult game, and is often the starting point when players start playing 'competitive' matches.

One very useful youth development tool, based around 5v5, is futsal. This indoor adaptation of the game, however, presents us with a unique contradiction in world football. Some coaches, and certainly some cultures, base their whole youth development programmes around it, whereas others seldom use it in any meaningful way, despite its championed benefits.

In its purest form, futsal is played indoors with a heavier ball that has a reduced bounce. The game has touchlines (rather than walls like other indoor variants of the game) and a four-second limit for players to get the ball back into play. Goalkeepers are traditionally used as a fifth outfield player, so need to have a skillset similar to that of outfield players – a trait that is now prevalent in the 11-a-side format.

In South America and parts of Eastern Europe, futsal is seen as being part of the course in the football upbringing of young players. Those who played it regularly, swear by its benefits when they graduate to the 11v11 game, even if not played in its purest form (it may be played outdoor, or with a slightly different ball, etc.)

"

Futsal is a collaborative / adversarial team game in which players are required to adapt to a changing, dynamic environment; one in which they have a restricted amount of time and space in which to make decisions and carry out actions that will provide solutions for their team. Futsal entails a high level of motor engagement and intense practices, with the tactical aspects (in terms of perception and decision-making) crucial to the effectiveness of each element of play.

"

UEFA Futsal Coaching Manual

---

[3] The four specific games used are available in *Making The Ball Roll*.

The nature of the game, outlined above by the *UEFA Futsal Coaching Manual,* should be a great sell to anyone involved in youth player development. It is quick, heavily technical, and contains elements of inherent tactical and team play. For coaches who live in countries where weather impacts regular training, futsal is the ideal solution. More leagues and organisations are now (or should be) using the format during winters where outdoor games are regularly cancelled. If this is a situation you find yourself in, pre-empt a bad winter and book an indoor hall or outdoor hardcourt to utilise futsal, either as a training tool or in a competitive game against other teams.

Larger Small-Sided Games (6v6 – 10v10)

If the small-SSGs are particularly effective for inducing technical outcomes in players, larger ones can be used to stimulate more tactical outcomes in older players. The further we move towards 11v11, the more it will look and feel like the competitive game that we see on TV each week.

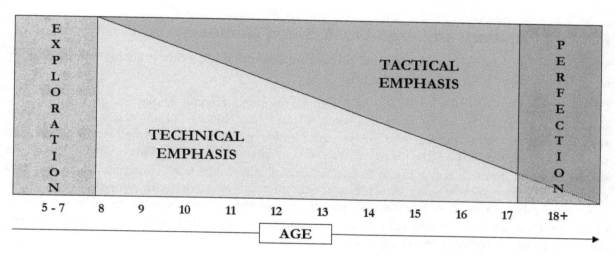

Belgian FA Technical & Tactical Objectives through the ages

The above diagram is taken from the Royal Belgian Football Association's *Philosophy of Youth Development* and concisely shows the relationship between technical and tactical development as young players progress through the age groups. The two are certainly interlinked, regardless of age – they just look different depending on the age of the players. The younger they are, the higher the focus is on the technical aspects of the game. The older they get, the more explicit tactical information can be layered into their game.

The use of small-sided games in our training regimes can reflect this nicely. The younger the players we work with, the more our SSGs should focus on the technical-laden small-SSGs. These produce more technical outcomes whilst also allowing players to develop tactically in an implicit way.

If the smaller-SSGs offer high technical and implicit tactical outcomes, then larger-SSGs increase in their tactical similarities to the 11v11 game. Although they allow less *on-the-ball* actions, they increase in tactical possibilities.

Six v Six – Ten v Ten

One of the greatest attributes of using SSGs is that *players are involved all the time*. Even when they are without the ball, they are still 'in' the game and are still making game-related decisions. For example, a centre-back's positioning will be affected by what their striker is doing with the ball, maybe 40 metres away. Contrast this to a bunch of players standing and watching, waiting for their turn in a queue-like drill.

The younger players' playing game formats that encourage ball contacts are important to develop them technically. Players in the 'Foundation Phase' do not need to spend too much time worrying about innate tactical nuances. The implicit tactical benefits are often enough. The players, as they develop through their teen years, however, can do so more and more when it comes to the tactically-focused aspects of the game.

In a conversation with Nick Cox, Academy Manager at Manchester United, we spoke about their use of the 4v4 format. Interestingly, though, he openly admitted that their Foundation Phase programme involves the players playing a range of formats up to 7v7 and 9v9. It is not 'just' 4v4. A mix of formats allows players a greater range of experiences, and your sessions can reflect the same sentiment. Not all your sessions with your Under-10s, for example, need to be 5v5 or below. Likewise, not all your Under-18 sessions need to be 6v6 or above. A mixture of formats is important.

Playing Positions in Large Small-Sided Games

Small SSGs, as discussed, ensure that all players are committed to both attacking and defending, regardless of their 'position' within the game.

Obviously, the closer you get to the 11v11 format, the more effectively players can practice their position in an SSG. In a *Sky Sports* interview, former Manchester United player, Gary Neville, revealed that in every training session, he would play at right-back in small-sided games. He would never venture into other positions like we often see players do. This arguably changed a self-proclaimed 'limited' teenage player into an expert adult right-back. Conversely, we can also experiment with players playing in other positions in a safe environment, something frequently done by the Head Coach at AFC Bournemouth, Eddie Howe. For example, playing a striker at centre-back allows them to see, experience, and appreciate 'the other side' of the game, and also allows them to appreciate what centre-backs *do not like*.

In these bigger games, you can also place players in combinations that will help the performance of the team. You can pair players that play on the same 'line' – two central defenders, central midfielders, or strikers together, for example, or indeed players who play on different lines: like wingers and full-backs, central defenders and holding midfielders. You can also link 'non-partnerships' together, for example, asking your central midfielder to 'connect' with one of the wingers with a pass, as much as possible. You could also, legitimately, play with a back four, midfield, or front three.

Constraints-Led SSGs

Largely, throughout this chapter, we have spoken about the *implicit* ways in which different types of SSG help to develop players. As the numbers evolve from low to high, we see a shift from a heavily technical influence to a more tactical one.

We can also manipulate the rules and setups of SSGs in a more *explicit* manner that allows us to elicit particular outcomes. By manipulating the rules of the game, we are changing some parameters and asking players to solve inherent problems.

It is important to be aware of what these changes mean for the game and for the players. Even with manipulations, the *primary rules* of the game, even if aspects of it have been manipulated, must remain in place. It must still 'look and feel' like the game of football. We may, however, alter the secondary rules that do not affect the essential make-up of the game.

Constraints-Led Coaching is a style of coaching where the coach takes a particular technique, skill or tactic from the 'whole' game, isolates it in a Small-Sided Game, and lets the players find the answers to solve the problem.

Connected Coaches website

Regardless of how we change the rules of games, or regardless of the practices we ask the players to take part in, we *compromise* the real game. 2v2 is not 11v11, but we accept the compromise as players get more touches. 4v4 is not the real game, but we accept the compromise as it allows players to practice technique under pressure and to both attack and defend. The ball mastery sessions you run look nothing like the game, but are worth it *so players can become comfortable with the ball.*

The constaints-led approach advocates that coaches can alter games in three ways – by manipulating the players (individuals), the task, or the environment itself. There are a multitude of ways in which we can do this, some of which we will look at below.

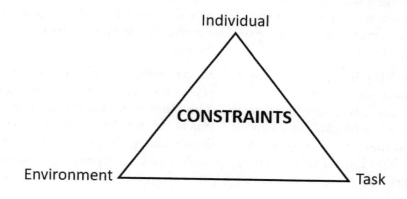

Constraining The Individual (Players) – Example: Overloads and Underloads

In Chapter 10, we looked at the work of Thomas Tuchel and the concept of *Differential Training*. In simple terms, it was about making training sessions more difficult than the players will experience in the real game.

Legendary Italian coach Arrigo Sacchi is notorious for his unique, compact, high-pressing defending style. He used a form of *Differential Training* with his team, often asking his defenders to defend against teams that heavily *overloaded* them – sometimes five defenders against ten attackers. There was so much stress and difficulty in these sessions that game-day, by contrast, seemed easier.

Football is full of underload/overload situations – where one team has fewer/more players than the opposition. There are countless situations in games where players have to deal with being outnumbered, or where players have to take advantage of situations where they outnumber the opponent. This may be the entire game (playing 10v11 after a sending off), but more commonly and more importantly, small segments of the game. If, for example, when one team is attacking in the final third, chances are the players who are defending will have more players than the attackers. Some teams actively attempt to create player overloads and achieve 'numerical superiority' in certain areas of the pitch.

By using these types of practices in our training sessions, we challenge the team with fewer numbers to compete through stress and pressure. We challenge the team with more players to take quick advantage of this superiority (we must remember that in-possession numerical superiority in games tends to only last a few seconds as the opposition will recover and reorganise to help their outnumbered teammates). So although the team with greater numbers has a numerical advantage, it is useful to constrain them in other ways.

In an excellent *Boot Room* video series, available online, former Sheffield United Academy Coach, Joe Sargison, takes his Under-14 team through a session that begins with even numbers before altering the numbers to 9v10 then 8v11. In a later video in this series, Sargison remains with 8v11, but places a 'constraint' on the team with 11 players – if they cannot get a shot away within six passes, the ball goes to the other team. The eight are practicing in a stressful environment against three extra players, while the eleven are also stressed by having to attack quickly.

Constraining the Task – Example: Scenarios

One method that is frequently used in training environments is the use of scenarios; the most common being the 'Cup Final' game. Team A is winning 1-0 with ten minutes remaining and therefore need to 'see out' the game until full-time. This team may focus on defending and counter-attacking, for example. The other team is losing 0-1 and will need to focus on attacking and chasing an equalising goal. Further scenarios can develop as off-shoots of this. For example, how do both teams react if the scores go to 1-1? Once they have played this game, you can ask players to discuss the outcome and play again, or reverse the scenario where Team A is now losing and Team B are ahead.

Rhys Barker (@rhys_b16) has posted a lot of varying scenarios of this ilk, where he uses professional teams as a way of engaging the players. One team will play as Barcelona, for example, and look to use possession-based tactics. The other team will play as Inter Milan who focus on defending in a low block. Using famous teams in this way allows players to resemble the players and teams that they see on a weekly basis. Barker kindly allowed me to use the scenario below as an example. You can, of course, come up with your own scenarios, or use more recent examples as inspiration.

BRAZIL (Team A)		**PORTUGAL (Team B)**
It is the quarter-final of the World Cup and into the second half of extra time. It is 2-2 and Portugal have a penalty kick.		
How will you come back from this if they score? If they miss, will this give Brazil the confidence to go on and win it.	**2 - 2** 105:00 minutes	Can you score and take the lead, then hold on for a memorable victory? If you miss, how will you react?

Sample scenario from Rhys Barker

Constraining the Environment – Example: Pitches

Largely, the environment that we can manipulate relates to the size and shape of the pitch we use, or how players score a 'goal'. To relate back to Chapter 10, and Tuchel again, we see he manipulated the shape of the pitch to force the players to attack centrally. Furthermore, I have seen coaches play SSGs on pitches that are big, small, short, long, skinny, fat, circular, rectangular, square, and more! Pitches may have one goal, two goals, four goals, or even six goals plus. I have seen coaches use end lines or scoring zones as a method of scoring (e.g., running the ball into an end zone, much like American Football). Maybe passing the ball to a target player or target players is the method of choice.

Each time we manipulate the environment in such a way, we will impact the performance and habits of the players. Understanding how these changes will affect the game is important. For example, if you train indoors, what are the impacts of rebound walls? Positively, they may allow players to be creative and combine with the wall, or negatively, it can encourage inaccurate passing as players know the ball cannot go out of play.

Playing an SSG on an overly small pitch will give players less time when in possession, forcing them to play quicker, scan earlier, pass, dribble or shoot more promptly, etc. Once the players are returned to a bigger pitch, they can take some of these habits with them. At Arsenal, it was frequent that Arsène Wenger would play 11v11 for 15 minutes[4] on a full-sized pitch, then 11v11 on half a pitch, then onto one-quarter.

Restrict, Relate, Reward

Ben Bartlett (@benbarts) is a former FA Coach Educator, and is currently the Head of Coaching at Fulham FC. He kindly contributed a story in the *It's Your Game* segment about how he came to designing training sessions and the use of constraint-based coaching. Bartlett does this by focusing on all three aspects (player, task, and environment) while planning.

First of all, he looks at how changing the environment or the "pitch parameters" will help induce the topic he wants to focus on. When coaching wide play, for example, he will use a pitch that is wider than it is long. His *Boot Room* article is available online for more information and examples.

He also constrains the players or the task by Restricting, Relating, or Rewarding players within these games:

	Explanation	Example
Restrict	This method generally involves restricting the actions of the players. This is how we traditionally approached 'conditioning' SSGs (two-touch maximum, one-touch finish, etc.). While useful in homing in on certain aspects, it often compromises the real game too much. For example, when we only allow players to score using one-touch, we are slicing away all the occasions where taking two+ touches are necessary, and where players turn down genuine opportunities to score as the restriction prohibits them.	To score, you must win the ball back in the opposition's half.

---

[4] Wenger was renowned for training practices that lasted 15 minutes, and not a second longer, before moving players to the next task.

Relate	The relate method is less about rules and more about asking players to recognise situations in which to perform a desired action. So rather than *insisting* on players finishing with one touch, you challenge them to do it, or ask them to get into positions where they can finish one-touch. What you may lose in repetition, you will gain in game understanding. The players are not just following rules, they are analysing the game.	Can you recognise when to press in the opponent's half?
Reward	The reward method is an excellent way of balancing both methods above. By giving players a reward for successfully completing a task, you home in on the skill, but without compromising other aspects of the game. I am certain that one of the best ways to ensure that players are motivated and performing intensely in training is by keeping score. If we want players to finish with one-touch, we can give them extra points for doing so, whilst also allowing them to score in other ways.	If you win the ball back in the opponent's half and score a goal, it is worth three points.

Conclusion

At the beginning of this chapter, I posed a football-related 'desert island' question. By now, hopefully, your answer is clearer. The game is the best way to teach the game to players. Players are implicitly practicing all four moments of the game, and will involve all elements of PPSTT. As we have seen, we can adapt the rules, numbers, and 'look' of these games to reflect the outcomes we want to induce. Other forms of practice can certainly be of use in terms of developing players, but if our sessions do not contain significant time when players are playing the game, then we are certainly limiting their development.

And the best thing is – the players love it!

Summary

- The single most important way for players to learn and practice the game is through the game.

- Through games-based coaching, we can recreate the benefits of street football.

- Small-Sided Games (SSGs) are reduced-numbers versions of the 11v11 game and the closest thing we get to the game in our training sessions.

- Do not bribe the players with the game – that is why they are here.

- Mastering the ball underpins all football actions, and being proficient in 1v1 situations allows you to bring ball mastery into the game.

- Players can work on their ball mastery skills when at home too.

- If we use a before, during, and after method, when looking at 1v1 situations, we quickly enter games of 2v2 or above.

- Data, and indeed logic, tells you that the fewer players you have playing in a small-sided game, the more football actions each player will perform.

- Using a mix of small-sided game formats can add value to player development. This includes small-SSGs like 2v2, 3v3, 4v4 and 5v5 including futsal, and also larger ones (6v6+)

- Small-SSGs are particularly effective for inducing technical outcomes in players. Larger ones can be used to simulate more tactical outcomes in older players. The further we move towards 11v11, the more it will look and feel like the competitive game that we are most familiar with.

- Coaches can use larger SSGs to play players (older players) in their defined positions, or to give them risk-free experience in new ones. The coach can also pair players together in different ways to help them 'connect'.

- The constraints-led approach to coaching advocates manipulating the game (the players, the task or the environment) to elicit certain outcomes. We must understand, however, that there is a compromise to changing the rules of the game. The game must still 'look and feel' like football, regardless of how you manipulated it.

- Examples of constraining players include the use of overloads and underloads. Coaches may use scenarios to manipulate the task or use different shaped and sized pitches to manipulate the environment.

- Ben Bartlett uses a method of Restrict, Relate, Reward, added to manipulating the pitch, to elicit certain outcomes in the game.

> ## It's Your Game #1
> # Another Tool for Your Coaching Toolbox
> ## Radek Mozyrko • @radekmozyrko
> ## Academy Manager, Legia Warsaw, Poland

The definition of small-sided games is to play with fewer than 11 players on each team. Playing with fewer players on the field means that players are constantly involved in the play and provided with more opportunities for touches on the ball. There are various ways of using small-sided games to enhance players' skills. I would like to mention one approach that I use when I work with elite players.

When a talented player plays 'up' an age-group, I usually ask him what the differences are between playing for his own age-group and playing for an older age-group. The majority of players usually say the same things, such as "I have less time on the ball," "the game is quicker," and "I struggle to find space on a pitch."

I asked myself what more could I do, to prepare players, before they move up an age-group?

My answer came when I was working with an Under-13's academy team. A few players were showing signs that they would be ready to play up soon, so I started playing 11v11 on a 7v7-size pitch in training and friendly matches. The environment was extremely challenging. Players had to be smart to find space. When a player received the ball, he did not have a lot of time, because someone was already closing him down. Therefore, the crowded environment forced players to create good angles of support; knowing what to do with the ball before receiving it. Their first touch had to be spotless, otherwise an opponent would steal it.

We decided to play these types of games regularly. This development tool was extremely good for the *best* players in a group. When players were finally moved up, they told me that they did not find the game quicker or more challenging than playing 11v11 football on a 7v7 pitch, and they felt confident when playing against older players.

There were, however, also negatives to this approach. 'Strugglers' in a group were often taken into the panic zone. They struggled a lot and did not have enough success in those games. Therefore, these players were overstretched and did not demonstrate improvement.

Balance, therefore, is important when using these types of small-sided games (or any other type of games or training methods), as *a part* of your coaching process, not as the main thing. Another tool for your coaching toolbox.

It's Your Game #2

Constraints

Ben Bartlett • @benbarts

Head of Coaching, Fulham FC

Several years ago, whilst delivering a coach development event in London, a coach approached me to thank me for the book of practices we had given him previously. He explained that some had been of great benefit to him and his players – and some of the ones that had worked less well. He proceeded to enthusiastically tell me that he had used all the practices by now and to ask if I had any more.

We discussed the reasons why he felt some had worked well and others less so, and particularly, the notion that, in many ways, the ones that had worked well were often, by accident, attuned to him and his players' needs.

This coach was recognising that to be an effective player developer, it was necessary to identify development experiences that reflected the aspects that were important to him and the players. The notion of practice books, where someone has decided what practice should look like for others was, it appeared at this moment, problematic. However, for many of us, constructing sessions from a blank piece of paper is incredibly daunting.

As a result, at that point, I committed to two things:

a. Identifying a consistent set of ingredients that I could combine in the design of football activity.

b. Openly and repeatedly rationalising the thinking that sits behind how and why these ingredients might be mixed at any point in time.

This supported me to blend my beliefs about the value of a constraints-led approach to coaching, where the design of the experience (e.g., playing area and distribution of the players), and the demands placed upon the players, gave them the opportunity to practice game elements in ways that are accommodating of their uniqueness.

The ways human beings playing football interact with these environmental conditions and tasks has the power to inform our observations and future coaching decisions, empowering us to break free of the shackles of coaching being limited by a finite resource of sessions and leading us into a more responsive, universal way of thinking.

> ## It's Your Game #3
> # We Need the Game
> ## Pete Augustine • @surrey_ccd
> ## FA County Coach Developer

Over the years, I – like many coaches – have strived to find the new coaching practice that nobody else has come up with. We all try to find that magic formula that will make our players world-beaters.

One day, on a long journey with one of my bosses, we were discussing the merits of different types of practice. He then claimed that there are probably only 14 different types of practice that you could create as they are all just a variation on a theme. This got me thinking – are there actually as many as 14?

If you think of a game of football – there are two teams, one ball, two goals, and one pitch. I will try to kick the ball into your goal and you will try to stop me, then you will do the same to me when you have the ball.

With that in mind, we then try to practise doing this in our training sessions. So what might this look like? It is far too simplistic to say, "Let's just play a match in training then that way we'll be good on a Saturday or Sunday." We first need to look at why we train, and what do we want to get out of it. When we look at a practice session, ideally we want to break the game down into its component parts – how will we do that? Well, we can divide the pitch into zones, we can have practices in circles, squares, rectangles, or even triangles if we see fit.

Would we design a practice in a hexagon or an octagon or a dodecahedron? No? Why not? I tell you why, because it is far too complicated and football is a simple game.

So the question, then, is why wouldn't we just do the same practices that everyone does time and time again? Why do we need creativity in our sessions? Why do we go onto the internet, buy books, listen to podcasts, and order DVDs? We are all looking for that 1% of inspiration to take back to our players.

The skill is then how we relate these sessions to our players. Do we actually look at our players before we decide which practice we are going to use with them? This is really where the magic happens – knowing what inspires and challenges *our* players; the thing that makes them want to come back time and time again. The truth is that if we know what we want from our players, we don't need hundreds of practices … we just need the right practices. We need the game.

It's Your Game #4
Wants and Needs; Freedom & Playfulness
Michael Beale • @MichaelBeale
First Team Coach, Rangers FC

I believe that the key to coaching is the merging of player 'wants' and player 'needs'.

We have all been a player that has come to training wanting to play the game or to practise something within the game that we like to do. We have also been the player who has taken part in a session where the coach has been insistent on working on a specific theme for the day that wasn't particularly fun or in-line with our motivation for being at the practice. Therefore, understanding players and what they *want* from a session and then merging this cleverly with what you, as the coach, feel the players *need* to improve is a key aspect of session planning. A rule of thumb for coaches should always be, "Would you want to play in this session?"

This underpins my style of coaching – understanding players' need to play the game and not complicate the learning via 'drills'.

I have been fortunate to work with a number of foreign players from the ages of Under-12 through to senior internationals. The period working in Brazil was particularly fascinating. It helped me to understand different cultures and how they impact football. The key thing that is evident in all top players is the love for just playing the game, trying out a new technique or skill and the contact time they have on the ball.

Therefore, the saying "train how you play" might be one of the worst things to promote. If you train how you play, then you will only play at the level of the last game. Training should be about improving, and about rehearsal and discovery. With this in mind, how often do you let your players have the freedom to explore and rehearse? Or are you always wanting the session to be intense and "perfect". If so, where will the creative spark and imagination come from?

The playfulness is understanding when to step back and allow the players time to be free in the session, to either work alone with the ball, or to just play a game as they would as kids. No coach ever gave players like Neymar the skills – playfulness allows them the freedom to practise and design the future of the game.

Chapter 16
Més que un ... Academy

They [the Academy players at FC Barcelona] are the future of Barça, but to get there they have to follow a path along which everyone must speak the same language; philosophy of football in which the ball, the greatest treasure of all, will accompany them on their journey. Learning to love it, respect it and above all enjoy playing with it. That is the key, what makes the difference.

www.fcbarcelona.com

First of all, apologies to the people of Catalonia for potentially butchering their language while I searched for a quirky name for this chapter. Barcelona's motto, 'Més que un Club', as many of you will know, translates to 'More than a Club' – a rallying call that unites the organisation, and inspires the feeling that it is unique. The intention for the rest of this chapter is to bring many of the things we have spoken about in this book, previously, to life.

Human beings, by nature, long to be part of something bigger than themselves – something greater that they can connect with. Think of Gianluigi Buffon in tears singing the Italian national anthem, Liverpool FC's famous Kop stand singing 'You'll Never Walk Alone' in unison, Borussia Dortmund's 'Yellow Wall' or The All Blacks performing the 'Haka'. On the pitch, this could be a club's adherence to a specific playing style, recruiting in a particular manner, or following a certain 'way'.

> For us, FC Barcelona is not a business;
> it is a feeling.
>
> **Sandro Rosell**

There is little doubt that the successes of the modern Barcelona teams are down to their academy. In 2010, all three players on the Ballon D'Or podium were not only from Barcelona – they were all graduates of the club's academy (Messi, Xavi, and Iniesta). Alumni since the turn of the century roll off the tongue – Carles Puyol, Xavi Hernández, Sergio Busquets, Andrés Iniesta, and Lionel Messi have all spent their entire top-level careers at the club. Cesc Fàbregas, Gerard Pique, and Jordi Alba all left Catalonia only to return, while career progressions saw Pedro Rodríguez and Bojan Krkić make an impact before moving on to pastures new.

At one point, under the late Tito Villanova, 17 of the 25 members of the first team squad (68%) were produced by the club. On one occasion, he actually selected an entire team of academy graduates (versus Levante in November 2012). In the 2011 Champions League final, seven of the 11 starting players came through the youth ranks. Furthermore, six of Spain's starting 11 in the

Chapter 16 – Més que un … Academy

2010 World Cup Final were from the FCB Academy (a seventh, Fàbregas, was introduced as a second-half substitute). Although in recent years such impressive stats do not quite stack up in the same way (at the time of writing, the last player to graduate from academy to first-team *regular* was Sergi Roberto, and he did so in the 2010/11 season), these achievements remain unprecedented, and, critically, their system produces some serious learning outcomes for coaches – both on and off the pitch.

Vision and Values

"

The first mission of the coaches is to help the boys with their behaviour; the second is to show them how to be good players.

**Albert Puig,
former FC Barcelona Academy Director**

"

In October 2011, Barcelona opened the 'New Masia' to expand their academy operations and develop a more modern facility. This replaced the more modest, old-school farmhouse that literally lived in the shadow of the Camp Nou stadium. A term frequently used to describe the Barcelona Academy is 'La Masia', literally translating to 'farmhouse', and that term will be intermittently used here also. Although modest in comparison to the new facility, it is crucial to remember that the original Masia housed the core of the Barcelona and Spanish teams that ruled and wooed the football world. The building itself is over 300 years old. It is not all about the cosmetics of a facility – it is about what you make of it.

What strikes you when you read the official press release about the new building, however, is a complete lack of initial reference to football, talent, or ability. Instead, the official FCB website referred to the facility helping with the "intellectual, personal, and social development of young sportspeople." Indeed, the Barca methodology lists "providing comprehensive care for players" before "promoting philosophy and style of play."

As important as the football training and style is in the process, their vision, values, and creation of 'something bigger' is central to the club's way. Very few clubs refer so frequently to their vision. Words like 'DNA', 'values', the 'Barcelona Way', 'ethos', 'philosophy' and such, are predominant in the material, and other messages that are emitted from the club. Because their identity is so robust and meaningful, "The players have an obligation to meet and defend the idea of the club," (former Head Coach, Louis van Gaal).

The Five Values of Barcelona's Academy

Effort	Teamwork	Ambition	Respect	Humility

Within the walls of La Masia, the five values that the club promotes roll off the tongue. They are constantly reinforced to coaches, players, and parents alike. In an interview for *Sky Sports*, a mother of an Under-10 player stated that "the values are so important here and are constantly cited, because they [the players] have to have values in life. They really hammer that home here." In the same interview, these values were explained without hesitation by the Director of La Masia, Carles Folguera:

> The value of humility. If I'm very good and have the ability to listen, I'll improve, progress, and become a better player. Then you have respect. That goes for teammates, the club, a model for playing the game which has made us great. Ambition – a Barca player has to be ambitious, want more, learn more and not simply settle. You have to try to go far and battle for your dream.

Carles Folguera, La Masia Director

While Barcelona have received some criticism for the lack of youth players making significant breakthroughs into the first team since 2011, the club still recognises its duty to perform away from the pitch. Barcelona acknowledge the fact that we discussed earlier – that many of their players will not make the step from academy player to international star and have come up with a comprehensive life skills programme known as *Masia 360*. As part of this, their *Athlete Integral Care Service* (SAIE) looks to support the player in ways other than football, including emotionally, educationally, and psychologically.

They learn skills around how to behave and are prepared for the job market outside of the game. Workshops are provided for parents, and lessons in nutrition and psychology are common. Even former professional players are supported in their retirement. The "Barcelona attitude" is as much about life skills as football skills. According to the European Club Association's 2011 *Report on Youth Academies in Europe*, 11 players in the Barcelona B team were studying at university alongside their playing and training programme.

If their football and non-football support are wholesome, so too is the language used at the academy. In recent years, they have moved away from aggressive words and terms often associated with the game with a preference for more positive, informational vocabulary, some of which are included below (with thanks to Cristian Colás (@crcolas) for the translation):

We talk about...	Instead of...
Create	Destroy
Recover	Defend
Winning the ball back	Stealing the ball
Opponent	Enemy
Competition, Game	Battle, War, Fight
Provide	Attack
Assertiveness	Passivity, Aggressiveness
To be better (than the opponent)	Humiliate / Underestimate
Enjoy, Learn, Compete	Only to Win
Empathy	Selfishness
Optimise	Improve

"   **"**

We believe in education based on values and attitudes that can be learned and, therefore, taught. Our team of professionals has an important role in providing information to the youngsters and conveying experiences and values that will guide their behaviour, helping them to live together and mature as individuals.

Displayed at the Camp Nou Stadium

Implications for Coaches
Football, and sport in general, is a great driver when it comes to life skills and education. Barcelona's five values – effort, teamwork, ambition, respect, and humility – could be the values of any organisation or institute. Instilling these values in young people assists them in life as well as football. Whether you coach as part of a programme that formally mixes football and education, or whether you coach part-time, instilling and promoting values and education is an extension of the role of coach. A career in professional football may not be the end goal for many players, like at Barcelona, (it may not even be something they are considering), but using the game to coach social skills, behaviour, and a respect for ambitious academic achievement remains possible. In the *It's Your Game* segment, at the end of the Chapter, Alex Clapham talks about seeing this at first hand with the young players at Barça.

Playing Style

"   **"**

Barça's style is unique in the world. The ball is always the reference. Our style is associated with technical excellence, plasticity and spectacle. But to get better, you need to enjoy the game. And that's what we do. That's the key reason why Barça is such a unique club.

Carles Folguera, La Masia Director

At the club, all teams are compelled to uphold the playing style that is considered the 'Barcelona DNA'.

In terms of formation, the focus is on a mix between 4-3-3 and 3-4-3. This very Dutch concept was imported to Barcelona by Johan Cruyff and his mentor, Rinus Michels. Having passing options – particularly angled passes, and the creation of triangles between players all over the pitch lends itself to concepts of short passes, support play, fluid movement, and the prevention of counter-attacks through immediate pressing. The diagram below is taken from Louis van Gaal's (another Dutch coach) *Barcelona Philosophy* document detailing the possible passing connections between players in their 4-3-3 formation:

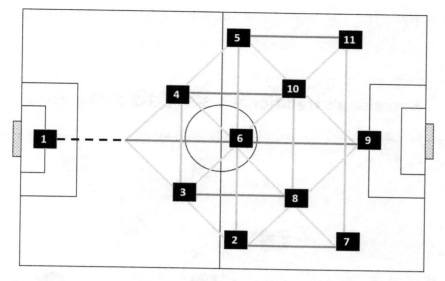

Slide taken from Barcelona Philosophy document written by Louis van Gaal, highlighting the connections between teammates and the triangles created when Barcelona are in possession

Their playing style is often referred to as 'tiki-taka',[1] which is characterised by dominating possession of the ball and the use of many short passes. Aimless or long, inaccurate passes are frowned upon. Movement off the ball to receive passes and create 'triangular' shapes all over the pitch is a central concept.

Even when in possession of the ball near their own goal, their instinct to use short passes remains. The central idea is to 'build-up' play and to advance up the pitch whilst maintaining these connections. Although not a 'rule' – as many will have you believe – the goalkeeper will also tend to use the same shorter passes when in possession, unlike the style of many others who will kick the ball directly into the other half of the pitch.

Although teams at Barça are duty-bound to uphold this style of play, there is also the suggestion of adaptability and unique styles that are influenced by the Head Coach. Luis Enrique placed a greater influence on counter-attacking than others, and the flexible 4-4-2 formation used by Head Coach Ernesto Valverde during the 2017/18 season is different to that of Guardiola, for example. The central point remains, however – when you watch Barcelona, you know you are watching Barcelona. If that identity disappears for too long, change to restore it isn't too far away.

"　　　　　　　　　　　　　　　　　　　**"**

Cruyff painted Barça's chapel; subsequent
managers must merely restore and add to it.

Pep Guardiola

The diagram below is again from the *Barcelona Philosophy* document mentioned above. Along with variations of the same theme that exist from coach to coach, van Gaal also suggested that they

---

[1] Some, most notably Pep Guardiola, do not like the term 'tiki-taka'. They believe it encourages the idea of passing the ball just for the sake of passing it. Guardiola once said that, "We don't pass the ball to move the ball, we pass the ball to move the opposition." In other words, they will keep the ball, 'recycle' possession, and be patient, waiting for the opposition to become disorganised, and then go for goal. Going for goal is always more important than anything else; keeping possession for long periods is just a vehicle for doing so.

were willing to adapt to the opposition, while still adhering to their own style and 4-3-3 or 3-4-3 formations.

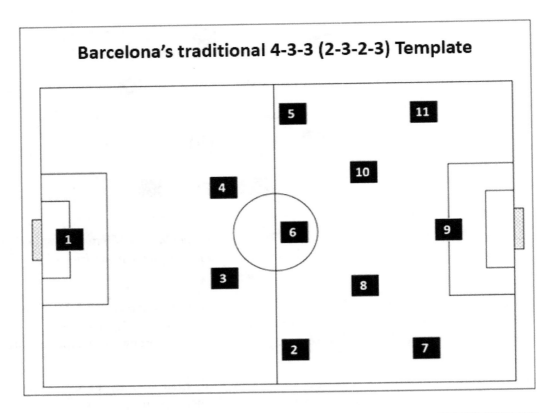

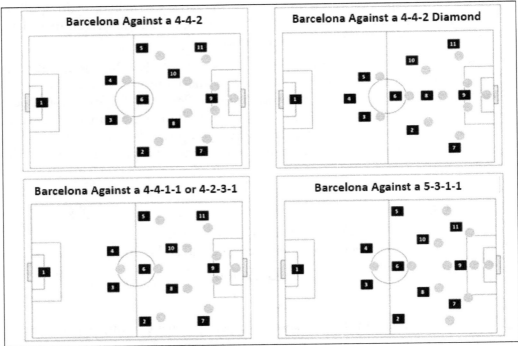

The same playing style and ethos that we see from the first team are also used throughout the academy. In fact, it is possibly more accurate to say that the first team has the same playing identity as the academy. This emphasis means that from a very young age, the academy players are indoctrinated into the way of playing that feeds into the 'Més que un club' mantra. By the time players graduate into senior football, they are educated in this style and system.

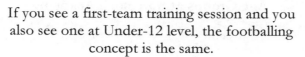

> If you see a first-team training session and you also see one at Under-12 level, the footballing concept is the same.
>
> We stick with the same methodology from a young age … They become better footballers. They have more of that Barça DNA.
>
> **Jordi Roura,**
> **Barcelona Head of Youth Coaching**

Implications for Coaches
In development football, this type of 'tiki-taka' play is generally accepted to be the optimum method in developing players. It encourages comfort in possession and a willingness to master the ball, plus inclusively mixing technical and tactical work. Playing out from the back, the use of short passes, mastering 1v1 situations, playing under pressure, sharing the ball but being creative as individuals, off-the-ball movement, etc. are all key concepts that are best learned and assimilated during youth phases.

Implications for Coaches
The methods of developing players at Barcelona is very much 'their way', something that the club is keen to point out. They openly admit and understand that it is *their* way and not *the* way. Having opened the Academy in 1979, the club are also keen to point out that their success in the 2000s was not a quick-hit. It was down to 30+ years of methodical work.
Having a single club philosophy from the youngest youth players to the first team is not always possible, although having one throughout a youth programme is achievable (depending on the ambition, togetherness, and foresight of the club).
Earlier in the book, Chris Ramsey asked the question as to whether coaches should produce players for the club, or for the game. There is also a forceful argument that developing players in one singular way is *not* optimal for their all-round football development. It may produce players who cannot adapt to any other style.

Winning … But Our Way

There is no academy league in Spain. All age groups at Barcelona play between 40 and 60 games per season, in local, regional or national leagues, depending on their age. Teams compete locally up to Under-12, and from Under-13 they compete at regional and national levels. Furthermore, promotion and relegation exist at all ages. Results and league tables are printed in newspapers and posted online.

Age Groups at Barcelona Academy

Juvenil	16 – 18
Cadet	14 – 16
Infantil	13 – 14
Alevín	11 – 12
Benjamín	9 – 10
Pre-Benjamín	7 – 8

Without a specific academy league system, you can imagine the competitiveness of any local or regional team that plays against Barcelona (or any other major club for that matter). A win for any club against Barça, regardless of age, is a feather in their cap. Producing players with the competitiveness to deal with this type of opponent, on a regular basis, and a winning mentality is vital.

"

Quality without results is pointless.
Results without quality is boring.

Johan Cruyff

"

At the academy in Barcelona, *winning is important and competition is promoted early*. They want to win – but insist on winning *their way*.

Although winning is highly valued, Barça stop short of the 'win at all costs' mentality that can pollute youth football. Their quest to win games does not resort to choosing players with strong physical characteristics over technical ones. They do not downscale to direct, aimless football when losing. Instead, they maintain their patient, possession-based style of play to negotiate difficult score lines. As Guillermo Amor, former Barcelona academy and senior player whose work at Barça spans both the academy and senior team, explains – "Even when we are losing, we stick to our beliefs."

To make their style of play work at senior level, it has to be believed in, and prized at youth level. It is during this period that players' technical foundations are laid for the future. Barcelona recognise the long-term aspect of this. If 'kick and rush' style football is the way to solve their immediate, short-term problems, they would not produce the technically superior players we have become accustomed to. If throwing a giant centre-back upfront and lofting the ball in his general direction is the answer, then Barça do not want to know the question.

Few players have epitomised the Barcelona way more than midfield maestro, Xavi. He had physical limitations as a young player, and could be considered diminutive as a senior professional. He did, however, thoroughly make up for these 'deficiencies' in terms of technical and tactical skills. In *La Masia: Developing People As Well As Players*, author Cristian Martin revealed a coaching review about the player when he was 14 and member of the 'Infantil A' squad:[2]

---

[2] Translation provided in article from Daily Mail Online.

Technical / Tactical Review	Physical Review
Control: Excellent. He compensates for his lack of speed with excellent ball control.	**Speed:** Average. He should improve his agility and speed of movement.
Passes: Very good. He should improve his left foot to better use this quality that he has. Shows real personality on the pitch.	**Aggression:** Average. His eminently technical game sometimes makes this aspect difficult.
Crosses: Good although he almost never needs to show this skill.	
Shot: Acceptable. He should improve.	
Running with the ball: Very good. He has a good sense of how to protect the ball. He almost never loses it.	
Dribbles: Good. It is not what he usually opts for, but technique is good.	
Positioning: Excellent. It is his best quality. He is always where he needs to be, always giving support and a passing option to his team-mates.	

Xavi Hernández Player Review as 14-year-old

Whilst the football world can seem obsessed with the physically big and strong players, Barcelona are more than happy to invest their time and belief in players who may have physical disadvantages, but strong technical ones. You will notice very quickly from the review above that Xavi's strengths lay in the technical and tactical aspects of the game over the physical ones.

Implications for Coaches
It is important here to understand that, although winning games and titles is prized at Barcelona, *the way they win* remains the most important thing at the Academy. It must not be confused with a 'win at all costs' mentality that can pervade a lot of youth coaching environments. Technical excellence remains the quality that is sought-after more than others, even under the pressure of every team that sees their encounter with Barcelona as a cup final.

Training Methodology

When you watch the youth players at Barcelona train, it is striking. Of course, the quality is evident – the technical excellence *shines through*. Barça can, of course, recruit from the best players locally, regionally, and nationally – even internationally when you look at Lionel Messi, and the arrangement with Samuel Eto'o's Cameroon-based Foundation.

As well as their intention to recruit well, the aim is to "develop players with technique, speed, and vision of the game" (ECA). As a result, the sessions are of high intensity and are a playground for the deliberate or purposeful practice that Daniel Coyle spoke about earlier in the book. All players are involved at all times during their training activities. Players are always busy, always involved, and always engaged, both physically and mentally.

To enable the development of players' game understanding, they are making game-related decisions and problem-solving throughout. When 12-year-old Infantil B player Cristobal Muñoz was asked (in an interview for a Sky Sports documentary presented by Guillem Balagué) what he enjoyed most about training, his answer –unscripted and surprisingly thoughtful for a pre-teen – was "the intensity, the rhythm and what we learn everyday." An answer right from the growth mindset catalogue.

Players at the academy train three times per week until they are 13, then it increases to four. The vast majority of training exercises over these sessions involve the ball. The players learn to love the ball, to prize its possession. Physical 'fitness' work is not considered until the age of 16, and weights are not introduced until players are 17. "You're on the ball all the time, and it's very fast-paced," commented a Benjamín player to Balagué.

This pace and deliberate practice is mentally challenging, as well as physically. In 2017, England women's international Toni Duggan made the move from Manchester City Ladies to Barcelona Femení. She immediately noticed the training methodology ingrained throughout the club. There was no passing from A to B and routinely following your pass. "In Barcelona, you don't go to B. You have to go to D, and then to F. It really works your brain."[3]

Around the Rondo

"

We'd spend most of the time in training working on passing, doing positional exercises and rondos. It was mainly skills work. The main idea was that the best kind of attack is to have the ball. We learned that the more you move, the more passing options your teammate has, but the real running is done by the ball. I've never encountered anything like that outside of La Masia.

**Víctor Vázquez,
former Barcelona youth player**

"

As coaches from across the globe descend on La Masia in search of the secrets of their success, they are often surprised. There is no particular mystery. One positive conclusion that many have come to is around their use of the 'rondo' and similar 'positional play' possession-based exercises.

Adrian Castro (@adribarca), who visited the academy, describes watching several age groups running similar practices and concepts, modified to be age-appropriate for each team. Practices detailed time, space, and quality of pass. Possession practices included numerical advantages with 'joker' or neutral players. Finding the free player was of great importance. "Whether it be 4v2, 6v3 or 5v4, there was always an opportunity to find an open man and create an advantage for your team," Castro added.

Below are four examples of these rondo/positional-play/possession-based practices used by Barcelona 'Juvenil A' coaches Álex Garcia and Marc Huguet, taken from their 2005/2006 *Programación Temporada* (Season Programme), bringing Castro's comments to life.

---

[3] If you are interested in sessions like this, check out the *Deliberate Soccer Practice* books.

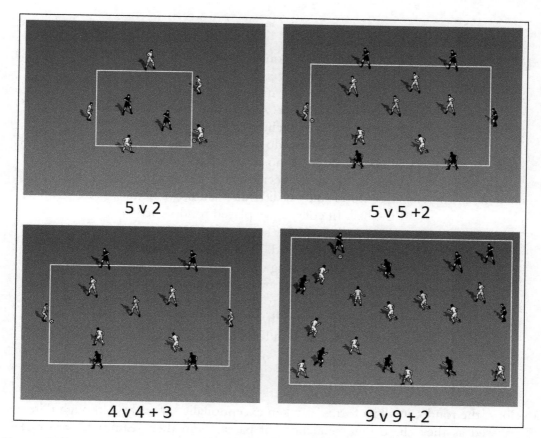

Four typical possession games used by Barcelona 'Juvenil A' coaches Álex García and Marc Huguet, taken from their 2005/2006 Programación Temporada (Season Programme)

In many football environments, the rondo practice is often, in its purest form (akin to the 5v2 above), just a bit of a fun. Players (and coaches) in some places do not take it especially seriously. It is a practice conducted before the 'proper' session begins, or by substitutes[4] while the rest of the team warms up. The quality is debatable and often players focus on being unnecessarily clever, or making fun of each other with bad, overhit, or poorly executed passes. Whilst advocates of the rondo insist on putting the defenders to the sword by completing as many passes as possible, those who use them for 'banter' will aim to embarrass them.

Although the traditional rondo is often seen as a 5/6v2 exercise, there are many variants. They can range from small 3/4v1 versions (see example from Barcelona's *Escola* below), to games that may involve two simultaneous rondos.[5] The rondo, performed well, should see both 'teams' working physically as well as technically/tactically. The inside pair have to work hard *without the ball* to ensure that players on the outside have to work hard *with the ball*. A rondo, if the area is too big, or the players are not applying themselves well enough, becomes sloppy and a slog.

---

[4] Re-branded as 'game changers' by US Women's National Team Coach, Jill Ellis – a positive spin on how we traditionally view those who are not in the first eleven. The term makes not starting a game easier to swallow, although you will need to ensure that all players have the opportunity to come on and 'change the game'.

[5] For further examples of rondos, and using them – whether it is for a technical warm-up, or for more tactical purposes – check out a presentation from Kieran Smith (@KieranSmith1) – *Rondos: How To Use Spain's Secret Weapon.*

"

"

I was introduced to rondo some twenty years ago as a player; however no one told me it was called 'rondo' nor did they explain the objectives of the game. At the time, there were actually coaches preaching what an unrealistic training exercise rondo was. They believed it taught the direct opposite of what you want your players to do because after passing the player stood still – it did not teach movement off the ball. In college, we played rondo once in a great while and only as a fun activity before training actually started. There was no intensity level or understanding of its real purpose. To us, it was just a keep away game with no real purpose. Now, twenty-three years later, as a seasoned head coach, I have a totally new appreciation and understanding of rondo.

Marcus DiBernardo, *The Science of Rondo*

At Barcelona, the rondo, in all its forms, is taken exceptionally seriously. Although defenders may be embarrassed as they chase long sequences of passes (and their teammates *will* make fun of them!), they understand the game-related benefits of this type of practice.

Indeed, it is the 'game-related' debate that has divided opinion about the theoretical effectiveness of the rondo. In US coach education circles, any type of 'non-directional' exercise is actually frowned upon. According to their system, opposed practices should all be directional – i.e. have one team playing towards a target, and the opposition playing towards another. There are no shortage of Barcelona coaches and players who disagree, of course, some of which we will address below. Football is, after all, a 360 degree game.

Pass 1 is known as a 'first-line' pass, where you play a pass to the player beside you. This, in a game context, refers to a pass in a 'retain & build' stage of attacking. Pass 2, a second-line pass (to a player other than the one beside you), could be considered a 'progressive' pass.
The third-line pass however (pass 3) is a directional, defence-splitting one, and ultimately the one in which is sort after.

For Player A, the directional pass is to player D or E. For player C, the directional pass would be to F etc. Albert Puig, former Technical Director at La Masia, in a video for his online football courses, speaks about there being an imaginary 'goal' that is constantly moving as the rondo changes direction. In the image above, the goal would be behind Players D and E. Should F have the ball, the imaginary goal is behind Players B and C – making those third-line pass more valuable.

Basic Rondo

Technical Outcomes – In Possession	Tactical Outcomes – In Possession
Playing with your head up	Breaking lines
Having a body position to see most of the pitch	Capitalising on numerical superiority
Playing with your back foot	Finding the free player
Focus on first touch	Recognising areas of overload (and therefore areas where players have more time and space)
Receiving away from pressure	Playing 2v1
Recognising passing lanes	Off-the-ball movements to support the player in possession
Playing using one or two touches	When to quicken the game, or when to slow it down
Selection, weight, and direction of pass	
Necessity for clever play (including using 'abnormal' areas of the feet and body – sole, thigh, for example)	

Some 'game-related' technical and tactical outcomes of rondos[6]

Implicitly, the rondo also promotes players' physical development – their general mobility, agility, and 'quick feet' to match the quick decisions necessary to complete the exercise effectively. Teamwork is necessary when both in possession, and out of possession, when seeking to regain the ball. Counting passes can also add to the competitive element, especially counting third-line passes.

Along with benefits *in possession*, the exercise can be used for out of possession (defending) elements. Liverpool first-team coach Pepijn Lijnders, for example, uses rondos to zoom in on concepts of pressing and counter-pressing within the group – one of the key tactical elements of the Premier League side. If the internal players can win the ball back within six passes, they receive the reward of both players being allowed to leave the centre of the rondo (normally only the player who regains the ball is entitled to leave). Skills around pressing, working together as a defensive pair, stopping forward passes (and maybe allowing other passes – the first-line passes that will not overly hurt them) are a constant here. Not being played through (third-line pass) is a key defensive quality that can be developed.

In line with their open, non-secretive approach, Barcelona exports its methods around the globe through their football school, *FCBEscola*. These schools are firmly based on the Barça DNA and training methodology (and, of course, the five values!).

Below is a full session held at one of their football schools. This is the first session of the programme, and the theme is to assess the players and thus group them according to ability. The essence of the sessions has a clear Barcelona imprint – the use of rondos, possession games, and small-sided games. Most of all, apart from stretching exercises, the ball is always in play.

---

[6] For more rondo-based practices, check out the upcoming edition of the *Deliberate Soccer Practice* series – *50 Rondo-Based Practices*.

Warm-Up (30 minutes)		
Juggling in Pairs (10mins) Juggling in pairs, any technique.	Stretching (10mins) As instructed by the coach. (stretching time will be used to explain the objectives of the session)	Possession (10mins) Players are split into two teams and aim to keep the ball for as long as possible. Ten passes equals a goal for the team.
Main Session		
3v1 Rondo (15mins) The ball should be passed from corner to corner. Players need to move to an empty corner to support the player on the ball.		
Possession Game 4v4+2 (20mins) In an area of 40x40, the players are looking for space. One team will keep possession of the ball, utilising two floating players. Coach focuses on players observing space, creating space, and making decisions.		
Small-Sided Game (2 x 20mins) Each team will have a defined shape. Free play. Coach will observe more than he will instruct.		
Cool Down (15mins)		
1. Stretching (As indicated by the coach) 2. Feedback (Have players enjoyed the session? What have they learned?)		

While there is clearly a huge emphasis on passing and possession at Barça, it is not limited to it. Sharing the ball is prized, of course, but individuality and creativity are encouraged. Long passing sequences, recycling the play from side to side, and counting connections between players is a normal part of the game, but Barça recognise that it is futile without the ability to finish moves with skill, cleverness, and creativity.

Implications for Coaches
Possession football is the optimal way of producing young players who are technically and tactically proficient. There is no doubt that the heavy focus on this at Barça is the reason they produce the players they do – you become what you practice. Goalkeepers are also included in these practices as having high technical ability is essential for them too.
Whilst youth coaches look towards playing out from the back and a possession-based game, individual creativity is often missed. The dribbler is forgotten and shouts of "pass, pass, pass" ring out around youth football pitches.
In the last chapter, we spoke of the importance of ball mastery and dominating 1v1 situations. Barcelona are a great example of how they use dribbling and mastery skills within a possession game. If they insisted on all players playing two-touches all of the time, we would have missed the mazy dribbles of Messi, the body feints of Iniesta, and the sight of Piqué advancing into midfield with the ball.

Lionel Messi

"

When you saw him [Messi], you would think: this kid can't play ball. He's a dwarf, he's too fragile, too small. But immediately you'd realise that he was born different, that he was a phenomenon and that he was going to be something impressive.

"

Adrián Coria, Newell's Old Boys coach

There are a number of videos floating around the internet of a young, creative Lionel Messi. He is, unsurprisingly, slaloming through defenders, scoring goals, showing the balance, agility, and deadliness that we now see on a weekly basis. While there is a certain trademark to what Messi does now, and what he did as a younger player running around the youth pitches of Rosario, there is much more to his story than that.

Messi joined the Academy in 2001 as a 13-year-old. The move from South America to Catalonia was not as smooth as his future career may suggest. He had been rejected by Newell's Old Boys, a professional club in Argentina, who refused to meet the financial costs of a young teen with a growth defect. Like De Bruyne, earlier – it is a decision that is hard to support in hindsight. Initially, in Barcelona, however, these sentiments were also shared.

Barca's first team director, Charly Rexach, however, wanted to sign him immediately. The story goes that Rexach, having been abroad and arriving late at a trial game, made his mind up to sign Messi in the seven or eight minutes it took to walk around the pitches to the dugout to meet the youth coaches. Distance learning was enough for him.

Other directors at the club, however, were not so keen. It was almost unheard of to relocate a foreign player of this age, adding to concerns about Messi's growth hormone deficiency. His medical issues caused two problems: one, his monthly bills were costing over $1,000; and, two – from a purely football point of view – they were worried about his physical capacity to translate his ability into becoming an effective first-team player, even with time on his side. Possibly the greatest ever story was secured though, when, with nothing else to hand, and an ultimatum from Messi's family, Rexach signed an agreement for the recruitment of Messi on a paper napkin.

"   **"**

First of all, he was foreign, and the law doesn't allow a foreign child to play in any national league. A considerable handicap. Second, he was a kid. He could end up not becoming a Barcelona player … Third, what are his parents going to do? We'd have to find work for them if they moved to Spain. And finally, the boy has a growth problem; he needs treatment.

Charly Rexach

When Messi arrived at La Masia, he was 4 feet 6 inches in height – a full foot smaller than an average boy at that age. Socially, the staff at La Masia also had concerns about him, as you would do for any resident that was so far away from home. Although Spanish is the native tongue in both Argentina and Spain, the regional differences remain abundant. He was exceptionally quiet and introverted, keeping to himself rather than mixing with the other players. His doctor in Rosario, Dr. Diego Schwarsztein commented that football, "was the only topic of conversation that would conquer the little boy's shyness." Suffering two notable injuries soon after arriving, and a licencing problem forbidding him to play in national competition as a foreigner (meaning he played with the 'B' team, rather than the 'A' team), led him to only playing two competitive games in his first season, which did not help.

Implications for Coaches
Resist judging a player too early in terms of their physical development. Although Messi is an extreme case due to his growth hormone deficiency diagnosis, there is still a temptation in youth football to judge and dismiss players prematurely. There is no danger in giving a player time to physically mature; nor is having a keen eye to appreciate technical and tactical qualities, even if the player is physically underdeveloped. There is, however, a danger in removing them too early.
In *Making The Ball Roll*, an anonymous coach contributed a story about watching a football session (shared again below), where creativity was stifled. Ensure you are maximising player ability.

Real Coach Experience

What if a Lionel Messi Arrived at Your Club?

(Observing a School Soccer Session - Anonymous)

What if a young Lionel Messi arrived at your soccer club? (I appreciate the obvious answer may be "great, my team will win more games!" but let's think deeper than that...)

How would you affect the development of this young soccer genius? I recently watched a junior school soccer session. There was one player who dominated the game. He scored goal after goal, and beat player after player. He showed an abundance of skill and seemed to cover every yard of the school playground. He was enthusiastic about the game and, like any young player, wanted to win.

The coach, however, saw this as a problem and commenced 'differentiating' within the game, but did so through positive discrimination. Firstly, he instructed 'James' that he was no longer allowed to score. James reluctantly accepted the challenge and commenced continually beating players and setting his mates up for easy tap-ins, something as an onlooker I found endearing, cheeky, but James was merely solving a problem set out by the coach and was living within the boundaries of the outlined rules.

Still dissatisfied, however, the coach conditioned James to a maximum of two touches, before making him go in goal and then confining him to his penalty box. All because he was *too good* for the session the coach had planned.

The coach differentiated but did so to meet his own needs. At times, it had the feel of a battle of wits, with the player determined to show his worth despite being handicapped, and the coach wanting to restrict James' ability so the session would be more manageable. You got the feeling that he would prefer if James were not there at all.

If a Lionel Messi arrived at your club, would you tell him not to score goals? Not to dribble? Would you restrict him to two touches? Would you banish him and restrict him to a 10-metre square box? I wonder how many extraordinary young players have been made ordinary in this way.

Conclusion

Due to their unwavering belief in *their way*, Barcelona have had some tremendous results and successes. After their 2011 Champions League Final win over Manchester United, Sir Alex Ferguson, not known for his willingness to openly praise opponents, described them as the best team he had ever faced. There was their 6-2 victory over Real Madrid in 2009 at the Bernabéu, when the pressure to win was tremendous, as Madrid, having won 17 of the previous 18 games, had cut Barcelona's lead at the top to four points; and the astonishingly late, late Champions League comeback against Paris Saint-Germain in 2017.

On April 17th 2018, with Barcelona cruising to yet another La Liga title, they earned a 2-2 draw with La Liga opponent, Celta Vigo. The achievement of sharing a point with a mid-table team was not significant. It did not secure or derail their push to the title. It did not quash any of the chasing title contenders or overturn a game with the away-goals rule. The point was not significant – but the team sheet was.

That night, in the north-western coastal town of Vigo, the Balaídos witnessed, for the first time in 16 years, the absence of an Academy graduate from Barca's starting XI. It took an hour for two to enter the game, in the shape of Messi no less, and local boy Sergi Roberto (who was sent off only minutes later).

To attribute the success of the late-noughties Barcelona team to a crop of exceptional academy products (which has now dried up) would be lazy. It is a factor, of course, but very few clubs, if any, would have handled and nurtured them as Barça did. Too few *youth* coaches are willing to play a bunch of little guys; FCB did so while competing at the top end of the game.

Summary

- The Academy at Barcelona provides players with stellar on-pitch learning, but also encourages and promotes vital life skills.

- The facility that housed the spine of their great team under Pep Guardiola came through a modest 300-year old farmhouse building – La Masia. Facilities are what you make of them.

- No club refers to their vision, values, and DNA as much as Barcelona. The players and coaches have an obligation to meet and defend the ideas of the club.

- Workshops are frequently carried out for both players and parents, including ones on nutrition and psychology.

- Their style of play is characterised by the use of 4-3-3 / 3-4-3, based around short passing and immediate pressure on the ball. This philosophy runs throughout the club.

- Having a winning mentality is crucial even for the young players at the club. League tables are maintained and published, and opponents treat them as their 'cup final'. They encourage winning at the academy, but not at the expense of their style.

- Barça are more concerned with players' technical attributes than their physical limitations.

- Their training aims are to "develop players with technique, speed, and vision of the game." Players are constantly working both physically and mentally.

- The rondo (and other possession and positional-based exercises) is taken exceptionally seriously at the club. Although the practice has its detractors, its game-relevance is not lost on Barcelona.

- Even the basic rondo has many relevancies to the game across PPSTT.

- Although passing and sharing the ball is prized and the club is well known for it, it does not forget about the clever players or the dribbler, even the goalkeeper.

- Upon signing a teenage Lionel Messi, the club had many reservations – but they saw the technician through his physical problems and limitations.

It's Your Game #1
The Day Pep Came to Class
Todd Beane • @_ToddBeane
Founder of TOVO Institute

I gathered my materials for another day of teaching.

Instead of driving to the Cruyff Institute, I headed to the FC Barcelona training grounds to conduct a seminar for the B Team players. This was a good group of guys much more accustomed to attending training on the pitch than in a classroom.

Handshake after handshake after handshake. One at a time, each player extended their palm to me in greeting as they passed. "Bon día," uttered the Catalans. "Buenos días," said the rest.

I crafted an interactive session of group work and individual reflection on the skills, knowledge, and values required to maximize their full potential. Each athlete had the same goal – to play on the first team, making Camp Nou their weekend workplace.

In the row to my right sat Pep Guardiola. It was not the first time we met, and it would not be the last, but I share with you why this day still resonates with me.

I had done this workshop in several countries and for several professional teams. The beginning almost always went like this... The head coach would show up to start the workshop, speak on the importance of intellectual development, and then promptly leave. All were invited to stay, and almost all coaches left the first chance they got. A hollow obligatory message of introduction and then an escape.

On this day, there was no preamble. The session began as Pep and his assistants participated as students. After class, we spoke for a while about the players and the challenges of promoting intellectual curiosity. Pep spoke of his mentor, Johan Cruyff, and how much he had learned from him.

Pep went on to become the head coach of FC Barcelona and to win countless trophies, and I went home to read to my kids.

I share this to highlight the importance of strategy and tactics. Not the 4-3-3 system of play. Not how to press high up the pitch. Not how to build out of the back.

I want to talk about the strategy to maximise our potential and the tactics that lead to sustained success. That day reminded me that a coach's results come from a commitment to learning. That learning provides us with a sense of perspective. That our accomplishments are directly related to our commitment. That good things come to those who respect what others have afforded them. Great things come to those that forge an identity of their own.

It's Your Game #2

Calm, Controlled & Patient

Sam Vincent • @SamJVincent

Academy Coach; Lead Futsal Coach

In 2017, we were lucky enough to be invited to spend a week at F.C. Barcelona. As one of the strongest futsal teams in the UK and ahead of representing England at the World Futsal Cup 2018, this was an incredible opportunity for Meglio United Futsal Club to learn from, and play against, the very best on the planet.

What an experience it was. In our under-14 futsal match, we found ourselves 2-1 up against all the odds. Yet FCB remained calm, controlled, and patient. No panic and no drama, just an intense and remarkable focus. Possession was everything; winning the ball back seemed an impossible task at times. FCB were happy to patiently rotate the ball, waiting for the right opening. Defending against this was the most intense experience, and we have adjusted our own game to follow elements of this philosophy. Ultimately, FCB came through to win the game and deservedly so; though we were proud to have given them a good run for their money.

A couple of the FCB coaches also delivered training sessions to the team during the week. The attention to detail was remarkable. Even with the language barrier, the coaches were able to communicate their messages clearly, using simple visual aids and/or practical demonstration when necessary. Again, everything was calm, controlled and patient, yet still incredibly focused, and the sessions were high on intensity and energy. Striking this balance is one of the key learning points I took away on the plane home. Nothing was left to chance, nothing was unclear, and nothing was ignored.

Perhaps the best moments of the week came in the hour or so before kick-off. We arrived to be greeted by an English-speaking security guard at the academy gates and parents/spectators were quickly ushered away to the viewing area. No distractions were allowed. As we entered the arena, the FCB boys were already engaged in an intense warmup. Yet not a coach in sight, as far as I could tell. The level of focus and discipline from players as young as 13 was truly remarkable. Yet, after the game, it was clear these boys were just typical young lads too. Happy and joking, posing for photos with our players and swapping *Instagram* details. Work hard, earn the right to play. Have fun once the job is done. An inspiring message for youngsters.

An experience to cherish.

It's Your Game #3

More than a Club

Alex Clapham • @alexclapham

Coach; Football Writer; Founder of @canofootball

In the 2015/2016 season, was I working within the academy of a club competing in the top category of the Catalan region. FC Barcelona were in our league and, as you can imagine, it was the first fixture I looked for on the calendar. I had spent many mornings at the *La Masia* complex, normally just watching in awe as the youth teams dismantled opponents without giving them a whiff of possession.

By the time game day came around, we were in a three-horse title race – the biggest horse being Barça. Our staff and players met outside the gates of the complex and, after bundling past the hundreds of fans and media who were waiting, we made our way into the preposterously nice dressing rooms.

We went out and put up a good fight, losing 6-3 in the end, but it's never easy when you're facing the kind of quality where if you concede a half-chance then the ball ends up in the back of your net.

After squirming through the screaming fans, who now knew first-team players had finished their session, a side-door opened just 50 metres up the side road. Four fancy cars pulled out – three of which shot past us. The last one pulled over, rolled down the window and waved us over for a chat – it was Sergio Busquets.

Fast forward to March and we were in the *Copa España* Final against, you guessed it, Barcelona. As it happened, we shared a hotel with them, and although we sat on parallel tables at dinner time and slept in rooms on the floor above, the staff and players were more than happy to mingle with us. Everybody wearing the *Blaugrana* badge was a real credit to the club. My colleagues and I sat discussing tactics with the Barça coaches whilst the boys were sat together chatting in the lounge.

One thing that will always stay in my mind is the Barcelona players ensuring that doors were consistently held open for hotel staff, waitresses were always thanked, and every single person they passed was greeted. The sharp haircuts were as neat as their polo shirts, buttoned up to precision. These were boys who were within touching distance of the fame and fortune that football offers, yet class never falters.

The final was played out in front of thousands in the stands and broadcast live on national TV. They beat us again; this time with a lot more comfort. As the full-time whistle sounded, the prodigies in blue and red spent less than 30 seconds celebrating together before joining our coaching staff in consoling our heartbroken runners-up, many of which in tears. As they say, "Més que un club."

It's Your Game #4

Changing Habits

Agustin Peraita • @MrPeraita

Coach; Author of *Play like Pep Guardiola's Barcelona*

I worked in the Arizona Barça Academy Residential Program in 2017 and 2018. It was the starting season of the project. Playing at Development Academy level with Barça's model of play was a methodological challenge for the coaching staff at first.

Training in small spaces was key to developing the tactical habits required. Rondos were our main weapon to sharpen ball-body coordination, to increase passing efficacy, and to improve body positioning. Rondos were not about fooling the defender, but about improving the time and space of the ball holder.

Positional games were the master formula to enhance the collective understanding of the game model. From 4v4 to 9v9, they were a constant activity. They helped players to improve their knowledge of the Barça playing principles.

Implementing this methodology with grassroots players is easier said than done. Players from 15 to 19-years-old struggled in their first experience training with us as it challenged their footballing norms. There were three main early concerns:

1. They were raised in a football culture of mistakes. Their playing mentality was something like, "We are not going to risk the ball close to our goalkeeper, and we are going to try to take advantage of your mistakes to score our goals." We had to change it to, "We are going to build our own playing advantage by possessing the ball, risky or not."

2. The large number of conditioned rules placed in rondos/positional exercises overloaded their cognitive training habit. It reduced technical efficacy and created some frustration. We had to be patient and positive.

3. Attacking players were frustrated because of the few balls that they were putting into the net during training sessions (because of poor understanding and execution of the playing model). We had to work on possession and penetration phases to get the ball forward effectively.

Belonging to FC Barcelona was a starting point that gave the players some faith in the process. However, it was only by witnessing their daily tactical achievements that saw players believing in the power of rondos and positional games.

Conclusion
For the Love of the Game

" Sport has the power to change the world. It has the power to inspire. It has the power to unite people in a way that little else does. It speaks to youth in a language they understand. **"**

Nelson Mandela

The fields of France were not a pleasant place to be in December 1914. The First World War pitted men and women, divided only by nationality, against each other. I am not talking about politics or foreign policy here at all; I am talking about the ordinary people who were thrust into the coalface of this conflict. Troops lay in dirty, uncomfortable, inhabitable trenches, shooting at each other across no man's lands, before ducking back down for cover. This brutality was to continue for four years, with only brief pauses in hostilities where soldiers from each side were permitted to collect their deceased comrades and repair their damaged trenches.

On December 25th that year, however, there was an impromptu ceasefire; one that was certainly not supported by those in higher-ranking positions. In the spirit of Christmas, German and English troops met in no man's land to celebrate their shared Christian commonality – they shared stories, gifts, and a game of football.

Football has a way of uniting people, of breaking down barriers, language difficulties, and social norms. Few things other than football can do this. I have been lucky enough to travel the world in the name of football, and the essence of the round ball is more powerful than we truly understand.

In Conclusion

Often coaches and sometimes parents will contact me through social media. They often to want to know what the "most important" aspect is when coaching young players. I often feel like my answer disappoints them. They probably want to talk about training, tactics, how to win games, how to solve behavioural problems, etc. However, my standard answer comes back to one thing – fostering a love of the game within players. This, I firmly believe, underpins everything.

If there is one thing that connects all coaches and players around the world, it is a love of the game. We may argue and debate training methods, game styles, and how to 'manage' players, but it is all bred from a passion for football. It is here, this romanticism around the game, where I would like to bring this book to its conclusion.

If you are having a bad day, a bad session, or have experienced a bad result, it is well worth remembering what brought you there in the first place. Maybe you were a parent who agreed to coach the local kids' team so that your son or daughter could play with their friends. Maybe your life, whether professional or not, was littered with the game – playing from kid to adult, avidly supporting a team, or watching every kick of a ball you can. Maybe it was a burning desire to make a career out of coaching. When things are going poorly, it is worth remembering why we started.

Always love the game.

> ## It's Your Game #1
>
> # I Just Want to Play
>
> ## Bastien Hery • @basmetys
>
> ## PSG, French Youth International … and US Torcy

When people look at my story, they see my years at Paris Saint-Germain and with the French Youth National Team. However, when Ray asked me about the coaches that helped shape me, the first to come to mind was the coach at my hometown club, US Torcy, East of Paris. It's an amateur club made famous by past players like Paul Pogba. I started there when I was six, and like every other kid I knew – I just wanted to play football, and we were fortunate to be able to train four times per week.

When I began playing, I wanted to be a goalkeeper. I laugh now, and those who have seen me play between the sticks will laugh too! I had lots of energy and wanted to dive, make saves, and was captivated by the keeper's role in the team.

I then transitioned positionally throughout my youth – my journey went from the last line of defence to the most prominent in attack – from goalkeeper to striker, back to goalkeeper, to striker again, and then, at 13 Stephane Albe – my coach – made a suggestion. He wanted me to play in midfield.

This was a year before my move to PSG, and I'm 100% certain that without this change, I would not have had the career I have had today. I would not have played for my country.

During my first game as a midfielder for US Torcy, I picked up the ball in midfield, and drove forward to score! I remember it so vividly, even today. Every kid will have standout moments like this – whether they played as a goalkeeper, striker, or wherever.

I trusted Mr. Albe so much that I would have played anywhere for him. When I think back to this today, I know that, deep down, there is still the kid inside me that loves the game and just wants to play.

It's Your Game #2

The Starfish and the Soccer Coach

Ian Barker • @IBarkerSoccer

Director of Coach Education, United Soccer Coaches

The competitive coach will accumulate wins and losses that very often pass from memory and can only be recalled from record books. There is also a parallel accumulation of names, faces, and human stories. Some of these stay longer with the coach than the results do.

Over 20 years ago, I co-directed a girls' residential camp. It was an era when camps attracted many of the most competitive players from good clubs, and this camp was of that quality. Over the years, we had repeat campers. One such repeat camper was a girl called Erin. She was ultra-committed and wanted to play college soccer.

At a mid-point in the camp, after a typically good quality session, I noticed Erin was extremely frustrated. Over several years, we had become aware of her ability, but also her self-criticism. It was powerful, indeed sad, to see this great young person so low. I chose to talk to her on the way from the field. I do not remember the detail, but I know that I expressed my belief in her ability and that she was a valued member of the "family" here, and that she could realistically achieve her goals. I recall Erin was grateful, if not completely convinced, and the conversation slipped from my mind.

Weeks after, I received a letter from Erin, and she shared an allegory with me:

Two people are at opposite ends of a long beach early one morning. They slowly walk toward each other. The beach is covered with thousands of starfish washed up by the tide and left to slowly die as the tide recedes. One of the people notices that every ten paces the other bends down, picks up a starfish, and tosses it back into the life-giving ocean. When they finally come together, they greet as strangers. The first person asks the other what they are doing. The response "saving starfish". The counter-argument was to question why, with so many starfish, what possible difference could it make? At this point, the person bends down, picks up a starfish and tosses it into the ocean and offers, "It made a difference to that one."

What Erin shared with me has stayed with me for over 20 years, and I refer to the allegory a lot. Erin did not play college soccer, but attended her dream college and had a fantastic experience. She is now a beautiful mother of four boys.

As an experienced competitor, and still active coach, wins and losses are central to some measure of my performance, but it is the personal relationships the game has given me that I have come to value the most.

> # It's Your Game #3
>
> # The Round Ball
>
> ## John Davies • @renegadestyle
>
> ## Life-Long Coach

It started simple. A lonely young man in a place far from home – and a ball.

Dribbling to and fro, along the pitch, in no particular order, like an artist grazing a brush along a canvas searching for inspiration, I could see the pitch was his home at a time he felt far from home.

I gave a wave, a welcoming "hello," then a "bonjour." He responded with a smile. The opening.

I sent a quick curling cross to him to him from 20 metres. He brought the ball down with skill and returned it quickly. Time moved by as we passed the ball back and forth, moving along the pitch against an imaginary eleven, slowly getting to know each other's habits, and quickly revealing his passion for the game.

He had recently moved from Africa and, as it so often is, the round ball was the constant in his life.

Within a few days, the once empty pitch – a miserable plot of hard-packed dirt and weeds – attracted many new arrivals to the area as word got out that it was *the* place to play. Don't ask me how, but such is the magic of the round ball. Within days, teen players, with their parents having immigrated to this far off place from across Africa and every stretch of Europe, arrived at "our grounds".

The differences were striking, the similarities remarkable. The Beautiful Game.

That year we would play nightly and through the entire day on the weekends. Through the cold, harsh winter, the torrential downpours of spring, and the blistering hot summer, it made no difference. This was our home, our friends, our grounds, our team. We played, took on all challengers, learned about each other's cultures, shared learning new languages, and grew. My, how they grew.

They grew not merely as players, albeit a number of them entertain fans on a far bigger stage now, but most importantly they grew as young men.

They learned, amongst a backdrop of a world so often divided with hate, that we are all the same. They learned that this magical ball is made of equal panels where, apart, they are of little strength, but together can make the world stronger.

This is the magic of the round ball, and this is why I coach.

It's Your Game #4

That'll Do Me

Bobby Madley • @BobbyMadley2

Former Premier League Referee

I am often asked why I referee. Why I started. How do I put up with the abuse, the constant analysis of decisions (whether right or wrong!), and the general frustration of it all. Especially when, in the end, you get little or no congratulations for your performance.

Despite the traffic-warden-type negativity a referee gets, I can honestly say that I have never woken up on the morning of a game without anything other than pure excitement for the day and game ahead. Maybe the enjoyment is a bit sadistic.

I didn't always want to be a referee. I would go as far as to say I had no interest in it at all. I wanted to be a player and, as a teen, I made some inroads at a couple of professional clubs, and, to this day, I hold a goalscoring record at my local club. In fact, such was my competitiveness as a player, I gave referees as much hammer as anyone! Often, when I play football even with some friends – I still do!

It was one of those referees I had given a hard time to who laid down the gauntlet, challenging me to take the referees qualification after I volunteered myself to help out with whistle-duties at a local football club gala. It was, more or less, "Don't complain at me until you know what you are talking about."

I took the course, along with my brother, who is now also making his way through the professional game too. I ended up on both the Premier League and international referee list, making the job everyone hates my 'bread and butter'.

I have been privileged to referee some of the biggest players, coaches, and teams on the planet. I have witnessed, at ground level, some of the greatest goals, performances, and matches you could wish to see. I have sampled and savoured some of the most extraordinary atmospheres at football grounds – both club and international – all over the UK and Europe. I have spoken with media personalities, club officials, and met some fantastic people from all corners of the game. I have worked with some exceptional referees.

And that probably takes us back to the original question. I cannot neatly list why I referee and happily carry all the baggage that comes with it. I do it now for the same reason I played as a striker in my youth, simply because I love the game.

That'll do me.

Other Books from Bennion Kearny

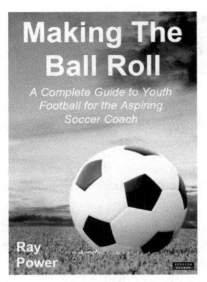

Making The Ball Roll: A Complete Guide to Youth Football for the Aspiring Soccer Coach

This focused and easy-to-understand book details training practices and tactics, and goes on to show readers how to help young players achieve peak performance through tactical preparation, communication, psychology, and age-specific considerations.

Each chapter covers, in detail, a separate aspect of coaching to give you, the football coach, a broad understanding of youth soccer development. Each topic is brought to life by the stories of real coaches working with real players. Never before has such a comprehensive guide to coaching soccer been found in the one place. *Making The Ball Roll* is for youth coaches, parents, and anyone who is thinking about becoming a football coach. It is a comprehensive one-stop-shop, filled with all the information and insights that readers need, to become a top class coach.

Deliberate Soccer Practice: 50 Small-Sided Football Games to Improve Decision-Making

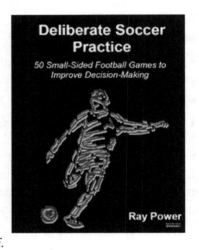

Small-sided Games are the epicentre of soccer improvement. Done right, they can play a huge role in the development of players. The environment created through these games makes it possible not just to 'let the game be the teacher,' but also to improve specific skills and tactics - all in the context of the real game. We do this by manipulating the secondary rules of the game, by either adding elements or constraining players in various ways. The ultimate alternative to the 'drill,' Small-Sided Games training promotes player autonomy through decision-making, problem-solving, and the much-heralded coaching technique of guided discovery. Small-Sided Games have the look and feel of the 'real' game where learning is made intrinsic by the game itself.

Defending

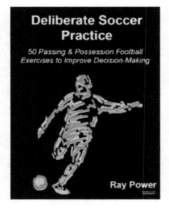

Passing & Possession

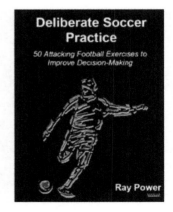

Attacking

Togetherness: How to Build a Winning Team

This concise and practical book – from Dr. Matt Slater, a world authority on togetherness – shows readers how to develop togetherness in their teams. The journey starts with an understanding of what underpins togetherness and how it can drive high performance and well-being simultaneously.

It then moves onto practical tips and activities based on the 3R model (Reflect, Represent, Realise) that readers can learn and complete with their teams to unlock their togetherness.

A must-read resource for anyone who is passionate about bringing individuals together to build top-notch teams.

Scientific Approaches to Goalkeeping in Football: A practical perspective on the most unique position in sport [Second Edition]

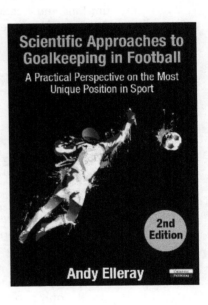

This fully updated, resized, and revised second edition of *Scientific Approaches to Goalkeeping in Football* builds upon the success of the original 2013 bestseller, offering both theoretical and practical changes that have emerged in the area of goalkeeping over the last few years. Written by goalkeeping specialist Andy Elleray, this book offers a 2019 update to his class-leading approach to goalkeeping in football. Focusing, in particular, on young goalkeepers, it sheds light on training, player development, match performances, and player analysis. New methodologies, training approaches, and development considerations are included, along with brand new content on goalkeeping in female football, performance analysis examples, and advances in practice design.

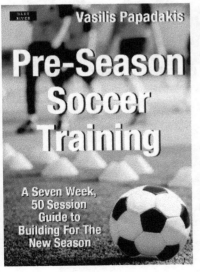

Pre-Season Soccer Training: A Seven Week, 50 Session Guide to Building For The New Season

Pre-Season Soccer Training covers the key elements of pre-season training including fitness drills, tactics, team understanding, skill development, set pieces, and transitional play. Using more than 165 illustrations, over 50 sessions, this book will help coaches of all levels to learn what a tested and effective pre-season can look like. The book is based on the current know-how and coaching being taught in UEFA classrooms, and sessions can be tweaked based on the age and experiences of your players.

Developing Skill: A Guide to 3v3 Soccer Coaching and Developing Skill 2: A Guide to 3v3 Soccer Coaching

In these books, coaches of all levels, working with players across all age groups and abilities, will learn to utilise the 3v3 method to develop skilful individuals and effective teams. Book 1 builds up from 1v1 to 3v3 through technical exercises that improve individual skills. Then, it moves beyond 3v3, adding in more players (including goalkeepers), as situations demand it.

In Book 2, Peter Prickett returns with the follow-up to his 2018 3v3 bestseller with new practices that link directly into finishing and creating goals. In this sequel, the advancement of the core principles of football through Small-Sided Games is explored further. This book's focus is on the creation and conversion of goalscoring opportunities, as well as deeper dives into session design to help coaches create better practices. *Developing Skill 2: A Guide to 3v3 Soccer Coaching* outlines how you can use and incorporate the 3v3 method into your training and provides more than 85 ready-to-use, illustrated practices. It also details how best to run warm-ups, how to work with different pitch sizes and shapes, and much more.

Blowing The Whistle: The Psychology of Football Refereeing

The football referee. Charged with controlling the players and enforcing the laws of the most popular and passionate game on the planet, they are often alone and always outnumbered. They ply their trade in the face of competitive athletes and a partisan crowd, all desperate to sway judgments in their favour. Along with players and coaches, they are the only people who can influence the result of a football match, yet despite such importance, there are many questions.

– Are referees influenced by the crowd?

– Do referees favour the home side?

– Do 'big name' players and managers get treated differently?

– Are referees arrogant?

– Do we really trust the referee?

– Do we neglect the mental health of referees?

– How can a referee prepare psychologically for a game?

In *Blowing the Whistle: The Psychology of Football Refereeing*, these questions, and more, are answered. A must-read for coaches who want to understand the behaviours and motivations of the man or woman in the middle.

Developing Soccer Players: Forward-Specific Practices

Aimed at football coaches of all levels, and players of all ages and abilities, *Developing Soccer Players: Forward-Specific Practices* seeks to develop, and enhance, the skills and functions of forward players through low numbers training. This includes the player on their own, with a coach, and in small-sided games. Detailing research into technique, psychology, and using the statistics of how goals are scored in the modern game, this book highlights where and how modern goalscorers get their goals, and serves up exercises to help players develop and excel accordingly.

101 Goalkeeper Training Practices

In *101 Goalkeeper Training Practices,* goalkeeping coach Andy Elleray follows up his previous trilogy of goalkeeping books to provide fellow football coaches and goalkeepers with a wide variety of new practices that cover many aspects of goalkeeping. Practices are broken down into three areas: working with an individual goalkeeper, small groups of goalkeepers training together, and fuller team-based exercises. The overall intention is to provide realistic, varied, relevant, and innovative practices that stimulate the goalkeeper in every element of their game and performance.

The goalkeeper training exercises in the book – illustrated with colour diagrams – focus on five main viewpoints – technical, tactical, psychological, physical, and social/environmental. Each practice is weighted to develop these elements to greater and lesser degrees, and exercises include 1v1 techniques, decision making, shot stopping from different angles/distances, travelling around the goalmouth, re-positioning, cutback scenarios, and more. There are also sections on key coaching observations and how to progress/regress the practices.

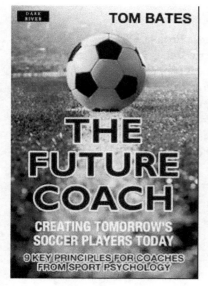

The Future Coach - Creating Tomorrow's Soccer Players Today: 9 Key Principles for Coaches from Sport Psychology

The Future Coach offers proven principles from soccer psychology for coaches to create winning cultures and re-define coaching excellence. Based around practically applied principles of performance psychology, coaches will gain the opportunity to explore how the values, beliefs, and expectations they hold, shape their coaching behaviour and end up defining the environment they work in and the players they work with. Coaches will learn new ways to design and implement their playing philosophy, identity, and style of play, on and off the field, with clarity and confidence.

Building a Successful High School Sports Program

In *Building a Successful High School Sports Program*, former High School Soccer Coach DeAngelo Wiser addresses the fundamentals of building a successful High School program. He covers numerous topic areas including how to choose team players, bringing them together, managing expectations, how to define success, working with administrators and colleagues, tracking progress, dealing with personal adversity, and much more. The book also includes contributions from a dozen highly successful High School coaches and Athletic Directors who offer decades of real-world wisdom and high-value advice. The book's foreword is by one of the world's leading and most recognizable Sport Psychologists - Bill Beswick.

Winning Your Players through Trust, Loyalty, and Respect

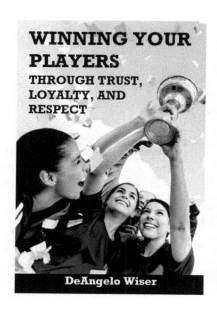

Coach DeAngelo Wiser is a soccer coach with more than 20 years' experience of working with high school players, during which time he has gathered District and Regional Titles, and Coach of the Year honors. In *Winning Your Players*, he offers accumulated wisdom, insight, and solutions garnered from years of developing players and working with them in competitive environments at key moments. His methods of building Trust, Loyalty, and Respect, give every coach the ability to have a positive impact in practice, the game, and - more importantly - in life. *Winning Your Players* offers a clear pathway for coaches who want to develop and nurture talent to the best of their abilities, and gives insight into situations that require strong leadership at key moments with your team. In those moments, they need every resource possible to clearly do what's best for their team. *Winning Your Players* is a must during those times.

Play Like Pep Guardiola's Barcelona: A Soccer Coach's Guide

Written by Agustín Peraita, FCBEscola Project Director at Sao Paulo FC Barcelona, this book is for soccer coaches looking to understand and implement Pep Guardiola's tactical approach and coaching methodology for that 2009-2010 Barça side. Containing more than 50 illustrations, detailing on-field drills, Principles/Subprinciples/Sub-SubPrinciples, tactical diagrams and weekly planning schedules, this practical and to-the-point book focuses explicitly on the preseason period as it lays the foundation for how a team will train, play, and perform over the season.

The Modern Soccer Coach: Pre-Season Training

When it comes to building successful soccer teams, pre-season is a critical time. It's the perfect time for the coach to create a team identity, set standards, develop effective training habits, and reinforce winning behaviors. Get it right and you can set the foundation required to catapult your team towards an excellent season. Get it wrong, however, and your season might never recover. This book looks at how pre-season has changed over the past 10 years, and offers ways for coaches to adapt their work and methods to deal with these changes accordingly. Pre-season is about much more than fitness testing, long-distance running, and gruelling physical work. *The Modern Soccer Coach - Pre-Season Training* looks at new, innovative ways to engage players so that they want to train at the maximum every day, and push towards new limits for the new season ahead.

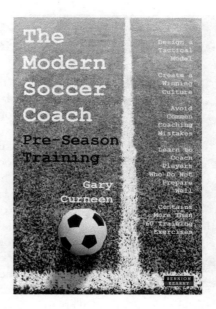

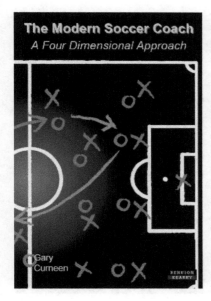

The Modern Soccer Coach: A Four Dimensional Approach

Aimed at Soccer coaches of all levels and with players of all ages and abilities *The Modern Soccer Coach* identifies the areas that must be targeted by coaches who want to maximize a team's potential - the Technical, Tactical, Physical, and Mental sides to the game. Readers will see how the game has changed and what areas determine success in the game today. They will learn what sets coaches like Mourinho, Klopp, Rodgers, and Guardiola apart from the rest. Philosophies and training methods from the most forward-thinking coaches in the game today are presented, along with guidelines on creating a modern environment for readers' teams. This book is not about old school methodologies, or 'motivating' players by screaming at them - it is about creating a culture of excellence that gets the very best from players. Contains more than 30 illustrated exercises that focus on tactical, technical, mental, and physical elements of the game.

The Modern Soccer Coach: Position-Specific Training

Aimed at football coaches of all levels, and players of all ages and abilities, *The Modern Soccer Coach: Position-Specific Training* seeks to identify, develop, and enhance the skills and functions of the modern soccer player whatever their position and role on the pitch. This book offers unique insight into how to develop an elite program that can both improve players and win games. Filled with practical no-nonsense explanations, focused player drills, and more than 40 illustrated soccer templates, this book will help the modern coach to create a coaching environment that will take players to the next level.

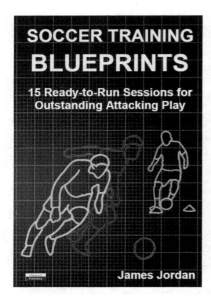

Soccer Training Blueprints: 15 Ready-to-Run Sessions for Outstanding Attacking Play

Utilising a game-based approach to soccer - where individuals actually play games rather than growing old in semi-static drills - author James Jordan offers 15 detailed session plans (comprised of 75 cutting-edge exercises) to help coaches develop attacking mindsets and improved skills in their players, and, most of all, nurture a love for soccer. Through his approach, James has won six High School State Championships and one Classic 1 Boys' Club Championship over the past decade. Aimed at coaches of both young male and female players, from 5-18 years of age, and adaptable depending on age group and skill set, Soccer Training Blueprints combines game-based soccer concepts with contemporary ideas from educational research on training and preparation to develop players who can think for themselves, execute their skills, and work to a plan. This is not about coaches standing on the touchlines yelling at their youngsters - this is about developing footballers to love and play the game as best they can.

Soccer Tough: Simple Football Psychology Techniques to Improve Your Game

Soccer Tough demystifies the mental side of football and offers practical techniques that will enable soccer players of all abilities to actively develop focus, energy, and confidence. *Soccer Tough* will help banish the fear, mistakes, and mental limits that holds players back.

In *Soccer Tough*, soccer psychology consultant Dan Abrahams shares the powerful techniques that have helped him develop reserve team players to become international players, guided youth team players from slumps to first team contracts, and helped young professionals win contracts at their dream clubs. This was achieved quite simply - by focusing on the power of the mind, and how it can elevate performance on match day to peak levels.

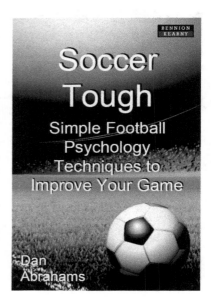

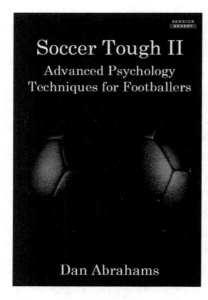

Soccer Tough 2: Advanced Psychology Techniques for Footballers

Global soccer psychologist Dan Abrahams follows up his ground-breaking, international bestseller *Soccer Tough* with his sequel title.

In *Soccer Tough 2: Advanced Psychology Techniques for Footballers*, Dan introduces soccer players to more cutting edge tools and techniques to help them develop the game of their dreams. *Soccer Tough 2* is split into four sections - Practice, Prepare, Perform, and Progress, and Dan's goal is simple… to help players train better, prepare more thoroughly, perform with greater consistency and progress faster. Each section offers readers an assortment of development strategies and game philosophies that bring the psychology of soccer to life. They are techniques that have been proven on pitches, and with players, right across the world.

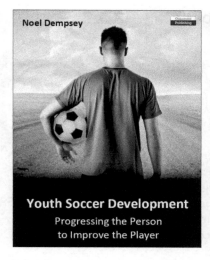

Youth Soccer Development: Progressing the Person to Improve the Player

In *Youth Soccer Development*, football coach Noel Dempsey examines where coaching has come from and where it is heading. Offering insights into how English football has developed, coaching methods, 'talent' in youngsters, and how a player's entire environment needs to be considered in coaching programmes - this book offers many touchpoints for coaches who want to advance their thinking and their coaching. Leaving specific onfield drills and exercises to other books, *Youth Soccer Development* digs deep into 'nature versus nature', players' core beliefs, confidence, motivation, and much more. Advocating that to improve the player, you must improve the person, Dempsey puts forward a case for coaches to be realistic with their players, ensure that they work positively across all facets of their lives - especially education - and to instil a mindset that leads to players being the best person they can be. By creating better people you are more likely to create better players.

The Bundesliga Blueprint: How Germany became the Home of Football

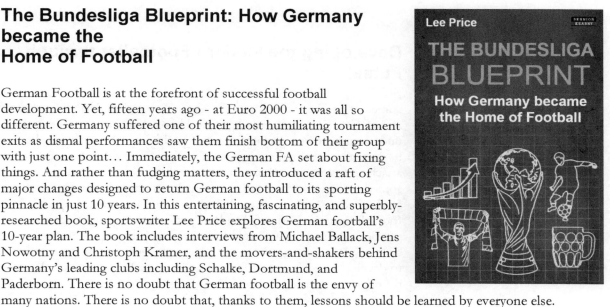

German Football is at the forefront of successful football development. Yet, fifteen years ago - at Euro 2000 - it was all so different. Germany suffered one of their most humiliating tournament exits as dismal performances saw them finish bottom of their group with just one point... Immediately, the German FA set about fixing things. And rather than fudging matters, they introduced a raft of major changes designed to return German football to its sporting pinnacle in just 10 years. In this entertaining, fascinating, and superbly-researched book, sportswriter Lee Price explores German football's 10-year plan. The book includes interviews from Michael Ballack, Jens Nowotny and Christoph Kramer, and the movers-and-shakers behind Germany's leading clubs including Schalke, Dortmund, and Paderborn. There is no doubt that German football is the envy of many nations. There is no doubt that, thanks to them, lessons should be learned by everyone else.

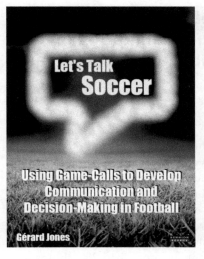

Let's Talk Soccer: Using Game-Calls to Develop Communication and Decision-Making in Football

Soccer coaches across all levels of the game share a common and simple dilemma: how best to improve their players. One of the best ways to do this is through improved communication and how we individualize our messages to our players. It's fundamentally important for coaches to provide quality communication with clear detail and, as the FA's Future Game Philosophy makes clear, "Mastery of innovative coaching methods that utilize communication styles is the mark of a gifted coach, and will be an essential requirement for the game of the future." *Let's Talk Soccer* introduces 'Game-calls', game-specific communication designed to enhance decision making and skill among players. Through Game-calls teams will become more organized, and players will understand - as individuals - how to play within a coach's playing philosophy.

Coaching Psychological Skills in Youth Football: Developing The 5Cs

Successful footballers are typically those who are best able to: regulate their emotions, fix their attention, utilise effective interpersonal skills, and remain highly motivated and self-assured in the face of consistent challenges. These behaviours are the hallmark of mentally tough, emotionally intelligent players, and can be grouped under the 5Cs of: Commitment, Communication, Concentration, Control, and Confidence. Written specifically for soccer coaches of all levels, *Coaching Psychological Skills in Youth Football* details each C in a methodical and practical manner with real-world exercises for training and matches. The book is relevant to soccer coaches working with 5-16 year old players, with individual techniques and practices marked for appropriate age groups. By weaving these techniques into their normal coaching practice, coaches will help educate young players to optimise their motivation, discipline, composure, self-belief and teamwork. A complete 12 month development plan is included alongside a case study from a youth coach who has actually experienced the 5C journey.

Coaching Psychological Skills in Youth Football
Developing The 5Cs

Chris Harwood
Richard Anderson

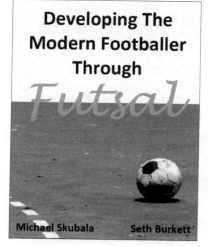

Developing the Modern Footballer through Futsal

Aimed at coaches of all levels and ages, *Developing the Modern Footballer through Futsal* is a concise and practical book that provides an easy-to-understand and comprehensive guide to the ways in which futsal can be used as a development tool for football. From defending and attacking to transitional play and goalkeeping, this book provides something for everyone and aims to get you up-and-running fast. Over 50 detailed sessions are provided, with each one related to specific football scenarios and detailing how performance in these scenarios can be improved through futsal. From gegenpressing to innovative creative play under pressure, this book outlines how futsal can be used to develop a wide range of football-specific skills, giving your players the edge.

Paul Webb Academy: Strength Training Books for Footballers and Goalkeepers

In this Strength Training Book Series, ex-professional footballer and renowned strength coach Paul Webb distils over 20 years of knowledge into books designed to train athletes to become stronger, faster, more explosive, and more resistant to injury. The method Paul uses is simple, and focused, yet extremely effective and unlike the vast majority of training programmes available has - at its core - the health of the athlete front and centre! Each book details: Beginner, Intermediate, and Advanced Training and Full Body Programmes. Dozens of exercises including Goblet Squats, Sumo Deadlifts and Turkish Get Ups explained so readers can start getting strong fast. Each book contains more than 200 photos that show the reader how to complete individual exercises. Dedicated Content on Nutrition and Supplements.

Soccer Tactics 2014: What The World Cup Taught Us

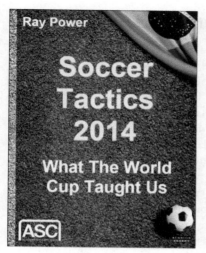

World Cups throw up unique tactical variations. Countries and football cultures from around the globe converge, in one place, to battle it out for world soccer supremacy. The 2014 World Cup in Brazil was no different, arguably throwing up tactical differences like never seen at a competition in modern times. Contests are not just won by strong work ethics and technical brilliance, but by tactical discipline, fluidity, effective strategies, and (even) unique national traits. *Soccer Tactics 2014* analyses the intricacies of modern international systems, through the lens of matches in Brazil. Covering formations, game plans, key playing positions, and individuals who bring football tactics to life - the book offers analysis and insights for soccer coaches, football players, and fans the world over.

Universality | The Blueprint for Soccer's New Era: How Germany and Pep Guardiola are showing us the Future Football Game

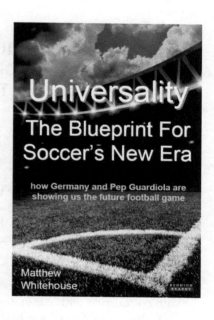

The game of soccer is constantly in flux; new ideas, philosophies and tactics mould the present and shape the future. Since the turn of the century we have witnessed dramatic changes in the beautiful game: new types of player, new coaching methods and tactical innovations have all enhanced and changed the sport of football. The technical, tactical, physical and psychological skills needs of the modern player - from the goalkeeper to centre forward - have all been enhanced. In this book, Matthew Whitehouse - acclaimed author of *The Way Forward: Solutions to England's Football Failings* - looks in-depth at the past decade of the game, taking the reader on a journey into football's evolution.

The Footballer's Journey: real-world advice on becoming and remaining a professional footballer

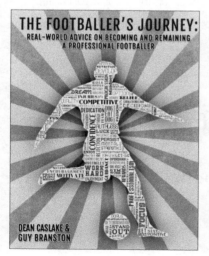

Many youngsters dream of becoming a professional footballer. But football is a highly competitive world where only a handful will succeed. Many aspiring soccer players don't know exactly what to expect, or what is required, to make the transition from the amateur world to the 'bright lights' in front of thousands of fans.

The Footballer's Journey maps out the footballer's path with candid insight and no-nonsense advice. It examines the reality of becoming a footballer including the odds of 'making it', how academies really work, the importance of attitude and mindset, and even the value of having a backup plan if things don't quite work out. Filled with real life stories from current, and former, professionals across different leagues, *The Footballer's Journey* provides readers with honest guidance and practical tips on what is required to give themselves the best possible chance of turning the dream into a reality.

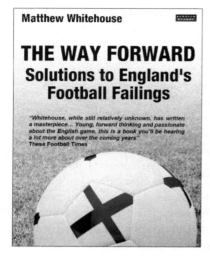

The Way Forward: Solutions to England's Football Failings

English football has been in a state of crisis. Until recently, it had been almost 50 years since England made the final of a major championship and the national sides, at all levels, disappointed and underperformed. In *The Way Forward*, football coach Matthew Whitehouse examines the causes of English football's historical decline and offers a number of areas where change and improvement need to be implemented immediately. With a keen focus and passion for youth development and improved coaching he explains that no single fix can overcome current difficulties and that a multi-pronged strategy is needed. If we wish to improve the standards of players in England then we must address the issues in schools, the grassroots, and academies, as well as looking at the constraints of the Premier League and English FA.

Soccer Brain: The 4C Coaching Model for Developing World Class Player Mindsets and a Winning Football Team

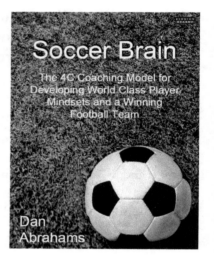

Coaching soccer is demanding. Impossible to perfect, it requires a broad knowledge of many performance areas including technique, tactics, psychology and the social aspects of human development. The first two components are covered in detail in many texts - but *Soccer Brain* uniquely offers a comprehensive guide to developing the latter two - player mindsets and winning teams. The environment that a coach creates, and the relationships formed with players, is the bedrock of performance and achievement. Coaches who are able to deliver students of the game, and who are able to help players execute skills and tactics under pressure are the future leaders of the world's most loved sport. *Soccer Brain* teaches coaches to train players to compete with confidence, with commitment, with intelligence, and as part of a team. The positive messages from each chapter of *Soccer Brain* help coaches to develop players through patience, repetition, reinforcement, re-appraisal and high value relationships.

See all these books, and our other football titles at:

www.BennionKearny.com/football

9 781910 5158